Pilgrims and Priests

Christian Mission in a Post-Christian Society

Stefan Paas

D1572400

scm press

© Stefan Paas 2019

Published in 2019 by SCM Press
Editorial office
3rd Floor, Invicta House,
108–114 Golden Lane,
London EC1Y 0TG, UK
www.scmpress.co.uk

Second impression 2022

SCM Press is an imprint of Hymns Ancient & Modern Ltd
(a registered charity)

Hymns Ancient & Modern® is a registered trademark of
Hymns Ancient & Modern Ltd
13A Hellesdon Park Road, Norwich,
Norfolk NR6 5DR, UK

Scripture quotations are from New Revised Standard Version Bible:
Anglicized Edition, copyright © 1989, 1995 National Council of the
Churches of Christ in the United States of America. Used by permission.
All rights reserved worldwide.

British Library Cataloguing in Publication data

A catalogue record for this book is available
from the British Library

978-0-334-05877-9

Typeset by Manila Typesetting Company
Printed and bound by CPI Group (UK) Ltd

Contents

Preface

In 2014 I presented my inaugural lecture at the Theological University Kampen, the Netherlands. While preparing it I had noticed how the manuscript, surprisingly, began to expand to rather fearsome proportions. Intuitions and thoughts that had been sown during my teenage years and early career, and that had apparently ripened during my years in Amsterdam, began to surface at last, exceeding by far the limits of a 30-minute lecture. The usual response of an academic to such unexpected abundance of ideas is to write a book, and that I have done.

After finishing it I discovered that the book had also become the answer to a question reviewers had asked about my other books, such as *Church Planting in the Secular West* (2016), namely 'What is your ecclesiology?' Better theologians than me wondered how I could write about matters like evangelism,[1] the initiation of converts into the Church,[2] or about planting new churches in secular soil,[3] without ever having systematically addressed the Big Question itself.[4] It may be typical of my theological methodology that I tend to work bottom-up, inductively, starting from concrete missional and other practical challenges and working myself up towards the more systematic questions of what Church and mission are about. Also, as a missiologist I find myself unable to write about any theological question separate from concrete challenges and isolated from particular contexts. Anyway, this is the book that, at this stage of my thinking, is my best shot at something that could be called a nuclear missional ecclesiology. It leaves much to be worked out later (hopefully by others), and it is highly contextual – but for that I do not apologize. I hope, though, that it will inspire others to work out a more in-depth approach of what it means to be a missional Christian community in a post-Christian society – or in other societies, for that matter. After all, the best way to learn contextual theology is to see how it is done in contexts other than your own.

The original version of this book was written in Dutch.[5] Much to my delight the book was reviewed very positively, and between October 2015 and July 2018 it has been reprinted no less than eight times. Even more surprising (and touching, I may add) was its wide ecumenical reception. Upon publication of the book I was invited to give lectures by virtually every denomination in the Netherlands: Roman Catholic or Protestant, Reformed or Baptist, liberal or evangelical. Apparently, the reality described in this book appeals to many Christians of very different stripes. That the large sections of biblical theology it contains have found a sympathetic ear among so many different churches, encourages me a great deal. I only hope that this will also be the case in other countries, especially those of the secularizing West.

For this English edition the book has been adapted to an international audience by removing and adding examples. Some sections have been completely rewritten, while others have been slightly expanded. Literature references have been updated, and some discussions have been improved. It has always been my intention that this book would be a helpful tool for students of missiology and for pastors and other Christians who face the challenges of a post-Christian culture. Therefore, I have found it necessary for the book to contain chapters that introduce readers to current missiological views of Western culture, and to questions of theology and spirituality that affect Christian mission in a secular age.

In different stages of writing I have been greatly helped by friends and colleagues who have read the manuscript and commented on it. They are in alphabetical order: Koert van Bekkum (Professor of Old Testament Studies, Evangelical Theological Faculty, Heverlee, and Associate Professor of Old Testament Studies, Theological University Kampen); Eddy van der Borght (Professor of Systematic Theology, Vrije Universiteit Amsterdam); Joost van der Does de Willebois (retired attorney); Pieter Gorissen (missionary worker in Groningen, the Netherlands); Rob van Houwelingen (Professor of New Testament Studies, Theological University Kampen); Martin de Jong (police officer, pastor, staff worker at City to City Europe); Gerrit Noort (Professor of Missiology, Theological University Kampen, director of Netherlands Mission Council); Gert-Jan Roest (evangelist, theologian in residence at Protestant Church in the Netherlands, and lecturer in missiology, Theological University Kampen); Daniël de Rooij (pastor of the Protestant Church in Zwartebroek, the Netherlands); Hans Schaeffer (Professor of Practical Theology, Theological University Kampen); Sake Stoppels (Professor of Church Development, Christian University for Applied Sciences, Ede); Paul Visser (pastor of the Protestant Church in Amsterdam); and Rikko Voorberg (pastor in Amsterdam).

Stefan Paas
Professor of Missiology and Intercultural Theology, Vrije Universiteit Amsterdam
Professor of Missiology, Theological University Kampen
Research Associate of the Department of Religion Studies, Faculty of Theology, University of Pretoria

Notes

1 Paas, *Jezus als Heer in een plat land*. See also several chapters in Noort, *Sharing Good News*.

2 Paas, *De werkers van het laatste uur*.

3 Paas, *Church Planting in the Secular West*.

4 My closest attempt were some chapters in my *Vrede stichten*, but as this was a work of political theology it went largely unnoticed by missionary practitioners.

5 Paas, *Vreemdelingen en priesters*.

Introduction

All my life I have been involved in 'missionary work'.[1] It started in my childhood. I remember that my father took me with him to a nearby village, when I had just entered primary school, to hand out evangelizing pamphlets. In the summer, when we stayed on a camping site, and after playing soccer, I sometimes had long conversations with other children about the Bible and faith. These things happened spontaneously; I loved being part of them. As a student I did children's ministry, I witnessed on the streets, and with fellow students I joined in door-to-door actions to tell people about Jesus. Later I organized exploration courses for those interested in Christianity, I worked as a mission consultant for my denomination, promoted new methods of evangelism like the Emmaus Course, conducted seeker services, and moved to Amsterdam with my family to help with planting a new church. I wrote several books on being a missionary church and on evangelism. And now I teach missiology at two universities. Apparently, this is a deep-seated thing for me.

No doubt this is partly a matter of DNA. My parents have worked as missionaries in Malawi (South-East Africa) for nine years, and in the nineteenth century one of my great-grandfathers moved to the the newly cultivated moor lands in the East of the Netherlands to minister among the poor and largely uneducated workers who had come there from various regions to make a scarce living under bitter conditions. However, when I was born 'mission' was not just in my blood, it was also in the air. Increasingly since the Second World War, the reality of the progressive secularization of their nations has dawned upon Western Christians, inspiring them to culture wars on the one hand, and revivalistic evangelism on the other. 'Can the West be converted?' the British missionary Lesslie Newbigin famously asked in his 1984 Warfield Lectures.[2] It was rather an ominous question, given the fact that the only 'conversion' of the West that we know of was connected to the ambivalent experience of Christendom. If that is not to be repeated, what then do we mean by the 'conversion of the West'? Can compass regions be 'converted'? Is it possible for cultures or nations to be 'Christianized'? But this is to run ahead of a discussion that will take place in the next chapters. At the time, Newbigin's lecture mirrored the dominant theological sentiment.[3] It echoed the report 'Towards the Conversion of England', issued in 1945 by the bishops of the Church of England,[4] while it represented the conviction of all major church bodies and virtually all leading theologians since the middle of the twentieth century: that Europe had become a mission field (America would follow somewhat later), and that churches should be missionary congregations.[5] This new missionary consciousness was expressed in a steady stream of analyses, models and methods that would help the churches of the West to evangelize, to grow, and to influence their societies. Much of these flowed from America to Europe, partly because mission-minded people had more reason to be concerned about the latter continent, and partly because churches in the United States seemed to fare so much better in a society that was in every respect just as modern as any European nation.[6] Only very recently, the rise of the 'nones' in their own country has caused Americans to look at European churches as possible sources of renewal for America, rather than the other way around.[7]

This was the air I breathed in the sector of orthodox Reformed Christianity where I grew up. It was a sector that was still relatively unaffected by ageing and church-leaving, and so could believe that it had a recipe against the increasing godlessness of the Netherlands. This feeling was boosted by the largely successful attempts of Dutch evangelical Protestants to build their own organizations during the 1970s and 1980s, through which they kept secularization at bay (at least, superficially), and from which they fought bitter culture wars against abortion and euthanasia in the 1980s and 1990s – wars that were all lost, by the way. Meanwhile, on the evangelistic frontier influential church models like Willow Creek and Saddleback crossed the Atlantic and helped us hope that there remained a market for Christianity even in a secular society. From the United Kingdom came the Alpha course, followed by other evangelistic courses. While these approaches have not been without results, by and large we failed to see that most of the evangelistic 'success' was achieved among people who were socialized in the faith already, and that churches grew mostly by drawing dissatisfied Christians from other churches. In sum, most of our evangelism was still largely revivalistic.

If I were to draw a graph from my birth year (1969) until now, the line would show a clear 'blip' in 2005. Until then I had lived and witnessed in places in the Dutch Bible Belt, where Christians were a majority. Many people who have only a tourist's knowledge of the Netherlands suppose that it is extremely secularized. To an extent this is true: currently, only about 35 per cent of the Dutch are members of a church, and no more than 8–10 per cent attend church with any regularity. In fact, there are more self-confessed atheists than Christians in the Netherlands. However, while the Western part is predominantly secular, most church-going Christians are concentrated in the central and eastern parts of the country. There you can find quite a number of villages and small towns where active Protestants are still a majority or a large minority at least.[8] Historically, in such locations the Dutch Reformed Church (the ancient national Church) has a prominent position, with a variety of newer, 'free' or 'independent' churches around it like moons orbiting Jupiter. In the local governments Christian political parties are well represented, sometimes even as a dominant force. Until recently, these parties still had the power in such Bible Belt places to keep shops, theatres and swimming pools closed on Sundays, for example, or to prohibit blasphemy in public spaces.

Of course, I knew agnostics and people of other faiths in those days. I wasn't raised in a Christian bubble. But all these contacts happened against the backdrop of a local culture that was profoundly impacted by organized Christianity. I am not saying that it was a 'Christian' culture throughout (whatever this may be), but in one way or another, it was 'normal' to be a Christian, or at least a church member, in these towns. Not 'normal' in the sense that it was unthinkable to be a non-believer (there were plenty of those), but in the sense that being a believer was not weird, not deviant; you knew that there were many other people just like you. As a consequence, many people 'inhaled' Christianity, so to speak. It could not be avoided. You encountered countless tacit affirmations of the faith: large posters of Christian parties on the streets during local elections (we have a multiple party system), friends from church who greeted you in the shopping mall, children collecting money for Tear Fund or other Christian organizations, the Bible club for children during the long summer holiday. And of course all shops were closed on Sundays, even though this is reversed rapidly now.

All this changed in 2005, when we moved to Amsterdam. In Amsterdam perhaps 3 per cent of the population attend church regularly, one half of which consists of immigrant Christians from Africa and the best part of the other half are immigrant Christians from the Bible Belt. In Amsterdam it is not 'normal' to be a Christian. On the contrary, Amsterdam is a secular Bible Belt: entirely its opposite and in many ways just as closed off to whatever contradicts its worldview. When we met our neighbours after we moved, they were surprised: 'Are you religious? You mean, really *strict* and all that? Interesting . . .' It felt like we practised one of those extinct professions, the kind you see demonstrated in open-air museums: blacksmith, basket-weaver, or letterpress printer. To them we were members of a lost tribe that had missed the boat to civilization somehow. Our opinions about God, Jesus or the Church might have been mildly interesting from an archaeological point of view, but of course they were completely obsolete.

Experiences like these affected us deeply. Of course, it was not as if you suddenly heard opinions that you never heard before. As I said, we had not been separated from the real world before we moved to Amsterdam. Rather than philosophical, our transition was primarily a social one, and because people are social beings to the core this will inevitably impact your faith as well. For the first time we lived in a place where our deepest convictions were not acknowledged at all, or even respected. Despite yourself, you begin to realize how completely self-evident it is for the vast majority in Amsterdam to live without God or the Church. In this profoundly secularized environment people do not even bother to be atheists. God is not interesting enough for one to have an opinion about him. Scholars of religion call this attitude 'apatheism'.

Especially for someone with a missionary heart this is a nagging realization. It undermines deep assumptions that you hardly ever thought about. People who are inspired by mission often think as entrepreneurs – at least in my experience. They believe that there is a real need for God and Jesus 'out there', but that the Church does not respond to this need because of its closedness. They assert that we now live in a 'post-Christendom' world, and that people are therefore finally free to choose their own religion, providing wonderful opportunities for missionary pioneers to 'play the market'. The Church could do better, and more people would come to the faith, if only the Church weren't so afraid to renew itself. Too often the Church leans back in fear or arrogance: people can come to us, as long as they adapt to our routines. As a matter of fact, I do believe that many churches could do better, but I also know that this is not the whole problem. Such revivalistic assumptions make sense in cultures of 'nominal' Christianity, or in religious parts of the world. But deep secularization means that mission work is not just a matter of a renewed or refreshed supply; you also face a decreasing demand. Regardless of how inventively or creatively you wrap it, there are many people who simply do not find the product all that interesting. My impression is that mission-minded people often do not really dwell on this. But in Amsterdam this reality will hit you, inevitably.

We had come to Amsterdam to contribute to mission in that city, to try and plant new churches. And while we did that, I soon noticed that all dreams about mass conversions were based on thin air. While Christianity certainly continues to prove itself as a vital life option to some people – sometimes with high-profile conversion stories by leading authors and thinkers[9] – these stories are a far cry from a so-called 'people movement'. Rather than a continuing stream we saw drops here and there (beautiful drops, for sure!). I entered that typical faith crisis that comes with a radical change of life. Only if you become a real minority will you find out how much your faith is intertwined with your social context, how much it depends on plausibility structures that *affirm* this faith. You ask yourself the question what it actually means to trust in God, to believe in Jesus and his kingdom, when virtually nobody shares this faith or is even vaguely interested in it. You start to wonder whether it really is worth your time to invest so much in one seeker who knocks on the front door, while so many others leave through the back door. These questions hit you with double strength when you notice that people can be really happy without religion, and that they do not need God either to care deeply about their fellow humans, or to give to charity. In most of them you do not find this sense of emptiness, or the vague sense of guilt that can be found among non-believers or ex-churchgoers in more religious areas. In Amsterdam, faith has nothing to do with 'doing the decent thing' or 'following tradition'. If you want to go to religion, you are absolutely free to do as you like, but it is purely a matter of individual appeal. And this appears to happen to only a few.

In those days the insight became more important to me that the Bible was written by minorities. For the New Testament this goes without saying, but for the Old Testament it is just as true that this is the voice of a minority tradition in ancient Israel. This appears crystal clear from the lamentations and criticisms of the biblical prophets, and recent historical research confirms this picture.[10] In that time certain parts of the Bible that had not meant much to me before began to speak to my heart. Especially the story of Daniel in exile became very meaningful. Daniel managed to develop a positive faith identity in a context that did not support or affirm his faith.[11] If your faith survives in exile, it will only happen by being thrown back on the nourishing narratives of the Bible, and by being connected with a faith community. The rest will soon become insignificant, or fade away. The story of Daniel and other stories from Israel's captivity went with us also when we left Amsterdam, and moved to the deeply secularized rural area south-east of the city. Again, the faithful formed small groups here amidst a rather disinterested world.

Of course, I do not contend at all that Christian life in such a place is miserable. On the contrary, it is often very salutary indeed.[12] In some respects, following Christ in an almost completely secular environment is easier. For starters, the paralysing culture wars, so characteristic in nations and locations where Christians feel threatened on the one hand, and are still strong enough to wield power on the other, have disappeared together with all their ensuing bitterness, Christian inferiority complexes, unholy political alliances, or struggles to stay in power. There is no significant Christian politics in the secular city, usually there are no Christian schools, and meeting a fellow Christian makes you happy enough as it is, no matter to which church he or she belongs. Secularization and the loss of cultural power tend to burn away all minor debates; they are great tools to help us concentrate on core issues, and forget about everything marginal. There are no ways to keep the 'world' at a distance or under control. Personal spirituality, your family, a few intimate friends, the faith community, a modest mission – that is what it takes. If you have children, they will recognize at a pretty young age that they do not 'belong' completely. They are living in a 'foreign' city with new, seemingly superior gods. Most of the time they will be loners as far as faith goes, or they will be part of a small minority. I think we will not really understand secularization unless we see that educating our own children into the faith is also evangelism. There is nothing self-evident about children becoming Christians, even if they have been raised in a Christian family.

In short, everything is very basic in a secularized culture: it is virtually impossible to just 'go along', based on habit or routine. If the message does not find a place in your heart, it will wither away sooner or later. It is as simple as that. Peer pressure will smother the faith of those who are not actually caught by the good news. And this throws Christians back on the core of their religion, the deepest sources of their tradition. I do not contend that this situation is ideal, or that it is superior to more religion-friendly contexts, but it is the situation in which more and more Western Christians find themselves. Increasingly, they will have to learn how 'to sing the LORD's song in a foreign land' (Ps. 137.4).

These experiences also provoke questions that keep me occupied every day in my work as a missiologist studying the secular West. However we articulate it, mission is about impact. Mission is born from the desire that the gospel will have an influence on human lives and societies. But what will happen with missionary ideals when the world around us changes so rapidly? Which models have we received from the past, and can they really help us in this new age? Are there biblical sources that have anything to say in a post-Christian culture? Can we learn from non-Western Christians who now have discovered the West as their mission field? And above all: how can you keep a positive Christian identity, while knowing at the same time that the majority of the people around you does not share this identity, nor ever will?

Over time I have become impressed by how profoundly our thinking about mission and evangelism is flavoured by the connection between Christian faith and cultural power. In a certain way, this connection even stamps the missionary initiatives of Africans and Asians who have come to the secular cities of the West in order to evangelize and plant churches. I think we need to analyse this connection critically, and should look for new approaches. In so doing we can learn a great deal from the biblical narratives of exile and diaspora, but also from the experiences of Christians who have lived as minorities for centuries, in societies that are largely indifferent or even hostile to their convictions. I think that it is possible to have an inspiring missional vision, while knowing that you will not be able to convince the majority of the people around you that your faith is worth the effort.

So, what kind of a book is this? That is not easy to say. It contains social science, historiography, a bit of systematic theology, quite a lot of biblical theology, and some tentative exercises in practical theology. But though it may be difficult to categorize, I am quite sure about its purpose: essentially this is a study about missional spirituality. To me this is a most crucial matter, especially in a context where 'mission' is difficult and often without much visible result. Decades of post-war missional thinking have been characterized by finding the most effective missional 'structures' and 'models'; but in the end there are no missional *structures*, only missional *people*.[13] It is impossible to engineer ourselves into the mission of God; instead we need to have a clear picture of what it means to be involved in this mission when human standards of success seem hardly applicable. In a sense, we need to find out what it means to receive mission as a gift rather than a task, as a way of being that has its reward in itself rather than in what it produces. We shouldn't take a missional spirituality for granted, as so often happens in mission literature. We shouldn't idealize 'missionary congregations' as if they were somehow impregnable to the acids of modernity. If successes are few and far between, mission-minded Christians may lose heart like any other person. The faith of a missionary is just as fragile (maybe even more so) than that of other Christians.[14] In other words: we shouldn't think of secularization as the enemy 'out there'. It seeps into the Church, into the very foundations of faith, and it may eat away courage, trust and joy unless it is checked by a renewed experience of God's love and grace.

What do we need for such a spirituality? To begin, we need a sober, hard look at what it means to live in a secularized society. I have met far too many church leaders who tend to look away from the hard facts of decline, using phrases like 'the Holy Spirit has his own statistics'. Denial will not help the Church. If faith is 'a living, bold trust in God's grace' (Martin Luther), we shouldn't be afraid to gaze into the intimidating complexities of our culture. This is God's world, and to look away from reality is to alienate ourselves from God. So, Chapters 2 and 3 are devoted to an analysis of our cultural situation in the West, and to a critique of existing missionary models such as 'church growth', 'countercultural community', 'revival' or 'transformation'. I am not writing these models off altogether, but I sincerely believe that they are far too indebted to the Christendom dream of '(re)converting the West'.

Second, in order to keep or to regain a joyful confidence amid secularization we need a narrative that helps us make sense of our situation, and locate ourselves on the map. Where are we? Why are we here? And especially: what does God have to do with it? Might he be involved in the secularization of the West? I look for answers to these questions mainly by exploring the biblical traditions of exile and diaspora. We should remind ourselves that in a sense the biblical prophets were much closer to our experience than our own ancestors. Until very recently Western Christians lived in an unbroken world of Christendom, where Christianity was both self-evident and superior. But similar to ourselves the prophets lived as a contested minority, surrounded by people who sincerely doubted or ridiculed their beliefs, and routinely followed other gods. So, we might find something in their words that helps us find our bearings in our world. Chapters 4 and 5 delve into the narratives of diaspora, both in the Old and the New Testament, eventually arriving at the first letter of Peter and his wonderful vision of a people who are both 'exiles' and 'a royal priesthood' at the same time. These two concepts – reflected in the title of this book – display the impotence of being a small Christian community in a largely secular context on the one hand and a positive missional vision on the other. They present a hopeful perspective: even if you have become an 'alien', it is perfectly possible to mediate between the story of God and the story of people.

Finally, we need a vision of what it might look like to be a small Christian community in a largely indifferent world – that is *God's* world nonetheless. In Chapters 6 and 7 I venture into some tentative descriptions of such a community. Nothing of this is too concrete or programmatic, in the sense of 'seven steps towards a vital missional community', but I hope it is concrete enough to be inspiring as a theological map for revisioning the congregation in a deeply secular society.

Further reading will reveal even more that I am a Protestant, with a Reformed background. It remains to be seen if this book rings a bell in more churched areas of the West, or in more religious areas of the planet. Also, I am curious whether Roman Catholics and Pentecostals will find here anything they can use. There is no voice from nowhere, and no vision can be translated to other contexts without serious challenges. So, this book is deeply contextual and autobiographical, even where I present historical analysis or biblical theology. Far from seeing this as an embarrassment, I believe that this is necessary. I think that, to some extent, all theology is autobiographical (even though many theologians try to hide the autobiographical nature of their own books!), and as a missiologist I wouldn't know what it means to write non-contextual theology. Therefore, in this book I do not pretend to give a universally valid description of the mission of the Church, and I certainly do not suggest that the deep secularization of Western European cities is the future for all societies where Christianity has made its inroads. Yet, I do believe that the Church especially in a context where she has little or no impact can learn something about the significance of Christian faith that may be important for the global Church. It may be the particular task of small communities in a secularized environment to learn these lessons for all of Christianity, just like other churches in other circumstances learn other lessons for the whole Church. Thus, I can only humbly present to the wider Church what I have discovered in my context, hoping that it can speak to other contexts and to other traditions as well. With this in the back of my mind I have done my best to write as ecumenically as possible.

I write this book as a theologian and researcher, who is at the same time involved in missionary practice. This makes it a dilemma of the kind C. S. Lewis once described as 'either to taste and not to know or to know and not to taste'. It is an intellectual dilemma of all times, but particularly in cases where you love to be engaged in what you want to understand by critical thinking. 'As thinkers we are cut off from what we think about; as tasting, touching, willing, loving, hating, we do not clearly understand.'[15] Just think of enjoying a hamburger while at the same time trying to analyse its ingredients, or reflect on the moral and ecological aspects of beef production! People are most efficient when they can separate themselves – at least for a while – from inconvenient, critical questions, so that they can be totally absorbed by practical challenges. Many good missionaries and evangelists I know are such people: go-getters with strong convictions. Researchers, on the other hand, are at their best when they can keep their distance from practical issues, and are able to look critically at what is precious to them. Many of my academic colleagues are wired like that. Often these two groups find it difficult to interact fruitfully, in spite of much good will on both sides. Lewis thought that myth is the partial solution to this 'tragic dilemma': a narrative that helps us to *feel* and *understand* at the same time. While I do not pretend to be a myth-writer, I will try to compose a narrative that conveys something of the thrill of witnessing while asking critical, sometimes painful questions about why and how this is done. Either way, my purpose is to sustain and improve missional practice.

Above I have outlined the content of this book. However, before focusing on the particular challenge of the secularized West I will present as briefly as possible my views of missiology, namely the science that studies (Christian) mission. After all, this book deals with a missiological question: what does it mean to be 'sent' as the Church and as Christians in this world? So let us turn to this question first.

Notes

1 In recent English missiological literature a distinction is sometimes made between the adjectives 'missionary' and 'missional', the latter being presumably less burdened by colonial history and less predicated on a dichotomy between Church

and mission. While I appreciate the attempt to surpass an ecclesiocentric approach of mission, the distinction does not work in most other languages, including my own. Also I am not sure if changing an adjective is the solution, if the new adjective still refers to the contested term 'mission' – where the real problem seems to be (more about this later). Therefore, I have chosen to use both adjectives, for the sole purpose of literary variation. For discussions, see Guder (ed.), *Missional Church*; Wright, *The Mission of God*, pp. 24–5; Bolt, *The J.H. Bavinck Reader*, p. 116 fn. 8 (with special attention to the translation of the Dutch adjective *missionair*, the term that was used in the original version of this book).

2 Newbigin, 'Can the West be Converted?'

3 And not just in the 1980s. See the recent, largely sympathetic reflection on Newbigin's question by Harvey Kwiyani on https://harvmins.com/2017/10/28/can-the-west-really-be-converted-a-non-western-reflection-on-the-newbigin-question-part-1-of-2/ (published 28 October, 2017).

4 Archbishop's Commission on Evangelism, *Towards the Conversion of England*.

5 See Paas, 'The Making of a Mission Field'.

6 In fact, the awareness of the United States as a 'mission field' emerged somewhat later in time. See for example Craig van Gelder, 'A Great New Fact of Our Day'. The first mentions of European nations as 'mission fields' happened already around the turn of the twentieth century (see Paas, 'Making').

7 See, for example, Tim Keller in *Movements of the Gospel: Experiments in Ministry in Unfamiliar Places* (City to City Conference Reader, Krakow, Nov. 2018), p. 4: 'No one knows if North America and the great global cities of Asia, Latin America, and Africa will become as secular as Europe, but it feels to me as if Europe is the missional frontier for the whole Christian church.'

8 In general Dutch Catholics are far less observant than Protestants. The Dutch Bible Belt is predominantly a Protestant phenomenon, even though there are nominally more Catholics than Protestants in the Netherlands.

9 Think of journalist Peter Hitchens (brother of atheist author Christopher Hitchens) and author Francis Spufford in the United Kingdom, prize-winning writer Willem-Jan Otten and journalist Stefan Sanders in the Netherlands, or the former atheist-become-priest Tomáš Halík in the Czech Republic. While they are more or less famous and influential people through their writings and their high level of public self-reflection, they certainly represent many others who have less or no access to the media.

10 See a.o. Van Bekkum, 'Coexistence as Guilt'.

11 I reflected on this in a booklet containing sermons from our first period in Amsterdam. See Paas, Wierda, *Ontworteld*.

12 Here one might want to compare the insightful comments by James, *Church Planting*, pp. 23–9, about Christian vitality in one of the more secular cities of the United States, Seattle.

13 Here I fully agree with the German missiologist Henning Wrogemann, who writes: 'The talk of "missionary structures" (still in the 1960s) always leads us astray, because it is never structures but rather inspired, radiating – that is to say, reflecting God's light – people who do the work of misson' (*Den Glanz wider-spiegeln*, p. 73; my translation).

14 See, for example, Paas, Schoemaker-Kooy, 'Crisis and Resilience'.

15 Lewis, 'Myth Became Fact', p. 42. Lewis has reflected more extensively on this dilemma in his autobiography *Surprised by Joy*, pp. 253–6.

I

Mission in a Secular Nation

1.1 A Contested Idea

A wind of mission is blowing through Europe. Its first breeze was felt in
the United Kingdom where the period of the 1990s was declared to be
the Decade of Evangelism. Since then, an impressive interdenominational
collaboration has taken shape, resulting in countless initiatives pursuing 'fresh expressions of church',[1] embarking on engaging studies and
introducing training strategies. While this spirit came upon Germany a
little later and with somewhat diminished force, even there all manner
of innovative impulses bloomed in the new century.[2] Meanwhile, the
Netherlands does not remain behind, as the sound of 'mission' and 'com-
missioning' rings from every crack and cleft in the church building. There
appears to be a general awareness in the nations of Western Europe that
the churches should turn outward more intentionally, deliberately reaching out to a rapidly changing society. This requires renewal of the entire
ecclesiastical enterprise, from organizational structure to leadership
training, from liturgical practice to theological reflection. Such sentiment
is expressed by all Christian traditions today, and not just in Europe.

Being one of the most secularized areas on the planet (and still counting), Western Europe may be a good case study of how this rediscovery of 'mission' works out in a post-Christian context, and which
challenges it has to face. Clearly, the winds of mission arose partly in
response to decades of ecclesial decline, but not everybody agrees that
mission is the *right* response. Part of this lies in the problematic history of the word 'mission'. The American missiologist Michael Stroope,
for example, has recently argued that the word 'mission' as a label for
cross-cultural evangelism and ministry arose among the Jesuits in the
sixteenth century, and as such is deeply implicated in the crusading and
colonializing mindset of that time. He makes the case that the 'modern missionary movement' was invented by Protestants at the end of
the nineteenth century, and was subsequently projected back on the
Bible and early church history. In this way a great diversity of historical
and cultural experiences was lumped together under one flag and thus

homogenized, while at the same time an imaginary historical continuity of 'missions' was invented. He concludes that the 'mission' label has become too problematic for further use, and suggests another label: 'pilgrim witness'.[3]

However, while I appreciate much of his rich, detailed historical description, and have nothing against the words 'pilgrim' or 'witness' (as the title of this book shows), I am not convinced by his main argument. Obviously, words have become tainted during their long march through history. The word 'mission' is no exception, and unless we invent new concepts every decade or so this cannot be helped. Interestingly, Stroope himself shows that his own favourite label of 'pilgrim' was used as their most popular self-definition by the European crusaders when they went to the Holy Land to slaughter Muslims and Jews in the name of Jesus![4] But to argue, as Stroope does, that 'mission' is exhaustively defined by its connection with the violent history of crusading Christendom, and that all previous and subsequent experiences of boundary-crossing witness therefore should not be called 'mission', sounds like an overstatement. Of course, the Apostles and many early Church Fathers did not speak Latin and thus did not use 'mission' and its derivatives, and certainly early Latin translations of Greek words for 'sending' (as, for example, in John 20.21)[5] should not be read as if Jesus commanded 'mission' in the sixteenth- or nineteenth-century sense of the word. Also, it is most certainly true that 'mission' needs to be redeemed from a history of colonialism and violence. But the point is, when we talk about 'mission' we talk about a *tradition*, developing over time, and referring to a wide cultural variety of practices and concepts, some of which change in meaning or are supplanted by others. Like any tradition, the tradition of 'mission' contains discontinuities and dark chapters, but I am quite sure that Paul or Patrick or Boniface would have recognized something familiar in each other's practices of boundary-crossing witness, and that they together would have recognized the work of, say, Hudson Taylor and Gladys Aylward as related to their own despite some real differences. Speaking of a 'tradition', rather than a timeless essentialist concept, also helps us to criticize historical and contemporary practices of 'mission' by comparing them to other practices in the same tradition. At least, that will be my approach of 'mission' throughout this book.

Meanwhile, negative associations with 'mission' abound, even among those of whom you can safely say are inspired by the missionary spirit. Examples from my own context are the clergymen Ruben van Zwieten and Ad van Nieuwpoort who together have established an initiative among bankers, lawyers and consultants in the *Zuidas* (South Axis), the booming financial district in Amsterdam. Their ministry seeks to refamiliarize their professional audience with Bible stories. In an interview with a Dutch daily, they clarified immediately: 'We are not missionaries; we don't speak in terms of conversion here at the *Zuidas*.' Yet a few phrases later, they do precisely that, but claim that by the term 'conversion' is meant a 'return to humanity'.[6] Evidently they mistrust the desire to be missional, which they associate with a diminution of humanity and the subjection of people to the ecclesiastical system. Clearly, this echoes the sentiment expressed above by Stroope.

If anyone thinks that this aversion against the 'M-word' is only typical for so-called 'liberals', they should think again. In my own country similar reactions can be heard on the orthodox side of the spectrum. Some years ago in a conservative Christian daily the Reformed theologian Jakob van Bruggen said that all the talk about a 'missional congregation' is evidence of an ecclesial inferiority complex. Apparently, the Church is so upset about the fact that society does not find her relevant any more, that she is prepared to do anything to be as agreeable and accessible as possible. But this ignores a more fundamental question: why should the Church be 'relevant' in the first place, and who sets the criteria for this relevance? Wouldn't this mean to subject the Church to worldly standards? Surely the Church exists for the pleasure of God, and that should suffice.[7] Interestingly, 'mission' on this view is not associated with power play at all! On the contrary, it symbolizes bending over backwards to be as nice as possible to an unsympathetic audience.

More or less in similar terms, another Dutch Reformed theologian, Abraham van de Beek, contends that the current missionary storm in the Church hides the real problem: there is a profound crisis, a divine judgement on the Church and on Western culture. Rather than working feverishly with the purpose of propping up its institutional frame, the Church should concentrate on prayer, repentance and conversion. The crisis must be sounded out in much more depth.[8] Van de Beek and like-minded critics seem to consider 'mission' as a cover-up for the spiritual poverty of church and society, a denial of the real problem. Rather than a remedy, the word 'missional' is a symptom of this spiritual disease. Again, a criticism shimmers through of a Church that no longer knows why it exists in the first place, and hides this by emphasizing its own institutional survival.

I could mention more examples, but this suffices to show where the problems are felt. By way of summary:

- 'Mission' is egocentric: it sets the Christian religion and the Church in the centre, rather than the world, compassion and humanity. It wants to 'win souls', if necessary at the expense of human beings.

- 'Mission' is shallow: it means to adapt your message to whatever people want to hear, in order to be seen as 'relevant' by a society that is in fact not the least interested in the Church.
- 'Mission' is activistic: it does not sit well with theological and spiritual depth. It is managerial and focused on institutional survival, so that a missional course betrays the Church's identity.

The picture emerging from this is quite confusing. On the more progressive side of the Church 'mission' is apparently associated with a Church that has *too much* self-confidence. The Church possesses the truth, and therefore it must proclaim it to the world. 'Mission' is associated with an attitude of arrogance, with looking down condescendingly on a lost world, with prioritizing the ecclesial institution, with forcing people into a moral straitjacket. On the more conservative side, however, 'mission' seems to be connected with a Church with *not enough* self-confidence. That is to say, a missional church convulsively seeks the favours of the world, it dumbs down its own message and liturgy, no longer believes its own sources, it avoids confrontation, and it is far too eager to be liked and appreciated by an indifferent outside world.

This is a rather contradictory picture. Frankly, I can't avoid the impression that ideological prejudice is influencing these objections. Of course, nobody will have a hard time trying to find examples of the problems that are mentioned here. Obviously, a deeply secularized and pluralized society can and will provoke spasmodic responses from the Church's side. In fact, we see this happening everywhere in institutions that feel threatened by late modernity, such as labour unions, the art sector, and political parties. It is also quite clear, in my opinion, that the rhetoric of growth and conquest is neither appropriate nor realistic in the current situation in the West. But does this mean that we have exhausted the concept of 'mission'? Are these objections doing justice to the missional wind that is blowing through many Western churches?

I am concerned that theologians in particular are doing away with 'missional' thinking through one-sided analysis. Those people in particular who have been trained to contribute thinkingly to the necessary renewal of the Christian tradition in the West seem determined to keep staring stubbornly in the rear-view mirror. The temptation to do so can be understood, especially when looking at the difficult cultural conditions in which 'mission' must be reinvented. But such criticism renders it almost impossible to think of 'mission' with an open mind. That would be a shame, because Christianity is undeniably missional by its very nature. The fact that we live in circumstances which necessitate the revision of much traditional missionary thinking does not change that at all. Whoever abolishes mission, mutilates the Christian faith, regardless of how deeply he or she is sounding out church and culture. Moreover, this theological desertion would mean to abandon many people who passionately and self-sacrificingly invest themselves in Christian mission. What we need is a theology that does justice to the deep secularization of many areas in the West without saying goodbye to the missional nature of Christianity. We must look for a new and at the same time recognizable shape of being a missional Church and being a Christian in a post-Christian society.

In this chapter I embark on this task. First I will sketch the missional foundational structure of the Christian faith, a structure that is non-negotiable as far as I am concerned, regardless of the justified criticisms that we can level against many historical examples of mission. Subsequently, I will describe a number of recent developments in the discipline of missiology. Under the influence of non-Western Christianity and the evolution of the ecumenical discussion we can now see a revaluation of this missional, evangelizing DNA of Christianity.

1.2 What Do We Mean by 'Mission'?

Long ago Christians used to speak Latin, and earlier still they spoke mostly Greek. That is where our vocabulary about 'mission' comes from. The word 'missional' is derived from Latin *mittere* ('to send') and *missio* ('mission'). These words in turn are translations of Greek *apostellein* ('to send') and its derivations. In this way we have received terms like 'mission', 'missionary' (a person sent out for mission), 'apostle', 'missiology' (the science of mission), and adjectives such as 'missionary' and 'missional' (everything concerning 'mission').

So, to be 'missional' has everything to do with the sense of having a 'mission', to be 'sent' or 'commissioned'. It points towards attempts to establish meaningful contact with other people with the purpose of influencing their lives. This is not an exclusive obsession of Christians or even of religious people in general. Our secular society teems with 'mission'. Surely, the principle of mission is universal: when a community thinks that it knows something, that it has certain important practices, or that it possesses something that more people should know, or do, or possess, a form of 'mission' kicks in. The examples are literally countless, because 'mission' is in every capillary of human existence. Think of education, development aid, training programmes in Afghanistan, marketing, charities, blogs and vlogs, scholarly publications, advertisements, op-eds, buddy projects, food banks, websites or journals with tips for computer users, cooking shows, and so on. In all these examples there is a form of transfer or communication: one person or group tries to teach or convince or help another. Sharing is deeply human.

The motivations behind all these forms of mission are diverse, and not all are virtuous. But eventually almost all of it boils down to one of these: a sense of *responsibility* or *enthusiasm*. The vast majority of people experience these motives now and then. Our Western wealth creates a sense of responsibility among many: after all, we did not 'deserve' to be born in a relatively affluent society. And others, for that matter, did not 'deserve' to be born in Bangladesh. Prosperity thus creates a sense of obligation, especially so because we often experience having such prosperity as – at least to some extent – a matter of grace. Also, seeing other people's suffering, or that of animals, can arouse this sense of responsibility. Not for nothing do NGOs and charities like to show heart-rending images. Furthermore, a sense of duty can emerge from the conviction that your own opinions or your own culture are in some way superior to those of others. Saying this is still rather unpopular in civilized post-colonial circles, but we cannot escape the fact that peace missions and actions for human rights and international justice have something to do with the idea that our Western societies are better than others in some areas at least. More than was previously the case, leading Western commentators dare to say that other cultures would benefit from a functioning democracy, more transparency in public offices, less corruption, the rule of law, and so on.

Besides a sense of duty, enthusiasm or *Entdeckungsfreude* is a source of mission. People who get enthusiastic about something are usually also inclined to point others towards this new insight, product or recipe, or whatever it is that they are happy about. Modern marketing makes use of this principle. Products are disseminated 'virally', through countless users who upload video-clips, organize parties (Tupperware), or post tweets. 'Evangelism marketing' is now a familiar phenomenon. Wikipedia defines it as 'an advanced form of word-of-mouth marketing in which companies develop customers who believe so strongly in a particular product or service that they freely try to convince others to buy and use it'. Positive reviews by satisfied users are called 'testimonials' in this marketing lingo. Large companies like Apple and Starbucks speak unreservedly about 'evangelists' who recommend their products without asking a reward, purely on the basis of their own enthusiasm.

Clearly, we live in 'a culture of conversion' (Bryan Stone).[9] Human life is inescapably missionary. Everybody evangelizes. Whenever people become impressed by certain experiences, views, products or services, they feel the need to commend them to others. Whenever people are struck by their own success or by the failure of others, they feel the responsibility to share something of their own blessings with others. Clearly, there is nothing high and lofty about 'mission' as such. It is fully wedded with our social nature; we are witnessing, sharing, helping beings. 'The word is near you, on your lips and in your heart . . .' (Rom. 10.8).

In the New Testament this sense of mission is directly associated with the experience of Jesus Christ, and what God has done through him. A calling for 'mission' is intimately connected with this experience. In fact, this does not even require a 'Great Commandment'. Mission flows forth logically and spontaneously from the awareness that in Jesus Christ something unique and important has happened. Mission is inescapable when this event impacts us. 'Mission begins with an explosion of joy,' writes Lesslie Newbigin.[10] The shockwaves of this explosion continue until today; they are vibrating in innumerable human lives. 'With Christ,' says Pope Francis, 'joy is constantly born anew.'[11]

We see this throughout the New Testament. Like all people in all times and places the first Christians were social beings; they were steeped deeply in all kinds of communicative behaviour. It would certainly amount to over-theorizing in most cases to ask about the missionary 'methods' that they used. They did what all people do: they bonded with friends, talked with relatives, raised their children, they ate together, played together, worked together. And of course they shared the 'tidings of great joy' they had heard; they 'gossiped the gospel'.[12] Jesus' first followers, the twelve Apostles, 'proclaimed' the good news about Jesus in the Roman Empire. The apostle Paul is busy with 'persuading' his fellow Jews in the synagogues of Asia Minor. He talks about his desire to 'win' people. Also in other ways the Apostles distribute, as it were, their experiences with Jesus. For example, they heal the sick, 'in the name of Jesus', and more than their contemporaries the first Christians were concerned with the poor, slaves, women and children.

Throughout the history of Christianity we recognize these drivers of enthusiasm and responsibility that are characteristic for every 'mission'.[13] Let me mention a few motives that emerge both from the Bible and from later Christian literature:

- The awareness of having received a great privilege (election, grace, blessing), and that this creates responsibilities with regard to those who do not yet know this salvation;
- love for and compassion for people who are, in whatever way, 'lost' (because of sin, poverty, injustice, sickness, addiction);
- concern about the direction in which the world or the nation is heading; the idea of an imminent 'judgement' or 'crisis';
- joy: simply being incapable of remaining quiet about it;
- the awareness of having a vision of truth that – if accepted by others – will bring tremendous change in persons and societies;
- and the conviction of being part of an advanced (Christian) culture, that spreads blessing and wealth, which should not be begrudged to other parts of the world.

As I have mentioned, as far as *structure* goes these motives are not specifically religious or Christian. In fact, they are entirely natural or human. Of course, their *content* does make a difference. Needless to say, evangelizing for Apple is not the same as evangelizing for Jesus. And warning that the world is heading towards an ecological crisis of immense proportions should not be completely identified with the biblical concept of God's judgement. Still, I have trouble understanding why the idea of 'mission' encounters so much resistance these days. It goes without saying that much can go wrong in processes of persuading and proclaiming. Such processes can and almost certainly will be stained by arrogance, short-sightedness, lust for money or power, inner uncertainty, fear, rigidity, shallowness, despotism, and what not. Nobody will deny that Christian mission has taken its share from all these vices. Undoubtedly, such experiences have determined the criticisms of 'mission' mentioned above. But in my opinion it is rather sterile only to criticize missionary desire, or to play it out against other interests. Mission is part of life; as humans we cannot *not* 'missionize'. Moreover, mission is intrinsically connected with the Christian core experience of Jesus and his story. They cannot be separated. In short:

- If you are even remotely enthusiastic about Jesus, his story and his kingdom, it does not make sense to always censure people who recommend this experience to others;
- if you are even remotely convinced that unique truth can be found in Jesus and his story, you can't always oppose attempts to persuade others of this truth;
- and if you even remotely believe that Jesus and his story are relevant for the concrete needs of all sorts of people (or even for the future of the planet), you can't always criticize people who, consequent on this belief, commit themselves to helping their fellow humans.

There is a missionary logic in the heart of Christianity. This basic belief structure is what permeates this book. In the pages to come I will crack more than enough nuts about various examples and models of Christian mission, but in my view these beliefs are non-negotiable.

1.3 In Search of an Intercultural Missiology

So, to me 'mission' has everything to do with processes of influencing and change, based on a sense of responsibility and enthusiasm about the gospel. Mission takes place eminently at the boundary of faith and unbelief, and it normally happens without much 'technique' or 'method'.

Now, one should always be a bit careful with striving for 'influence' and 'change'. For example, it is easier to influence people when they depend on you. I started my career teaching religion to children between 12 and 18 years old at a high school. Friends who knew me from missionary practice sometimes suggested that this was an excellent opportunity for evangelism. I did not think so, and I still don't. Children are at school because they must attend. They will be punished if they don't attend. For their graduation they depend on the teacher's evaluation of their work. So, there is a clear imbalance of power. In my opinion this does not sit well with what is traditionally called 'a free offer of grace'. And it agrees even less with the way the Apostles in the New Testament spoke about the 'weakness' and 'foolishness' of the gospel. Of course, my students (at least some of them) will have noticed that I am a Christian. And if they asked questions about it, I was more than happy to answer them. But I have tried not to misuse the hierarchical relation between teacher and student for evangelism.

On a larger scale, missional work was and is often embedded in such relations of dependency. Particularly when these differences are very large, the risks of violating the integrity of the work increase. I remember, for instance, an activity where homeless people received a free meal. But prior to the meal there was a Bible study with an exposition. In order to get hot soup, the visitors had to sit through this evangelistic talk. Regardless of how good their intentions were, in my opinion the mission workers misused the homeless people's dependency.

Many will agree that such examples are indeed problematic. However, when we look at an even larger scale, we might wonder whether the entire concept of 'mission' suffers from this dependency problem. As we have seen, 'mission' is often associated with the time that Western nations could impose their version of Christianity on their colonies in the South. Now that the non-Western world has become emancipated, while at the same time secularization and pluralization have increased in the West, mission can easily be considered as obsolete, or even a direct threat to world peace.[14] Moreover, we have to face the fact that former colonies are often more Christianized than Western nations. What kind of 'mission' should Americans or Dutch people do in Kenya or Brazil?

Processing this makes it easy to understand why 'mission' has become rather dubious for many people. For some time, therefore, there has been a trend to look for a term that does more justice to equality and mutuality. It has been suggested, for instance, that missiology should be renamed 'intercultural theology'. Whereas missiology previously focused on 'cross'-cultural or 'trans'-cultural questions (with the implicit assumption that the roles of 'sender' and 'receiver' were well defined), the preposition 'inter' suggests mutuality. So far as 'intercultural theology' pertains to relationships between Christians and churches from different cultures, this is indeed a valuable and necessary correction of older models of transfer and dependency. The self-theologizing nature of non-Western churches may be respected better by this term.[15] Surely, Christian theology is no longer the exclusive possession of Western churches; Christians from all cultures are contributing to it.

At the same time, the question arises what happens to the classic emphasis on faith transmission with this rebaptizing of missiology. Has 'mission' become so suspect that we need to get rid of it altogether? Has it become so entangled with a problematic history that mission is now merely a source of shame and embarrassment? Has 'conversion' become a dirty word? But how do such feelings relate to the countless ways in which 'mission' happens in our societies? Why does every government, organization, company or individual have the right to influence others, and should the Church refrain from it? Is that not an invitation to hypocrisy? Would such a renaming of the discipline of missiology not also imply that theologians separate themselves from 'ordinary' Christians, who (in some sectors of the Church, at least) certainly are engaged in mission and evangelism? Are academic theologians called to look down their noses at Alpha courses, and apologize to their secular colleagues for their less enlightened fellow believers?

It is clear that we live in a new, post-colonial era. Western Christians have to realize that they are no longer (and never were) the guardians of 'mission'. But what is the consequence? What does it mean to take this new reality of non-Western Christianity seriously? Rather than abandoning mission in every traditional sense of the word, it means in my view that we will have to develop an *intercultural* missiology.[16] And precisely such a missiology will show a renewed emphasis on faith-transmission as the heart of mission. Of course, this evangelistic transmission must be redeemed from its unilateral colonial past. After all, if anything has become clear during the last decades, it is this: mission is no longer a movement from Christian nations in the West to their non-Christian territories in the South. In recent literature two crucial concepts constantly come to the fore. The first is that we nowadays speak of 'World Christianity'.[17] The second implies that mission is increasingly a matter of 'mission from everywhere to everywhere'.[18] These two concepts should inform every conversation about mission today, including our use of traditional terms like 'mission field'. Christianity has found a home in many cultures, so that this world is no longer one of 'senders' and 'receivers'. No longer is Christian faith produced in the West and received in the South; in many places it is produced, rebuilt, assembled and shipped. Mission is not a one-directional movement any more; it has truly become intercultural.

In this new reality of mobile 'mission fields' and 'mission bases', Europe has become a 'mission field' too.[19] This discovery, together with the emancipation of the non-Western Church, has contributed to the awareness that Christianity is a world religion and that mission moves to and fro over the planet. Whoever takes this seriously – and we cannot turn this clock back – will have to accept that the discipline of missiology can no longer be defined unilaterally by Western theologians, based on their own cultural experiences (or frustrations). We must do full justice to the fact that tens of thousands of Africans and Asians see the West as a mission field more or less in the same way that has become an embarrassment to Western Christians themselves. They are coming to Europe, and increasingly to America as well,[20] as a continent that should learn to know Jesus anew, that should be converted from its servitude to the powers of darkness, that must be rescued from its cynical and hyper-critical mindset, its coldness and moral decadence.[21] In this context a Malawian missionary in the West, Harvey Kwiyani, speaks about 'the evangelisthood of all believers'.[22] It strikes one as odd when Western theologians, out of their (largely justified) sense of guilt about the era of Western colonial missions, want to establish a new form of Western domination by stripping missiology from everything that smells of faith-transmission and conversion. This fails to do justice to Christian mission itself, that is endlessly older, wider and more coloured than the period in which white Westerners missionized in Africa, Asia and Oceania.[23] And it fails to do justice to the theological self-understanding of a large number, perhaps the largest number, of Christians on this earth.

That is why I think that a truly intercultural theology – engaging intensively with Christians from other cultures – should make us accept 'mission' as boundary-crossing witness, proclamation and persuasion.[24] Far from being a religion that has accidentally become multicultural somewhere on the road, Christianity has always tended to multiculturality. Exactly Christianity's missionary nature is the cause of its mobility and diversity.[25] Therefore, it is more than strange when a justified attempt to give more weight to interculturality results in the neglect of mission. The vision of a worldwide connection of persons and peoples is first and foremost realized by mission, by the simple yet revolutionary thought that everybody does not just have the right to receive the message that has been revealed to few, but is capable in every way to understand, accept and process this message. Nobody is too stupid, too smart, too barbaric, too uncivilized, too traditional or too modern for the gospel of Jesus. If this thought is abandoned, mission stops and tribalization begins.

1.4 Evangelism as the Heart of Mission

Thus, a missiology that is interculturally sensitive and historically conscious should centre on faith witness, or evangelization. On this particular point a new impulse has emerged. Since the 1970s we see on different sides a renewed focus on evangelism as the heart of Christian mission. In 1982 the World Council of Churches published *Mission and Evangelism: An Ecumenical Affirmation*, seeking a re-evaluation of evangelism alongside its traditionally strong emphasis on social justice. The report *Together Towards Life: Mission and Evangelism in Changing Landscapes* (2013) continues this line, whereby the influence of the Pentecostal movement and Eastern Orthodoxy should be noted.[26] Illustrating this development is also the document *Christian Witness in a Multireligious World* (2011), in which the World Evangelical Alliance, the Roman Catholic Church and the World Council of Churches present a common code of behaviour for evangelism, and mention witnessing as the heart of Christian life. Moreover, for the first time in its history the World Council has published a handbook on evangelism in Europe (2017), meant for theological education and formation, and containing a large number of case studies.[27] Among evangelicals a more or less reversed movement happened: in various manifests we see a growing attention for holistic or integral mission (social justice, ecology) in addition to evangelicalism's traditionally strong emphasis on evangelism.[28]

Looking at Europe in particular, it cannot be denied that contextual developments have contributed to this renewed promotion of evangelism. Now and then, prominent Christian-Democratic politicians suggest that we should revive Europe's Christian 'soul'.[29] Theologians and other intellectuals point at the growing 'speechlessness' with regard to religiosity in general and Christianity in particular. The pluralization of European nations, among other factors caused by the immigration of non-Western Christians to this continent, leads to questions of a missionary nature. Equally remarkable are the developments in the Roman Catholic Church. Post-Vatican II documents like *Ad Gentes* (1965), *Evangelii Nuntiandi* (1975), *Redemptoris Missio* (1990) and *Evangelii Gaudium* (2013) accelerated theological thinking among Catholics about mission and evangelism. Moreover, since the early 1990s different popes emphatically concentrated on what has been named the 're-evangelization of Europe'.[30]

It thus seems that the heart of Christian mission is recovered everywhere. This does not mean that the breadth and depth of mission that was rediscovered in the twentieth century is lost, but more than has been the case for some time mission is regaining its authentic focus – especially in the secularizing countries of the West. Here I do not intend to venture into precise definitions of 'mission' and 'evangelism'. Instead, let me present three complementary statements that can be found among many missiologists.

First, it must be recognized that 'mission' is wider than 'evangelism'.[31] The Roman Catholic missiologists Stephen Bevans and Roger Schroeder show how three theological paradigms have become important as sources of missional thinking in the second half of the twentieth century: (a) mission as participation in the mission of the Triune God (*missio Dei*), reflecting early Christian ecumenical teaching on the doctrine of God; (b) mission as liberating service of the reign of God, drawing on the synoptic Gospels – particularly Jesus' kingdom ministry; and (c) mission as proclamation of Jesus Christ as Universal Saviour, continuing the preaching of the Apostles in Acts and the Epistles.[32] Together these theological paradigms provide a rich biblical and theological support of a variety of activities, such as for example have been expressed in the 'five marks of global mission' by the Church of England: (a) 'to proclaim the good news of the kingdom', (b) 'to teach, baptize, and nurture new believers', (c) 'to respond to human need by loving service', (d) to seek to transform unjust structures of society', and (e) 'to strive to safeguard the integrity of creation and sustain and renew the life of the earth'.[33] While these five marks are not meant to be exhaustive, they do present a fair picture of what Christian mission is about. Thus, we can summarize 'mission' as everything the Church is called to say, do and be in this world, as a witness to what God has done in Christ with a view to the coming of his kingdom.[34]

Second, although 'mission' is large and wide, it is not infinite. 'The missionary task', says the famous South African missiologist David Bosch, 'is as coherent, broad and deep as the need and exigencies of human life.'[35] Of course, such a wide definition renders it difficult to delimitate 'mission'. Some would say: if everything is 'mission', nothing is 'mission' (Stephen Neill). But that is a risk, according to Bosch, that we should be prepared to take. Greater risk may lie in the attempt to limit something which is in fact infinite.[36] I agree with Bosch. If there is truth in the great discovery of the twentieth century that the Church is missionary by its very nature, we should really not be too concerned about the question of where exactly the Church's work is still 'mission' and where it becomes something else. At the same time, I think that it is somewhat vulnerable to let 'mission' correspond with the 'need and exigencies of human life'. It is theologically more adequate, in my opinion, to describe mission as participating in the realization of 'God's purposes in the world, *as these are demonstrated in the ministry of Jesus Christ*' (Andrew Kirk).[37] This focusing of 'mission', based on Jesus' ministry in the Gospels, is important in order to keep mission close to its source. Jesus' life, death and resurrection – not the need and exigencies of people – are the normative lens on God's purposes with his world. As far as I am concerned this still means a wide definition of 'mission': Jesus proclaimed the news of the kingdom, healed the sick, gave bread to the poor, included marginalized people, prophesied against those in power, formed a community around himself, and encouraged a sober lifestyle. Wherever we do this in his name, we are doing 'mission'. Still, this definition indicates a certain limitation of what we can call 'mission'. For example, Jesus did not take up arms, not even for a good cause, and he kept himself rather distant from matters of earthly politics – not rejecting them as such, but treating them with a certain indifference. Also Jesus seemed remarkably uninterested in the question of whether he had a large crowd of followers, even if he desired to see people find their destination.

Third, having said all this I want to reiterate that the best way to maintain a recognizable and intelligible form of Christian mission is to take evangelism as the heart of 'mission'. Rather than trying to describe carefully where 'mission' ceases and other Christian work begins, we should keep stressing where the heart, the magnetic pole, of mission lies. This lies in testifying about God's news in Jesus Christ. This does not necessarily mean that evangelism always precedes everything else, namely that it has *priority*. It does mean, however, that evangelism has *ultimacy* in relation to everything else that is mission. Although, everything missional has integrity in itself and is good because of itself (just like raising children consists of all sorts of activities which are all good in themselves), 'mission' has reached its purpose only when people are invited to respond to the gospel of Jesus Christ (just like faithful parents want to see their work completed by their children's choice for faith).[38] In the previously mentioned World Council of Churches report *Together towards Life*, evangelism is defined as that 'mission activity which makes explicit and unambiguous the centrality of the Incarnation, suffering, and resurrection of Jesus Christ'. Evangelism, according to this document, is what the Church discovers when it explores its identity as a missionary community.[39] Mission, agrees the American Lutheran missiologist James Scherer, 'means the *specific intention* of bearing witness to the gospel of salvation in Jesus Christ at the borderline between faith and unbelief . . . [T]he heart of mission is always making the gospel known where it would not be known without a special and costly act of boundary-crossing witness.'[40] To be clear, this evangelism is not limited to a testimony by words alone. The gospel is proclaimed and demonstrated; it is a matter of words and deeds. But regardless of whether it happens through words or actions, it is characteristic of evangelism that it invites people to follow Jesus, to become disciples. And this 'becoming disciples' means to be commissioned for God's mission – 'teaching them to obey everything that I have commanded you' (Matt. 28.16–20).

In my view these reflections indicate the direction an intercultural missiology should go that is at home in the Western context. 'Mission' takes place in a field of motivations, intentions and creative verbal and non-verbal practices with the intention of giving witness to God's actions in Christ at the borderline of faith and unbelief. Since especially in the secularized parts of the West religious speechlessness is widespread, we must emphasize that Christian mission should not be ashamed of naming the Name.

1.5   The Receptivity of Christianity

In his deceptively simple reflections on the Incarnation, the British theologian Rowan Williams writes about the receptivity that is part of the Divine being. 'Jesus (to put it crudely) isn't God just when he's being strong and in control; he's God when he speaks lovingly to God the Father, when he submerges what his human nature fears or longs for in love for the Father.' We could say that Jesus' mission is not just 'divine purpose, power and action', but also 'humility, responsiveness, receptivity'. If the Incarnation is indeed the source of Christian mission, its most profound pattern, this Spirit-filled movement between the Father and the Son, should render mission as not simply giving but receiving as well.[41] To participate in Jesus' mission means to be part of this giving and receiving. God's love works both ways.

To follow Jesus in his mission is to become part of this divine relationship of giving and receiving. If that is true, Christians should accept that through mission they are not only teaching others how to be disciples, but they are learning as well. More precisely, there is a theological order here, in which receptivity *precedes* purpose, power and action. 'What do you have that you did not receive?' (1 Cor. 4.7). It should be clear that this receptivity must not be isolated from the action part of mission, as if receiving were primarily a matter of prayer and contemplation after which the 'real' work of giving must be done by 'us' serving 'them'. Rather, evangelism and social ministry are always disciplines of becoming dependent on God before being anything else. When Jesus sends out his disciples in pairs, he commands them to go without purse, bag or sandals, and depend on the welcome that is offered by 'people of peace' (Luke 10.1–12). Through their vulnerability the missionaries receive a deeper sense of God's grace. They learn to understand what God is up to in the lives of those they engage with, and thus the stereotypical framework of 'givers' and 'receivers' is broken. By contrast, both the missionaries and their hosts are given the opportunity to find their place in God's mission.

Thus, what 'mission' is in this particular situation, how God is to be known and worshipped in this specific context, and what the good news is for this person or community, can only be discovered in a genuine encounter. Rather than knowing all the answers in advance, the missionary embarks on an adventure of learning to know God's intentions through participation in God's mission. Precisely the fact that sharing is in the heart of the Christian faith, renders this faith receptive to others. This is inevitable: a missionary religion seeks to establish contact with people who think and live differently. And a genuine contact means that you open yourself up to other people and cultures – there is no other way. The receptivity of Christianity thus implies that there is a deep relationship between not being 'ashamed of the gospel' (Rom. 1.16) and a true interest in others, their language and culture, a sincere willingness to learn from them. Again, we should point to the life and death of Jesus who gave himself completely without losing his identity.

Because this relationship is profound and bound up with a healthy spirituality, it is easy to lose sight of it. There is a risk that interest for others becomes a means to an end rather than a learning experience. Just think of the infamous example of 'friendship evangelism'. Conversely, there is a real possibility that mission runs out of steam when a genuine relationship with the 'other' is established. It is easy to have strong opinions about 'Islam' in general, but what about the nice Muslim woman next door or your sister's Iranian husband? Yet, in mission it is crucial that we know how to inhabit the tensions between the desire to influence other human beings and to be influenced by them at the same time.

Christianity's receptivity becomes visible in two ways. First, since the earliest days of Christianity we see the gospel entering all sorts of cultures. Surely, these cultures are criticized, but they are not erased. On the contrary, the Gambian missiologist Lamin Sanneh contends that in the colonial era African indigenous cultures were protected by the missionaries against self-contempt and cultural erosion. If the words of the highest God could be expressed in their language and cultural repertoire, their culture wasn't so insignificant as slave traders and colonizers had told them.[42] There is something quite remarkable in a religion that so effortlessly 'writes itself away', as it were, into all kinds of languages and cultures. Behind this lies a deep confidence that God is truly the God of all the earth, and that he has not left himself without a witness in any place or culture. Christians rarely give it a thought, but what a wager is it to translate God's Word! Still, the first Christians immediately embarked on it; even the words of Jesus are no longer available in their original Aramaic. Every proclamation demanded a patient, intense interest in the receiving culture. This culture had to be 'listened to' attentively, so as to 'look the words out of the mouths of the mothers at home, the children on the street, and the common man on the market place' – as Luther wrote in his letter on Bible translation (1530). Every translation created an indigenous expression of Christianity, with all its ensuing enrichment and risk.[43]

In this context, the Scottish missiologist Andrew Walls uses the metaphor of a theatre. Imagine life, he suggests, as a play (the 'drama of life'), with a key scene that may be called the 'Jesus Act'. It is obvious that your perspective on this vital development depends on your position in the auditorium. '[E]veryone sees the stage, but no one sees the whole stage. People in the auditorium view the Jesus Act on the part of the stage most open to them where they are sitting.' Nobody has a full, unobstructed, 'objective' view, even though he or she may see more than somebody else. Yet, everybody has something unique to share from his or her own position in the theatre. Precisely the universality of the gospel – it is an offer to everyone – requires a multitude of responses. This is the inevitable consequence of the way this gospel has been revealed: *within* the drama of human life. The divine Word has become 'flesh'; it is incarnated. It has accepted an ethnic identity, a shoe size, gender, DNA, body length, hair colour. Jesus could not become abstract 'humanity'; he became human, a Jewish man. This concrete cultural revelation requires a concrete 'incarnate' response. Therefore, a 'pure' supracultural Christianity is impossible; Christianity only exists as an ever-increasing variety of cultural expressions.[44]

Another aspect of missional receptivity is bound up with this. If Christian faith can enter many cultures, then it will also return to its sender from these cultures. 'Feedback' is part of serious mission. Precisely because of its missional nature, Christianity is not just a teaching but also a learning religion.[45] Of course, this has not always been acknowledged by Christians; often it has emphatically been denied in an attempt to safeguard the 'purity' of Christianity. Also it should be noted, as Philip Jenkins explains, that Christians may have learned most from others where they have been a minority, for example in Asia during the first millennium.

> [W]e are used to the idea of Christianity operating as the official religion of powerful states, which were only too willing to impose a particular orthodoxy upon their subjects. Yet when we look at the African and Asian experience, we find millions of Christians whose normal experience was as minorities or even majorities within nations dominated by some other religion. Struggling to win hearts and minds, leading churches had no option but to frame the Christian message in the context of non-European intellectual traditions. Christian thinkers did present their message in the categories of Buddhism – and Taoism, and Confucianism – and there is no reason why they could not do so again.[46]

Thus, the Christian Church has learned from the traditions of Israel by accepting and embracing the Tenakh as the Word of God; it has also learned from the Greek stoa, from Plato and Aristotle, and from the great religious traditions of Asia and Africa. This learning attitude flows from the conviction that God is sovereign. 'Did you bring God to us', Africans asked the first Western missionaries, 'or has he been here all along, before you came?' The answer is obvious: God was there long before the missionaries came, and he has worked there. But then it is inevitable that God's Spirit will somehow encounter the missionary from the 'receiving' culture. People and cultures are no passive receivers of the gospel; they appropriate it, and work it into their own cultural repertoire. They notice things that went unnoticed by the missionary, and they return their insights consciously or unconsciously to the worldwide Church. Countless are the examples of missionaries who started their work with all sorts of theological and moral expectations – delivered to them by their own cultures, and were totally surprised by the way in which other peoples accepted and appropriated the gospel. For example, they expected that converted Africans would quit drinking alcohol, but the new Christians kept holding drinking bouts while meanwhile releasing their slaves – unnoticed by the disappointed missionaries.[47]

Here we find the roots of the intercultural theology that I mentioned above. Mission can and must lead to mutual learning and receiving. In one way or another the gospel always returns to its sender. This is a process that requires much trust, sensitivity and patience. It cannot be controlled. Eventually, the missionary has to hand over the gospel to others, and trust God to do his work.

Fast-forwarding to the next chapters, it is fascinating to ask to what extent mission can learn from those who do *not* accept the gospel, because they don't understand it or because they do but reject it. Especially in the secularized cultures of the West this is an important question. Can missional Christians learn from the experiences of church-leavers, from the stories of people who simply are *incapable* of believing it? Is it possible for Christians to get a new view of the gospel when they listen carefully to people who vehemently criticize the Church and Christian faith? Can our faith be enriched, purified and deepened by a respectful confrontation with a non-believing world?[48] Does the gospel return to us in a special, indirect way via its advised rejection by others, and could this lead to a new cultural expression of Christianity? Are there truths about God that we can only sense through contact with somebody to whom God remains hidden? These may be the most important questions for Christian mission in a post-Christian society.

1.6 Summary and Conclusion

Although nowadays increasing attention is being paid to the missionary nature of the Church, at the same time much theological criticism with regard to 'mission' exists. Even though this criticism may be partly justified, it appears to suffer from caricature. Whatever we may have against particular instances of mission, Christian theology will have to maintain that there is no turning away from Christianity's missionary nature. This nature arises from the experience with Christ, the conviction that unique truth is found in him, and the belief that his life, death and resurrection have relevance for the needs of the world. Abandoning this means not merely to reject mission, but eventually also Christian faith itself. At the same time this underlines the heart of Christian mission: although mission is wide and deep, evangelism is its core. Recent developments in missiology, influenced by the worldwide Church and ecumenical discussions, also point in this direction. Finally, this heart is open towards the other, because Christianity's receptivity is intimately related to its missional desire.

Notes

1 A 'fresh expression of church' is 'a form of church for our changing culture established primarily for the benefit of people who are not yet members of any church'. It involves the conscious stimulation of various experimental ways of doing church, alongside (and in cooperation with) traditional means, with the goal of reaching as many and as dissimilar a people as possible. For a description and analysis of this phenomenon see, particularly, chapters 1, 3 and 4 in my *Church Planting in the Secular West*.

2 The *Arbeitsgemeinschaft Missionarische Dienste* or the Evangelical Church in Germany (EKD; the national Protestant church) initiated a number of church-planting projects in 2001, inspired primarily by developments in England. More on this is found in, for example, Roschke, *Gemeinde pflanzen*; Bartels, Reppenhagen, *Gemeindepflanzung*; and Baron, 'Back from the Brink'. The developments in this area have since then continued.

3 Stroope, *Transcending Mission*.

4 Stroope, *Transcending Mission*, pp. 169–72.

5 '*Sicut misit me Pater, et ego mitto vos*' ('As the Father has sent me, so I send you'). Latin *misit* and *mitto* are derivates of the verb *mittere* ('to send'), from which the noun *missio* is derived.

6 Dutch daily *Trouw*, 3 January 2012.

7 Dutch Christian daily *Reformatorisch Dagblad*, 1 December 2011.

8 Van de Beek, *Lichaam en Geest van Christus*, pp. 179–80.

9 Stone, *Evangelism after Christendom*, pp. 258–9.

10 Newbigin, *The Gospel in a Pluralist Society*, p. 116. See also his *The Open Secret*, p. 3: 'The story [of mission] begins with the vast explosion of love, joy, and hope released into the world by the resurrection from the tomb of the crucified and rejected Jesus.'

11 Apostolic Exhortation *Evangelii Gaudium* ('The Joy of the Gospel', 2013), §1. For a more extensive exploration of the meaning of joy as a motive for mission, see §§4–10 and §§264–7.

12 See Paas, 'Evangelism and Methods'.

13 See, for example, Van den Berg, *Constrained by Jesus' Love*.

14 Skreslet, *Comprehending Mission*, p. 1. For a profound and extensive analysis of the crisis of (Western) mission, see Scherer, *Gospel, Church, & Kingdom*, pp. 21–38.

15 Cf. Wrogemann, *Interkulturelle Theologie*, a.o. pp. 37–41.

16 For this section, see also Paas, 'The Discipline of Missiology'.

17 The missiologist Lamin Sanneh wants to distinguish between 'world Christianity' and 'global Christianity', whereby the first concept is defined as 'the movement of Christianity as it takes form and shape in societies that previously were not Christian, societies that had no bureaucratic tradition with which to domesticate the gospel', and the second as 'the faithful replication of Christian forms and patterns developed in Europe' (Sanneh, *Whose Religion*, pp. 22–3). See further a.o. Walls, 'The Rise of Global Theologies'.

18 Walls, 'Afterword', p. 202. See also Walls, 'The Ephesian Moment'.

19 The first European theologian who (to my knowledge) called his own country a 'mission field' (*Missionsfeld*) was Gerhard Hilbert, Professor of Theology in Rostock, Germany (1916). See Paas, 'The Making of a Mission Field'. For a critical discussion of the term 'mission field' from a post-colonial perspective, see Hof, *Reimagining Mission*, pp. 89–96. While I am aware that the history and usage of 'mission field' are 'intricately connected with the construction of the other in concrete and fixed localities' (p. 96), I retain the concept, reiterating that it should be used against the background of the two leading concepts of 'world Christianity' and 'mission from everywhere to everywhere'. Mission fields are floating islands nowadays; they are constantly on the move.

20 See, for example, Kwiyani, *Sent Forth*.

21 For a discussion of recent studies of non-Western mission in Europe ('reversed mission'), and the images of Europe that are held by missionaries from other continents, see Paas, 'Mission from Anywhere'.

22 Kwiyani, *Sent Forth*, pp. 58–60.

23 The heyday of Western colonial and post-colonial missions lay approximately between 1490 and 1940. For surveys of non-Western, early Christian, and later missionary movements, for example from Africa, India and China, see Irvin, Sunquist, *History of the World Christian Movement I*, and *History of the World Christian Movement II*. This series aims at presenting a non-Eurocentric mission history.

24 Feldtkeller, 'Missionswissenschaft'.

25 See Paas, 'Intercultural Theology and Missiology'.

26 For a comparison and an analysis of both documents, see Jongeneel, 'Mission and Evangelism'.

27 Noort et al., *Sharing Good News*.

28 For a survey of this development, see Padilla, 'Integral Mission'. See also his *Mission between the Times*.

29 See Krause, *A Soul for Europe*; Hogebrink, *Europe's Heart and Soul*.

30 See, e.g., Dulles, *The Reshaping of Catholicism*, pp. 144–9; Üffing, 'Catholic Mission'. See also *Redemptoris Missio*, a.o. section 33.2, on the 're-evangelization' of 'countries with ancient Christian roots'.

31 E.g., Bosch, 'Evangelism'. Reprinted in: Chilcote, Warner, *The Study of Evangelism*, pp. 4–17. See also Bosch, *Transforming Mission*, pp. 409–20.

32 Bevans, Schroeder, *Constants in Context*, pp. 283–347. They base these three paradigms on their analysis of ecclesiastical statements by Roman Catholic, Eastern Orthodox, ecumenical and evangelical churches.

33 Walls, Ross, *Mission in the 21st Century*, pp. 1–104.

34 Cf. World Council of Churches, *The Church*, p. 33.

35 Bosch, *Transforming Mission*, p. 10.

36 Bosch, *Transforming Mission*, p. 512.

37 Kirk, *What Is Mission*, p. 21 (italics added).

38 This distinction between the 'priority' and 'ultimacy' of evangelism I borrow from Wright, *The Mission of God*, pp. 316–19. Theologically, this approach seems balanced to me, and is it also practicable.

39 Keum (ed.), *Together towards Life*, p. 29.

40 Scherer, *Gospel, Church, & Kingdom*, p. 37 (italics in the original).

41 Williams, *Tokens of Trust*, pp. 64–5.

42 See Sanneh, *Translating the Message*.

43 A famous example is the Old Saxonian Gospel harmony *Heliand* (c. 830), where Jesus is presented as a feudal lord, and his Apostles as his vassals (knights).

44 Walls, 'Culture and Conversion', pp. 43–4.

45 For extensive reflections on this 'learning' and 'receiving' in mission, see for example, Bevans, Schroeder, *Prophetic Dialogue*.

46 Philip Jenkins, 'When Jesus Met Buddha', *Boston Globe*, 14 December 2008. Online: http://archive.boston.com/bostonglobe/ideas/articles/2008/12/14/when_jesus_met_buddha/?page=1

47 Cf. Newbigin, *The Open Secret*, pp. 135–8.

48 See, for example, Westphal, *Suspicion and Faith*.

2

An Always Elusive Majority

In Chapter 1 I argued that evangelism is the heart of mission. However, it goes without saying that 'mission' never happens in a vacuum. This book is not about China or Egypt, but about the secular areas of the West – Europe in particular.[1] This is the part of the world that is termed by some as the 'missional frontier for the whole Christian church'.[2] What does it mean to evangelize there rather than somewhere else? What is really to be expected when we evangelize here? And what should we aim for?

I have written that 'mission' is everything to do with influencing. Individuals or groups, driven by a sense of responsibility or sheer enthusiasm, address others with the purpose of changing their beliefs and ways of life. Historically this has always played out on two levels. Mission can focus on individuals, but also on institutions and structures. In Europe – and in all places where Europeans have evangelized – mission was always about these two dimensions of conversion: changing humans and cultures.[3] This dual conversion process has often been called 'Christianization' – the making of Christian people and Christian societies. Here we may recall Lesslie Newbigin's question, 'Can the West be converted?', mentioned in Chapter 1. This question clearly reflects the traditional missionary emphasis on Christianization as the purpose of mission.

In the present chapter I will show by a historical overview that there has always been a certain distance between these two levels of mission in Europe. This is not hard to understand. After all, it is easier to declare a country formally 'Christian' by law than to really win people's hearts and minds. Although Europe as regards politics and culture oriented itself formally towards Christianity for centuries, for much of the time only a minority of people were devoted Christians. This relatively limited interest in serious Christianity became clearly visible only when in modern times the formally Christian framework of Western societies began to crumble away. I conclude this chapter with some missionary reflections based on these historical observations.

2.1 The Church as a Hospital and a Restaurant

Christianity in Europe has always been characterized by the relation between a committed minority and a large majority that was much more distant to the Christian faith, or even rejected it. This pattern appears to be very old, in spite of all attempts by churches and governments to change it. The British scholar of religion Grace Davie sees this typical relation between minority and majority recurring in two different religious 'economies' that are dominant in Europe.[4]

The first 'economy' she describes is determined by the Church as a public utility, an institution for the common good. This system operates on the basis of what Davie calls 'vicarious religion', that is, 'religion performed by an active minority but on behalf of a much larger number, who (implicitly at least) not only understand, but, quite clearly, approve of what the minority is doing'.[5] For modern Americans[6] and other non-Europeans this system is difficult to grasp, as it is connected with a history of Christianity as a national or cultural identity, combined with state churches. However, for Europeans from Helsinki to Madrid 'vicarious religion' definitely rings a bell. For many of them the Church is like a hospital. In principle you try to stay out of it, but it should be there just in case you need it. And of course there must be people to keep the Church going should you need it.

This vicarious role of the active minority is most clearly visible in what the Dutch call 'faith on wheels'. Traditionally, most Europeans will be rolled to a church three times: once in a pram for baptism (hatching), once in a coach for their wedding ceremony (matching), and once for their funeral (despatching). Also there is usually a role for the Church during national catastrophes or celebrations (like a coronation). In such moments countless Europeans appreciate that there are people who keep the business running, so that they can make use of the services of the Church when it is necessary.

However, vicarious religion also functions in other, less obvious ways. For example, Davie points to the fact that publicly confessed unbelief on the part of church leaders or their lack of moral behaviour provokes a more than usual irritation among many Europeans who do not darken the doors of any church. Even the priests don't believe it! It almost seems as if many people find that priests, pastors and bishops *ought to* believe, and that they of all people are to represent a high moral standard. Conversely, it seems that even non-members are interested in ecclesiastical authorities who live out Christianity credibly and sincerely. The wave of sympathy for Pope Francis speaks for itself in this regard. Finally, Davie pays attention to the symbolic significance of church buildings. Clearly, many people value these historic buildings, and want to keep them open as long as possible.[7] For example, in the quite secularized village where I live the restoration of the ancient church building was supported financially by almost all citizens, while a good number of them were prepared to give a helping hand. Many of these people never attend on Sundays, nor would they consider themselves as believers.

This is the oldest form of religion in Europe (with echoes in the early stages of the American republic), and it is supported largely by the more or less formal connection with church that most Europeans still have, through infant baptism, confirmation, a vague sympathy for Christian culture, and the like. Alongside this system, and partly overlapping it, we find another, newer and more international form of Christian religiosity that increasingly characterizes the active minority as well. Davie calls this a form of commitment based on choice ('consumption') rather than 'obligation'.[8]

> In Europe as well as America, a new pattern is gradually emerging: that is a shift away from an understanding of religion as a form of obligation and towards an increasing emphasis on consumption or choice. What until moderately recently was simply imposed (with all the negative connotations of this word), or inherited (a rather more positive spin) becomes instead a matter of personal inclination. I go to church (or to another religious organization) because I want to . . . so long as it provides what I want, but I have no obligation either to attend in the first place or to continue if I don't want to.[9]

In the performance of their faith, active Christians in the West will be inspired far less than they used to be by social and familial pressure, or a sense of 'what is the decent thing to do'. When I was in primary school, some 40 years ago, one could hear parents and teachers say: 'Behave a bit more like a Christian!' Here, 'Christian' was simply an equivalent of 'decent' or 'civilized', without much religious resonance. This identification of Christianity with generally accepted cultural codes has now evaporated, even among most Christians. Instead, their commitment to the Church is driven by what attracts them, or touches their senses (the 'feel-good factor'). This is everything to do with the disappearance of a formally Christian framework in secular societies. When being a Christian is no longer felt as standard behaviour or as the unquestioned heritage of the nation, fewer people will pay attention to it. Put differently, if believing is no longer 'obliged' and 'normal' it becomes an option, something that can be chosen or rejected. Faith becomes a matter of the *will*.

Of course, this is not everywhere the case yet, not even in the more secularized parts of the West. There are all kinds of individual, local and regional differences. But I clearly recognize this shift from obligation to consumption in Amsterdam and similar contexts. When I am leading a worship service on a Sunday morning in my own church, I know one thing for sure: these people are not here because their parents dragged them out of bed, or because they fear the sanctions of not going. They are here because they *want* to be here; their commitment comes from the inside. I do not contend that this is necessarily a 'better' way than a more traditional religious life; I merely observe that this has become the normal way of believing in a secular context. For better or worse, Christianity is consumed rather than assumed.

Davie asserts that this shift from obligation to choice does not necessarily imply an increasing shallowness in religion. 'Consumption' is not the same thing as 'consumerism' or 'selfishness'. Indeed, late modern people can have very serious reasons to choose something, perhaps even more so than in the past.[10] They can go on a pilgrimage, become fundamentalist or liberal, or take monastic vows. One can also decide to subordinate her own needs to those of others, to become a vegetarian, or adopt an ascetic lifestyle. However, people will no longer do these things because it is the village tradition, or because someone is the third son in the family (who is supposed to become a priest), or because he is afraid not to be a good citizen otherwise. In one way or another all these ways of life are carried by choice, often a vulnerable and contested choice, that must be nourished and affirmed over and over again.

Also, this model of religious consumption overlaps with the older model of vicarious religion. Even in a society where faith and church attendance are supported entirely by individual choice, there will be need of a minority that keeps the churches open should it happen that seekers feel the urge to attend. Also this minority is necessary to keep a reservoir of religious language – 'God talk' – at everyone's disposal. After all, if people have lost the vocabulary that allows them to engage with religious experience, it will be difficult for them to have this experience at all.[11]

Commitment to the Church does change, however, when individual choice becomes the motor of a Christian life. In the model of 'vicarious religion' the Church is like a hospital for which people who do not really participate are still prepared to foot the bill. In some European countries this even happens quite literally through a church tax. In this model people maintain a formal membership with the Church should bad times happen, but they will only show up when there is an urgent need to do so. In the emerging pattern of 'religion-as-consumption' the Church is more like a restaurant. You do not become a member of a restaurant, and you do not pay for it when you are not attending.[12] Also you are completely free to go to another restaurant, or to eat at home. But you can be very enthusiastic about your favourite restaurant, and you may be prepared to dig deep into your pockets for an unforgettable culinary experience.[13] Conversely, churches can profile themselves with their own 'kitchen', and present themselves proudly and self-confidently as places with a unique language, symbolism and tradition. This consumption of religion shows itself among other things in the rise of evangelical churches, televised worship services, Internet churches, the increasing attendance of cathedral worship, and Christmas Eve worship, and the dramatically growing interest for pilgrimages, festivals and retreats.

These two models differ most in how they frame the way people are connected with the Church. In the first model, this connection is formal, more or less in the same way people can be (sleeping) members of a labour union or political party. Such formal bonds can be very tough, but usually they generate little fire. In the second model these bonds are more emotionally charged. Therefore, one's relation with the Church is more vulnerable to societal changes (a restaurant can be 'out' just like that), and to ruptures in someone's biography (for example, by moving to another place or after a divorce). At the same time, a bond like this can be very intense, at least during certain periods in someone's life. However, both models have this in common: they assume an actively religious minority and a large majority that is passively or latently religious. This pattern is confirmed by longitudinal surveys in Europe, which indicate time and again that churchgoing and orthodox Christian beliefs are in retreat (although the process seems to level out in the most secular countries),[14] but that simultaneously the majority does not seem to have become predominantly atheistic.

2.2   An Ancient Pattern

At first sight, the pattern I sketched above based on Grace Davie's work looks like a new development. After all, our memory usually does not extend further than one generation. Therefore, we are inclined to compare the current situation in Europe with the period between 1850 and 1950, when a large part of the population in many countries attended church regularly. In fact, this is also the self-evident and rather uncritical point of departure of virtually every study into the religiosity of Europeans. The conclusion thus seems straightforward: everything is now far worse than in those golden days.

However, if we study European history over a longer stretch of time, this period of massive ecclesial mobilization appears the exception rather than the rule. The model of vicarious religion – an active minority keeping the Church going for the benefit of a large majority – seems to do more justice to the history of Christianity in Europe. This does not mean that nothing has really changed, but it does mean that the underlying pattern remains unmistakably European. In this section I will present some examples, by way of a general impression.

Historians will point immediately at the problem, clinging to every attempt to find such a contemporary pattern of religiosity in history. Whenever we try to trace this relation between an actively Christian minority and a passively Christian majority through the centuries, we run into the problem that the word 'Christian' did not always have the same meaning. A soldier of the Frankish king Clovis who called himself a 'Christian' in the year of our Lord 510, did not convey exactly the same meaning by this label as a follower of John Wesley in 1780 or novelist Marilynne Robinson in 2019. If I would try to apply this differentiation through a number of periods in European history, I run the risk of projecting a modern (evangelical) distinction between 'born again' and 'nominal' Christians on times in which nobody would have understood this distinction in the first place. I am aware of this risk, but at the same time I think that it is possible to make a careful distinction between Christians with mostly intrinsic motivations, and Christians for whom secondary motivations are predominant – and that this distinction albeit with some reserve can be found throughout history. Even in a culture that is completely soaked in religion there are creators of culture and mere followers.

For example, we can reasonably assume that Christians in the Roman Empire preceding the conversion of the emperor Constantine (AD 312) were generally intrinsically motivated, because being a Christian could cause you trouble at that time. One's Christianity could be a reason for discrimination, and one's life could even be in danger. To me it also seems reasonable to assume that the explosive growth of Christianity in the fourth century, after Constantine's conversion, can be explained at least in some part by the influx of people for whom Christianity had become a matter of social desirability (good citizenship, career). Christianity was, after all, declared a privileged religion first (313), and subsequently the state religion of the Roman Empire (380). This meant among other things that everybody who aspired to a position in public service had to be a Christian. Ambition for success and status will have inflated the number of conversions considerably.

Finally, I believe it is reasonable to assume that people whose Christian identity is not so much the conclusion of an existential quest or a choice against all odds but rather an adaptation to changing political and societal conditions, will generally look for a performance of their Christianity that creates as little tension as possible with the rest of their lives. There are, in short, people whose Christianity is the sun in their universe around which everything else turns, and people for whom their Christianity is one of the planets in a universe that orbits another centre. And I think that this – admittedly typological – difference has always existed.

At this point it is tempting to make a comparison between estimations of the number of Christians in the Roman Empire immediately before the conversion of Constantine (10 per cent),[15] and the number of people (Christians, Muslims, others) who regularly visit a religious worship service in secularized Western nations. In the Netherlands, for example, 17 per cent of the population attend a religious ceremony at least every month.[16] A figure around 10 per cent might very well be what we could expect of the size of Jesus' 'little flock' in a culture that does not propagate Christianity as some sort of obligation. Apparently, the Dutch theologian, journalist and politician Abraham Kuyper thought something like this in his Stone Lectures on Calvinism at Princeton University in 1898.[17] In one of the lectures, titled 'Calvinism and the Future', he said:

> Then, again, the Calvinistic confession is so deeply religious, so highly spiritual that, excepting always periods of profound religious commotion, it will never be realized by the large masses, but will impress with a sense of its inevitability only a relatively small circle.

Yet according to him this was not at all a reason to lose heart. '[T]he smallness of the seed need not disturb us, if only that seed be sound and whole, instinct with generative and irrepressible life.'[18] Of course Calvinists are not the only Christians, but I think Kuyper's observation can easily be applied to the wider history of Christianity in Europe – or the West in general. A serious, demanding Christianity will not receive big cheers from the large majority of people in most times. In their time Martin Luther and John Calvin knew this just as well.[19] The Dutch confession (*Confessio Belgica*) from 1561 speaks of the 'Catholic or universal Church' that 'sometimes for a while appears very small, and in the eyes of men, to be reduced to nothing', and is 'spread and dispersed over the whole world' (Article 27).

2.3 Christendom as a Missionary Ideal

Of course, all this does not mean that there are no differences between those days and ours. The current secularization of Europe displays an ancient pattern, but this pattern plays out against a changed cultural background. The most striking difference is the degree to which Christianity for centuries has been the political and cultural norm for society. In

English studies this historical connection between Christian faith and culture is often labelled as 'Christendom', the English translation of Latin *christianitas*. In an authoritative study Christendom is defined as

> a society where there were close ties between the leaders of the church and those in positions of secular power, where the laws purported to be based on Christian principles, and where, apart from certain clearly defined outsider communities, every member of society was assumed to be a Christian.[20]

For those who are familiar with the anti-Christendom rhetoric of much contemporary missiological literature, it may come as a surprise that for many Christendom was a *missionary* ideal. In his Encyclical *Immortale Dei* (1885) Pope Leo XIII described this ideal in rather nostalgic terms:

> There was once a time when States were governed by the philosophy of the Gospel. Then it was that the power and divine virtue of Christian wisdom had diffused itself throughout the laws, institutions, and morals of the people; permeating all ranks and relations of civil society (section 21).

Even if Leo's once-upon-a-time picture of Christendom rings a bit too anti-modern and romantic to our ears, there is an inevitable missionary logic in the Christendom construction. If indeed the Christian message contains a transformationist ideal, and if indeed it is true that 'there is not a square inch in the whole domain of our human existence over which Christ does not cry "Mine!"' (to cite Kuyper again),[21] then Christendom may be the more or less expected outcome of such a message when it takes root in human societies. This is exactly how Oliver O'Donovan in his *Desire of the Nations* describes the transition under Constantine. The 'gentile mission' of the Church in the early Roman Empire had two frontiers: society and rulers. 'Its success with the first was the basis of its great confidence in confronting the second.'[22] For O'Donovan this is partly a matter of historical apologetic. It would be anachronistic and, in fact, rather priggish to reproach the Church of the fourth century that it took up the challenge created by respectability and power. 'The church of that age had to do contextual theology just as we do.'[23] After all, if the North Korean rulers today would turn to the Church, inviting it to cooperate towards a more just and peaceful society, would it then be more authentic to remain in the catacombs?

Of course, embarking on such a mission would also lead to rather unexpected and likely unintended results, since the world is never completely under control, but it seems that a good case can be made that

Christendom was historically inevitable. That is, if a transformationist ideal is indeed part of the Christian missionary enterprise. Accepting this transformationist ideal would imply more than just a historical apologetic defence of Christendom; it would render Christendom *theologically* inevitable as well. To be clear, that is not O'Donovan's argument. To him Christendom was not a missionary project or mission's justification; it was rather a *response* to the Church's witness to the kingdom of God, and a sign that this mission had been blessed.[24] If I understand him correctly, O'Donovan would argue that the Church should witness about the kingdom rather than strive for worldly influence, but that at the same time it should be responsive to any sign that the world has become attentive to this witness.[25] However, as modern missionary literature often revels in language of 'growth', 'change' and 'transformation', the question must be asked how this relates to the counter-Christendom rhetoric of the same literature. How can one seek the 'transformation' of society and at the same time avoid a restoration of some form of Christendom? Also it should be asked to what extent this dream of a transformed society under the lordship of Christ tends to become particularly popular in contexts of beginning secularization and culture wars.[26] I will discuss this further in the next chapter.

2.4 The Creation of a Christian Culture

All this said, with this formally Christian structure of European societies lies an important difference from today, at least where the more secularized countries are concerned. For a long time through this structure the religiosity of the majority was centred on Christianity rather than a plurality of worldviews, as is currently the case. But if we think away this formal framework and concentrate on the extent to which people are actively committed to their religion, the difference between then and now begins to fade. Time and again a pattern of an active minority vis-à-vis a rather passive majority becomes visible.

For example, paging through a number of historical studies into the rise of Christian culture in Europe immediately reveals how the process of Christianization in Northern and Western Europe was politically inspired to a high degree, and often a concurrent feature of military conquest.[27] Admittedly this led to the formal Christianization of these societies, but not to a passionately confessed Christianity of the masses. Here we should take into account the tribal nature of the Germanic kingdoms: whenever a king converted to Christianity (either by inner conviction or by political calculation), it went without saying that his subjects followed him. After all, they had sworn him an oath of fealty. It is very unlikely that a Saxonian warrior had any articulate idea of tribe members choosing autonomously a different religion than their chief's. Therefore, we must be very careful with modern and liberal emotions connected with concepts like Christianity being 'forced' or 'imposed' on these ancient Europeans. Evidently this was a societal order that was created through military conquest, and it was maintained with violence if necessary. But the latter is true for every societal order, and the first for most – including many modern societies (if we look back far enough). The crucial issue is: is this order being supported generally, is it eventually internalized by those who are part of it? Do they understand the making of this order as going against the grain of how things should go (as most liberal citizens of modern societies would), or do they see it as more or less the usual ways of the world (as undoubtedly our ancestors would)?

In this Christianization process the unity of Christianity and Roman culture played a role too. In North-Western Europe mission was to a high degree a civilizing project, and Christianization often entailed first and foremost that a layer of civilization was painted on the Germanic barbarians. This cultural varnish consisted of marriage laws, political arrangements, formal religious duties, taxes, and the like.[28] Even then it was not always easy to keep the converted pagans on track. Boniface (ca. AD 672–754), the apostle of Germany and the Low Countries, wrote to his good friend Daniel of Winchester:

> Without the patronage of the Frankish prince I can neither govern the faithful . . . nor protect the priests . . . nor can I forbid the practice of heathen rites and the worship of idols in Germany without his orders and the fear he inspires.[29]

Daniel on his part reminded Boniface that the pagans 'were frequently to be reminded of the supremacy of the Christian world'.[30] Thus, partly by their fascination with the splendour of Romanized Christian culture, and partly by the military superiority of the Frankish kings, the Germanic tribes accepted a formally Christian identity as their societal order. This however did not entail that they had a deep understanding of or even a great sympathy for Christianity. To a large extent this early Christianization period was a top-down process.

As far as we can ascertain, this form of mission produced a rather unintensive form of mass Christianity, often mixed with pre-Christian religiosity. An important factor in all this was that the Church, now that it had come to understand itself as the religious framework of entire societies, had to lower its standards of Christian life and faith.[31] As regards the political elites, from their position in the centre of power they would have felt, at least formally, a stronger connection with the Christian religion.

Their awareness of the role of Christianity for their own careers and societal order is not to be confused however with sincere faith and good works. The tradition of liberal Christian elites in Europe, who were prepared to set the good example, but at the same time saw to it that their subjects were not given too much to 'enthusiasm', is likely as old as the first stage of Christianization. In this context Thomas Cahill mentions the fifth-century Gallic patrician and career diplomat Ausonius as a typical example of the elite culture towards the end of the Christian Western Roman Empire. Formally Ausonius shared the religion of the emperor, like every ambitious person. But materially things looked quite different: 'His real worldview glimmers through all his work – a sort of agnostic paganism . . .'[32] In this sense Ausonius had more in common with early-modern elite Christians like Machiavelli and Montaigne than with his contemporary Augustine of Hippo.

At this point the question arises as to what extent the Christian ideal of discipleship – sincere love for God and one's neighbour, imitation of Christ, self-denial, loving your enemies – can be reconciled with the mundane life of labour, marriage, having children, working the land, paying your mortgage, maintaining order, doing politics and waging war. The Canadian philosopher Charles Taylor emphasizes that in every world religion there are different 'speeds' or 'levels': one for the minority who feel called to a radical commitment while distancing themselves from ordinary life, and one for the large majority who need to compromise and therefore must settle for a more moderate religious practice.

Undoubtedly, in medieval times there were those among the laity who sincerely and with great effort tried to practise the ideal of Christian discipleship. Otherwise it would remain unexplained how movements of renewal and revival were often so successful – even if only temporarily. But notwithstanding such movements, the minority ideal of discipleship was represented primarily by the monasteries. True conversion (*conversio*) entailed that one renounced the world and entered a religious order in order to live the 'perfect life' (*vita perfecta*).[33] Here Taylor speaks of 'hierarchical complementarity', a religious system characterized by at least two different ways of being a Christian, one of them 'higher' than the other (hence 'hierarchical'), while supporting each other in some way (hence 'complementarity').[34] Thus the different ways of being a Christian (the one more radical, the other more willing to compromise) were not played out against each other; they belonged to the same system, and they supplemented each other. Knights protected the monks and the farmers, the farmers fed the knights and the monks, and the monks piled up prayers and good works for everybody.

It is not hard to see the logic in this, when Christianity is the national religion. How else is it possible to unite a whole people in the same faith community? Also it is not hard to see in this concept of hierarchical complementarity the historical equivalent of what Grace Davie calls 'vicarious religion'. Apparently, this is a deeply ingrained and ancient way of dealing with Christianity in Europe.

Unique to Europe, at least according to Taylor, is that here great effort was made to replace this system by another system: a religion in which everybody has the same 'speed'. From the late Middle Ages until modernity Christian mission in Europe happened through a series of reformations and revivals with the purpose of leading the masses to a deepened and more intensive form of Christianity. This 'Christianization of Christians' as the Dutch historian Peter Nissen calls it,[35] happened against the background of a generally shared ideal of a Christian nation and usually with the active support or benevolent consent of governments. While 'reformations' can be considered as more or less planned attempts to further Christianize the masses through large-scale catechesis, juridical measures and ecclesiastical reorganization, 'revivals' may be seen as rather spontaneous 'contractions' of the multitudes around commonly recognized values.[36] Especially in the period of beginning secularization in the eighteenth century, nostalgia for an undivided Christian society played a role in attempts to revive semi-Christian masses ('baptized pagans') into personal faith (a 'religion of the heart'), church attendance, and sanctity.[37] While it had appeared increasingly difficult to enforce a Christian order upon society through the government, this could perhaps still be done in a democratic way via the conversion of the people. In modern evangelical movements this eighteenth- and nineteenth-century revivalistic concept of culture change through individual conversions has maintained its vitality. Take, for example, the motto of the International Fellowship of Evangelical Students (IFES): 'Change the world, one student at a time.' This historical matrix of revivalism and moral restoration is also one of the roots of twentieth-century culture wars, both in America and Europe.

Of course it is impossible in a few brief paragraphs to do justice to these prolonged and constantly repeated attempts to involve the majority of Europeans in intensive Christianity. It also matters from which angle one looks at this history. Roman Catholic historians and cultural observers like Charles Taylor and, more recently, Brad Gregory[38] tend to emphasize the typically Protestant aspects of rationalization and disenchantment, which according to them have contributed to the secularization of the masses. Briefly put: if you remove all magic from the world and offer people the unrelenting choice of being a Christian radically and personally or not being a Christian at all, many people will choose not to be Christians. Protestants, for their part, like to dwell on the authoritarian style of Catholic mission and the persistence of 'superstition' in Catholic territories. At the very least we can conclude that, despite centuries of reformation and revival, the attempts to lead the majority of Europeans to orthodox Christian beliefs and regular church attendance has failed. Also the eradication of superstition has only been partly successful.[39]

To mention just one example, the practice of the Reformed Church in the Netherlands after the Reformation is revealing in this respect. Around 1600 only one-fifth of the population in the Northern provinces were active church members (both Catholics and Protestants), whereas the majority were not or barely involved in church.[40] The church council minutes of the city of Haarlem from 1581 report that the largest part of the population in the city consisted of 'children of the world who are to be brought to Christ'.[41] The Dutch historian Van Deursen writes that the Reformed Church in the sixteenth and seventeenth centuries had two types of membership: 'full members' (*lidmaten*) and 'sympathizers of the Reformed religion' (*liefhebbers van de gereformeerde religie*). The first category had made a public profession of faith, they stood under church discipline, and were thus allowed to participate in Holy Communion. The second group was more distantly involved, for instance by contributing financially to the building of churches, and the like. This group was not submitted to church discipline, and was not admitted to Communion. What we see here is an interesting attempt to gradually initiate the masses into Reformed religion and church life. On the other hand, it is telling how few people actually became 'members'. There was no place where the group of members consisted of more than 15 per cent of the local population, and usually it was far less – sometimes not more than 1–2 per cent.[42] Only when the church considerably relaxed its requirements for membership in the course of the seventeenth and eighteenth centuries, and when somewhat later church membership was made mandatory, did the group of members begin to increase steeply. By the end of the eighteenth century practically every Dutch person was a member of one of the recognized faith communities. Moreover, it is not to be ignored that not merely confessing members with their children belonged to the 'public church' (the Dutch Reformed Church), but also 'the religiously inactives who could not be classified anywhere else', as the Dutch historian Fred van Lieburg points out.[43]

So, throughout the entire period of European Christianization we do see a missionary drive among the actively Christian minority. They certainly tried to permeate the masses with Christian beliefs and a Christian lifestyle (however this was understood). At the same time we see that this Christianization always happened against the background of a generally embraced ideal of a Christian culture, while the threat of force (in milder and heavier forms) was never far away.[44] Christianity, in other words, was always the soul of a societal order that could and, if necessary, would be maintained with violence. Finally, we see that in times or places where this threat of force (from outright oppression to social ostracism) could not be deployed effectively there was no large influx into the church.

Although every comparison between Christendom and late modern liberal societies is inevitably flawed, we might try to understand this religious constellation by comparing it to the modern attitude towards democracy. In Western nations the overwhelming majority of the population supports democracy as a system. There are very few people who seriously want a dictatorship or a good old-fashioned oligarchy. Nevertheless, only a minority is actively involved in politics, registered as a voter, or member of a political party. In the Netherlands, for example, only some 300,000 of 17 million citizens are members of a political party, while only 30,000 are *active* members. While general elections and referendums usually draw more attention, the actual turnout in many countries is often only a minority or a small majority of the population; apparently, sympathy can sit well with indifference. Also, waking an average citizen of a democratic nation in the middle of the night, and asking him or her to mention three cabinet ministers together with their proper departments would most likely result in interesting yet disappointing answers. Moreover, a large majority of citizens would not know about current debates in the parliament on anything beyond the most obvious issues. As Winston Churchill once said: 'The best argument against democracy is a five-minute conversation with the average voter.' However, despite the indifference and notwithstanding this lack of knowledge, democratic values are widely embraced, meaning among other things that most democratic citizens condone or actively support an aggressive tactic against undemocratic groups (like radical Muslims), to the extent of ignoring their rights and treating them violently. So, although the large majority is only superficially interested in the political system, they do support it – including punitive measures against its 'heretics'. Also, the minority who are actively involved in politics can count on some sympathy at least. And if this sympathy is lacking, the criticism is usually not directed against the democratic system but against the 'corrupt' politicians who are not interested in 'what the people want'. Suspicion against politicians, which is admittedly widespread, does not translate into widespread suspicion against politics or democracy as such – at least, not yet.

We could see the position of the Christian religion during the largest part of Western history more or less in this way. Only a minority was actively involved, but this minority was supported in some way or another by the majority – even if the grumbling against church and clergy could be heard in every tavern of a medieval city.

2.5 Foolish and Weak

A while ago I had a conversation with a missionary who had returned from a long stay in an African country. On his return in the Netherlands he had become involved in evangelism activities of his church. When we talked about it, he sighed: 'In Africa it was very easy to see the evil we had to fight. I could preach against it, I could point it out, I could build structures to restrict it. I could show people how Jesus could make a difference for them. But here, in the Netherlands, it is so difficult to see what the evil is. There is so little to improve, so little that Jesus can do for us.'

In my view this quote accurately indicates the crisis of Christian mission in the secular West. This crisis is not primarily to do with greater freedom of choice, as if people would immediately abandon Christianity the minute they are allowed to do so by law. As I said before, it would be a mistake to draw the conclusion from the history of European Christianization that people 'in those dark ages' were 'forced' to believe, while we in a time of post-Christendom are finally free to believe what we want. Such a simple binary between coercion and freedom, which sometimes appears in popular missionary literature (and in anti-theistic writings, for that matter), does not do justice to history. Christian Europe was no North Korea. Normally, governments can only enforce something by legislation when there is general support for what is enforced. Europe would not have had 1,000 years of Christian cultural history if Christianity had been shoved down people's throats during all these centuries. Indeed, it does not make much sense to assume that mass conversion in the first stage of Christianization or the great revivals in later stages were merely the products of violence or opportunism. Apparently, the overwhelming majority accepted the system, even if they were not thrilled about it. For better or worse, Christianity was generally considered as the 'soul' of Western culture; there was no coherent way to conceptualize the divorce of European civilization and Christianity. Thus, the crisis of mission in the West does not lie in freedom of choice as such, but in something else. Contrary to earlier times, many people no longer experience Christianity as self-evident or necessary.

Throughout the centuries people have always had personal reasons for becoming Christians. This is the case even today, also in Europe. But in order to get a sense of the cultural position that Christianity once had in Europe, we should not focus on reasons that are unique to individuals; rather, we should focus on reasons that many individuals have in *common*. Massive church growth (by conversion or revival) is to be expected only when Christianity – to cite Kuyper again – will impress a large circle 'with a sense of its inevitability'. In my opinion, this 'inevitability' (the Dutch original says *noodzaak*, namely 'necessity')[45] of Christianity entailed this: with the exception of the first three centuries Christianity was the 'soul' of a Western culture that was superior in almost every respect. The Germanic kingdoms accepted Christianity in the twilight of the Roman Empire primarily as the religion of the late Roman civilization, with its aura of literacy, impressive architecture, military hegemony, astounding degree of organization, and overall cultural refinement.[46] The Christianization of the North-Western European tribes was inseparable from the military superiority of the Frankish kings, who considered their struggle 'against the pagans' (*adversus paganos*) above all as a civilizing mission.

Thus, far from being a later colonialist invention, this *mission civilisatrice* has always been in the DNA of Western Christian powers; the idea of Christianity as the spiritual component of a superior civilization has never been far away.[47] The same mindset can be found in the early colonial missions of the Portuguese and Spanish *conquistadores*, whereby the necessity of 'civilizing' the barbarian tribes who lived overseas was seen as sufficient justification for military conquest.[48] Later, in the heyday of the British Empire there was a strong consensus among intellectuals, theologians and missionaries that it would be impossible to offer European civilization to the uncultivated tribes of Africa and Asia without also sharing the soul that animated this civilization – Christianity.[49] On their part, many 'pagan' rulers, if not attracted by Christianity as such, were certainly interested in the advantages of Western culture, and accepted that Christianity somehow was part of the package.[50] So, whenever Europeans sent their missionaries overseas, they did so as colonial powers with a dizzying lead in medical science, military and technology. I am not contending that every missionary took advantage of this; the point is that for those living in the so-called 'mission fields' the gospel always came with plows, antibiotics, schools, cars and guns. Inevitably, the Western missionary was a representative of this culture. Not much force was needed to persuade people that Christianity was a religion that led to prosperity in many dimensions. When push came to shove, one could benefit from becoming a Christian.

Even the great revivals of the eighteenth and nineteenth centuries were inspired on the one hand by a wide nostalgia for an unbroken Christian nation, and on the other hand they brought an unrivalled success in 'the reformation of manners', such as resisting alcohol abuse, slavery, child labour and the promotion of cleanliness. Something of this dynamic can still be observed in the Pentecostal revivals in Latin America.[51] The sober observation of sociologist Steve Bruce is worth citing here: '[R]eligious conversion works best when potential converts can see in the adherents of the new religion who evangelize them people who are like themselves but better.'[52]

All this does not mean that such conversions are not 'real'. The authenticity of conversions is not the point here. I am just saying that most people will be prepared to consider Christianity as a realistic option only when there is a strong cultural appeal that drives them to do so. Furthermore, we can assume that such a sense of cultural inevitability will also render Christianity more attractive to people who are not completely convinced in their hearts, or to people who are inclined to ground their choices especially on what benefits them most at this particular moment. The latter group will likely be the first to turn away, when the balance shifts to Christianity's disadvantage. And finally, the use of force to promote Christianization or, reversely, to fight 'heresy' will be possible over a longer stretch of time only if there is a cultural logic that justifies this coercion in the eyes of the majority of the population.

When Christianity does not have this wind in its sails, there will still be people who convert for individual reasons, but mass conversions and great revivals will most likely not occur. And everything indicates that such a favourable wind is now lacking in the West. At most some whiffs may be felt, now and then. For example, a certain number of people in the West, including those who do not call themselves Christians, are concerned about the sustainability of the civilization that has been built here. Can this culture persist without a vital Christianity? Also there are people who, mostly through the arrival of Islam, have become more conscious of the historically grown and unique character of Western culture, and the role Christianity has played in bringing it about. Although I cannot produce any hard data, I have the impression that with some regularity such conservative deliberations (of course, besides other and more personal reasons) are active in conversions of people who return to the church of their childhood. Where I live this seems particularly the case with conversions to Catholicism. But these examples are few and far between. Moreover, there are other strong cultural forces which keep people away from Christianity. So, for evangelism in Europe (and increasingly in the West in general) we are predominantly depending on the intrinsic motives of individuals to (re)convert to Christianity, more or less against the stream of our culture. This often produces extremely fascinating and moving stories, but no long queues of baptism candidates.

In my view, here we find the heart of the crisis of Christian mission in the West. For the first time in its long history Western Christianity has to learn what it means to do mission without in almost every respect being 'stronger' than the receiving culture. Even more, in the receiving culture Christianity finds what is in some way its own product. The West is, after all, in all sorts of ways stamped by Christianity. In such conditions it is extremely difficult to say what – apart from purely religious reasons – is the 'added value' of a conversion to the Christian faith. Virtually all blessings of earthly life – including those blessings that have been produced by a Christian culture – are perfectly available in Western societies without faith in God. Anybody who wants to believe that the good news of Jesus Christ is also *true*, is free to do so, but it does not 'yield' anything extra in this world. Hence Christian proclamation has become vulnerable. The message of Christianity no longer speaks from the centre of culture; it is no longer a voice that is supported by inevitability and necessity. More than ever before it has become a *witnessing* voice, easy to be ignored and ridiculed.[53]

Although European theologians have called their continent a 'mission field' since the beginning of the twentieth century, I have the impression that this truth still has difficulty penetrating our minds. The rhetoric of 'revivals', 'restoration' and 'crusades' is still very much alive, both among Western (evangelical) Christians and among immigrant Christians who come to do mission in the West.[54] The reality is that this rhetoric is not justified given the current cultural conditions of the West in general, and Europe in particular.[55] For example, a colleague and friend of mine who is an inspired evangelist, told me not long ago that his church in Amsterdam has more than 200 good missionary contacts, as the result of years of hard work. Moreover, through its missionary work this church meets dozens of new people every year. Nevertheless, his church has baptized 'only' 12 adult converts in the past few years. Another very gifted evangelist from the same city told me that he has on average 100 evangelizing conversations on the street each week. Usually, however, this does not lead to more than one contact with somebody who wants to explore Christianity further. And so, lately, after over a year of hard work and hundreds of conversations, he was able to baptize six people.

What these examples from an admittedly very secularized context show is that unless a church can tap into a population that is more than averagely receptive (as is sometimes the case with immigrants), mission in the more secularized areas of the West is a matter of harvesting one by one, after an infinite amount of cultivation, sowing and watering. Conversions are happening, for sure, but little by little.

Writing this down is no lack of faith; it is the simple refusal to take the explosive growth of Christianity in China, Korea (until recently, that is) and sub-Saharan Africa as the missionary standard of all things. After all, there is a Christian mission narrative to tell about other areas as well – for example, the Middle East, North Africa and Indonesia. Stories can also be told about Christian mission by churches and groups who were at the margins of Western societies, and who generally developed much more modest concepts of mission.[56] We should remember, too, that missionaries in the past were certainly not harvesting many conversions when they addressed the cultural elites of self-confident and resistant cultures like India and China. Thus, there are more than enough analogies from mission history to learn from about doing mission in today's secular West. In conclusion, missionaries in the West may have to learn again what seems to have been forgotten a long time ago: what it means, with the apostle Paul, to be 'foolish' and 'weak' in the world (1 Cor. 2.1–5).[57]

2.6 Summary and Conclusion

The history of evangelizing mission in Europe has always been characterized by the difference between an active minority and a passive majority. For centuries these were connected in the same formally Christian cultural framework. Within this framework mission presented itself initially as a civilizing project from the late Roman Christian culture towards the North-Western European tribes. Later this evangelizing mission mostly assumed the face of 'reformation', that is, the conversion of Christians. In the first stages of secularization of Christian culture, mission happened through revivals, whereby the latently Christian masses – at least for some time – 'contracted' around still commonly shared Christian beliefs and standards. In our time this formally Christian cultural framework has crumbled. Being a Christian is no longer a matter of cultural routine or decency. Active religiosity, particularly in the most secular areas, is entirely a matter of personal choice and taste. Here becomes transparent what in fact has always been the case but remains hidden when Christianity has the cultural wind in its sails: only a minority of Europeans (and Western citizens in general) are interested in serious Christianity. At the same time this means a serious crisis for Christian mission, because for the first time in a long time Christians must learn what it means to be 'weak' and 'foolish'.

Notes

1 'Secular' can mean many things, among which the least contested meaning is that in modern societies social differentiation takes place: 'religion' becomes disentangled from other domains (like politics, education, etc.), and receives its own (ecclesiastical) domain. See further Paas, 'Post-Christian'.
2 See Chapter 1, note 7.
3 For this, see extensively Paas, 'The Crisis of Mission in Europe'.
4 Davie, 'Religion in Europe in the 21st Century'.
5 Davie, 'Vicarious Religion', p. 22.

6 I am not sure about the United States in the eighteenth and nineteenth centuries. According to Fitzgerald, *The Evangelicals*, for example, eighteenth-century America may have resembled this European pattern more than modern evangelicals care to believe. Especially the Second Great Awakening seems to have changed this.

7 Davie, 'Vicarious Religion', pp. 23–7.

8 Davie, 'Religion in Europe', p. 281.

9 Davie, *Sociology*, p. 96.

10 This point is emphatically made by Joas, *Glaube als Option*, pp. 129–48.

11 I have reflected on this in 'Religious Consciousness'.

12 Cf. Hollinghurst's remarks on the emergence of 'client religion' in the West (*Mission Shaped Evangelism*, pp. 52–6, 221–3).

13 For a discussion, see Paas, 'Mission among Individual Consumers'.

14 For a survey of recent developments, see Burkimsher, 'Is Religious Attendance Bottoming Out?'

15 Of course, this is a very rough estimation. See Stark, *Rise*, pp. 4–13.

16 www.cbs.nl/nl-NL/menu/themas/vrije-tijd-cultuur/publicaties/artikelen/archief/2014/2014-4115-wm.htm (in the most secular areas of the Netherlands this is 12 per cent). Another statistical agency, using different measures, has monthly attendance figures around 12 per cent, which is comparable with other Western European nations. One could object that there are also nations (like Sweden) where the churchgoing rate is much lower, and countries (like Poland) where it is much higher, but the Roman Empire was a huge territory with considerable regional differences (prior to Constantine the number of Christians was much higher in the Greek-speaking East than in the Latin-speaking West). The average monthly churchgoing rate in all of Europe is still much higher than 10 per cent of the population.

17 Kuyper, 'Calvinism and the Future', p. 115.

18 Kuyper, 'Calvinism and the Future', p. 117.

19 Luther, *Von weltlicher Obrigkeit*, pp. 12–13; Calvin, *Institutes*, I.4.1.

20 McLeod, 'Introduction', p. 1.

21 Kuyper, 'Sphere Sovereignty', p. 488.

22 O'Donovan, *Desire*, p. 193.

23 O'Donovan, *Desire*, p. 194.

24 O'Donovan, *Desire*, p. 195.

25 However, it must be said that O'Donovan's description of the early Church's missionary ideal is sometimes a bit ambiguous: '[Society] is to be transformed, shaped in conformity to God's purpose; [rulers] are to disappear, renouncing their sovereignty in the face of [God's]' (p. 193). This could be read as a statement of intent, a blueprint for a Christendom society. I suspect that we should take the Church here as the prolepsis of a transformed society, and O'Donovan is quite clear about the right order in all this (*first* society, *then* the rulers), but still the statement may sound a bit too programmatic in the light of what he writes on p. 195: 'It is not, as is often suggested, that Christian political order is a *project* of the church's mission, either as an end in itself or as a means to the further missionary end. The church's one project is to witness to the Kingdom of God. Christendom is *response* to mission, and as such a sign that God has blessed it.'

26 Note that both Leo XIII and Abraham Kuyper lived and worked in the twilight of Christendom, and that their invocations of a completely transformed society under the lordship of Christ cannot be read separately from the general feeling that Christianity was in decline.

27 On the political dimension of Christian mission in early medieval Europe, see especially Smith, *Europe after Rome*, pp. 217–52 ('Kingship and Christianity'). The Christianization of Ireland was an exception, since this country was never part of the Roman Empire, and was ruled by pagan kings during the pilgrimages of Patrick/ Patricius (c. 389–461). Cf. Bury, *St. Patrick*.

28 Too much has been written about the Christianization of Europe than can be summed up here. See, e.g., Fletcher, *Barbarian Conversion*; Brown, *Rise*; Kendall, *Conversion to Christianity*.

29 Brown, *Rise*, p. 424.

30 Brown, *Rise*, p. 419. Cf. Smith, *Europe after Rome*, p. 238.

31 There is much literature on this as well. See for example Kreider, *Origins*; Hamilton, *Religion*. From a missiological perspective: Wessels, *Europe*.

32 Cahill, *How the Irish Saved Civilization*, pp. 21–2.

33 For example, Michael, *Vita Perfecta*.

34 Taylor, *Secular Age*, pp. 80–1, etc.

35 Nissen, 'De kerstening van christenen'.

36 I have further elaborated on this in 'The Making of a Mission Field' and 'The Crisis of Mission in Europe'.

37 Walls, 'The Eighteenth-Century Protestant Missionary Awakening', p. 41.

38 Gregory, *The Unintended Reformation*.

39 Cf. Cameron, *Enchanted Europe*.

40 Cf. Israel, *The Dutch Republic*, p. 366.

41 These and other examples can be found in Stoffels, 'Opkomst en ondergang', pp. 13–15. Regarding the city of Haarlem, see Spaans, *Haarlem*.

42 Van Deursen, *Bavianen en Slijkgeuzen*, p. 128, etc.

43 Van Lieburg, 'Nederlands protestantisme', p. 8.

44 Even in the Netherlands, where the religious regime was rather mild compared to other European nations, the Reformed Church was highly privileged over other churches. For a discussion, see Van Rooden, *Religieuze regimes*.

45 Kuyper wrote his Stone Lectures in Dutch, and had them translated by the English nanny of his children.

46 Cf. Fletcher, *Barbarian Conversion*, p. 236 (mission worked 'from the top downwards').

47 Cf. Brown, *Rise*, pp. 426–7, and further.

48 More discussion of the 'civilizing' motif in early modern Portuguese, Spanish and French missions in Stroope, *Transcending Mission*, pp. 244–8.

49 See, for example, the illuminating essays in Van der Veer (ed.), *Conversion to Modernities*.

50 Cf. the incisive study of nineteenth-century British Nonconformist missions among the Tswane in South Africa, by Comaroff, Comaroff, *Of Revelation and Revolution*. Similar observations in Peel, *Religious Encounter*.

51 On this revisited 'Methodism', see Martin, *Pentecostalism*.

52 Bruce, 'Secularization', p. 289.

53 I explore this further in section 4 of Chapter 4.

54 For this last group, see the surveys of Burgess, 'Bringing Back the Gospel', p. 435: 'restorationist agenda'; Knibbe, 'Nigerian Missionaries'. See also Paas, 'Mission from Anywhere to Europe'.

55 In this context, what Steve Bruce writes on secularization in the United Kingdom may be relevant. In his opinion, secularization is not 'inevitable', but the trends causing secularization are certainly 'irreversible' ('Secularization').

56 Here we may think primarily of the Moravian Church or the Herrnhut Community, under the guidance of Ludwig Graf von Zinzendorf (1700–60), that is widely recognized as the first Protestant church that ventured into overseas mission. See Callagher, 'Integration'. Background on the Herrnhut Community in Paas, *Church Planting in the Secular West*, pp. 69–74. Another source of reflection may be St Patrick's work in Ireland (see Lockhart, *Beyond Snakes and Shamrocks*).

57 For a nice study of Paul's reflections on his 'weak' and 'foolish' performance in Corinth, see Tomlin, *The Power of the Cross*, pp. 87–101.

3

From Folk Church to Conquest

The shift from a culture of obligation to one of consumption or choice, and the concurrent erosion of the Christendom ideal, bears major consequences for church and faith. In fact, all familiar religious and ecclesial structures will inevitably go into revision. Theology and Christian spirituality will be affected too, as I intend to show in this chapter and the next.

A change like this is often expressed by (older) believers in terms of loss: churches are losing members, Christian faith has less impact on new generations, other religions are emerging, and the number of atheists is on the rise. These are all unmistakeable trends, which have not reached the end of the line yet. But all this should not make us blind to the fact that Western societies have changed strongly *as a whole*. Most of these countries have abolished military conscription, political parties are in decline, parliaments are ideologically fragmented, volunteers for charities and sport clubs are increasingly hard to find, the number of television channels has exploded, and shopping has been changed dramatically by the Internet. In my own country the impressive and widely ramified culture of societies, associations and clubs has suffered enormously, and church denominations are among its last, surprisingly tough survivors. Another scene is emerging in its place: a landscape of continuously intermingling and clashing minorities, 'tribes' if you will, facing the task of how to relate to each other now that it is no longer possible to unite everybody under one single 'lordship' – religious or secular.

A cultural landslide like this can release much creativity, especially because it makes us question what seems natural and straightforward. Europe, says Philip Jenkins (and I agree), 'is a laboratory for new forms of faith, new structures of organization and interaction, that can accommodate to a dominant secular environment'.[1] At the same time we know that something that is genuinely new never appears out of the blue. Paradoxically, innovation that burns all the bridges towards the old and traditional will not be recognized as innovation. Renewal is always the renewal *of* something; it is no creation out of nothing.[2] If a car factory innovates to the extent of producing baby powder, it will have innovated itself out of business. So too with the renewal of the Christian tradition in the West; eventually this is about rendering the tradition of Jesus and the Apostles visible and tangible in a convincing and recognizable way. This may occur when a creative interaction is happening between traditional insights and new circumstances.

In the present chapter I discuss six ways in which the churches in the West have responded to the secularization of their societies: the folk church; the Church as a counterculture; church growth; the Church as an agent of culture transformation; the Church inside out; and the Church as a powerhouse for spiritual warfare. I will argue that all these models are still too implicated in the gradually disappearing culture of Christendom. At the same time, they contain building blocks for a renewed missionary view of the deeply secular culture of many Western contexts.

3.1 Folk Church

Folk church, with its deep roots in the Christendom experience, can be considered as the *Ur*-model of ecclesiology. Memories are still lingering throughout the European continent, while the model has been planted in Latin America and the British Commonwealth in the era of colonial missions. North Americans may recall how their republic began with a series of attempts to create a European-type 'established' Church, and there are regions where there is some continuation of European folk church culture even today.[3] Generally, the folk church is associated with massive, albeit largely nominal, church membership, a formal relationship between church and state, establishment clauses privileging one church of the realm at the expense of other churches and religions, a prominent role of said church in *rites de passage* and during national celebrations or catastrophes, and usually some form of state support by a church tax (*Kirchensteuer*) or other means. As folk churches – either in 'pure' or 'mixed' forms – exist in many countries, their historical and cultural diversity is huge. Also, the rapid pluralization and secularization of many Western nations has led to revisions of the model. An accurate phenomenological description is, therefore, impossible to give.[4] In the present context, however, I am primarily interested in some theological features that are associated with the folk church tradition.

The Classic Pattern

To begin with, the English word 'folk' is a poor translation of what is implied by concepts like *Volkskirche* (German), *folkekirken* (Danish) or *volkskerk* (Dutch). The word *volk* has overtones of 'people', 'folk', 'culture' and 'nation' all at the same time. In a brochure about the Danish Evangelical Lutheran Church, for example, various suggestions to translate *folkekirken* are mentioned, such as 'church of the people' or 'church by the people', but in the end the word is left untranslated.[5] So, while 'folk church' is an accepted, popular translation, caution is advised in using it.

As a general feature we might say that in the folk church tradition the *volk* (all the citizens) are church folk at the same time. Or to put it more dignifiedly, in a genuine folk church the religious identity of people coincides with their national identity. A folk church is associated with statements like 'Italians are Catholics' or 'Greece is an Orthodox nation'. In such countries the vast majority of the population (sometimes more than 90 per cent) are members of the same church. In many other countries this is not the case on a national level, but there you can often find villages or regions with strong folk church traditions. Wherever there are more or less self-evident associations of ecclesial identity and cultural or ethnic heritage, one can speak of a folk church culture.

Predicated on this fusion of ethnicity and religious identity, a number of theological characteristics follow. First, folk church theorists emphasize that *God works through what is socially 'given' and 'natural'*. This makes sense, if we understand what a people (*volk*) is. It is construed from what precedes us as individuals: a shared history, tribal and familial bonds, regional and local identities. God is supposed to be present in such 'natural' givens, and he uses them to build his kingdom. God thus associates himself with a national history, he takes sides in patriotic liberation wars, and he works through the chain of generations. This connection of salvation and *volk* is usually legitimated with the help of the Old Testament or, more accurately, the history of God with Israel. Often the idea prevails that God has made a covenant with this particular people, analogous to Old Testament Israel ('Dutch' or 'British' Israel). Other elements of folk church thinking, like a theocratic theology and an uneasy dealing with 'sects', result from this almost automatically (see below).

Second, folk churches are rather *relaxed about church membership*, or, more precisely, about *active* church membership.[6] Again, this goes without saying. After all, membership of a *volk* (or any 'natural association') is received by birth rather than choice – especially in nations where mass immigration is a very recent phenomenon. It more or less *happens* to you. The consequence of this approach is a wide practice of infant baptism, even to the extent of not requiring parents to meet any standards of faith. In Denmark, for example, baptism is 'in many parts of the country the normal way of marking that a new member has been added to the family'. It is a 'cultural norm'[7] just like in many other European nations, especially among members of the traditional national or mainline churches. Another illustration of this relaxed approach of membership was the former Dutch Reformed Church – traditionally the national Protestant church, which until recently even had so-called 'birth members': unbaptized children of baptized parents who would be categorized as church members even though their parents would not go to church or believe in God. Just like with families and villages, you belong to the Church more than you are aware of – or even care to be. You are involved in all kinds of associations into which Christianity is woven. You learn, more or less unconsciously, that you 'belong', that prior to yourself and around you there are multitudes who believe the same things (or, in any case, who also belong). A certain relaxedness plays through all of this. One does not take each other incessantly to task in the folk church. Being part of a faith community is less vulnerable in this model; one does not drop out of it just like that. Christianity is a cultural identity before anything else; it can't be shaken off easily.

Third, folk church theologians usually pay much attention to *political and societal structures*. After all, a people is not just a crowd; it is also a political entity. A group will become a people (*populus*) only when there are laws, institutions, a recognized government. Such structures are the skeleton of the *volk*, so to speak. Thus, folk church thinking is not merely concerned with persons; it also deals with the laws and symbols of a political society. These are to be symbolically 'charged' with Christianity. Therefore, many theologians in this line of thinking are given to some form of theocracy. They find it important that the head of state is a Christian, or even a member of the dominant church, that coins and bills bear a religious inscription ('in God we trust'), that council meetings open with prayer, that courthouses display symbols of the 'Judaeo-Christian' tradition such as a plaque of the Ten Commandments, that marriage ceremonies remain rooted in Christianity or in 'religion' at least, and that shops are closed on Sundays. Governments should be addressed by the Church to remind them of their task to keep the people centred on their Christian roots. Some of them may nowadays respond to the presence of Muslims in many Western nations by recalling that these countries are 'Christian', and that Muslims therefore should not expect to have the same rights as Christians.

Finally, the folk church tradition lays much emphasis on the *institutional unity* of the Church. Folk church thinking is determined by the explicit or implicit assumption that the entire people in fact hides under one religious umbrella; that is, that similarities are more important than differences. Christianity has forged Germanic tribes into nations, and therefore the crucial role of Christianity is that it will perpetually 'hold things together'. There is no room for a vision in which different denominations (religious 'tribes', as it were) bring to expression the cultural wealth of Christianity together. The fear of division and the recurrence of tribal wars is too deep to allow this. There is an inbred conservatism as well. Folk church thinking is averse to radical plans for innovation, since experience teaches that prophets and visionaries all too easily split the people into leaders and laggers. This institutional conservatism shows itself in an uncomfortable handling of alternative (Christian) movements. They are easily considered as less 'legitimate', because they divide the *volk* along religious lines. In such cases folk churches like to speak of 'sects'. In the past this led to persecution and discrimination; nowadays it usually remains limited to dismissive rhetoric. However, in a number of European countries there is still an official policy regulating the degree to which religious organizations are permitted, usually resulting in a restriction of groups that fall outside the traditional religious establishment.

The Folk Church in a Pluralistic Society

As a descendant of a long lineage of Saxonian farmers there is enough 'tribal blood' in my veins to help me understand the strengths of the folk church – at least in some parts. Personally, I believe that the folk church has been used by God to connect many people with the gospel, in ways appropriate to a collective culture – a culture where individuals were defined by the community they belonged to. But times have changed dramatically, as many church leaders have observed. The increasing pluralization of Western societies means that religion now is consumed rather than assumed. At this point we should not fool ourselves, as even a self-confessed traditionalism is chosen and cultivated rather than unwittingly adopted from our ancestors. Also, populations have become more diverse due to immigration. What does 'folk church' mean when 10 per cent of the population belongs to another religion, and when a large minority or even the majority do not want to belong to any religion? Does folk church thinking make any sense in countries where church members are distributed over dozens of denominations, while a considerable number of them were born in Africa or Asia – as in many Western cities today?

One response to this is a revival of some sort of Christendom rhetoric. For example, recent research shows that many people in Eastern Europe have embraced religion as an element of national belonging, but without becoming highly observant. In post-communist Russia and Poland majorities say that being Orthodox or Catholic is important to being truly Russian or truly Polish.[8] This also creates a basis for politicians to restrict immigration, especially from Muslim nations, and to insist on the 'Christian' character of their states. However, these nations have always been ethnically and religiously more homogeneous than the old colonial empires in Western Europe or an immigrant country like the United States. I remember while visiting Prague (Czech Republic) and Budapest (Hungary) how it struck me, being used to Amsterdam, that virtually everybody around me was white. By contrast, a city like Amsterdam contains around 170 ethnicities, while the majority of children under fifteen is non-white. Whatever we may think of the attempts to reinforce an ethno-religious culture in the Central and Eastern parts of Europe (and as a theologian I am rather critical), this is not a realistic option for, say, France, Germany, the Netherlands or the United Kingdom. In these nations the isolationist, vaguely Christian, and explicitly anti-Islamic rhetoric is carried out by nationalist minority parties who often draw on strong culture-war traditions. Many of these movements have felt a strong surge from the surprising victory of Donald Trump in the United States (2016) who was massively supported by evangelical Christians. However, even if there are enough Christians to make a political difference and willing to support a restorationist policy (as seems to be the case in the United States, but definitely not in Europe), an incidental power grasp by Christians in nations that are rapidly secularizing will likely backfire on them. Thus, evangelicals in the United States seem to have wasted most of their credibility by their stubborn backing of Trump's erratic and vulgar behaviour. What, after all, will it profit Christians if they gain the whole world and lose their souls?

Be this as it may, the restoration of Christendom does not seem a realistic path for most Christians in secularizing nations. This raises a serious dilemma for folk church thinkers. Think of a wheelbarrow full of frogs. As soon as the frogs start to jump out of the wheelbarrow in large numbers, one can do two things: put a lid on the wheelbarrow, or make the wheelbarrow so large that the frogs can never find its edge. As to the first strategy: the use of political force left aside, it may be possible to maintain the folk church rhetoric in certain isolated areas or villages where cultural Christianity still has a great influence. There are places in the West where folk church thinking still bears some plausibility, in the sense that the church is at least a 'village church' – more or less the sacred centre of a local community.

Wherever this does not work any more, while simultaneously maintaining the folk church tradition, there is only one way to go: to expand the boundaries of the Church to such an extent that virtually everybody fits in. Inevitably, this creates frictions with late modern individuals who refuse to be counted as church members – by whatever trick in the book – when they do not consider themselves as Christians in the first place. Currently, there are even people who have themselves 'unbaptized' as a protest against what they sense to be an annexation of their bodies by the Church. The same problem arises with other strategies to make the wheelbarrow as large as possible. Take, for example, the somewhat patronizing and fiercely criticized term 'anonymous Christian' coined by the Roman Catholic theologian Karl Rahner (1904–84). The problem with this is that people are labelled as 'Christians' against their knowledge and will. However kindly it may be meant, it shows a lack of respect to call your Muslim neighbour an anonymous Christian. He is not a Christian, and he does not feel himself a Christian. If he did, he would have called himself a Christian.

As secularization continues, the basis for this religious imperialism crumbles away. However, there are other ways in which the folk church tradition casts its shadow even in deeply secularized societies. In what we might call 'homeopathic' folk church theology, categories are thinned out to such an extent that people really have to do their best *not* to belong. For example, by the term 'religion' one can maintain that the whole nation, despite secularization and pluralization, still feels at home under one roof. Even atheism is thus almost triumphantly redefined as a 'religion'. 'Spirituality' is often used in a similar way. After all, most people are 'spiritual' in some way. This strategy only works, of course, when concepts are kept vague (football is a 'religion' too, and gardening can be 'spiritual'), and especially when 'religion' and 'spirituality' are limited to the domain of feelings and rituals. Almost everybody has some feelings, now and then, that could be called 'spiritual', and rituals are everywhere. I don't mean to ridicule serious studies of ritual and spirituality,[9] and I am not contesting the point that these can be indicators of late-modern religiosity somehow, but it should be clear that such large and poorly delineated categories relativize considerable differences in worldviews and lifestyles between groups and individuals. In this way, a seemingly new 'we' can be created, which is actually a rather old European 'we'. Surely, it is not hard to recognize the last gasp of the ancient folk church in all of this. It is the urge, whatever it may cost, to keep everybody within the same religious boat under the flag of a concept of 'religion' that is defined in terms as universal as possible.

More or less the same can be said of missional initiatives whose purpose is primarily described as 'connecting' people. On inquiry this often appears to amount to gathering people around shared activities or interests, regardless of whether these make any reference to God or Jesus.[10] Apparently, the fear of returning to tribal identities is so deep that 'connecting' becomes a purpose in itself. To be sure, nothing is wrong with connection (it is good for people to like each other), but it is a rather shallow missionary agenda if it does not contain more than this. Actually, what would be against saying that Christians in some respects are *not* like other people, and that they are to find their own motivations to live in peace with their neighbours? Why couldn't Christians be a 'friendly tribe'?

It thus seems that all those who are alluding to some version of anonymous Christianity (or anonymous religiosity) find it difficult to say goodbye to a Christianized nation. Even at a time when the majority of people have no functional relationship with the Church, it seems to be crucial that this majority is kept within the same worldview somehow. But, plain and simple, many people do not follow Jesus, and they don't want to. That is the reality that has become visible by the loss of Christendom. There is little point in trying to ignore this through redefinition. Moreover, it is counterproductive in missional terms. Many people will experience it as a lack of respect if the Church tries to frame them as 'members' in some way, while they emphatically distance themselves. And many people refuse to see themselves as 'religious' or even 'spiritual'. In my opinion, a more bounded view of the Church does more justice to this modern consciousness, and it will – paradoxically – create more room for a genuine encounter than the vague concepts of religion held by some late-modern theologians. Church and world must be distinguished theologically, even though clear sociological boundaries are usually impossible to draw.

Church for the People

Folk churches will have to learn how to be minority churches, not just in terms of numbers but also in terms of their mission.[11] As for the latter, in my own country the folk church tradition has undergone a remarkable revision through the hands of Reformed theologians who began to use the term 'church for the people' after the Second World War.[12] At the same time this development is a clear warning as to the structural problems of retaining a folk church theology in a post-Christendom age. These theologians recognized the reality of secularization to some extent, and admitted that the Church will never comprise the whole nation. Nevertheless, in its practice and theology the Church is to be guided by the desire to reach the whole nation with the gospel. Already during the war the Dutch Reformed Church stated that it considered itself as a 'Christ-confessing folk church (*volkskerk*)'.[13] In the church order of 1951 this was expanded in a missionary and theocratic way – the so-called 'theology of the apostolate'.[14] The order said that in its evangelizing work the Dutch Reformed Church 'will address those who are alienated from it, in order to bring them back to the communion with Christ and his Church', it 'will struggle for the Reformed character of the state and the people in all its components', and 'in its work of Christianization' it will address 'government and people in order to arrange life according to God's promises and commandments'.[15]

In the words of one of its contemporary advocates, this is not a quantitative but a qualitative approach of the folk church. It is not the number of people who are members which defines its character as folk church, but its theology, its desire to Christianize the world, and its accessibility for outsiders. In this way a minority church can perfectly well be a folk church. Even stronger, in the words of the Reformed post-war theologian Arnold van Ruler: 'The church is a folk church or not a church at all.'[16]

What are we to think of this attempt to modernize the folk church? Of course, it is good that the Church wants to reach out to people with the gospel, and excludes nobody in advance. But folk church theologians do not speak of 'people' in general; they speak of '*a* people' (*volk*), and that is not the same thing. After all, 'a people' is not merely a mass of human beings; it is a political entity and a cultural community. In the sentences from the Reformed church order cited above, for example, the '*Reformed character* of the state and the people' is mentioned. It is precisely a formula like this that carries so much historical baggage. Saying that most Italians are Catholics is a neutral statement of fact. But claiming that Italy is a Catholic *nation*, or that *true* Italians are Catholics, is ideology. Unfortunately, such ideological features are intimately associated with the use of the word 'folk'.[17] In the Netherlands, for example, the ideology of the 'Protestant nation' made it difficult to see Roman Catholics as truly Dutch until the twentieth century. Similar discrimination against Catholics has occurred in other nations, such as the United Kingdom or the United States. The same happens in countries with Roman Catholic or Orthodox folk church traditions. Some years ago, for instance, I had a conversation with a Portuguese Baptist (a very tiny minority in Portugal) who told me that his neighbours called him a 'fake Portuguese' on account of not being Roman Catholic and not having his children baptized. There is no need here to recollect more, and often far worse, stories in the same category; they are all too well known.

The problem with this updated 'church-for-the-people' theology is that the structural problem inherent in folk church thinking remains untouched, namely the relationship that is assumed between civil and religious identity. Thus, folk church theology inevitably involves delegitimizing other religious identities, including other Christian churches or denominations. If the 'character' of our nation is indeed 'Reformed' or 'Catholic' or 'Orthodox', or even 'Christian' for that matter, what does this mean for all those who do not belong in these categories? Can one be a true member of the 'Reformed' nation if she attends Mass on Sundays, or if he is a Ghanaian Pentecostal immigrant? Could Muslims or atheists ever be true members of a Christian state? If the church is always a folk church, as Van Ruler thought, does this then also mean that the true 'folk' (*volk*) is always Reformed (or Catholic, Orthodox, Christian) *church* folk? Doesn't that amount to a Balkanization of ecclesiology?

All this shows is that it is not as easy as it seems to differentiate between the church 'of' the people and the church 'for' the people. The problem does not lie as much in the preposition that is used, but rather in the word 'people' itself. Thus, the church *of* the people – together with its fierce rhetoric against 'sects' and 'separations' – remains a background tune in this tradition of Christianization. Also the theocratic desire – an ecclesiastical glow over law and state – keeps exerting its influence. I fear that this will remain so, as long as the word 'folk' (*volk*) has a place in ecclesiology. It is therefore a big step ahead that the church order of the Protestant Church in the Netherlands (into which the Dutch Reformed Church has merged) has abandoned the folk church concept. The Church calls itself a 'Christ-confessing faith community' that 'in conversation with other churches' wants to 'witness to persons, powers, and governments about God's promises and commandments'.[18] In this revised version of the old order the sting has been removed from the tradition. The presumption that there is only one legitimate faith community for the whole nation has been abandoned.

Contributions of the Folk Church Tradition

Even though many, or perhaps most, readers of this book may not be familiar with a folk church theology or a historically Christian nation, nor consider it very relevant for their missional context, I have spent some room describing this tradition nonetheless. Later we will see that the current missional conversation contains many implicit references to the folk church tradition, and that it has influenced our concepts of mission enormously. Moreover, this book is about doing mission in the secularized West. Especially in this context the folk church tradition with its strong roots in the Christendom experience looms large in almost every debate.

Meanwhile, there are certainly valuable elements in the folk church tradition that can contribute to a missionary ecclesiology in a secular age. More than many other missional thinkers, folk church theologians are serious about the bonds, traditions and communities that give us our identities. 'The heart is historically formed!', said Van Ruler.[19] A Christian identity is not only, or even primarily, supported by our individual choice. I consider this as an essential accent for a missional church (more on this in Chapter 6).

With folk church theologians I like to emphasize that the Church should be present and accessible in as many places as possible, even if this will not always be the *same* Church in our contemporary reality. By the end of the nineteenth century the German missiologist Gustav Warneck compared this presence with the parable of the sower. Just like the sower throws the seed in all directions, knowing that only a minority will bear fruit, the Church will try and reach as many people as possible with the gospel, by being an inviting presence in as many places as possible.[20] This presence is not always evangelistic in the strictest sense of the word; attention should also be paid to a wider cultivation of society through all kinds of Christian and theological activity. Today we find these folk church intuitions in conscious attempts to speak theologically in the intellectual debate in Western societies (public theology and apologetics). Also these intuitions can be seen in initiatives of missionary pioneering, inspired by folk church traditions, such as the 'fresh expressions of church' movements in England and Germany, and the pioneering projects of the Protestant Church in the Netherlands.[21] These projects are authorized by referring to the pluralization of society: the people (*volk*) have become so diverse that a wide variety of church forms is required to reach out to them. As always this is still a church that sets itself the task of being present and accessible in all corners of society. At the same time, by this diversity of forms, the institutional frame of the old churches is stretched to such an extent that we might better speak of a 'mixed economy' of church (Rowan Williams).

Another important contribution of the folk church tradition is the insight that the boundaries of the Christian community should not be drawn too sharply.[22] Here the folk church impulse is an important correction of a dogged search for a church that is completely 'pure'.[23] Theologians inspired by folk church thinking often assume a number of 'circles' of participation around the core of actively involved churchgoers.[24] In Chapter 2 we have already seen that some traditional churches in Europe, like the sixteenth- and seventeenth-century Reformed Church in the Netherlands, recognized different degrees of participation. Furthermore, especially in old urban estates and villages in rural areas, the folk church traditionally has many formal bonds with people, bonds that may be actualized with baptisms, marriages, funerals, and the like. Sometimes this creates opportunities to further involve people into the life of the congregation.

Finally, it is an important folk church insight that the Church should never think that its own members are sufficiently Christianized. In a church with a large fringe this may be recognized better than in somewhat triumphalist free churches. Every congregation is to constantly work at the missionizing of its members, for example through good education, accessible and relevant preaching, and home groups.[25]

3.2 Countercultural Church

If the Christian nation has disappeared, and the classic folk church is no longer an option, what then does this mean for the Church? One possible strategy is, of course, to design programmes of restoration or revival. I will discuss such approaches later in this chapter. An entirely other possibility, however, is to redefine the challenge. What if the nation was never 'Christian' in the first place? What if the Church was always destined to be a minority community representing entirely different values from the world?

The countercultural church is the most consistent outworking of this approach to missional ecclesiology in the post-Christian West. Just like the folk church it is a family rather than a single model. Interestingly, the countercultural approach of ecclesiology has emerged in different traditions more or less at the same time, which points to its relevance for the debate on mission to the secularized West. This does not mean, however, that it was somehow plucked out of thin air. In fact, modern advocates of the countercultural model draw extensively on ancient forerunners of this approach, such as early medieval monastic life and the so-called 'Radical Reformation' in the sixteenth century. Take, for example, the highly influential works of the Catholic philosopher Alasdair MacIntyre. While MacIntyre's main argument is against modernity's claim to be a universal narrative that is independent of tradition, he combines this with a very critical analysis of today's Western societies. Intellectually and morally these societies have become corrupted to such an extent that we should expect little from modernity's own capacity to restore its vitality. Rather we should invest our hopes in the creation of small communities that can function as reservoirs of decency and morality, and from which the possible restoration of our culture may begin some day. Here MacIntyre points to the historical role of the monasteries in the so-called 'Dark Ages' after the decline of the Western Roman Empire. These countercultural communities kept the flame of civilization burning amid tribal wars, massive destruction and large-scale people movements. According to MacIntyre we are waiting 'for another – doubtless very different – St. Benedict'.[26]

Another influential stream in the countercultural family can be found in the works of neo-Anabaptists like John Howard Yoder and Stanley Hauerwas. Much contemporary literature on the missionary challenge posed by the post-Christian West draws extensively on these authors.

They draw their inspiration from a revival movement that emerged in Switzerland and Germany in the 1520s, and whose adherents were called 'ana-bapists' (those who baptize 'again') by their opponents. The Anabaptists accused the mainstream Protestants of compromising with Scripture in retaining, for example, infant baptism and thus the idea of a Christian nation. According to the Anabaptist view, people could be considered as Christians only if they lived holy lives, according to the practice of the earliest church in the New Testament. Infant baptism was therefore to be rejected; only faithful adults could be baptized. The early Anabaptists believed in the imminent return of Jesus, and therefore they went to great lengths to evangelize their 'pagan' fellow citizens, so as to save as many as possible. Because of fierce persecutions in the first stages of their movement, and increasing wealth in the later stages, their missionary zeal waned towards the end of the sixteenth century. Anabaptists survived here and there as small, often quite closed communities in regions with somewhat more religious freedom than the average in Europe. Also many crossed the Atlantic to the New World, to escape persecution and marginalization. Today, the Amish in North America may be the best known descendants of this Radical Reformation movement.[27]

Characteristics

The revival of monasticism and Anabaptism has had great influence among missional writers.[28] It is easy to see why. After all, the crumbling of Christian nations invites us to look for missionary strategies that are less dependent on universalizing narratives and political force. This tradition of Christianity as a minority option presents itself as a logical candidate. Elsewhere I have described the sources and advocates of the countercultural model in more detail.[29] This does not need to concern us here. At the risk of lumping together separate currents in the countercultural family and thus presenting a more coherent picture than is the case in reality, I list the most important characteristics of this model.[30]

First, most advocates of the countercultural model take their point of departure in some sort of cultural 'fall' that has happened in history, and that is seen as the root cause of much that has gone wrong since. However, proponents of the model do not agree on where this fall must be sought. Authors who are inspired by the neo-Anabaptist take on Christendom usually trace the root of Christianity's problems to Constantine's rise to power in AD 312 (see section 2.2). They reject the union between church and state that was forged within Christendom. This union leads the Church to understand itself erroneously as the moral department of a 'Christian' society, and as an institution that somehow bears responsibility for the future of the state. The fundamental problem with this 'constantinianism' (Yoder) is its assumption that the meaning of history lies in the world rather than in the Church, and that it is therefore crucial for the Church to find out where the world is going. This view disagrees considerably with the 'MacIntyrians' within the countercultural paradigm who locate the 'fall' rather *after* Christendom, in early modernity. Here, the collapse of a Christian society is the root of our current problems, such as secularism and relativism. So, while both streams advocate the establishment of countercultural communities or congregations, their reasons and purposes differ considerably. For neo-Anabaptists this means a return to the Church as it was always meant to be: a minority community within the world that is called to witness to the world. For many others it is rather an emergency measure: a temporary withdrawal in the hope of restoring a Christian society once the cultural tide has changed.

Second, the countercultural stance implies that the Church should not expect too much from earthly politics. For those who sympathize with Christendom this distance from politics is rooted in a negative (or even cynical) evaluation of 'modern' or 'secular' politics. A frustrated nostalgia for the Christian nation (see section 3.1) seems here the source of resentment and feelings of cultural exile. A more principled rejection of politics as an instrument for Christianization and a source of moral reform is found among the neo-Anabaptist authors within this paradigm. Governments and societal institutions are seen as part of what the New Testament calls 'powers'. These powers are created by God (Col. 1.15–17), but they have rebelled against him (Eph. 2.1, etc.; Gal. 4.1–11). In his earthly ministry, through his life of service, his death and resurrection Jesus resisted and unmasked these powers, represented by religious and political authorities. After Jesus' victory political order is sustained by God for the time being (Rom. 13.1–4), but it does not have a future in his kingdom. Therefore it makes no sense to strive for a Christianized social and political order.[31] Therefore, the traditional stance of Anabaptist Christians has been to refuse political office or military service. Even though governments play a role in God's rule of the world in this dispensation, their use of deadly violence and coercion characterizes them as representatives of the old order that is destined for destruction. To be sure, all this does not mean that neo-Anabaptists are blind to any influence of Christ outside the Church.[32] It basically means that they leave the world to Christ, and trust him to rule it properly without the interference of the Church. Also, Anabaptist theologians certainly accept that the Church, by being faithful to its witnessing task, will have an impact in the world. But this is not part of a 'strategy', nor is it the justification of the Church's existence.[33]

This brings us, third, to the mission of the Church in the world. For the 'MacIntyrians' this mission would be focused mostly on 'guarding the good treasure' (2 Tim. 1.14). In other words, in this approach the countercultural community is first and foremost a sanctuary where certain beliefs, ways of thinking, habits and virtues are protected against a majority culture that should be kept out as much as possible, and that should be engaged critically through debate and possibly through social and political action. Here the two versions of the model may become indistinguishable, as neo-Anabaptists also maintain a rather negative view of the world as the place where defeated 'powers' rule. The Church has the task to be a witness of the new 'politics' of God's eschatological order, and to remind the powers-that-be of their temporality, their rebellion and their inevitable demise.[34] It does so primarily through the quality of its own existence. The Church is a holy and visible community of believers. These local communities are the universal Church of Christ in diaspora: resident aliens who 'seek the peace of the city' but not through political or cultural control.[35] Rather than trying to be *effective*, says Yoder, Christians should try to be *obedient* to Christ in a world that they cannot and need not control.[36] The world is in God's hands, not ours. Therefore, the Church's primary missional strategy is not to try and influence this world, but to be a witness to the *new* world of which it is a foretaste.[37] What makes Christianity unique is not the fact that it is a faith as such, but that it is a unique community. Christian beliefs about God, Jesus, sin, humanity and salvation are only intelligible against the background of a church – a community of people who have been set apart from the world with the task to worship a God whom the world does not know.[38] Especially by being itself and by concentrating on shaping a Christian lifestyle, the Church makes an offer to the world; it represents God's order, it displays an alternative practice. 'Only a believing community with a "thick" particular identity has something to say to whatever "public" is out there to address.'[39]

In my view the neo-Anabaptist version of the countercultural model is the more interesting one when it comes to thinking about mission to the secularized West. I cannot escape the impression that many defenders of the model who think along the lines of MacIntyre are actually homesick for Christendom. Their ideal is and remains a Christianized world, but for the time being (due to secularism and such) this ideal cannot be realized. The neo-Anabaptists, on the other hand, seem to present us with a more principled rejection of the folk church (section 3.1), and their influence on missional literature seems more substantial. These writers point out that there have always been churches who thought that they lived in a pagan society, even in the Christendom era. These churches have been marginalized and persecuted, but they are the best evidence that there has always been an awareness among Christians that church and world are not necessarily friends – not even in so-called 'Christian' societies. Perhaps the best way to characterize this approach is to see it as an 'anti-folk-church model', in the sense that it rejects everything that is typical of the folk church: the relativization of church membership, the sacralization of the nation, and the urgency of finding a theological voice that is relevant to everyone.

Idealism

I have great sympathy for the neo-Anabaptist contribution that gives voice to the suppressed alternative Christian tradition within Christendom. It cannot be denied, in my opinion, that this 'free church' tradition in particular has kept the tradition of the essentially apostolic and evangelizing task of the Church in the world, even if this world seems Christianized. Indeed, its radical and justified criticism of theocracy – the idea that political power is the primary instrument for Christians to change the world – deserves to be heard. Its vision of evangelism as, first and foremost, an apology of Christian communal life, is a lasting contribution to Christian mission in the West. Finally, its unmasking of the desperate search for 'relevance' and 'realism' among Christians as a betrayal of authentic Christian witness is crucial in a secularizing society. If Christians have nothing to tell that the world does not know already, they will end up offering cumbersome and esoteric versions of what the world is perfectly able to express in much clearer and attractive words. In short, Anabaptists retain the crucial theological distinction between 'church' and 'world' that is lacking in the folk church tradition. Readers of this book will soon find out that this tradition has influenced my own proposals in some important ways.

Yet, I have some reservations.[40] Part of these have to do with my hesitation about an ecclesiology that speaks about the concrete, local, witnessing community all the time, but without really addressing the social, psychological, cultural, organizational and other empirical dimensions of this community. This gives a somewhat docetic feel to the countercultural model.[41] The issue of power, especially, should be tackled in more depth. How can the church, for example, be a place where people are shaped as disciples with the intensity that Hauerwas and Yoder seem to have in view?[42] It would assume a great degree of openness and vulnerability, strong examples of Christian maturity, a limited respect for privacy around matters of moral importance such as sexuality or finances, and willingness to submit to the authority of leaders. How would such a church deal with diversity of opinion, dissent, or pluralism in general?

How would it handle power differences responsibly? As churches tend to be 'very conforming places',[43] one wonders how this model could avoid producing rather dependent people who are anxious about the world. And when wounded and fragile people are shaped into discipleship by church leaders, one wonders how such people are protected against abuse and oppression? While this is a concern that has been brought forward against Yoder's ecclesiology, and not without reason,[44] the same could be said about Hauerwas's.[45] To what extent does this approach create conformity to a group rather than Christian character?

What we need here is best practice that demonstrates how a strong formative rhetoric can be combined with safe spaces, diversity and some pluralism within the community of the church. By 'best practice' I do not mean books by church leaders presenting their own experiences and advocating their own models. I mean a series of good ethnographic studies of congregations that are successful at creating countercultural, strongly formative communities while avoiding the pitfalls of unhealthy relations and authoritarianism.

Next to this rather somewhat over-theological approach of the church itself, the countercultural model has difficulties in articulating its relationship with the world in a consistent manner. This is the topic of the next section.

Church and World

The idea that the Church can be described as somewhat unrelated to 'mundane' issues addressed by sociology or psychology may be less of a problem for the 'MacIntyrian' model of a protected community. However, it is a problem for a community that claims to have a mission in the world that goes beyond safeguarding a tradition. We have seen that modern Anabaptists stress that the Church separates itself from the world in order to witness to the world, and that it may trust that this witness will be heard now and then. Ethnographic research suggests, however, that church groups with a strong theological identity may excel in missional rhetoric, while at the same time finding it very difficult to establish meaningful relationships with people outside the Church. In a sense, the countercultural approach with its idealistic vision of the Church may lead to a missiology that draws only on its 'own' resources without having a real place for learning about God's mission in and through contacts with outsiders.[46]

So, next to the issue of power within the Church, the issue of how the Church is related to the world outside must be addressed. If this is refused the result will be, at best, a highly abstract and idealized picture of a church that is nowhere to be found in real life. It would be similar to a description of marriage from an exclusively theological perspective, without consulting biology or culture. Very likely no actual human being would recognize his or her marriage in such a description, even if they would consider it valuable and inspiring. It is important to be clear here. The point is not that the Church can be defined in purely theological terms first, whereafter this definition should be made 'concrete' within or 'applied' to the empirical realm. This is not about 'application'; the point is that the Church can only exist *within* this empirical realm. The Church is made out of visible and tangible material. It is a part of the world that has turned to Christ. In other words, it is impossible to define the Church (i.e., Christian beliefs and practices) without having a thorough engagement with our context, and without reflecting on the degree to which Christians themselves are 'made' by this context.[47]

If this is true, one cannot expect that in a post-Christian nation church-goers and those outside the Church are entirely different. There must be cultural overlap, common interest, echoing desires and shared insights. Christians are humans and fellow citizens after all. Thus Robin Gill, after an extensive study of sociological data, writes:

> [T]here are broad patterns of Christian beliefs, teleology and altruism which distinguish churchgoers as a whole from non-churchgoers. It has been seen that churchgoers have, in addition to their distinctive theistic and christocentric beliefs, a strong sense of moral order and concern for other people . . . None of these differences is absolute. The values, virtues, moral attitudes and behaviour of churchgoers are shared by many other people as well. The distinctiveness of churchgoers is real but relative.[48]

This is not just true in a post-Christian society; it was also true for the sixteenth-century Anabaptists from which many countercultural writers are drawing their inspiration. Their 'culture' was connected with the surrounding culture in many ways. Anabaptism did not come forward as a Christian movement in a non-Christian world; in that sense it was not a return to the New Testament church.[49] The 'countercultural' communities of the Anabaptists were *intensive* Christian communities in a *formally* Christian world. In this respect they may be best compared with the monasteries in the Middle Ages. Just like the monastic movements, the Anabaptists were not outside the system, but they formed a counter structure within the system. The early Anabaptists lived and formed their theology in a society where people believed in God, knew about

Jesus, and to whom the Bible may have been largely unknown but not unloved. Moreover, in this culture there was a certain respect for a radical Christian lifestyle, even if this lifestyle was mostly admired from a distance. If 'countercultural' means a community that opposes the cultural values of its context, the Anabaptists were not countercultural at all. On the contrary, they embodied an intensive form of cultural values that were almost universally *endorsed* if not practised. Precisely that determined the force of their witness.[50]

Being part of the religious and theological intuitions of the surrounding world also plays out in the realm of morality. The advocates of the countercultural model have a high view of the calling of the Church, and rightly so. However, part of this calling may be to take the world more seriously than this model tends to do – especially in its critique of the Church. This may be particularly true in a post-Christian society where the Church by its mission has generated an enormous number of cultural memories and moral intuitions that are mirrored back to the Church. Thus, some of the best and most challenging understandings of the Bible and Christian practice in a post-Christian society come from 'appropriations on the frontiers of the Church and beyond' (Rowan Williams).[51]

If this is ignored, the countercultural approach may alienate Christians from certain human moral intuitions; it may breed a misguided aristocratic rejection of the wisdom of the 'world'. An illustration may be John Howard Yoder's response when he was disciplined for his sexual abuse. He claimed that criticism of his predatory behaviour revealed 'the consensus of our respectable culture'. In other words, Yoder rejected criticism coming from outside the Church as merely a reflection of secular middle-class values. Against this, Stanley Hauerwas points out that in a post-Christian culture many 'worldly' intuitions about marriage are not that secular at all. Moreover, there may be truth in the ancient notion of 'natural law', that is, true moral knowledge may come from outside the gospel. Hauerwas continues with some crucial sentences:

> The point I am trying to make – a point not easily made – may entail a criticism of Yoder's work that I am only beginning to understand. I worry that Yoder may have made too extreme the duality between church and world, particularly when it comes to dealing with our everyday relations with one another.[52]

Of course, the model of the countercultural church does not rest on Yoder's work alone, and it as such does not become suspect only because one of its architects used it to immunize himself against justified criticism from outside the Church. Nevertheless, the term 'countercultural' must be used with great care, as its negative view of the world (or its aristocratic view of the Church) can easily lead to rather misguided and even destructive conceptualizations of the relationship between church and world. Something of this also plays out in the field of mission, as we will now see.

Mission and the Preparation of the World

The neo-Anabaptist view of the church's mission runs into a dilemma if we look at the question of how the world should recognize the 'thick offer' that the church invites the world to accept. The dilemma is caused by neo-Anabaptism's rather harsh rhetoric about the world's evil.[53] In all forms of this reinvented Anabaptism we find a strong, almost absolute opposition between the Church and the dominant culture. As James Davison Hunter writes, '[i]n the writings of the neo-Anabaptist theologians, there is little good in the world that deserves praise and no beauty that generates wonder and appreciation'.[54] In a way this follows from Anabaptist theology: if you understand yourself as a 'counterculture', the world can only be painted in unattractive colours. The 'world' in this literature is mostly an arena of power play, violence, capitalism, consumerism, oppression and selfishness. There is really little good in it, and almost nothing to learn from it.

But if this is true, it is hard to imagine how the world can ever accept the offer that the Church makes. There is no natural capacity on the part of the world to recognize and appreciate the gospel lifestyle and the prophetic witness of the Church in her midst. On the other hand, if the world does have some capacity to value and accept this offer, then we must assume that the world has after all some degree of inherent goodness, wisdom, desire to know God, and morality.

Here we encounter again neo-Anabaptism's inconsistent relationship with the world. If the world is really as evil as is suggested, the Anabaptist missionary vision is sterile. But if the mission of the Church is indeed a hopeful enterprise, then the world cannot be as bad as neo-Anabaptists think – at least, not all the time. Of course, there are periods in history, and certain places in this world, where there is a strong opposition between church and world. We may think of the role of the Confessing Church in Nazi Germany, when it was necessary to take an uncompromising stance against the politics of blood and soil. Perhaps it is important to stress this contrast also when nostalgia for Christendom and its accompanying culture wars is still very much alive, and as such the neo-Anabaptist literature is a welcome prophetic voice in many areas of the West where Christians are still tempted by power. But is the world always such a bad place? And is it always wrong for the Church to accept the submission of the rulers of the world, and the invitation to help them create a Christian society? And if the Church stops being a threat to the post-Christian world, because it has become too small and weak and because it has learnt some lessons, might there come a time – at least in some places – where the world welcomes the Church again, even if completely differently than during Christendom?

What we need here is a more dynamic, contextually sensitive view of the relationship between church and world. To me it seems that an Anabaptist ecclesiology is too dependent on a pessimistic picture of the world in which the Church lives, and out of which it is made. In rejecting the theocratic vision of Christendom with its rigid optimism about the Christian character of the world, Anabaptism has embraced an equally rigid pessimism. Thus, if there is anything in the world that deserves praise, this immediately puts into question the Church's nature as a 'counterculture'. For everyone who is seriously involved in mission work this is hard to believe.

In order to be really missional in a post-Christian world we must abandon timeless, supra-cultural constructions of the relationship between church and world – either theocratic or countercultural. The world is not always a hostile place, but on the other hand there is always the possibility of a Pharaoh who has never heard about Joseph. I have discussed the theocratic position in the previous section. As for the countercultural stance, there is something wrong with a Christian identity if it depends on almost entirely negative depictions of the world. As we have seen, even the monasteries did not see themselves primarily as a 'counterculture', but as a radical department within a wider Christianized society with different 'speeds'. Looking back on the Middle Ages and early modernity we can observe that conversions to a monastic vocation or to the intensively Christian lifestyle of Anabaptism occurred against the background of a widely shared ideal of a Christian culture, and on the basis of the – albeit shallow – Christian formation of the largest part of the population. It seems that neo-Anabaptism has insufficiently taken into account that the Anabaptist vision was born in a world that was Christian enough to recognize the truth and goodness of the holy community of disciples in its midst.

This is important to consider, because the question must be raised: how can the world be prepared to recognize the offer of the gospel made by the Christian community? 'Natural' goodness aside, this cannot happen without some vision of broader cultural evangelization. The idea that Christian mission in a post-Christian society should be done by making the world the offer of a 'thick community', an alternative community that represents the future reality of God, may make much sense from the inside out – from the Church's self-understanding. But from a missiological perspective the question is equally important how this community is perceived by the *world* – from the outside in, so to speak. In the radically pluralist societies of the late modern West, there is a persistent rejection of unifying grand narratives or national myths. The current social order is presented as simply the most efficient 'technique' to keep the peace and to produce prosperity for a population that is deeply divided on the level of values and worldviews. Thus, in the words of Rowan Williams, modern societies 'can evade the question of *why* this social order should be respected, preserved and defended'. Worldview differences are redefined as various 'lifestyles', and are as such easily absorbed into the prevailing social order. 'In the context of these societies,' Williams continues, 'indeed, *style* is everything: with massive commercial support, cultural options – even when their roots are in would-be dissident groupings – are developed and presented as consumer goods. And religious belief is no exception.'[55] The most likely response of late modern societies to the so-called 'countercultural communities' of the neo-Anabaptists is to trivialize them as examples of consumerist lifestyles.

In other words, if Christians think that mission can and should happen through the creation of 'thick' communities alone, they should think again. Doing so would simply reinforce the secular absence of a common good, it would amount to abandoning the vision of a redeemed world. Clearly, there is no way for the countercultural tradition to avoid the question of Christian public discourse, of Christian participation in the world of politics, science and the arts. Only in combination with a public discourse that is somehow influenced by Christian notions (however fragmentary) can the witness of strong, countercultural Christian communities make an impression on the world.[56]

All this leads to the paradoxical conclusion that Anabaptism's missionary vision makes sense only against the background of Christendom. That does not necessarily mean a world ruled by Christian governments, or a majority Christian population, but it does imply a world where the gospel has had enough impact to make a home for the countercultural community. And this means, in turn, that this community is not so 'counter'cultural after all. It is a community whose witness depends on the extent to which the gospel has found a hearing in this culture. Thus, the folk church (see section 3.1) and the Anabaptist 'counterculture' are two sides of the same coin. They are predicated on each other like the weekend and the working week, like Carnival and Lenten. Both assume a Christianized world that must be Christianized further. The one does so by uniting the whole population in one structure (the folk church), the other does so by forming an 'anti-structure' as a radical version of the dominant culture (the monastery).[57] The mistake of new Anabaptists is that they take literally the rhetoric that unavoidably accompanied this structure, such as 'pagan', 'world' or 'a godless Babylon'. This creates the false impression that this model is at home in a non-Christian world. By contrast, it seems most comfortable within a (nominally) Christian world.[58] If copy-pasted in a post-Christian world, the countercultural model would (without revision) merely lead to the abandonment of the public square and the reinforcement of the consumerist view that religion is just another lifestyle.

Missiological Conclusions

In a deeply secularized culture churches that draw their inspiration from Anabaptism will have to respond to a completely different cultural context. An anachronistic appeal to the presumably countercultural character of the early Anabaptists will be counterproductive; it will only lead to a disruption of communication with a post-Christian environment. In my opinion this means four things for the Anabaptist path to be fruitful in a secular world.

First, in their relations with other churches Anabaptistically inspired churches are not to present themselves as a 'counterculture' but as an 'intensive' culture. In other words, they should not play the sectarian card, but the monastic card.[59] Here the various movements of 'new monasticism' seem a worthy and missionally relevant heir of this Radical Reformation tradition.[60] Such movements do not present themselves so much as a totalizing ecclesiastical model (not every Christian is expected to become a monk), but as an opportunity for Christians to radically commit themselves to an ideal of discipleship by keeping a certain distance from late modern culture of consumption. Such Christian communities serve their cities and they display to the rest of the Church an ideal of radical discipleship and prophetic critique, without separating the bond that connects them with other churches.[61] In some way this means to accept the structure of 'hierarchical complementarity' (Charles Taylor) that I have discussed in Chapter 2. There are different, complementary ways of being a Christian, and some ways are more radical than others. Traditionally, this principle is mostly expressed in terms of vocations: one Christian has the vocation to remain single and to live without possessions, while the other is called to marry, to have children and to start a business. This is much like in the Old Testament, where the prophet Elijah and the courtier Obadiah both tried to live faithful lives in very different conditions (1 Kings 18.1–15).

Second, in their dealings with the world modern Anabaptists will have to incorporate 'transition zones' in their church life; they will have to provide opportunities to gradually become part of the congregation. After all, in a deeply secularized world the Church cannot simply wager on sudden conversions to a radical Christianity or hope for revivals of people who have no understanding of nor sympathy for the Christian message. The early Anabaptists could profit from the gradual slopes that were present between their communities and the Christianized world around them; churches in the secularized West do not have that advantage. So, even 'countercultural' churches will have to create stepping-stones, ways of belonging without yet really believing or behaving. This they will have to connect with their traditional emphasis on holiness, which makes them face essentially the same challenges as the folk churches which they have rejected.

Third, these communities will have to develop a vision for the formation of a Christian background culture ('cultural Christianity') as a preparation of the gospel. After all, you cannot just harvest; you must be prepared to work the soil and to sow as much as you can – and to accept that most of the seed will bear very little fruit if any. If they are not prepared to do this cultural preparation, countercultural communities are doomed to a sectarian existence. Perforce they will focus on dissatisfied Christians from other churches, as they have no clue how to witness to those without a Christian formation. And their public communication will inevitably be characterized by a judgemental attitude and a lack of humility, because their implicit 'other' are so-called 'mainline' and 'liberal' churches rather than the world.

Finally, the Anabaptist approach leaves us with the ancient question whether Christian mission may require different ecclesial structures alongside the congregation. Here Ralph Winter's proposal about 'two redemptive structures of God's mission' comes to mind. Winter asserted that there have always been two structures working in the mission of God: the modality and the sodality. The first is open to everybody, and is represented by the parish church or the congregation. The second, however, is open only for those with a special vocation and who are prepared to make special vows. This structure is represented, for example, by Paul's company on his travels, by the medieval monasteries, or by the missionary 'societies' that emerged by the end of the eighteenth century.[62] Without going into detail now, I tend to agree with Winter's analysis by and large, but obviously much ecclesiological work still needs to be done given the almost universal preference in the worldwide missiological conversation to the *congregation* as the single most important instrument of God's mission in the world.[63] And this concentration on the local church at the expense of possible other ecclesial structures may be part of the explanation of the popularity of neo-Anabaptist proposals – and of much frustration among pastors about the actual quality of their congregations.

Protestants in particular have a task here, as they continue to wrestle with the Reformation's abolition of alternative ecclesial structures next to the parish church or congregation. This neglect of the 'monastic' dimension of church comes with a vengeance, though, as the Anabaptist tradition shows.

3.3 Church Growth Theory

Both the folk church and the Anabaptist model strike their roots deeply into the Christendom era. Consequently, the crumbling of this formally Christianized society in modern times leads both models into a crisis. In fact, they can only be realized in areas where remnants of Christendom are still to be found. However, there are also models that have emerged later, in the evening glow of Christendom. This would lead one to expect that they contain good answers to the missional challenge posed by a secular society. On a closer look, however, these models are also profoundly shaped by the Christendom dream. The difference with both previous models is that they do not assume Christendom as a static background culture, but rather as an ideal that should be achieved or restored by strategic action. This lends to both models a more dynamic and for many also a more motivating character. Both models can be differentiated by their emphasis on the two dimensions of the mission of Christendom: 'society' and 'rulers' (Oliver O'Donovan).[64] The one model aims for individual conversions (church growth), while the other concentrates on the conversion of the structures and institutions (cultural transformation). In this sense, these two models too are sides of the same coin.[65]

The Purpose of Mission according to the Church Growth Movement

To begin with: in the so-called 'church growth movement' numerical church growth is put centre stage. The world in this model is not a semi-Christianized front portal of the temple, but neither is it necessarily a hostile 'opponent'. First and foremost the world is a fishing pond of 'lost' people who are to be drawn into the Church. Reversely, the success of witness must be assessed by its numerical results. Regardless of anything else that mission may produce, in the end what really matters is growth in numbers.

This idea has been explored most persistently by the American missionary Donald McGavran. In his well-known book *Understanding Church Growth* (1970; reprinted in 1980), McGavran stated emphatically: 'The chief and irreplaceable purpose of mission is church growth.'[66] Opposing contemporary developments in the World Council of Churches where mission was increasingly defined in terms of social action, McGavran demanded a renewed attention to the winning of people as the heart of mission. He did this not to underestimate the importance of 'the Christianizing of the social order' but to set priorities straight. 'Our social causes will not triumph unless we have great numbers of committed Christians.'[67]

This approach in itself does not necessarily depend on Christendom thinking, because it can be applied anywhere in the world. But in Europe and other parts of the West, where church growth centres were established in ever-growing numbers since the 1960s, the ideal of church growth functions in a context of restoration. The main thought seems to be that Europe (and possibly the United States as well) has been insufficiently Christianized by the existing churches, so that churches must be renewed and new churches must be planted in order to meet the religious demand. Only thus can the mass of European 'Christo-pagans' be (re)converted.[68]

Church Growth and Eschatology

McGavran's church growth theory has been criticized many times, especially because of its highly pragmatic character. After all, if the *growth* of the Church is the purpose of mission, rather than faithful testimony, it needs to be asked to what extent this purpose justifies all means. Would this mean, for example, that it is allowable to manipulate people, to exploit their weaknesses, and to turn the gospel into a consumerist commodity in order to get as many 'decisions for Jesus' as possible? Unfortunately, many worrying stories could be told at this point, as I have set out elsewhere.[69] But here I want to focus on the *theological* premise of McGavran's theory that is mentioned above: the purpose of mission is church growth. If indeed the numerical growth of the Church is the goal of mission, its logical consequence is that the world must become church. After all, as long as there is a 'world' outside the 'church' the Church can still grow, which means that mission has not yet reached its purpose. The conclusion is that mission's purpose is the 'erasing' of the world, that is, to change it into 'church'. Only when all people are baptized and enfolded into a church has mission come to its completion.

The question is whether this does justice to what the Bible tells us about mission. Is the world really to become church? In some way, the answer is clearly 'yes'. After all, Jesus is Lord of the Church *and* of the world (Eph. 1); the Church confesses that his significance is universal in scope (Acts 4.12). The Church was never meant to be a particular sect, offering an identity that may be important to some but meaningless to others. If indeed the Church represents the new humanity, it must be emphasized that this humanity belongs together. Even if there is no (Christian) way to enforce this unity prematurely, it must be said that '[t]he Christian community is potentially the whole world' (Rowan Williams).[70] At some point this vision of the unity of humanity must enter our theology of mission. The question is, at what point? Surely, it is God's mission that all people will bow before Jesus, and join in the glory which the Father will give him (Phil. 2.9–11).[71] But clearly this is an eschatological promise, that is to say a promise that will be fulfilled when Jesus returns. All Christian mission testifies to the future gathering of all people under Christ's lordship, but Christian mission itself is not an instrument designed to achieve this. In other words, it is important to make a careful distinction between God's mission and ours. We are not the ones to write the final chapter of world history. It is not our task to gather all of humanity into one worshipping community. We do not even know how God is going to achieve this. It is this eschatological tension that is removed by church growth theory: God's future is drawn into the realm of human expertise and planning.[72]

Advocates of church growth theory may object that this contradicts the so-called Great Commission in Matthew 28.18–20, which unambiguously says: 'Go therefore and make disciples of all nations.' Regardless of whether this specific mandate is given to each individual Christian or only to the twelve Apostles, the text seems to say that according to Jesus the purpose of mission is indeed to make every human being a disciple. And that would invite us to accept quantitative measures as a standard of the Church's faithfulness in mission.

There are different ways to answer this objection. For starters, we should note that within the Gospel of Matthew this text's thrust is clearly the breakthrough of the good news to the gentiles. It is about salvation history rather than numbers. Matthew emphasizes time and again that the Messiah comes to the people of Israel first (for example, Matt. 10.5; 15.21–28, etc.). Only after his resurrection does humanity as a whole come into view. So, the Great Commission marks the great leap of the gospel towards the wider world of nations, fulfilling the promise to Abraham in Genesis 12.1–3 through him who is called 'the son of Abraham' (Matt. 1.1).

In addition we should also question the rather modern and individualistic assumption in this reading of 'disciples of all nations'. Does Jesus really mean that each and every individual citizen of the planet is to become somebody who 'obeys everything that I have commanded you'? In all fairness we must say: that is impossible. After all, in this world four people are born and three die, every *second*. Apart from this pragmatic comment, a more serious theological response is to point out

that there is in fact a deep relationship between the eschatological promise in Philippians 2 and the Great Commission. Jesus gives this mandate
after his resurrection, while anticipating 'the end of the age'. It is in this
intermediate period, awaiting the time that 'every knee will bend', when
mission happens. Rather than interpreting 'disciples of all nations' as a
modern description of *purpose*, it should therefore be read as an eschatological *promise*. No act of witness will be lost; everything will contribute
to that glorious scene in the last of days.

This shows the importance of evangelism as an eschatological activity.
Every church must take up the challenge to further evangelize its environment. The apostle Paul certainly seems to expect this from 'his' congregations (for example, Rom. 1.8; 1 Thess. 1.9). After all, God 'desires
everyone to be saved' (1 Tim. 2.4). In many of Jesus' parables it is said
that the kingdom of God entails that people are 'invited' or 'gathered'.
Even if such expressions are primarily referring to the eschatological
future, this future is present among us somehow. Therefore, the entrance
of new believers into the Church is certainly a sign of the coming kingdom.[73] Wherever the kingdom gospel is proclaimed conversions are to
be expected – even though the Bible does not tell us how many.[74] The
Church is to be an inviting church; she must yearn for new people to
join her ranks.[75] But all this is not the same as church *growth*. We must
learn to separate evangelism and conversion from seeking church growth.
Mission is not an instrument of (numerical) growth; evangelism and conversion are good enough as they are, especially because they point to a
future reality that we don't create. There are many situations when the
entrance of new Christians is not sufficient to replace those who died,
moved away or lapsed. There may be churches that are not growing
because of all sorts of practical reasons, even though they are faithful
in sharing the gospel and even though they welcome new converts now
and then.[76] Such churches may fight an uphill battle, but they are fighting
nonetheless. They are true churches in the New Testament meaning of
the word, even if they are declining in numbers.

Thus, the Great Commission points to the eschatological future shining
on every single act of mission: the bending of every knee, the discipling of
all nations. It extends the promise of Christ's presence to every Christian
who is involved in witness: 'I am with you always.' And it makes it abundantly clear that the Church should reach out to the nations, and that it
should be willing to cross all sorts of ethnic and cultural boundaries.[77]
But it does not say that the purpose of the Church's mission is to disciple
each and every individual. Clearly, the Apostles as the first receivers of
the mandate did not succeed in doing so, and it did not seem to bother
them very much. In fact, the apostle Paul could say that his task was finished and that there was no further work for him in an area when he had

planted a number of churches there, as the first fruits of the harvest of the nations (Rom. 15.17–23).[78] We will remain closer to the language of the Bible if we don't formulate the purpose of mission in terms of church growth but as the *planting of a church* that confesses Jesus as Lord, and applies itself to further proclaiming the gospel, to the glory of God. In so doing we participate in God's mission, but it is not our task to establish his kingdom.

Church Growth and the Church as a Little Flock

Next, there is an uneasy tension between speaking of church growth as the purpose of mission and a series of New Testament texts speaking of the Church as a *minority* in the world. The predominant desire of the church growth movement – a church that engulfs the world – does not seem to motivate the writers of the Bible very much. Time and again Jesus and his apostles speak about the Church as 'salt', 'light', 'residents and aliens', a 'colony of heaven', the 'first fruits', or a 'little flock'. New Testament images of the Church do not suggest a community that is somehow destined to rule the world or to swallow it up, but they point towards a community that leads a precarious life amid the world. God calls the Church *out of* the world, not to swallow it thereafter, but to testify to the world as God's 'kingdom of priests'. In his careful study of biblical growth metaphors Charles van Engen emphasizes that the image of the Church as a 'little flock' is 'not derived from some pessimistic perspective of secularized Europe'. It is a 'realistic appraisal of the situation of the Church in the world'.[79] The New Testament seems very clear about this question: being a majority is an exception for the Church, and often it is a dangerous exception. In my view this image of a minority church in the world bears great missional significance, on which more later in this book.

From the perspective of small Christian communities in a secularized society more realism can be found in the Gospels than in church growth theory. In such a context Christians need to find a way to have 'joy over one sinner who repents' (Luke 15.7, 10) rather than being obsessed by quantitative success. There is, after all, something very dangerous in rejoicing in *growth* (the result of a statistical calculation), instead of rejoicing in the salvation of a *person*. I do not mean to say that church growth enthusiasts do not love people or are uninterested in individuals, but focusing on the abstract category of 'growth' makes it very difficult to have joy over one repenting sinner (only *one?*) when the Church is not growing numerically. In other words, in this approach lies a great risk of instrumentalizing Christian witness to the supposedly higher purpose of church growth. Here I'd like to refer again to the Parable of the Sower that I read as a part of Jesus' missionary teaching to his disciples (Matt. 13; Mark 4). The parable makes three things very clear: (1) the gospel must be sown as widely as possible, (2) we should expect that the majority of the people will not respond, or only superficially, and (3) we are to believe that the minority who do respond will bear fruit in abundance. This is a message for a hopeful minority, and not for a people that will conquer the world in Jesus' name. The dream of a constantly growing church is not dominant in the New Testament. On the contrary, Jesus asks: 'When the Son of Man comes, will he find faith on earth?' (Luke 18.8).[80]

Church Growth and God's World

Finally, we can wonder what actually is the significance of the *world*, if church growth is the purpose of mission. It appears that the world, according to church growth theory, is nothing but a collection of lost souls that must be drawn into the Church. Apart from being a fishing pond for evangelists, the world does not have any *theological* meaning. God 'does' nothing in the world, except moving people to become members of the Church. But doesn't the Church need the world somehow in order to be the Church? Some of this is seen in the biblical images of the Church as a minority in the world. If the Church consists of the *first* fruits of the harvest, then what is the world in God's eyes? If the Church is a community of 'residents and strangers' or a 'colony of heaven', then what is the theological place of the world as the Church's 'host' society? Should the guest take over the house of the host? Is the mission of the stranger accomplished only when he or she has achieved domination?

Besides theology we can also look here at the recent history of the post-Christian West. The world has come into the picture more emphatically as an independent force that puts pressure on the Church out of its own secular motives. This can be embarrassing for the Church, but it seems to me that this pressure is needed sometimes to purify the Church. What would the position of women in the Church be without criticism from the outside? Would the abuse scandals in the Roman Catholic Church have been exposed and dealt with if this would have been left to the Church's initiative? Can the current sensitivity to the fate of LGBTQ people in the Church be explained without reference to the changed mood in the host societies of the Church? And doesn't the growing ecological consciousness in our times have a salutary influence on the missionary conscience of the Christian community?

In my view we should consider to what extent Christians need the world – especially the powerful world of the secular West – to remain humble, dependent on grace and constantly surprised by the measure of God's love. The world is not just the dark background of our evangelizing mission. It is *God's* world. Just like God uses his Church to witness before the world, God uses his world to teach the Church and to keep her close to him. This may be the reason why God does not want the world to disappear into the Church before Jesus returns. The Church can only be church if there remains a world outside her; a world that is challenging her, posing critical questions, threatening her, and sometimes welcoming her (Luke 10.5–6).[81]

3.4   Church as a Transforming Power in the World

The next missionary model I want to discuss is related to the church growth movement, in the sense that it has emerged in a culture of beginning secularization, while being focused on restoration. I am under the impression that this model is currently often embraced by younger missionary Christians who have become disappointed with the possibilities of quantitative church growth, and the shallow methods that are sometimes associated with it. By rebound, they turn to alternative strategies to expand the gospel's impact on the world. In short, this model entails that the Church has the calling and task to 'change' or 'transform' the world with a Christian vision.

For convenience's sake I distinguish two currents in this model even though I have to add that they overlap in practice.[82] One current has its roots in the revival movements of the eighteenth century that form the foundations of modern evangelicalism. These revivals took place in a culture of beginning secularization, when Christian intuitions and cosmological ideas were still widespread among the population. Growing urbanization and industrialization, together with the massive uprooting of rural populations, caused a widely shared nostalgia for the restoration of a Christian society.[83] The revival movements presented spiritual renewal as the key to this restoration. In this sense they were *modern* movements. Christians in the seventeenth century would first have looked at the government in order to Christianize their societies, but the eighteenth-century Christians sought a 'democratic' approach. If only enough people would be personally converted and discipled, the structures and institutions of society would change as a matter of course. As we have seen above, this is what church growth theorists hold to be true as well. Eventually, the conversion of society is nothing but the sum of countless changed lives.

However, it is the second current in this model of mission as transformation of the world that will concern us here. This approach of mission emerged in the twentieth century, and is becoming increasingly popular within missional literature. Part of its popularity lies in its more sophisticated analysis of how societal change happens. Cultural conversion according to this model is not merely Wilberforce's 'reformation of manners' writ large; a society is more than the sum of its people. Individuals and groups are embedded in and shaped by structures and institutions, while cultural elites represent a power far exceeding their force in numbers.[84] A missiology that aims for cultural conversion must meet these challenges head-on; it must have a theory of institutions, and it must address the issue of cultural and political power. This also becomes very clear in concrete experiences of (evangelical) missions that have concentrated on increasing the number of converts before anything else. As Chris Wright notes, often, 'successful evangelism, flourishing revivalist spirituality and a majority Christian population did not result in a society where God's biblical values of equality, justice, love and nonviolence had taken root and flourished likewise'.[85] In short, while retaining the ancient ideal of a Christianized society many Christians felt that there was need of a more responsible, holistic approach of cultural conversion.

Roots and Influences

Like so many other approaches of missional ecclesiology this one is not a seamless tunic, woven in one piece. For example, as Ruth Padilla DeBorst explains in her lucid introduction of the transformation model from a Latin American perspective:

> [I]t drew on the stores and strengths of various strands: radical discipleship and the priesthood of all believers from the Anabaptist tradition, socially committed pietism from the Wesleyan tradition, a comprehensive affirmation of Christ's lordship over every last dimension of existence from the Reformed tradition, and an appreciation for the diverse gifting of the Holy Spirit from the Pentecostal tradition, among others.[86]

While DeBorst's description refers to a specific context, this citation mirrors a general sentiment in contemporary missiology. In its background lies what sometimes has been called a 'Copernican revolution' in missiological thinking: the *missio Dei* theology that came up in the 1950s and 1960s. Taking its cue from the neo-reformed theologian Karl Barth (1886–1968), *missio Dei* theology entails a radical theocentric perspective on mission.[87] While previously mission could be described as essentially a task of the Church, and aimed at the preservation and expansion of the Church, *missio Dei* means that God is the centre of mission. God's mission is his plan of salvation, defined in the broadest terms. God is on a mission to reconcile the world with himself, to heal his broken creation, and to repair the effects of sin. Consequently, the Church becomes instrumental to this mission. It is to 'participate' in the 'movement of God's love towards people' (David Bosch).[88] Also, the scope of mission widens: '[s]ince God's concern is for the entire world, this should also be the scope of the *missio Dei*'.[89]

This rooting of mission in the doctrine of God, and the decentring of the Church, have become almost common sense in contemporary missiology. This is not to say, however, that everybody means the same thing with *missio Dei* terminology.[90] In an important article, Thormod Engelsviken points out that, while all adherents are more or less agreed on the theocentric character of mission and the decentring of the Church, there are important differences between those who see God's mission as his all-encompassing work of providence and those who think that God's mission is bound up with a specific history represented by the people of Israel in the Old Testament and the life, death and resurrection of Jesus in the New.[91] Roughly speaking, one could also differentiate these approaches from one another by the emphasis of the former on the Holy Spirit (God's ubiquitous presence in creation), and the emphasis of the latter on Jesus Christ (God's particular presence in the Incarnation).[92] These positions are not without consequences, especially for the role of the Church in God's mission. If God's mission happens primarily through his providential care for the world, the Church tends to dissolve. Its main task seems to be to identify where God is working in the world, and then join this movement of the Spirit. This leads to all sorts of problems that will be discussed in the next section. More influential in contemporary missional literature, however, is the second position. Here the Church is the community that emerges from the history of salvation in and through Jesus. Even though God's mission is not about the Church itself, the Church is his privileged instrument to bring his salvation about. This position combines quite naturally with the Anabaptist perspective that was discussed before. After all, if the world must indeed be 'healed' and 'reconciled' then there is evidently something wrong with the world as it is. This invites us to adopt a countercultural and critical model of mission, and if the Church is indeed to play a role in God's mission then this church must be countercultural and critical as well.

DeBorst's reference to the 'Reformed tradition', however, hints at another and somewhat older reformed current in missional theology:

the so-called 'neo-Calvinism', founded by Abraham Kuyper (1837–1920). Today, this tradition is an increasingly popular resource to draw from among missional writers. One of its core ideas, as already mentioned in Chapter 2, is Kuyper's slogan that there is 'no square inch' of this earth over which Christ does not claim dominion. Another important concept is the so-called 'cultural mandate', which is based on the task given to humanity in Genesis 1 to cultivate the earth. Thus, Christians are called to embody their faith in such a way that a particular part of the world (for example, the workplace) is 'transformed' with a view to Christ's rule over each aspect of life. At this point Kuyper made a distinction between the Church as 'organization' (institution) and 'organism'.[93] With the first he meant the outward form of the Church, as being built by human beings; with the second he meant the inner organic life that flows directly from the Spirit of God. Both dimensions of the Church must be kept together, as they both represent what the Church is about. But they are not identical. Thus, Kuyper could also distinguish between the visible organization of the church as an institution, and the countless ways in which Christians and their organizations are active in society. To Kuyper, the purpose of this activity was missional, in the sense of a restoration of Christian culture. As salt and yeast Christians would permeate society with Christian values through organizations such as schools, universities, labour unions, political parties, newspapers, and so forth.

Something that often goes unnoticed by those who are inspired by Kuyper, however, is that he believed that his model would no longer be possible in a time of advanced secularization. Already in the early decades of the twentieth century he saw this more deeply secularized culture emerging in the Netherlands. According to him this would mean that a reflourishing of Christian culture was not to be expected any more. In his work are indications that Kuyper would then recommend a more 'Anabaptist', countercultural model for the Church's mission to society. In other words, the mission of the Church would be much more exclusively bound up with the church as an institution, the local congregation.[94] Given this original context of Kuyper's thoughts, it would not surprise me if at least one explanation of neo-Calvinism's popularity among the more intellectually inclined evangelicals in the United States should be sought in the increasing awareness of secularization in the country. If this is true it would also mean that this revival of Kuyperianism will not last long, rooted as it seems to be in a context where the restoration of a 'Christian culture' still makes sense.

Be that as it may, it is interesting to see to what extent these two neo-reformed currents – though representing different generations of thought – touch the same sentiments. Both see a kind of 'bipolarity' in Christian life, in the sense that ecclesial existence is lived out both in the gathered community of worship and in the dispersed people of God in various walks of life. While the neo-Barthian approach may be more at home in a secularized society, the Kuyperian vision has a much more concrete philosophy of what it actually means to permeate society with Christian values. Fleshing out a 'transformationist' mission in all its concreteness remains the challenge for its adherents in post-Christian societies, where their cultural and political power is limited.

Neo-reformed perspectives are currently extremely influential in literature on Christian mission in secular societies. At the time, Lesslie Newbigin (1909–98) already threw the weight of his considerable reputation into advocating a missional ecclesiology in which 'Anabaptist' and 'Reformed' motives were combined.[95] In his view the Reformed tradition offered a building block that was lacking in Pietism and Anabaptism: an inspiring vision and a good practical description of the significance of the 'ordinary' Christian in modern society. Newbigin's theology has influenced Reformed missiologists in America like George Hunsberger and Darrell Guder.[96] Other important evangelical theologians working from this framework could be mentioned, such as Chris Wright in his monumental book *The Mission of God* (2006), and his namesake the New Testament scholar N. T. Wright, whereas one generation earlier David Bosch emphasized that Christian identity and conversion mean, first and foremost, that we are being turned towards God's world and apply ourselves to its flourishing and future.[97] All these theologians are well read by missionary Christians, both theorists and practitioners. The same is true of Tim Keller from New York, one of the world's most influential missionary practitioners, who in speeches and writings has proclaimed himself a Kuyperian time and again. In his book *Center Church* (2012) he presents a powerful ideal of cultural transformation: God wants the restoration of his creation, the cities are the most influential engines of cultural change, and therefore Christians should try and reach the cities for Christ.[98]

A third influence, occupying a somewhat different territory by its association with non-Western and usually less secularized societies, is found in a range of critical theologies emerging since the 1960s, and somewhat loosely defined as 'liberation theology'.[99] For our purposes it is important to point out that these theologies take their point of departure on the one hand in the experiences of injustice and oppression suffered by the poor in so many nations, and on the other hand in the kingdom ministry of Jesus (particularly in the synoptic Gospels). Thus, the mission of God has a concrete face in Jesus who faced the powers of this world in order to bring justice, forgiveness, communion and healing to those who were oppressed and excluded. The Church is to participate in this kingdom mission, and this means that it sides with the poor against their oppressors. A mission that is content with preaching individual conversion and a salvation after death betrays this mission of God, since it leaves unjust structures unaffected.[100]

This particular prophetic dimension of mission has impacted evangelical Protestants, especially through the works of Latin American Protestants such as René Padilla and Orlando Costas, who time and again demanded a more holistic approach of mission by evangelicals. In Spanish they called this approach *misión integral* ('integral mission'). The Church, according to a key text in this tradition, 'is to incarnate the values of God's kingdom and witness to the love and justice revealed in Jesus Christ in the power of the Spirit and for the transformation of human life in all its dimensions, personally and communally'.[101] In this quotation we see traces of the same bipolarity as in the neo-reformed currents, but the element of 'transformation' is emphasized much more. This emphasis has found its way into a wealth of reports and studies, much of which is compiled in Vinay Samuel's and Chris Sugden's *Mission as Transformation* (1999).[102] 'Fundamentally, Transformation is the transformation of communities to reflect kingdom values.' Kuyperian overtones are not lacking, as the authors make clear that this holistic approach is 'centred in the rule of Christ over the whole of life'.[103] Also the increasing influence of the Pentecostal movement is pointed out, besides kingdom theology, as this movement has brought to the attention how crucial the experience of the Spirit is in transformation.[104]

Transformation as a Missionary Purpose

This ideal of a church shaped by gospel values that participates in God's mission to heal the world is found in virtually every capillary of the modern missionary movement. It is easy to see why. This model builds on crucial insights in twentieth-century missiology, that is, the nature of mission as God's mission, the ensuing characterization of the Church as an instrument of this mission rather than its purpose, and finally the holistic and prophetic character of mission in a world full of structural injustice. Also, from a practical perspective, this approach is attractive. It is, after all, hugely inspiring to believe that you and your small community play a role in a worldwide story, to trust that your life contributes to an eternal project.

So, what to think of this model? Let me be clear that I have no intention whatsoever to criticize integral mission or the theocentric character of mission. On the contrary, as I explained in Chapter 1, I believe that these are crucial developments that cannot and should not be reversed. Also, there is nothing wrong with a theology that inspires Christians to serve their neighbours and develop a responsible approach of the workplace, ecology, poverty and politics. Moreover, there is nothing wrong with a theology that tells Christians that their labour is not in vain (1 Cor. 15.58), and that all the good that we are doing contributes in one way or another to the coming of God's kingdom. Finally, even if I would like to see a bit more restraint in the use of words like 'change' and 'transformation' (see below), it is of course true that mission produces changes. If somebody is converted, healed or restored in her rights, something real and concrete is happening; if an institution changes its policy or if a government issues new laws a genuine transformation occurs.

My concern with this model is, therefore, not structural. It is, rather, that concepts like 'change' and 'transformation' tap into a linguistic field full of hazards.[105] This happens especially when the relationship between God's mission and ours is not articulated properly. As regards God's mission (*missio Dei*) with his creation, we find a wealth of metaphors and descriptions of God's purpose in the New Testament. There will be 'new heavens and a new earth, where righteousness is at home' (2 Peter 3.13), God will be 'all in all' (1 Cor. 15.28), 'every knee will bend and every tongue confess that Jesus Christ is Lord' (Phil. 2.10–11), and so forth. Let us assume, then, that 'transformation' is indeed an apt term to summarize what God's mission (*missio Dei*) is about, even though the term itself is not found in the Bible. But what does this mean for our mission? How are we to 'participate' in God's mission? Christians are called to love their neighbours (even their enemies), by concrete acts of witness in words and deeds. These acts receive their significance from God's future reality; they are inspired and empowered by the Spirit who is given as a 'first installment' (2 Cor. 1.22) of this future. I believe this is the primary meaning of our 'participation' in God's mission. By loving and serving others, even their enemies, Christians build 'signs' (however vulnerable) of God's 'transformed' future, and they witness to the inbreaking reality of God's kingdom.

So far so good. My question is this: is it helpful to call *our* witnessing activities 'transformationist' as well, or should we restrict this terminology to God's own work?[106] An immediate problem arising from using this term for our mission is that it may lead to the instrumentalization of witness. If a 'changed society' rather than faithful witness is the purpose of mission, all separate deeds of neighbour love and service are to be justified based on what they contribute to a different world. Also, how do we avoid the sacraments or worship being reduced to 'tools' for 'building up the saints for mission'?[107] Just like the concept of 'growth' in church growth theory, the concept of 'transformation' in this paradigm can suffocate authentic mission. Everything is about cultural transformation! Change the world! When this strategic ideal begins to dominate mission, it will irrevocably lead to a perversion of mission, and possibly to the exhaustion of Christians.

Another problem is that 'transformation' and 'change' are not innocent words; in one way or another they are associated with the exercise of power. In this context it always strikes me how the desired outcome of transformationist mission is usually left vague in much missionary literature. What exactly should the 'conversion of the West' (Newbigin) lead to? What does a society look like that is 'transformed' by the gospel? And, most importantly, how do we avoid identifying our own dreams and projects of transformation with the purpose of God's own mission? This last question is important because, consciously or unconsciously, and especially in post-Christian countries, nostalgic agendas of restoration tend to become identified with the mission of God in our societies. Thus, in very subtle ways God's mission is transformed into our own mission after all.

Sometimes I ask my students to close their eyes and think of what they consider the most 'Christianized' place in their country. Then, after some time, I ask them: 'Would you like to live there?' Almost always this question provokes embarrassed smiles. It appears very difficult to imagine such a place without at the same time having memories of a rather dull and legalistic culture, focused on issues such as 'observing the Sabbath', and without the creative tensions brought about by living among those who do not share your worldview. Idealistic pictures of a more 'just' and 'equal' society do not help us very much here, so long as these pictures do not seriously engage with the heritage of Christendom, and issues of how (political) power is used in a Christianized society especially with regard to those (minorities?) who dissent from Christian orthodoxy.

Of course, enthusiasts of a 'transformationist' approach are quick to admit that we should not repeat the Christendom experience. Ruth Padilla DeBorst makes that very clear, for example, when she emphasizes that the rule of Jesus is different from the authority exercised by earthly rulers. 'The fundamental problem with Christendom projects is that they confuse the kingdom of God with the institutional church, the gospel with culture, and the power of the cross with the power of the sword.'[108] That is well said, indeed. But I wonder if this is really an adequate response against concerns about the concept of 'transformation'. How exactly do we prevent that 'the transformation of human life in *all* its dimensions' results in a Christian social order, after all? And how are Christian rulers not also *earthly* rulers wielding earthly power? How can such a Christian state deal with its dissenters and minorities if not in the ways governments have usually dealt with them? To be sure, DeBorst sees this danger, and that is why she writes: 'The church has not been called to manage the world, but rather to bear witness to the kingdom of God in the world.'[109] I agree, but what does this mean for 'transformationist' mission? Is it really possible to 'transform' the world without 'managing' it? I don't see how one can embrace a 'transformationist' approach to mission (especially in the rather totalizing form sketched above), and at the same time persist in a prophetic minority position of the Church. In short, I do not really see how the 'transformationist' approach can escape the Christendom temptation.

Confusing God's Mission and Our Mission

While reiterating that there is nothing wrong as such with a missionary ideal that inspires Christians to work towards a more just society, I want to point out a number of additional problems that are often overlooked by advocates of this model, without assuming that they would necessarily disagree with what I write here. All these problems flow forth from the lack of differentiation between God's 'transformationist' mission and our 'witnessing' mission.[110]

To begin with, the whole idea of mission as cultural transformation bears the stamp of the modern age. It is charged with modern optimism about humanity, such as that we have the *wisdom* to know what the world should look like, and that we have the *power* to steer it in this direction. This is not what the Bible teaches about human beings, and it is not what the Church Fathers believed either. God is a mystery, the world is messy and unpredictable, and we are very limited beings indeed. Time and again people have thought that they knew which way the world was going, only to find out a generation later or so that they had miscalculated completely. This is the rule rather than the exception. It even happens to American presidents who are able to surround themselves with the brightest analysts and experts, and who possess an almost unlimited power. Whence, then, do we assume the arrogance that we can 'plan ahead' more or less what a Christian culture change should look like? Virtually in every instance we lack the knowledge to see how witnessing can be an *instrument* of God's coming kingdom. But isn't it sufficient if we can erect a *sign* that points to it? Often a sign is transient, like a sand-castle on the beach that is washed away with the first tide. Nonetheless it can encourage us and others for some time; it can inspire us and keep our hope alive. It mirrors God's future world even if only dimly.

Next, a missional strategy that is inspired by the 'change' it is supposed to bring about easily leads to us hampering the Holy Spirit. Our own idea of what a transformed society is to look like begins to shape our missionary practice. Every action, every conversion is supposed to be one step on the ladder that leads us to this missional utopia. In order to achieve this we are to focus on people with power and influence. After all, they are the ones who, if converted, are going to change the culture. In such a strategic ideal the conversion of a lawyer, a politician or a popular artist is much more important than the conversion of an asylum seeker or a prostitute. We must concentrate on the *leaders*, who are living in the *cities*, and as we all know it is the cities that determine the course of the *world*. And so on. All this has little to do with a healthy theology of mission. On the contrary, in the Bible we see time and again that the Spirit seems to prefer the *unstrategic* places for the mission of God to happen. Abraham is called out of the influential city of Ur to wander about in the desert; the people of Israel are guided out of the world's leading power of Egypt in order to find a place for themselves in a mountainous and infertile strip of land squeezed in between the major political centres; and Jesus was born in a stable in Bethlehem rather than in the royal palace in Jerusalem. If anything gives the lie to missional strategies aimed at transforming the world's leading institutions, it is the gospel itself. Quite simply, this is not how the Spirit works most of the time.

Third, this brings us to the rather naive view of institutions in this model. If changing the world is our purpose, we will seek to become involved in 'relevant' institutions. We want to be there where it 'matters'. What could be better than a Christian president, a Christian CEO, a Christian Olympic athlete? Just imagine the good that these people can do, the power they can wield. But Christians often realize insufficiently that these institutions are part of the rationalized world of modernity. If politics can be 'Christian', then Christian faith can be 'politicized' just as well; it can be sucked up into the power-play of laws, corruption, compromises and negotiated rulings.[111] Every bridge that is built towards the 'outside world' also invites all sorts of influences to enter the 'inside world'. This is not something to avoid anxiously (the Church is in the world), but let us not think that we can control this process or even steer it towards projected outcomes. As far as I am concerned there is nothing against a Christian political leader, but I do not see much reason to be very happy about it either. In any case, such people need much prayer, not so much to be 'successful' as to be protected against what St Augustine once called the *libido dominandi* – the lust for domination.

Fourth, this idea of cultural transformation as a missionary strategy is simply too big for human beings. There is something deeply misguided, perhaps even idolatrous, in such far-reaching visions. In modern societies a vision is never big enough; we are always expected to aim higher. The German missiologist Theo Sundermeier says: 'We live in an age that is pushing for perfection and completeness.' The Church is no exception. It is tempting to construct the mindset of the kingdom as a big plan to change the world by focusing on influential locations and relevant people. But regardless of how attractive it may be for many people to be part of such a grand scheme, is this really what God asks of us? Perfection becomes a form of tyranny if we are to achieve it. We will only reach perfection in God's kingdom. 'Mission is patchwork', says Sundermeier. 'We are not forced to change the whole world or even to Christianize it.' If this is true, there will be room for small and local witness, free havens of spontaneity and creativity.[112] Refusing grand schemes of 'culture transformation' may open our eyes for what the Holy Spirit does through inspired people in the most unexpected and unstrategic places – such as Nazareth in Galilee. We could do with less planning and more surprises.

Finally, rejecting an ideal of strategic culture change may also be the best contextual approach of mission in the post-Christian West. After all, Europe and some of its former colonies are the best examples of a Christianized ('transformed') culture in history – and with very mixed results. Most citizens of modern Western nations are very wary of repeating this experience even if they agree that it was not all bad. To assume that a programme of cultural change by the churches will somehow be attractive for secularized societies is deeply mistaken. Of course, many people will appreciate it if churches do something about poverty or speak out against social injustice. As long as churches articulate the morality of the majority it is all fair and square. But a large and growing majority of Western citizens will draw the line as soon as churches interfere with 'private' matters (like sexuality), or if they fail to echo the latest political fashion on the left or the right. If kingdom-minded action still feeds on the dream of a homogeneous Christian society, it must be said loud and clear: *this dream is over*. The only kind of sympathy that the Church will get in secular societies is when it has neither ambition nor power to restore Christendom. After all, Jesus assigned his disciples with the task to be salt in the world, not to change the world into a salt desert.

Changing the World and Missional Spirituality

Within this strategic discourse of Christian culture change lies, in my opinion, a deep conflict with Christianity itself. The question remains, then, what will be the effect of the current shift towards a new Kuyperianism among younger Christians who are in search of an inspiring ideal. In my estimation this could very well accelerate the process of secularization. Charles Taylor describes how the rise of secular humanism in the West cannot be explained without a theological prehistory.[113] Some historians would even claim that the so-called Enlightenment was a radicalized Christian movement before anything else, and that modern unbelief in fact emerged from the disappointment and frustration with Christendom on the part of dissenting and free-thinking Christians.[114] This is a long and complicated history, but an important part of it is the gradual fading of the view that the meaning of our earthly existence is to be found elsewhere (after this life, in heaven, in the future). On this traditional view, the purpose of life on earth, individually and communally, was not primarily the flourishing of humanity but rather the glory of God. This did not mean that God was against human flourishing, but it did mean that God's will could not be *reduced* to human flourishing. This life was not all there was.

This perspective begins to shift in early modernity towards an accent on the life here and now. According to Christian thinkers in the seventeenth and eighteenth centuries God's plan is primarily to do with a social order in which everyone finds his right and destination – a right and destination that were coloured in economic and juridical terms to a high degree. In short, this meant that the weight of life moved from heaven to earth, from conversion to development, from God to humanity. The image of God followed suit. First and foremost, God has become a loving God who desires the good and happy life for his children above anything else. Within this theological framework not only does suffering become unintelligible (Lisbon, 1755); it is also a path towards secularization. After all, as soon as people begin to think that a better world can also be built without prayer, God moves to the background. This evolution is characteristic of all modernity, both with regard to the mega-trends and a number of smaller and more localized developments in all sorts of countries. Every time, we see the same pattern: first, the Christian faith is instrumentalized in the service of earthly goals, and then it turns out that these goals can also be realized without Christian faith. In this way one gets 'Christian' countries without Christians.

The American philosopher James Smith sees a similar development in contemporary evangelicalism, 'which is increasingly casting off its "otherworldly" piety and becoming newly invested in the flourishing of this world'.[115] Obviously, young Christians and especially those who have been raised in 'fundamentalist' families, will often experience this turn towards the world and towards creation as a liberation and a source of inspiration. It is inspiring to discover that you can be an orthodox believer and at the same time fully engaged in the world; that you can be *relevant* to art, politics, science and business. It is, at last, possible to escape this escapist cocoon, to crawl out of your world-denying spiritual cabin, and embrace all goodness and beauty of the world as God's gifts. The energy that is discharged when the two continents of faith and culture are no longer grinding against each other but slide over each other smoothly, provides a new impulse for the life of faith. Indeed, this can be a salutary and healing experience. But there are risks involved. It is to be expected, says Smith, that these Protestants will go through the same process that many before them have gone through already. Young Christians will lose their perspective on eternal life and conversion, and they will move towards Protestant liberalism or, perhaps more likely, post-Christian spirituality. And since such people usually only have barely enough oil for their own lamps, their children in turn will probably become entirely separated from church and faith.

Another possibility, and certainly one for which Smith hopes, is that these younger evangelicals, when they get tired of the lack of enchantment and the constant activism of this transformation ideal, will turn from a Christianity that craves recognition and relevance and turn to a more 'old-fashioned', liturgical, sacramental, 'catholic' type of Christianity. And who knows if just a revival of a vital catholicism (with a small 'c') may not be more attractive to many of their secularized and individualized peers than a Christianity that constantly seeks to demonstrate its superiority in terms of world improvement, that time and again argues modernistically that it has been right all along, and that moreover always seems to seek a renewed control over society.[116]

3.5   Church Inside Out

Finally, I will discuss two newer models that have both emerged in the twentieth century. I set out with a model that became enormously popular as of the 1960s, particularly in mainstream Protestantism. Again, I will concentrate on the main issues without trying to map this movement exhaustively. The model is strongly associated with the Dutch missiologist Johannes Hoekendijk (1912–75). It displays similarities with both the folk church model and the transformationist model that I have discussed above.

From the Ends of the Earth to the End of Time

According to John Flett, the position that the Church is an 'instrument' for missionary witness 'finds classic expression in the work of Johannes Christiaan Hoekendijk'.[117] In this section I follow his careful reconstruction of Hoekendijk's missionary ecclesiology. Hoekendijk's contribution must be situated in the Dutch theology of the apostolate, which was developed in the decades preceding and following the Second World War.[118] An increasing awareness of the secularization of Europe and the ensuing collapse of Christendom led to an emphasis (associated with, among others, Hendrik Kraemer) on the formation of congregations that were up to the challenge of witnessing about Christ in a post-Christian context. Here the 'bipolarity' emerged that was mentioned in the previous section as a characteristic of twentieth-century Reformed missiology:

Christian mission required a witnessing community on the one hand and a witnessing 'dispersed' presence in society on the other.

While Hoekendijk, despite his free church background, found much of his theological inspiration in this tradition, he opposed its strong folk church dimension that envisaged the re-Christianization of the Netherlands (see section 3.1). What does it mean, then, to be a missional church that does not aim at restoring Christendom? The answer, for Hoekendijk, lay in a thorough critique of the territorial character of Christendom, and its (mostly colonial) mission.[119] By identifying the kingdom of God with a specific territory, its history and its culture, Christendom had turned the God of the Bible into a tribal God, a 'Baal'. Its mission was to repeat this constellation by planting it in other territories, and by projecting categories from its own social history (such as 'civilization' or '*Volk*') onto the 'mission fields'. Thus, mission's purpose was to expand Christendom until the ends of the earth. Hoekendijk's response was to recategorize mission as *historical* rather than geographical. Mission is not about expanding a certain realm until it covers the whole planet; it is about being attuned to the eschatological reign of God that draws the world towards his future *shalom*.[120] For Hoekendijk this removal of (expanding) space as a defining characteristic of the Church also means that the Church ceases to have a separate role apart from the apostolate. 'Church' is what *happens* in the encounter of the kingdom and the world; it is therefore in constant transition towards the end of time. Or, in Hoekendijk's famous words: the Church is 'a function of the Apostolate, that is, an instrument of God's redemptive action in this world'.[121]

This does not mean that Hoekendijk has no place for churches.[122] Wherever the kingdom meets the world, communities and their structures emerge. However, since Hoekendijk allows no existence for the Church prior to its involvement in mission, these churches will be pluralistic, sometimes even contradictory in form, they will be mobile, and they will usually be small and dedicated to creating 'signs' of shalom. 'Church' is, after all, what 'happens' in the manifold encounters between the coming kingdom and the world; it takes shape only where *shalom* happens, and, as history is always on the move, this shape is volatile by definition.

At this point, serious questions emerge. 'History' is, after all, a rather abstract category in itself. It may be trivial to say, but it must be said nonetheless: history is always the history *of* something, and we can only experience history because we are embodied creatures who experience change. We are indeed constantly moving towards the future, but we are also made by the past; we are historical, but also spatial. Where, for example, do the people come from who are dedicated to God's *shalom*? How are they to be formed, or discipled, in such a transitory, amorphous, mobile 'apostolic event' like the Hoekendijkian church? As Flett aptly says, 'Absent from Hoekendijk's church is a certain human texture.'[123] According to Flett, this has something to do with the absence of *divine* texture in Hoekendijk's missiology. God seems to disappear into the apostolate, and thus into history. 'God's being becomes, through God's own act, somehow secondary to the historical process itself.' Against this, Flett quotes Karl Barth's axiom: 'God gives Himself, but He does not give Himself away.'[124] I agree, and I think that this inadequate doctrine of God is reflected in Hoekendijk's isolation of 'history' as the domain of mission. Mission and, for that matter, the Church do not just *happen*; they also have a *being* that is not exhausted in their actions. Without embodiment *nothing* really 'happens'. Important problems follow from ignoring this, as the next section will show.

Secularization of Mission

Ironically, Hoekendijk's rejection of folk church thinking falls into the same trap of thinking the world together under one religious category – the 'apostolate' of eschatological 'shalom'. In the folk church tradition (that was revived in the Dutch theology of the apostolate) the difference between the Church and the (Christianized) world is minimal: the ruptures among humanity do not really define us, not even here and now. This can lead to attempts to 'churchify' the whole world, but of course it can also go in the opposite direction: the Church must become 'worldly' in some way. It is subsumed into the history of the encounter between God's eschatological shalom and the world, without a being of its own. As a consequence of its complete instrumentalization, the Church does not have a separate or unique place. Its mission is not to invite people in (church growth) or to influence secular communities with gospel values (transformation). As a 'function' of the apostolate the Church can only identify struggles for shalom in this world, and join them. It is not to be focused on itself and its own future, but it is to turn itself 'inside out' – thus a famous book title of Hoekendijk's.[125] Thus and only thus can it serve the mission of God's shalom (peace, well-being, reconciliation) in the world.

Already during Hoekendijk's life, this vision came to be intimately connected with a particular theology of the kingdom of God. Since the beginning of the twentieth century theologians have often emphasized that the kingdom has 'already' arrived in Jesus' ministry on earth, but has 'not yet' been realized completely. This will not happen before the last judgement, when Jesus returns and God will be all in all. This also means that we have already received an, admittedly limited, vision of the kingdom. Even though most of it is still to be discovered, there is something 'behind' us, something we can point to and draw normative perspectives from. The radical historicizing of God's mission in the model of the 'inside-out church', however, may easily lead to a separation between the kingdom and the person and work of Jesus. 'Kingdom' and 'Messiah' threaten to become *chiffres*; symbols, so to speak, of some eschatological future of *shalom* without concrete historical and scriptural substance. Instead, they coincide with the gradual realization of God's will in his creation, on the road to the world's humanization. In this way the kingdom of God is identified with political and social 'progress' – however that is measured.[126] What the kingdom is (and what it is not) becomes increasingly difficult to say, if limited historical realizations of the kingdom – especially those recorded in the New Testament – are ruled out as being normative for today. Rather than consulting the Gospels, we will have to discover it by involving ourselves in the desire for *shalom* that is found everywhere, particularly among the poor and oppressed. Insofar as the Church plays a role in this mission of God, it is to support it, together with other people of good will.

The problem with this line of thinking is that it leads to Christian speechlessness. How, after all, do we recognize God's work in the world if there is no normative realization of it? How can we distinguish the movement of God's kingdom in other movements? Which criteria do we have by which to assess the work of Christians and others in the world? If we respond to these questions by pointing to the Bible and the Christian tradition, then we also say that apparently there is a higher norm than 'worldly' wisdom – regardless of how true and wise it often is. In other words, as soon as we turn to the Bible or tradition in order to make sense of something, or in order to evaluate it, we are saying that God is not just generally active in the world, but also in a particular way. He has made himself and his intentions known in times, places, persons and institutions with a special, 'elected' or 'inspired' status. Apparently, they provide the standards by which we can make distinctions between the mission of God and other missions, between kingdom activity and other activity.

But if this is true, then the Church is more than just an instrument. It then represents a perspective that ontologically precedes its activity in the world. Everything the Church does, it performs by reference to a reality that is the source of its actions. And these actions cannot be judged solely by asking if they contribute to a more humane world. If we, by contrast, reject every form of special revelation we will have to look for other criteria by which to assess the Church's mission. And these criteria can only be provided by the world itself. Every movement that is deemed good and just by the world (or by certain parties within it) is to be accepted as such by the Church. This robs Christians of their own voice and agenda. They cannot tell the world anything that it does not know already.[127] Hence the rather boring nature of a certain type of theological liberalism that says the same things you can hear everywhere but with a Christian coating. The world can welcome the Church (Christian citizens) in its struggle with injustice (as the world sees it), but it does not really need the particular narrative of Jesus and his kingdom to define this struggle or to legitimate it. The 'Church', if we still need this outdated name, would be nothing but a different label for something that can be described just as well (or better) in political or sociological terms. If the world delivers the criteria by which the Church's usefulness is determined, Christians do not bring anything universal or supracultural into the world. Also they would not be capable of testifying to anything that transcends the wisdom of the world.

If we take seriously that the Christian faith makes a unique contribution to the world in one way or another, we cannot avoid distinguishing 'church' and 'world', and giving each their own integrity. A church that turns itself inside out will dissolve into the world, and this will paradoxically result in both the world and the Church losing their identity. Thus, in many studies this model has been debated and criticized as a missiological dead end.[128] Christian mission cannot merely be defined as 'protest', 'critique', 'counter movement', and the like. It is pointless to speak about the mission of God if the question is not asked who God is, and how we can know about him in the first place. And it is impossible to use the language of the kingdom of God if in doing so there is no reference to the Lord Jesus Christ who demonstrated this kingdom on earth by his concrete life and by his death and resurrection.[129]

The Inside-Out Model and Evangelicals

Hoekendijk's ideas have become associated mostly with so-called 'ecumenicals' and 'mainline' Protestants, but it should be noted that his model reflects intuitions that are shared in much wider circles. As I have discussed more elaborately elsewhere,[130] the inside-out model seems to get some traction in the contemporary 'emerging' conversation. Without going into details, I want to point out two interesting similarities between the inside-out model and the modern evangelical movement, including its late modern 'renegates'.

First, the idea that God's mission is somehow to be discerned in the movements of the world is something that many evangelicals have in common with those who have followed Hoekendijk. This often goes unnoticed as evangelicals have been such vehement critics of ecumenicals who championed social justice at the expense of evangelism. But the church growth movement, which has been so hugely influential among evangelicals, breathes the same spirit of the 1960s, namely that careful observation of the world will provide the key for mission activity. Thus, Christians should analyse demographics, wars, famines, and so on, in order to see where people become 'receptive' to the gospel and deploy missionaries accordingly. This is not so different, in fact, from the ecumenicals' emphasis on watching where God works towards 'humanization' of the world, so that the Church can join this mission. We can also think of voices majoring on 'postmodernism' as the new spirit of the era, which presumably changes everything for the churches.[131] Apparently, evangelicals (including most younger evangelicals) and mainstream Protestants want to be relevant before anything else.[132]

Second, Hoekendijk's criticism of ecclesiocentrism sits well with the contributions of late modern evangelicals such as Alan Hirsch, Michael Frost, Brian McLaren, Pete Ward and many others. The main thought is that the Church should reject a 'come-to-us' mentality, and should take seriously that it is sent into the world as a people with a mission. With this belongs an 'incarnational' lifestyle, that is not focused on the maintenance of the church as an institute, but radically associates itself with the needs and questions of this world, demonstrating the love of Christ in word and action.[133] Christian mission is not about growing the Church; it is about 'following Jesus in the real world'.[134]

This turn towards the 'real world' actually reflects the lack of ecclesiological substance in much of the evangelical tradition. As we have seen in our discussion of the church growth movement, which has been so hugely influential for mainstream evangelical missions, there is a tendency to instrumentalize mission and everything ecclesiological in the interest of winning souls. Consequent on this supreme purpose the Church itself must be simple, transportable, ready to multiply at any time. The Church is to be stripped for battle rather than bother itself with all sorts of 'internal' debates. While the so-called Hoekendijkian 'liberals' and the church growth-driven 'evangelicals' seem worlds apart, their ecclesiologies are thus very similar. In both approaches the Church has no 'being' prior to its 'acting' in the world; the only difference is that this 'acting' is aimed at individual conversions in the one model, and at establishing peace and justice in the other. The essential structure is the same: in both models the Church is an instrument for action.

This problem basically remains the same when younger evangelicals become frustrated with the shallowness of church growth practices, and turn towards other forms of action, such as helping the poor, developing green worship, promoting gender equality, and so on. Now the Church's success is not assessed based on the number of baptisms, but on its capacity for creating an eco-friendly lifestyle or welcoming gay people. Still this means that the Church 'is' nothing before it 'does' something. It does not have a story of its own; the Church coincides with its performance in the world. 'Incarnational', however, does not mean much if the Church does not know its own story first, the story of the Incarnation of Christ. If this story is forgotten or turned into an empty symbol, the term 'incarnational' will be nothing but a somewhat jargonesque alternative for 'solidarity' or 'engagement'. Unfortunately, this can be seen more often in those sections of the Church that want to be relevant above anything else: Christians who, by using lofty theological words, try to say things for which the world had excellent terms all along.

Here, I think, the necessity of a more 'catholic' ecclesiology becomes visible. The Church 'is' before it 'acts'; it is 'in Christ' before it is in the world; and it is 'in the world' but not 'of the world'. To be sure, this 'before' is not meant as if we can speak about the Church without referring to the world out of which it is called. It should be taken ontologically rather than chronologically. Nevertheless, the Church's identity is to be distinguished from its acting in the world. The Church is not just there to be effective, but to witness about Christ and to be a foretaste of the coming kingdom. If the Church is not more than a tool for achieving a better world, then this means in fact that the Church tells the world in a cumbersome religious way what the world was well aware of to begin with.

Lessons

What can be learned from this model, in my opinion, is its recognition of the world as *God*'s world. There is no other model where the receptivity of Christianity as a missionary religion has been stressed with the same force (see Chapter 1, section 5). The model strongly resonates with the experience of many missionary practitioners that people 'out there' often have a deeper understanding of life than many Christians, and that they may draw surprising and humbling conclusions from the gospel. Regardless of whether they become Christians, such people often become teachers for the Church. It must be stressed, time and again, that God *loves* the world and that the activity of the Holy Spirit precedes the engagement of Christians. This underlines again that Christians are not on earth to establish a Christian culture based on their own blueprints, or to draw the whole world population into the Church. God is going his own way with his world, and much of this will remain hidden from the Church. Christians don't have to ground their contributions to justice and peace on an idea of their own superiority; there are many people outside the Church who have understood at least as much of this.

This model thus shows that it is unacceptable if the Church fixates on itself as a 'counterculture' by definition or if it thinks that the world is to become church. Where this model is mistaken, however, is in its under-estimating of the distinction between God's general providence over his creation and his special action through Jesus Christ. In this way God's kingdom becomes a general expression for everything that serves *shalom* (by whatever definition), instead of being a concept that is directly associ-ated with what God has done, still does, and will do through Jesus. I have the impression that an ancient European folk church ideal plays in the background of this attempt to keep the distinction between church and world as vague as possible.[135] If the world cannot be church anymore, then let the Church be world! However, if we can truly leave behind our captivation with centuries of Christendom, the necessity to collapse church and world disappears. We can give the Church and the world each their due, without sliding them into each other.

3.6   Church as a Powerhouse

While perhaps less present in standard theological textbooks, this sixth model is extremely influential in today's world, and it is spreading at lightning speed. In fact, almost all the so-called megachurches on every continent are now associated with this particular type of Christianity. We are talking here about something that goes by different names, but is mostly referred to as 'neo-Pentecostalism'.[136] The neo-Pentecostal model is represented by a worldwide network of churches, ministries and para-church organizations that have all appeared to be effective at engaging the globalizing contemporary world.[137] Essentially, it is a 'style of spiritu-ality' rather than a denomination.[138] It shares many characteristics with 'Old' Pentecostalism, like speaking in tongues, Spirit baptism, healing, prophecy, and the like. In addition, however, it consists of a loose set of features that can be emphasized or toned down depending on con-text. The following characteristics are generally recognized as typically 'neo-Pentecostal'.

Characteristics

Neo-Pentecostalism is characterized, first, by a *this-worldly orientation*. While classic Christianity (and many other religions) tended to empha-size the difference between the 'temporal' and the 'eternal', presenting the 'eternal' as the somehow more 'real' and meaningful realm, neo-Pentecostals designate the here and now as the arena where salva-tion happens. The meaning of human life must be found in this world rather than the next. Instead of considering this life as a preparation for encountering God in the hereafter, God is seen as the great Provider of blessings for the faithful in this life of work, family, self-development, and so forth. The main framework in which God-talk functions is not the framework of truth, but of relevance. God 'works', and that is what makes him true. Therefore, many commentators consider neo-Pentecostalism as an example of a truly modern, even 'secular', religion.[139]

Second, this style of faith promotes a *holistic (and materialistic) view of salvation*. Jesus came, died and rose again, not primarily to bring souls from earth to heaven, but to bestow all kinds of goods on his people on earth. He became poor to make us rich – quite literally, in fact. Salvation in neo-Pentecostal terms is not just (or even primarily) salvation from sins, but it is also (and predominantly) healing, material blessings, success in work or relationships, inner balance, and so on. Therefore, conversion is not in the first place a transformation in order to be saved after this life, but it transforms the body into a receptacle of divine gifts, a place of worship, spiritual battle and encounter with God. We are 'really' and 'radically' to believe that God is eager to bless us. This is where terms like 'prosperity gospel' or 'health and wealth movement' come in, although proponents of the movement prefer the name 'Faith Movement'.[140]

Neo-Pentecostalism is, in the third place, characterized by its emphasis on performative language, called *words of power* ('name it and claim it'). There is a great, almost 'magical' confidence in (and fear of) the power of words in neo-Pentecostalism. If a word is spoken in order to make positive changes, it can be called 'positive confession'. Simon Coleman defines this as 'a statement that lays claims to God's provisions and promises in the present'. Words spoken in faith enable the believer 'to assert sovereignty over multiple spheres of existence, ranging from their own bodies to broad geographical regions'.[141] Of course, there is also a negative side to this. Words of criticism can be explained in very material ways as a form of 'contagion' or even as 'curses', standing in the way of God's blessing. Either way, this lends great power to human beings, since simple words spoken in (bad) faith can do great things on earth. Other typical concepts are connected to this belief in proclamation power, such as for example the idea of 'territorial spirits' hindering evangelism, which must be fought by loud formulaic prayers.

Finally, *performance, theatre* and *personalization* are important ingredients of what neo-Pentecostalism is about. The movement has a highly theatrical outlook. It is fond of dramatic faith healings, massive worship concerts with a great variety of body movements (laughing, falling, dancing, crying, lifting hands, etc.); public baptisms in a swimming pool (sometimes inviting bystanders to get baptized on the spot); multimedia spectacles; Jesus marches; and many more visible performances. Also, neo-Pentecostalism tends to emphasize heavily the role of leading pastors ('apostles'), who collect a lot of airmiles, and function in many ways as role models of 'spiritual careers'. Thus, religion is not just performed; it is personalized. In a way, this may be part of the 'materiality' of salvation in neo-Pentecostalism. There is something sacramental about this: salvation becomes tangible by booming basses, flying banners, performances of the body, and receiving words and healing touches from anointed leaders.

All these characteristics are extremely flexible; they can adapt to any circumstances. With young professionals in the West this faith-style usually concentrates on dimensions of salvation that have to do with therapeutic questions, self-acceptance, career issues, dietary problems, sexuality and family matters. With less successful people or in the majority world the emphasis lies more often on prosperity, demonic influences (exorcism), spiritual warfare, or on discrimination and racism.[142] Such features have allowed the movement to spread with unprecedented speed in all continents, and to feel at home among all social classes.[143] One could say that this movement, for many people at least, somehow succeeds to make visible and tangible the 'inevitability' (Kuyper) of Christianity for this life. With this the language of evangelism is transformed: rather than vulnerable and witnessing it is demonstrative, proclamatory and triumphalistic.

Neo-Pentecostalism and Mission in a Post-Christian Society

It is extremely difficult to provide a good description of a movement with so many faces that is expanding so rapidly. As such, neo-Pentecostalism is rather a moving target. Here I will concentrate on the way the movement manifests itself as a missionary presence in the secularized areas of the West.

At first sight, its missional practice belongs in the evangelical family. There is a clear affinity especially with the church growth model and the transformationist model: to change the world through as many conversions as possible. Moreover, the missionary rhetoric of many neo-Pentecostal churches (as, for example, African diaspora churches) comes across as deeply revivalistic, oriented to the restoration of a Christian culture. Core elements seem to be that the West used to be Christian, and that the majority of secularized citizens in these societies can still be 'revived'. Also the connection between individual conversion on the one hand and the improvement of society on the other has been a recurring theme in evangelical mission practice since the eighteenth century. So far, the movement does not add anything really new.

In terms of methodology, however, neo-Pentecostals do seem to provide a distinctive contribution to the evangelical tradition. Key is the idea of 'power' that must come from above, and that is deemed crucial for successful mission. Of course this is in itself not a new concept for Christians, but it is typical of a neo-Pentecostal vision that this power can be 'summoned' by believers, particularly through shared prayer and worship.

This idea is processed differently, depending on culture. In West African immigrant churches, for example, we often find a concept of 'spiritual warfare'.[144] This is essentially a form of prayer by which through loud voices and various bodily gestures battle is waged against invisible spiritual powers who (supposedly) hold Western societies captive. African neo-Pentecostals reproduce this vision within a traditional West African cosmology. Salvation is viewed as holistic and earth-centred, but always in peril. Jesus wants to give every believer a life in fullness. However, early death, illness, poverty, infertility, misfortune, racism and accidents show that satanic powers (or witchcraft) are still active to hinder the believer in achieving the life that Jesus promises. The concept of spiritual warfare thus strongly depends on a dualistic worldview: two empires are constantly fighting over souls and countries; believers can contribute to this fight by intense, continuous and collective prayer. Neo-Pentecostal Africans see this as an important contribution to the re-evangelization of the West: there are as many demons in Europe and America as in Africa, only Westerners do not want to realize it. Evangelism is a 'power encounter': if nothing happens in the spiritual realm, no conversion of individuals and cultures can be achieved.

A very interesting illustration of this concept is described by Claudia Währisch-Oblau. During a meeting, some West African pastors asked their German counterparts: 'What makes the Germans tick? We want to understand this so that we can evangelize more effectively.' The Germans answered their request by organizing a seminar on the great minds that have shaped modernity in Europe, especially in Germany. So, a professor came and he explained, with good German, *Gründlichkeit* to the Africans, the philosophies of Ludwig Feuerbach, Karl Marx and Sigmund Freud. What happened next may be best quoted in full:

After the full day seminar, the participants gathered for dinner. During the meal, they announced that they would convene a special prayer meeting later that night. Now that they had understood what was blocking evangelism in Germany, they were going to wage spiritual warfare against the spirits of Feuerbach, Marx and Freud. The prayer meeting that night lasted almost two hours and was one of the most intense I ever witnessed. The participants, migrant pastors from Ghana, Nigeria, Sierra Leone, Ethiopia, Nepal, Vietnam, and Indonesia screamed and shouted at the top of their voices, jumped, shook their arms and raised their fists until they were streaming with sweat. They clearly waged a battle – their prayers were not supplications or intercessions, but 'authority prayers': 'In the name of Jesus, we assert authority over Germany! We declare that the spirits of Feuerbach, Marx and Freud have no right to oppress this country! We totally bind the spirits of Feuerbach, Marx and Freud and all spirits who have been following them! We declare that they will no more mislead the Germans, in the name of Jesus! We cleanse Germany from the spirits of Feuerbach, Marx and Freud, in the name of Jesus!'

The researcher remembers how she was sure that the Germans had completely failed to make the participants understand the meaning of Feuerbach, Marx and Freud. However, the colleague who had been teaching 'wondered aloud whether perhaps an exorcism of the spirit of religious criticism might be exactly what Germany needed'.[145]

In a Western neo-Pentecostal church like Hillsong this concept of 'power' is approached somewhat differently. Its mother church was founded in Sidney in 1983, and has since then grown to a membership of 20,000. Currently, the Hillsong branch has expanded into a large number of major cities all over the world. Here the accent lies less on spiritual warfare in the service of evangelism. Instead we find another element of the neo-Pentecostal movement, an element that is more prominent in wealthier cultures, and that we have encountered already in a somewhat different tune in the transformationist model. The idea is that God impacts the world through the successful lives of influential believers. Whenever people meet a Christian who is obviously blessed, they encounter the Holy Spirit. And the presence of such Spirit-filled people can eventually change whole societies.[146] This also pertains to politics. The view is widely shared in neo-Pentecostalism that nation-states are God's design, and that every state has its own calling in the world. Only after a nationwide revival can the state respond to this calling and exert its unique spiritual influence in the rest of the world.[147] The path towards such a national revival runs through the planting of (preferably large) churches as centres of worship. These churches function as powerhouses, emitting renewing energy into their societies – like the water that flew from Ezekiel's temple (Ezek. 47.1–12).

Logically, this leads to a view of mission that is oriented first and foremost towards worship and church planting. Through the Church, and especially through massive, exuberant praise, God will become, as it were, 'tangibly' and 'audibly' present in society.[148] To what extent this is combined with actual missionary activity on the streets and on weekdays is not always clear. Undoubtedly neo-Pentecostal churches do their fair share, for example in offering prayer for healing,[149] but from a missiological point of view the emphasis seems to lie on creating spiritual 'power centres' through communal praise and prayer. Core to this seems to be to enfold people into a Sunday celebration and invite them to share in worship. This worship in turn is supposed to lead to a life in the service of society and neighbour, even though this is not always clearly articulated. The power of God is, as it were, 'sucked down' in a thundering worship gathering, whereupon this power finds its way into the world via the changed lives of a large mass of believers.

Finally, special mention must be made of neo-Pentecostalism's excessive emphasis on 'apostolic' *leadership* as a prerequisite for effective church growth and cultural transformation. Much of this has to do with the idea of spiritual warfare as the key concept of mission. In the so-called 'spiritual mapping movement' that came up in the late 1980s, the idea became important that certain territories are controlled by evil spirits, and should be 'taken' or 'claimed' by (symbolic) acts and persons of authority.[150] The movement received a new impulse from C. Peter Wagner, who introduced the 'new apostolic reformation' (1996), claiming that only a focus on highly influential pastors and leaders (apostles) could lead to the 'transformation' of cities.[151] For this to happen, the egalitarian models of older evangelicals (such as Billy Graham) must be abandoned as these stifle the impact of 'aggressive, initiating, risk-taking leaders'. The unity of a (local) Christian mission movement does not come from citywide cooperation among a variety of churches, but from recognizing the authority of apostolic leaders who each commit themselves to a specific 'sphere' – similar to the New Testament Apostles such as Paul and Peter who worked in different regions and with different social and ethnic groups.[152]

Evaluation

Clearly, this model has a strong appeal to people of all cultures and walks of life. It is easy to understand why. Neo-Pentecostalism is 'earthly' and concrete, it makes salvation tangible and visible (sacramental), it empowers people so that they can change and improve their lives. Moreover, many neo-Pentecostal churches are entrepreneurial, they know how to participate in a global world, and they engage often rather impressively with the latest trends of a late modern, media-savvy culture.

Naturally, this has all sorts of shadow sides as well. The reports of pastoral abuse and authoritarianism in these circles are hard to keep up with, signalling the lack of checks and balances in neo-Pentecostal churches, while travelling leaders tend to support each other even in the face of serious and well-founded accusations.[153] It is also concerning to see how their obsession with 'success' and 'power' has caused leading neo-Pentecostals to embrace the authoritarian politics of Donald Trump in the United States and Jair Bolsonaro in Brazil. Apparently, neo-Pentecostalism's revivalist theology and its focus on 'warfare' renders it very vulnerable to accepting culture wars as the way to do mission, and to buy into scenarios where the forces of evil represented by worldwide 'Islam' encounter the armies of heaven, which are in these circles usually associated somehow with the politics of the modern state of Israel. Also, there are plenty of stories of people who have been damaged by a shallow and optimistic doctrine of healing (those with true faith will heal), or who have run aground on an atmosphere of competition between (more often than not) self-concocted spiritual experiences. In spite of all the fascinating sacramentality of the movement (which may be a correction to an all-too-cerebral Protestantism) there is a genuine risk as to the authenticity of worship in the bombardment of stimuli that is poured on people in many neo-Pentecostal celebrations. There is little room for reflection; either you allow yourself to be swallowed by it, or you leave. Finally, it remains to be seen if this movement will be capable of holding secularization at bay, given its almost exclusive concentration on the here and now and its lack of theological reflection.

Be this as it may, this is not the place for an overall evaluation of neo-Pentecostalism or the various types of 'prosperity' teaching. Here a few comments may suffice on the missionary substance of this model with regard to Europe, and I trust that at least some of these comments pertain to other parts of the secularized West as well.

Most studies of these churches in Europe conclude that they usually fail to attract significant numbers of genuinely secular people. This is true both for their Western-based branches and for immigrant churches.[154] Their attraction seems effective primarily among people from their own cultures or with a Christian background. In this regard, neo-Pentecostals certainly do not seem to do a 'better' job than other churches, and given their frequent 'sheep stealing' they may in fact do worse. This should give pause, given the strong missionary rhetoric and criticism of other churches that characterizes the neo-Pentecostal movement. In this context religious scholar Simon Coleman even speaks of 'a formal ideology of sectarian self-righteousness'.[155] This lack of missionary success (at least, a failure to have more success than other churches) may be explained in part by the fact that neo-Pentecostal churches have little to offer that is genuinely new in missional terms. Their approach moves by and large within the classic evangelical revivalist model, while their claim to have found more effective means to bring this revival about has so far remained unsubstantiated. In deeply secularized areas there is little to 'revive', to begin with. Rather than endlessly repeating revivalistic strategies that are more appropriate in an early post-Christendom era, churches should concentrate on the hard work of contextualization and mission among 'nones'. A genuine mission model is not yet found by the neo-Pentecostals.

While this criticism more or less affects most if not all churches in the West, there is another problem that pertains more specifically to neo-Pentecostalism. Its concept of spiritual warfare might be counter-productive especially in very secularized areas, as it easily fosters a disengaged approach to mission. If one approaches evangelism primarily as a war that is to be fought in prayer meetings, Jesus marches and intense worship events, one could easily forget that legwork and creative thinking are needed just as much. Especially when evangelists are culturally, socially and economically less powerful than those they reach out to, like many immigrant missionaries, the risk exists that evangelism is 'spiritualized' at the expense of real involvement in society. This risk becomes even worse when mission is seen first and foremost as building large, attractive and spectacular churches designed to invoke God's power through multimedial worship. After all, the mega-church potential of neo-Pentecostalism has already led to the creation of virtually self-sufficient 'prayer cities' in some places.[156] Their 'unwaveringly forward-looking, growth-oriented vision'[157] renders them especially vulnerable to concentrating on building centres of visible power and wealth that are somehow supposed to benefit their societies. Consequently, members are invited to spend as much time as possible within the church, supporting it, participating in prayer meetings, taking classes, and so on. Especially in an unreceptive society the temptation seems huge to withdraw from society in this way, by building what is in fact a series of micro-Christendoms. I do not intend this as a criticism of prayer meetings or celebratory worship events (far from it), but I want to stress that mission is a matter of 'beautiful feet' (Isa. 52.7) just as it is a matter of 'ceaseless prayer' (1 Thess. 5.17). Recent research shows that the main difference between churches that regularly attract converts and churches that don't does not lie in theology or missionary rhetoric, but in the actual amount of time and energy invested in the world outside the church.[158] There is, after all, a difference between singing that you are 'history makers' and 'planet shakers',[159] on the one hand, and giving soup to the homeless or visiting the lonely on the other.

3.7 Towards Mission in the West

For the first time in history we have entered a cultural stage where Christianity is no longer an 'obligation'. The Christianized societies of the past are rapidly disappearing in the rear-view mirror, and we will have to find a new missionary vision for the West. The models that have been discussed above can contribute much that is valuable, but each one of them is still too implicated in the Christendom experience. In searching for a new missionary vision for Christians and churches, three elements seem of great importance to me. Successively: the difference between church and world must be respected; we must take our distance from ideals of reconstruction and conquest; and we must discover a Christian spirituality of mission fit for a deeply secular culture. Here follows a discussion of each of these three elements.

Respecting the Difference

All of the six models that were discussed are premised on a grand vision of unity somehow. Christian mission is intimately associated with a world where to a large extent the same values prevail, the same desires are held, and where people essentially believe the same things. On a closer look they break down into two groups of three: the one group assumes this grand unity to be present already, whereas to the other group this unity forms an ideal that is to be restored.

As regards the first group, it goes without saying that the folk church belongs here. Much in this model, if not everything, amounts to keeping as many people as possible under the same religious umbrella as long as possible. With the model of the Church inside out, basically the same happens, but in the reverse direction. Here the Church should gather itself under the banner of secular movements. In both models the emphasis lies on keeping humanity together under one common denominator, regardless of whether this is called 'folk church', 'religion', 'shalom' or the 'kingdom of God'. This minimizing of the difference between church and world may be the least obvious in the Anabaptist model, due to its emphatic 'countercultural' rhetoric. But it cannot be denied that this model presents a radicalized version of generally shared values rather than a counterculture. Its significant 'other' is nominal Christianity rather than the world as such. Hence this model should belong in the first group too, even if it occupies a place somewhat at the boundary.

The other three models are more modern, in that they accept the post-Christendom distinction between the 'church' and the 'world'. They have all originated in a time when the 'world' already began to slip away from the 'church'. However, all three suppose in different ways that we must return to the previous situation. 'Church' and 'world' are emphatically distinguished (perhaps even too starkly), but this happens in order to make the task clear: the world is to be reconquered, revived or transformed after a Christian vision.

The shadow of Christendom, with its homogeneous religious culture, hovers heavily over all these models. Of course, in a modern era these overarching concepts are less laden with confessional or specifically Christian notions. 'Christendom' becomes 'kingdom', 'confession' mutates into 'religion' or 'spirituality', and 'theocracy' becomes 'righteous structures'. But in one way or another a vision of unity is assumed. Even the model that is most averse to Christianization, the model of the Church inside out, carries the DNA of this vision. Distinctions between 'church' and 'world' are undesirable; they are to be ignored or erased. If the Church cannot overarch the world, then let it turn itself inside out, and 'empty' itself into the world.

Seen from the perspective of a small Christian community in a deeply secularized society this vision of unity is completely unrealistic. This vision, insofar as it is considered as a missionary ideal, comes across as obsolete and undesirable. Is it even possible, a world that hides under the same worldview umbrella? Is this really a mandate that is put into our hands? Such a thing may be imaginable in a world that is successfully dominated by one religious regime. As long as nostalgia for this earlier society (or the place where we grew up) is captivating us, such a vision might be inspiring. But in my opinion there is little to say, theologically, in support of the idea that this should be a missionary ideal for Christians. Can one really apply the word 'Christian' to such unequal entities as human beings and churches on the one hand, and cultures and societies on the other? Is a 'Christian' nation even conceivable? Do 'Christian' villages exist? This entire assumption that 'church' and 'world' can be brought under one and the same denominator is theologically suspicious.

This becomes manifest from a number of early church metaphors that designate the relation between church and world.[160] The below table lists a few:

Church	World	Relation
Soul	Body	Animating, giving life
Yeast	Dough	Rendering edible, easy to digest
Salt	Food	Rendering tasty, preservable
Light	Room	Revealing, shining upon
Sheep	Wolves	Being threatened, vulnerable
City on a hill	Valley	Being visible, admired

All these metaphors indicate the dynamic *difference* between church and world. The world is not yeast, but dough through which the yeast is to be mixed in order to make the bread light and edible. The Church is not food, but it gives taste to the food. Whoever wishes to bring the Church and the world under the same Christian (or alternative) denominator will lose this dynamic. Mission begins with the recognition of differences. This includes also the recognition of unbelief, not to condone it or to be happy with it, but to face the fact that there are people who do not want to belong to you nor think like you. We should not cover this up by elastic definitions or try to solve it with violence. The human world is divided and will remain so until the end of time.

At the same time it must be said: to take our distance from a vision of unity does not mean that we should always oppose the world. Church and world are not necessarily *against* each other. Their relation is situation-dependent and contextually determined. Sometimes the world is threatening and hostile; sometimes it welcomes the Church and asks for its counsel. But the world is no church, and it will not become one.[161] For the Church this is not some tragic fate, but rather an important building block of its identity. Without a body the soul leads a ghostly existence; without food the salt has no use. Being a missional church in a deeply secularized culture begins in my opinion with these two points: (1) the world will never be Christian, and (2) until the last day the Church and the world will remain in a dynamic, complicated and hopeful relation with one another.

Some of this dynamism and messiness can be found in all six models that were discussed. From the folk church tradition it can be learned, among other things, that mission will always be necessary within the Church as well. There is a distinction between church and world, but this does not mean that we can make crystal clear who belongs and who doesn't. The neo-Anabaptists make it clear that the Church does not need to control the world in order to be the Church. Although this model insists too much on a counterculture, it has understood well enough that the Church can perfectly well operate from the bottom or the margins of society. Like no other model, the church growth approach has emphasized the cruciality of evangelism. Conversions are important signs of the kingdom. The transformation model directs the attention to the importance of a Christian vision of culture, and the equipping of Christians to be salt and yeast in the workplace and in politics. The ecumenical model of the Church inside out stresses like no other that the world is God's world, and that the Church has much to learn from the world. The neo-Pentecostals, finally, show the importance of prayer and a message that concretely addresses the questions of people.

The way ahead, as I see it, is that churches in the West give up their historical privileges – everything that suggests that these nations are 'only for Christians'. As Wilbert Shenk says: in order to do mission in the West, we must be prepared to become strangers again in our own societies.[162] Only if we become weak will people be prepared to listen. Only if people do not feel threatened by an institutional grasp for power by Christians will they feel free to appreciate what Christians have to tell. And only in this way will Christian communities have the room to develop a 'prophetic' alternative voice. In Amsterdam, for example, there are few churches and only a small minority of the population darkens the door of a church regularly. But it is interesting how, especially in more recent years, while the church has become smaller and weaker, Christians in the city have experienced that the local government and other parties in society have warmed up to the churches. There is more appreciation of the good work that is being done, especially because everybody knows that Amsterdam is *not* a Christian city, and is very unlikely to become one.[163]

Abandoning Hegemonic Ideals

In modern missionary theology it is often said that the Church is an 'instrument', a 'sign' or a 'foretaste' of the kingdom of God. With this the Church stands in an exciting, hopeful relationship to the coming of God's reign. She contributes to it, witnesses about it and demonstrates something of it in her own life. I do value such insights. They are an important fruit of the recovery of Christian eschatology in twentieth-century Western theology. It is a problem though that these theological findings can become mixed up in practice with dreams of restoration and revival. Especially, the thought that the Church is an 'instrument' of the kingdom can easily come to play a role in a restoration programme of a Christian culture. Especially in the West this can happen, since our theological imagination is so profoundly shaped by the memory of this culture. For us it is very difficult to speak about mission without having a grand dream of unity in the back of our minds. I have pointed this out in my discussion of the models of cultural transformation and the Church inside out. The church growth model also shares this pursuit of a world that is Christianized (again). Thus, under the guise of 'changing the world' and 'revival' the Christendom ideal is being revived.

As language tends to influence the way we look at the world, it is important to notice that Western missiology has a long history of using militaristic language, inviting Christians to conceive of the non-Christian world as a 'territory' that must be 'brought under control' or 'occupied' by 'well-trained armies' of missionaries. Such language is not innocent; it distorts the way we look at other people and societies.[164] It tempts us to create 'enemies' out of opponents, it frames Christian contributions to the public debate as 'battles' for the soul of the nation, and it makes us very reluctant to admit our own failures as this would be to admit 'defeat'. While most Christians, including evangelicals, have stepped back from this 'spirituality of conquest' (or, like the neo-Pentecostals, have spiritualized it),[165] there still is a great deal of 'strategic' planning and purposeful action involved in missionary language. Perhaps the metaphors of the business world have replaced the language of soldiering, but the essential outlook remains the same: through our action we have to change the world into a more Christian place, reflecting Christian values and Christianized structures. Of course I do not want to lump all the representatives of this model together; some of them speak with much more finesse than others. Also I do not want to get rid of the word 'instrument', since our work in the Lord will not be in vain. I believe that everything that is good in our actions and words will be used by God to build his kingdom. But in general the risk does exist that the 'instrument' character of the Church is emphasized to such an extent that the kingdom of God is, in fact, identified with our own blueprint of an ideal society. Thus it comes within our reach, and it is only a matter of time before we achieve it. And thus all the worrying memories of power play and its concurrent militaristic metaphors rise once again.

By contrast, I want to stress that mission is not a project or a strategic enterprise. The justification of mission must not be sought in its contribution to the realization of a grand vision of unity. There will be a time that God is all in all, but it is not our task to achieve this. Therefore it seems good to me to emphasize in the West the 'sign' and 'foretaste' character of Christian mission rather than its 'instrument' character. Conversions resulting from evangelism are not 'instruments' to bring a churchified world one step closer, but they are first and foremost 'signs' and 'foretastes' of the coming kingdom. They point towards the interrupting and future reality of God's reign that breaks into our world in surprising, counterintuitive and often rather unspectacular ways.

The same counts for all successes that the Church achieves – together with other parties – in the areas of justice, reconciliation, poverty reduction, unity, peace and dialogue. Here too we find signs and experiences of the coming salvation that become visible here and there, even in the deepest chaos. But all these matters are good in themselves, or rather: they are good because they reflect the pattern of Jesus' life on earth. This life is resurrected by God from death, and therefore everything we do in Jesus' name testifies to the hope that our deeds will also be resurrected with Christ. Without the resurrection, everything that Jesus did would be – at best – a good story of a good man whose life was tragically terminated. Touching perhaps, and inspiring to those who love heroic self-sacrifice, but essentially a dead end. Let's face it: it is very difficult not to become cynical if you think of how many noble human deeds of self-sacrifice ignited a flame of hope for a moment, only to realize how quickly the world shrugs its shoulders and continues its course. What is left of the India that Gandhi envisioned? Shouldn't we conclude now that Mandela failed in bringing about a just and harmonious South Africa? What are the results of the self-sacrifices and self-burnings that once inaugurated the Arabic Spring?

If Jesus had not been raised from the dead, everything we do in his name would at best contribute something to a better world. Then we would have to draw our motivation from the effectiveness of our actions and the success of our strategies. After all, what else could motivate us? Also, we would need the people whom we have helped to be very grateful to us. What else could give us joy? But speaking and living as a witness points back to Jesus' life, death and resurrection, and at the same time it points forward to the reality of which Jesus' resurrection is a foretaste and a sign. The mission of the kingdom is God's, not ours. Therefore all these missionary things that we can do are good and meaningful, even if we can't possibly see how they contribute to a greater good on this earth. We can be happy with what we have done, even if we don't hear any words of gratitude. 'Never grow weary in doing what is right', writes the apostle Paul (Gal. 6.9–10). And Jesus said that 'there is joy in heaven over one sinner who repents' (Luke 15.7). Of course, we are allowed to believe that changes in people and societies will be 'instruments' of the coming kingdom in some way, but hardly ever will we be able to see how this happens. Often, we will notice that the signs and foretastes that have been established collapse behind our backs, and are washed away. People relapse into their former patterns; forces of injustice and indifference suffocate the wheat that was sown. All this fits into the pattern of Jesus' mission, who ended with fewer people than he began with, and died on a cross – before God's life washed over him from the other side. This pattern is the penultimate reality of Christian mission, a reality that is determined more by hope and joy about what God is doing than by optimism and complacency about what we are capable of.

Thus, I advocate a new language that stands at a distance from expressions like 'changing the world', 'redeeming culture', 'transforming society' or 'building the kingdom'. These words may not be wrong in themselves, but in my view they are too burdened with conquest and domination, precisely what God did not call us to do. Strategic plans rise eminently in the minds of those who have power; they reveal the spirit of dominion that has held Western Christians captive for so long. The stronger the 'instrumental' character of Christian mission is emphasized, the stronger the temptation to do mission through manipulation and pressure. We must resist the call to concentrate our mission on places where we can be 'relevant' and 'influential'. I would like to see culture change much more as 'micro-resistance': Christians are invited to 'cut out' small niches of hope, reconciliation, forgiveness, beauty and health in the world. Rather than using the functionalist language of business and project management, we may consider adopting a different language, perhaps that of art. There is something entirely non-instrumental in a work of art; it is 'just there'. It is not good 'for' anything; it just radiates goodness, beauty, challenge and mystery. 'Beauty', says Alexander Schmemann, 'is never "necessary", "functional" or "useful".' It is there, simply, to be loved and enjoyed, and it fans our longings and expectations. 'As long as Christians will *love* the Kingdom of God, and not only discuss it, they will "represent" it and signify it, in art and beauty.'[166] Perhaps mission is rather like making art. We are not to expect that a beautiful sculpture will change the world into a paradise, but it will give the world something to think and talk about by just being there, inviting love and longing. Art reflects value that cannot be expressed in 'instrumentalizing' language; as such it is at the same time a critique of a society that has no genuine concept of non-monetary value. So, this may be our task: a mission of small things – things that will be redeemed when Jesus returns.[167]

Spirituality

One question constantly emerging in this chapter, and also suggested by the concluding lines of the previous section, is the question of spirituality. I suspect that many of the faith challenges Christians struggle with in a secular culture are produced by a theology that leans on one or more of the models that have been discussed. If one presumes that the world is or should be Christian, he or she will have a hard time in a secularized environment. This can be clearly observed in the folk church and the Anabaptist (free church) model. Whoever believes that God prefers to work collectively, through generations and village communities, may stumble into a crisis of faith the very moment he or she enters a more individualized and more profoundly secularized context. After all, here in particular you will be confronted with the fact that being a believer in such a context is a *choice*, and usually not the most obvious choice. Also, if you think that your own 'countercultural' ideal is intelligible or even attractive to your environment, you might be disappointed when you start living in a place where Christianity is no longer society's conscience but rather its suppressed memory. It can be a shock to discover that people here are not at all interested in the evangelical package that attracts so many people in more traditional, folk church cultures: testimonies, enthusiast worship, therapeutic warmth, 'radical' commitment, miracles. All of a sudden you don't belong to a cool and growing church that is admired or envied by other churches from the same Bible Belt location, but you are rather looked at as a member of some weird sect.

I have seen this in Amsterdam, for example with students who came to the city from one of the villages and small towns in the more churched regions of the country. Often, they tried to keep the faith for some time within the bubble of a Christian student club, but when they finally had to leave the Christian pond, they lost their faith almost immediately. To a great extent their faith was socially embedded; first and foremost it was a way of belonging. I do not intend this as a judgement, since a collective faith has been an authentic form of Christianity for centuries. But unfortunately, it is a form that usually does not survive for long in a secularized consumer society.

'Revivalistic' mission models are the first prominent victims of this cultural shift. The idea that the West must be brought back to its Christian roots, either by a moral *réveil* or by maximal church growth (or both), clashes immediately with the harsh reality of a secularized society. There is nothing to 'revive' here, and church growth only happens where churches are successful at attracting migrants or people who have a churched background. Obvious spiritual damage resulting from this is discouragement or cynicism. One abandons mission (or even the faith) because it does not work anyway. More often, perhaps, a fake reality is created. Figures are blown up, successes are exaggerated and endlessly propagated, definitions are tampered with, so that the ideal seems to be achieved after all. Here the American researcher Gary Corwin speaks of 'mobilization rhetoric', a phenomenon we find all too often in newsletters and on websites of mission organizations.[168] Organizations that take their lead from church growth ideals have the unsavoury habit of connecting reputations, positions and salaries with numerical targets, encouraging even more the temptation to lie and exaggerate. Clearly this does huge damage to a healthy spiritual climate. Authentic Christian faith cannot flourish in an atmosphere that breeds convulsive concealing of the truth and a hysterical rhetoric of success. I wouldn't be surprised, therefore, if many missionary pioneers trying to achieve church growth targets among deeply secularized groups have more or less lost their faith already. The rhetoric may still smoulder, but the fire has gone.

The models that are oriented towards culture change or *shalom* also run great risks of spiritual shipwreck in a de-Christianized society. Initially, for people with a conservative Christian background the discovery of the relevance of Christianity for this world often releases much energy. Of course, there is something compelling and enthusing in struggling against sex trafficking, working for a better environment, fighting poverty, and so on. It is, after all, so immensely *relevant*. Also it is liberating to no longer be placed in a black-and-white opposition against the world, to engage with those of other worldviews just as fellow human beings, working together for the benefit of the world. There is nothing wrong with this; the more people apply themselves to it, the better. But if this work is seen without reservation as building God's kingdom, Christians will soon run into spiritual difficulties. This can be clearly seen in the model of the inside-out church. I have already said that whoever thinks that God works only in the world, while he uses (or tolerates) the Church as a mere instrument, in fact robs the Church of its own voice. In the end, then, the Church's contribution will consist of cumbersome reformulations of what the world has known already for a long time. Even though this may yield a sense of liberation at first, it is very unlikely to be a lasting inspiration for anyone. The inevitable consequence is that the word 'Christian' will gradually lose its meaning, and that the vision of God and his reign, Jesus Christ and the gospel, will be lost. A church that turns itself inside out in this way will likely dissolve into the world – often within the span of one generation.

Adherents of this model, however, are absolutely right about one thing: in projects of world improvement it is a rather naive thought that Christians are better at this or have more wisdom than other people. Christians have hope (as opposed to optimism), they can pray and worship, and as the only people in the world who have been given the task to love their enemies. This and more distinguishes them from other people. But Christians are not more effective at politics, development aid, organizing food banks, administering law, conducting science or doing business. If mission indeed equals world improvement without reservation, then eventually a Christian voice does not add any value of its own. This is often insufficiently noticed by adherents of the revivalistic or neo-Calvinist transformation model. Here the Church has its own and unique task to change the culture for Christ and his kingdom. But in doing so, this model immediately puts Christians in competition with non-Christians. This comes with important spiritual problems for Christians who let themselves be inspired by this model. After all, if it is indeed true that Christians have the God-given task to establish a Christian culture, then it is also true that Christians have the task to make a difference. They are to be better citizens, better politicians, better development workers, better nurses and better scientists than other people. Their enthusiasm and spiritual balance (partly) depend on whether they succeed at this. But whoever takes up this challenge seriously will constantly encounter people of other or no faiths who commit themselves much more radically to a better world than most Christians. So, in practice Christians will constantly run into this dilemma: if they indeed do a better job than others, they will immediately hear that you don't need God for this. In a secular society people simply don't believe in the moral superiority of Christians, and they know enough examples to support this. But if Christians don't do a better job than those around them (again: enough examples), then it appears that Christian faith is irrelevant where it really matters. This is a 'catch 22': regardless of how you achieve, it will never prove your point that Christians make a unique, irreplaceable contribution to a better world.

The spiritual consequences are easy to guess. Some believers will stubbornly stick to the supposed moral superiority of Christians, with disastrous consequences for their missionary impact. Surely, you can only maintain that Christians are better people when you avoid genuine contacts with non-Christians as much as possible. Whoever is not capable of doing this will soon discover that there is a good non-Christian for every good Christian, and that faith in God therefore seems to make little difference in improving the world. Doubt will creep in: if it is a Christian's calling to change the culture, while non-Christians appear to be at least morally equal to you and the Christians you know, what then is the added value of being a Christian? Why do we need God if we can improve the world without him just as fine? Why should we still pray?

Small churches in a secular context are facing the challenge of how they can nourish and protect the spirituality of their members. No longer can faith rest on self-evident cultural reflexes. When faith is no longer a matter of decency or obligation it will have to be supported and nourished from day to day. This subject is too big to discuss here. From what has been said in this chapter I outline three points without trying to be exhaustive.

The first point I have already mentioned: Christians will have to learn to make their spirituality independent of success in terms of church growth or world improvement. They will learn how to develop a spirituality of 'signs' and 'foretastes'. Christians must learn to do good without growing weary (even if it crumbles in your hands), and they must learn how to rejoice about every person who is prepared to follow Jesus (even if such persons are few and far between). Good deeds and conversion are not building blocks in a greater project; they are good in themselves. Ever again they are reasons to praise God and to rejoice in his future. He has not left himself without a witness, not even in the secular West. In a deeply secularized context I can only imagine such a Christian spirituality: one that is not overly bothered with far-reaching ideals, and that constantly finds an occasion to throw a party. 'An evangelizing community', writes pope Francis, 'is filled with joy; it knows how to rejoice always. It celebrates every small victory, every step forward in the work of evangelization.'[169]

The second spiritual note is bound up with this: Christians should learn to develop a spirituality that can handle failure and obstruction. Especially if you commit yourself to doing good in the world, you will soon find out how everything seems to cooperate so that evil may prevail. Time and again you meet malevolent people, indifferent bureaucracy, political interests that are squarely opposed to the interests of the poor, disappointing fellow Christians, resentful critics of religion, and polluters who don't care about the next generations. Therefore, idealists are very vulnerable to bitterness. The philosopher Charles Taylor writes how a Buddhist friend of his travelled about Europe. He was upset by his visit to the Green party in Germany: idealistic, self-sacrificing vegetarians – but so much anger and frustration![170] It is surprising how many enemies you get once you have embarked on improving the world. People who chain themselves to oil rigs, attack mink farms or hijack aeroplanes are not indifferent, nor are they necessarily evil. On the contrary, there is no lack of ideals or courage. What they may be lacking, however, are love and humility. In the Bible we meet such a person in the prophet Jonah. He, the righteous Israelite and member of an oppressed and suffering people, is called to prophesy against the cruel oppressors from Nineveh. Nowhere is Jonah's anger relativized, nowhere is it suggested that Nineveh's injustice is anything else than 'wickedness' (Jonah 1.2). Yet in the end Jonah is faced with an enemy who is equally loved by God as Jonah himself. Jonah is to learn that the hatred of the just does not fit into God's new world any better than the cruelty of the unjust.[171]

A spirituality of signs and foretastes is not crushed by failure, nor by the obstruction of evildoers. And if we are allowed to respectfully surmise that Christians may have an irreplaceable contribution to world improvement after all, then this contribution is not that they are more effective, but it may be this: Christians are called to love their enemies, and to pray for their own forgiveness (also for those sins that come from good intentions). The more idealistic we are, the more we will need this.

A third element of this kind of spirituality is the deep conviction that the identity of churches and Christians is not to be identified with what they are doing in the world. The Church 'is' before it 'acts', it is 'in Christ' before it is 'in the world', and it is 'in the world' but not 'of the world'. These are all traditional, perhaps somewhat worn-out, ways to express that Christian spirituality does not depend on its effectiveness at improving the world. Before anything else Christian spirituality is a spirituality of gratitude and praise. When Jesus called his disciples he did this for them 'to be with him' and 'to be sent out' (Mark 3.14). These two goals are not subordinated to one another; the one is not a means to the other. To be with Christ is not merely a way to be optimally equipped for mission. Conversely, Christians are not sent out just so that they can be with Christ. The first renders worship into an instrument for world improvement, while the latter renders mission into a ground for justification. The two goals are equivalent; both are essential.

Jesus speaks in a parallel way about love for God and the neighbour. When somebody asks him about 'the' greatest commandment (singular!), Jesus gives the beautiful answer: '*The* greatest commandment? There are *two* of them: love the Lord your God above anything else, and love your neighbour as yourself' (Mark 12.28–31). This juxtaposition of two commandments has often confused Christians. How can the love for God and for the neighbour be equivalent without being identical? The answer lies herein that our love, both for God and for the neighbour, is always an echo of God's love for us. Love begins with the one God and not with the human being who so often feels torn between contradictory goals. His love nourishes our love, and unites it. Just like God's love for us is non-instrumental (he does not *need* us; he *loves* us), so is this human love for God directed towards God because of himself and not because it wants to achieve something else. Our love for our neighbour drinks from this well too: God's undeserved and non-instrumental love for us. Therefore Christians can love their neighbours as they love God, for the sake of the other person and not in order to achieve something different (like changing the world). We love others with the love with which he first loved us. The order is important: God comes first, and his love for us creates our love for him and for our neighbour. To say that the Church is there 'for the world' is therefore a half-truth at best. The Church is there for God, and therefore it is also there for God's world. Whoever reverses this order, will soon be out of breath.

With this non-instrumental love we have arrived at the core of a missionary spirituality. In the previous section I compared mission with making art. Art is not good 'for' anything; it is not justified by its impact on the world. It is simply 'there', and by being 'there' it fulfills its destiny. Perhaps we can dig somewhat deeper now. Christian mission in a secularized culture is all about finding and keeping joy in small things. It is rejoicing with the angels about one sinner who converts – even if we know all too well that this one sinner will not convert our church statistics. It is about never growing tired in doing good – even if we know all too well that our good deeds are too insignificant to turn the world around, or even to be noticed. So what is the secret of finding joy in what is usually not very effective? Perhaps the secret lies with what many Christians have discovered to be the core of a mature spirituality: *do not try to achieve (by conquest or project) what can only be received.* The great mystics of the Christian tradition have developed this into what Rowan Williams calls 'a strategy of dispossession'. He describes it as follows:

> [A] search for prayer beyond deliberate and ordered meditation, the expectation of failure in coping with the 'truths of faith' when trying to use them for the stirring of devotion, essays in physical privation or isolation, scepticism or hostility towards internal and external props of devotion (pious sensations or edifying images).

This non-instrumental, non-strategic approach of spirituality often comes with 'a measure of emotional strain and disturbance, profound or even frightening depressing symptoms', but all this is 'preliminary'. Williams continues:

> The fruition of the process is the discovery that one's selfhood and value simply lie in the abiding faithful presence of God, not in any moral or conceptual performance; which is a radical affirmation of the *goodness* of nature.[172]

So, basically, a Christian missionary spirituality begins with the affirmation that there is One who is not good 'for' anything; he is simply good. Period. And so too with all the things that are done in his name, all the works and words of evangelism, service and justice. They may not be good 'for' anything, but they are good regardless, because they represent the goodness and mercy of God. And thus they can be done with joyful hearts, with creativity. Or, in Williams's beautiful prose:

> ['G]od' has ceased to be the interruption of our earthly action, because the self acts out of an habitual diffused awareness that its centre is God. The self is fully conscious (even if only at a rather elusive level) that it is the object of an unchanging creative love, conscious that for it to be itself is for it to be dependent on God's presence at its root or centre. To act from this centre is to give God freedom in the world, to do the works of God.[173]

Christians breathe God's love in and out: worship and mission are two sides of the same coin. With even more precision we might say that mission is an act of worship *especially* because of its non-instrumental character. Neighbour love does not subordinate serving the neighbour to supposedly higher goals; my neighbour is not an instrument for a 'greater' agenda. Certainly, mission happens with expectations; who knows what it will do in the world? Undoubtedly, we will be surprised when God reveals how our words and deeds have contributed to his kingdom. Even though changing the world is not our project, we may believe that the world does change sometimes by our efforts. But there is no *agenda* in

mission other than disinterested love. From the history of Christendom
we may learn that the world should not just be protected against evil,
but also against an excess of good intentions. Christianity is not primarily about establishing justice and peace in the world. Of course these
things are good, and of course we should not give up pursuing such good
things. But for Christians these things are never to be separated from
their source. God is our highest good and our first task is to worship and
honour him in everything we do.[174] And precisely this is why we work for
justice and peace, regardless of whether it changes the world. Our efforts
are fuelled by love, not by visions of growth, impact or transformation.
For the Church this means a renewed attention to the liturgy, the sacraments and community. More on this will follow later in this book.

3.8   Summary and Conclusion

Reviewing this long history of attempts to further Christianize the West,
we should wonder if mission in the West is an incomplete project or
something entirely different. In this chapter we discussed six models that
all view mission in the West as a project that needs completion. Seen from
this perspective, mission in the twenty-first-century West is business as
usual: still the large majority has not been successfully evangelized (even
less than ever before), and we set ourselves to change this – either by
action plans or by creative redefinitions.

If mission in the post-Christian West is not an unfulfilled project of
Christianization, but something rather different, a new possibility opens
up. Perhaps we can accept in some sense that the large majority of citizens in our societies have never been Christians, nor will they ever be.
Mission on this view is constant witnessing on the boundary. It means
to experience a foretaste of God's rule now and then. A mission like
that expects converts, but it also knows that their number will usually
remain small. This mission is not motivated by the question how large the
portion of the world is that can be transformed, and against what costs,
but rather by the question what it means to be a witnessing Church in a
world that does not recognize God, even though this world sometimes
surmises him in mysterious ways. When this perspective opens, we arrive
at a new stage of Christian mission in the West. We might realize that
the active minority of Christians will always be a minority, and that there
is nothing 'normal' (let alone 'decent') about being a Christian in this
world. It might be that we realize that the world will always be the world.

However, it is important to be aware that embracing this minority perspective is not business as usual either. For centuries the active minority

of Christians could cherish the thought that they admittedly did not succeed at recruiting the large majority, but that they somehow represented an ideal that appealed to the majority nonetheless. Now this is largely gone; the Christian minority is now really a minority without much prestige or influence. This raises the question where this active minority will find the confidence that it really means something for God's mission in the world. Therefore, we will have to look for a missionary spirituality, theology and practice that can motivate the Christian minority in the West to do mission with hope, but without illusions of conquest. Some remarks as to this have been made already in this chapter: we must abandon ideals of reconstruction and conquest, and we need a spirituality of signs and foretastes. In the next chapters we proceed with this constructive task.

Notes

1 Jenkins, *God's Continent*, p. 19.

2 See my extensive discussion of ecclesial innovation in *Church Planting in the Secular West*, pp. 181–241.

3 Cf. Patrick Keifert's description of his childhood in a Lutheran cultural pocket in the USA, in his *We Are Here Now*, pp. 32–5.

4 Cf. Jan van der Graaf, writing from a Dutch Reformed perspective in his *Volkskerk in de marge*, p. 12: ' . . . a deeply contested concept . . . that is filled in many different ways'. My translation.

5 Svenningsen, *Brief Guide*, pp. 10–11. See also Lodberg, 'Studying'.

6 Wolfgang Huber mentions as a persistent characteristic of the folk church its 'respect for distanced membership as a legitimate form' ('die Respektierung von distanzierter Mitgliedschaft als legitimer Form' – 'Volkskirche I.', p. 253).

7 Nielsen, 'The Danes', p. 48.

8 Pew Research Center, 'Religious Belief and National Belonging in Central and Eastern Europe: National and religious identities converge in a region once dominated by atheist regimes', 10 May 2017 (accessed 29 November 2017).

9 See, for example, Ammerman, *Sacred Stories*.

10 Of course, I don't mean that such activities should always be about God or Jesus. My point is that in these initiatives the evangelistic tension seems to be gone: it is just fine if they are never about God or Jesus at all.

11 Cf. for example (from a Roman Catholic perspective), the studies in Hellemans, Jonkers, *Catholic Minority Church*.

12 For example, Buskes, *Hoera*, p. 206.

13 Cf. Noordegraaf, *Vijf broden en twee vissen*, pp. 97–117.

14 For a programmatic statement of this theology, see Van Ruler, 'A Theology of Mission'. For a brief discussion of this publication, see Flett, *Apostolocity*, pp. 234–8

15 Cited in Van der Graaf, *Volkskerk in de marge*, p. 56.

16 Van der Graaf, *Volkskerk in de marge*, p. 11. It is impossible to separate this statement from the desire of restoration in the (still very Christian) Netherlands immediately after the war. After all, if the Church is a folk church by its very

nature, it becomes very difficult to see the Church in China, North Korea or Maroc as a true Church. On Van Ruler's influential position in this debate, see Janssen, *Kingdom*.

17 Cf. already Hoekendijk, *Kerk en volk*. Translated in German as *Kirche und Volk*.

18 *Kerkorde en ordinanties van de Protestantse Kerk in Nederland* (March 2015), articles 1.6–1.7.

19 Van Ruler, 'Theology of Mission', p. 224.

20 Warneck, *Evangelische Missionslehre*, p. 252.

21 These projects are discussed extensively in my *Church Planting in the Secular West*.

22 Van der Graaf, *Volkskerk in de marge*, p. 106.

23 See, for example, the parable of the weeds among the wheat (Matt. 13.24–30). Augustine may have been the first who applied this parable to people inside the Church (*corpus permixtum*). This text emphasizes, on the one hand, that there is a difference between 'wheat' and 'weed' (there are no liquid boundaries in this respect), but on the other hand it says that this difference is usually so difficult to see with human eyes that we should be extremely reluctant to try and create a community of pure 'wheat' before the last judgement.

24 For example, see the Dutch theologians Gerben Heitink (*Een kerk met karakter*, pp. 79–116, 176–81, 188, 190–225) and Henk de Roest (*Een huis voor de ziel*, pp. 142–3). I have written about this in *De werkers van het laatste uur*. There I accept the idea of different degrees of involvement in the congregation. But the metaphor of 'circles' around a 'core' I consider as being too static; instead I prefer the more mystagogical concept of 'paths towards the core'. More on this in Chapter 6, esp. section 6.4.

25 See also Herbst, *Missionarischer Gemeindeaufbau*.

26 MacIntyre, *After Virtue*, p. 238.

27 For an extensive missiological analysis of the Anabaptist movement in Europe, see my *Church Planting in the Secular West*, pp. 62–5.

28 As for MacIntyre's influence, see for example Wilson, *Living Faithfully*, pp. 68ff; Hart, *Atheist Delusions*, p. 241; Dreher, *The Benedict Option*, p. 2. Good popularizing examples of missional reflections inspired by neo-Anabaptism can be found in the books of the British theologian Stuart Murray, such as *Church after Christendom* and *Post-Christendom*. From a more North American perspective, see McKnight, *Kingdom Conspiracy*; Green, Krabill, *Fully Engaged*.

29 See my 'The Countercultural Church. The work of Karl Barth has played a major role here (see Bender, *Karl Barth's Christological Ecclesiology*, p. 285). Barth has influenced post-liberal theologians like George Lindbeck (see, e.g., his *Nature*, pp. 16–17, 125–6) and the early Stanley Hauerwas (e.g., Nation, 'Stanley Hauerwas', p. 29), while the neo-Anabaptist John Howard Yoder engaged extensively with Barth's work. Also the ecumenical debate on the continuity of the Church has contributed to thinking of the Church as a 'culture' (see, for example, John Flett's discussion of the ecclesiology of the Lutheran theologian Robert Jenson in *Apostolicity*, pp. 115–37).

30 For the following, see Paas, *Vrede stichten*, pp. 254–62.

31 Yoder, *Politics*, pp. 135–62. Also McClendon, *Ethics*, pp. 173–6.

32 See, for example, Yoder, 'Believers Church', pp. 150–3; Hauerwas, 'A Christian Critique', p. 471.

33 Hauerwas, 'Why the "Sectarian Temptation" is a Misrepresentation', p. 105. See also Yoder, 'Christ the Hope of the World', p. 215.

34 Cf. Yoder, *The Politics of Jesus*, pp. 135–62. See also McClendon Jr., *Ethics*, pp. 173–6.

35 Yoder, 'To Serve Our God', pp. 133–5.

36 Yoder, 'Let the Church Be the Church', p. 177: 'The Christian community is the only community whose social hope is that we need not rule because Christ is Lord.'

37 Cf. Yoder, 'The Believers Church', p. 159: 'We can't leave the world in peace with its commitment to other standards.'

38 Hauerwas, 'On Keeping', p. 72. See also his *After Christendom*, pp. 23–44.

39 Yoder, 'The New Humanity', p. 42. For an extensive missiological defence of this position, see Stone, *Evangelism after Christendom*.

40 After the completion of this book I received a PhD manuscript that is one of the best evaluations of John Howard Yoder's contribution to missional ecclesiology that I have read so far. This study (Daniël Drost, *Diaspora as Mission: John Howard Yoder, Jeremiah 29, and the Shape and Mission of the Church*, PhD dissertation VU University Amsterdam, 2019) not only discusses Yoder's history of sexual abuse in the context of his diaspora theology, it also adds extensive ethnographic case studies highlighting the strengths and weaknesses of this model, deepening and strengthening the more or less intuitive missiological points of critique that I have articulated below: idealism, the issue of power, a too rigid conceptualization of church–world relationships, and so on.

41 This kind of criticism, especially with regard to Hauerwas, typically goes in two directions. On the one hand, it is said that he overestimates the 'contrast-qualities' of actually existing church members, because of his lack of engagement with ethnographic studies of really existing churches. See, e.g., Healy, *Hauerwas*, pp. 78–85, 95–9, 101, etc., who claims that there is, in fact, little difference between church members and other people. On the other hand, Robin Gill, while voicing the same criticism of Hauerwas's 'bias towards idealized rather than actual church communities', sets out to show with the help of sociological data that there are actually significant differences – both in terms of beliefs and behaviour – between regular churchgoers and non-churchgoers (*Churchgoing and Christian Ethics*, esp. pp. 13–30). For a similar, albeit more impressionistic study on Roman Catholics, see Greeley, *The Catholic Imagination*.

42 Hauerwas, *A Community of Character*.

43 Savage, *Human Face*, p. 11.

44 Usually in the context of reflections on the history of his sexual abuse of more than a hundred women. See a.o. Goossen, 'Defanging the Beast'; Cramer, 'Scandalizing John Howard Yoder'. Online: https://theotherjournal.com/2014/07/07/scandalizing-john-howard-yoder/ (accessed 15 December 2017).

45 Cf. Mark Mason's critical discussion in 'Living in the distance'.

46 See Lichterman, *Elusive Togetherness*, e.g. pp. 136–7, 256–7.

47 For a more elaborate version of this argument, and other theological criticism of Anabaptism, see Paas, *Vrede stichten*, pp. 269–75.

48 Gill, *Churchgoing and Christian Ethics*, p. 197.

49 And even if it did, we should remember that the Christian communities of the first century also built their culture in interaction with their context. We cannot characterize the earliest Church as a 'counterculture' if that means that it could understand itself without reference to the world out of which it was called and from whose material it was made.

50 For a case study, see the fascinating description of local relations between reformed and Anabaptist Christians in the seventeenth-century Dutch village of Graft, by Van Deursen, *Een dorp in de polder*. Clearly, the attitude of outsiders against Anabaptists was not determined by animosity but rather by a form of reluctant admiration. Reformed pastors used the Anabaptists to warn their flocks: 'Do not become heretics like them, but do learn to imitate their ways!' In a sense, the Anabaptists did not remind the (Christianized) world around them of what it did *not* know (*pace* Hauerwas), but rather the contrary: they were an uncomfortable reminder of what it knew all along.

51 Williams, 'Judgement', p. 30. For such a 'chastened' vision of Christian spirituality and mission in a post-Christendom world, see for example Addison Hodges Hart's fascinating little book *Strangers and Pilgrims*.

52 Hauerwas, 'In Defence'. Online: www.abc.net.au/religion/articles/2017/10/18/4751367.htm (accessed 15 December 2017). Hauerwas's lack of ethnographic reflection on real congregations, however, renders him vulnerable to the same problem. His contrast between 'church' and 'world' (and thus between 'Christian' and 'non-Christian') is too sharp, and worked out inconsistently. See Fiddes, 'Versions of Ecclesiology', pp. 347–9, who agrees with Healy on this point.

53 For example, see the strong negative rhetoric in Hauerwas, Willimon, *Resident Aliens*.

54 Hunter, *To Change the World*, p. 164.

55 Williams, 'Judgement', pp. 34–5.

56 Cf. Willliams, 'Judgement', p. 36.

57 Interestingly, in most European countries (and possibly also in the United States) the most vital 'free churches' (drawing on the countercultural tradition) can be found in areas with relatively strong Christian vitality (the so-called 'Bible Belts'). This illustrates that the 'other' against whom one is defined and from whom one derives its identity is not so much the secular *world*, but rather the *Church* that is (in their opinion) liberal and assimilated.

58 Cf. the thorough analysis of the German 'free church' tradition by Bartholomä, *Freikirche mit Mission*. Bartholomä argues convincingly that the German Free Churches, while featuring a strong anti-Christendom rhetoric, are in fact just as wedded to the Christendom tradition as the mainstream folk church (*Volkskirche*) tradition. Their historical identity is shaped in this context, and the collapse of Christendom is a problem for the 'free churches' just as much as for the folk church.

59 See also my *Church Planting in the Secular West*, pp. 226–9, on 'free havens'. A 'free haven' is a place where Christians can work out radical solutions to certain questions together without having to compromise with middle-class values or bourgeois life. However, such groups become 'sects' when they consider themselves as everything the Church is about (thus rejecting other churches), while 'monasteries' keep the communication lines with the less radical centre intact (thus affirming the other churches' legitimacy while at the same time challenging them).

60 See Cray, *New Monasticism*; Marti, Ganiel, *The Deconstructed Church*, pp. 19–21, 148–53. The ideas of new monasticism are influenced by Alasdair MacIntyre (see above) and Dietrich Bonhoeffer with their pleas for communities where virtues could be practised.

61 An example is the L'Arche communities, where cognitively impaired people are considered 'core members' who live together with other people in a common search for a more genuine way to be human. Cf. Vanier, *An Ark for the Poor*, p. 99, etc.

62 Winter, 'Two Structures'. Cf. Sunquist, *Understanding Christian Mission*, pp. 303–4.

63 For an extensive ecclesiological reflection on the place of monastic orders in a Protestant (Lutheran) ecclesiology, see for example Dombois, *Das Recht der Gnade*, pp. 214–32.

64 O'Donovan, *The Desire of the Nations*, p. 193.

65 Most of my discussion below pertains to Protestant sources and developments, but the parallels with Roman Catholic discourse are many. Official Roman Catholic missiology tends to echo the Christendom experience more clearly, in keeping together both dimensions of Christendom in its core term 'evangelization'. This, according to the apostolic exhortation *Evangelii Nuntiandi* 18 (Paul VI, 1975), means: '[B]ringing the Good News into all the strata of humanity, and through its influence transforming humanity from within and making it new.' For discussion, see Worthen, 'What's New', esp. pp. 80–3.

66 McGavran, *Understanding Church Growth* (1980), p. 24.

67 McGavran, *Understanding Church Growth* (1990), p. 23 (citing George G. Hunter III).

68 *Understanding Church Growth* (1990), p. 262 ('christo-pagans').

69 For an extensive discussion of the church growth movement, see my *Church Planting in the Secular West*, pp. 37–42, 111–80.

70 Williams, 'Trinity and Revelation', pp. 137–8.

71 From a missiological perspective this text is primarily an indication of the essentially doxological nature of mission rather than of church growth as its eschatological result. For extensive reflections, see Wrogemann, *Den Glanz widerspiegeln*, pp. 86–113, and later in this book (esp. section 7.5).

72 It is telling how McGavran, in his defence of a 'theology of harvest' (as opposed to a 'search theology'), mentions several supposedly biblical arguments without once addressing the eschatological nature of the kingdom of God as both present and yet to come. Thus, he can read the gathering motives in the parables of Jesus as unequivocal instructions for church growth (cf. *Understanding Church Growth* [1990], p. 28).

73 Van Engen, *Growth*, pp. 416–19.

74 Although the book of Acts clearly rejoices in large numbers of converts (as church growth writers never become tired to emphasize), this accent is virtually absent in the Gospels and the Epistles (see, e.g., Luke 15.7). Jesus concluded his career with fewer disciples than he had at the beginning (cf. John 6.66–67). On numerical claims in the context of evangelism in the New Testament, see also Schnabel, *Urchristliche Mission*, pp. 711–17 (translated as *Early Christian Mission*).

75 Van Engen, *Growth*, pp. 448–53.

76 So too Van Engen, *Growth*, p. 451.

77 Cf. Stone, *Evangelism after Christendom*, p. 273.

78 Newbigin, *The Open Secret*, p. 128.

79 Van Engen, *Growth*, p. 446.

80 Cf. Matt. 7.13; 22.14.

81 A fascinating argument for the importance of secular Western culture to the integrity of the Church is given by Halík, *Patience with God*. An extensive engagement with atheistic criticism of Christianity with a view to prophetic ministry can be found in Westphal, *Suspicion and Faith*.

82 In passing I note that, while I limit myself here to Protestant developments, Roman Catholic missiology has kept an even stronger focus on 'transformation' of

humanity, as a core element of 'evangelization'. See Worthen, 'What's New', pp. 73–90.

83 Walls, 'The Eighteenth-Century Protestant Missionary Awakening', p. 41.

84 For an extensive discussion, see Hunter, *To Change the World*.

85 Wright, *The Mission of God*, p. 321.

86 Padilla DeBorst, 'Integral Transformational Approach', p. 85. Her description refers especially to the theology of *misión integral* by the evangelical *Fraternidad de Teólogos Latinoamericanos* (founded in 1970).

87 For a brief overview, see Bosch, *Transforming Mission*, pp. 389–93. An extensive historical and systematic analysis of *missio Dei* theology is provided by Flett, *Witness*.

88 Bosch, *Transforming Mission*, p. 390.

89 Bosch, *Transforming Mission*, p. 391. Cf. Flett, *Witness*, pp. 7–8.

90 See esp. Flett, *Witness*, for the inconsistensies and unclarities in this discourse.

91 Engelsviken, 'Missio Dei', pp. 481–97.

92 For this distinction and its consequences for missional thinking, see Fitch, 'The Other Missional Conversation'.

93 Kuyper, *Geworteld en gegrond*. Translated by Nelson D. Kloosterman as *Rooted and Grounded*.

94 On this, see De Bruijne, 'Not without the church as institute'; 'Colony of Heaven'.

95 Cf. Goheen, *As the Father has Sent Me*, esp. pp. 417ff.

96 See, for example, Hunsberger, *Bearing*; Guder, *Continuing Conversion*.

97 Bosch, *Transforming Mission*; Wright, *The Mission of God*. Of N. T. Wright's books I mention especially *Surprised by Hope* and *After You Believe*.

98 Keller, *Center Church*.

99 For a brief overview, see Bevans, Schroeder, *Constants in Context*, pp. 305–22.

100 For a classical introduction to the spirituality of liberation theology, see Gutiérrez, *We Drink from Our Own Wells*.

101 Padilla, Segura, *Ser, Hacer y Decir*, p. 15 (translation DeBorst, 'Integral Transformation', p. 77).

102 Samuel, Sugden, *Mission as Transformation*. More recent literature can be found in DeBorst, 'Integral Transformation', esp. pp. 87–90, who also points out how this approach has influenced Western movements like the Sojourners (Jim Wallis), radical discipleship, and new monasticism. International networks such as the Micah Network and increasingly the Lausanne Network also help to spread these views in the West.

103 Samuel, Sugden, *Mission as Transformation*, p. xii.

104 Samuel, Sugden, *Mission as Transformation*, pp. xi, xiii.

105 See also my comments on the militaristic language of Western missiology below.

106 Of course, I am not trying to create a gap between God's work and ours. This would imply a great risk of God and us becoming competitors. The Spirit works 'in us' and 'through us'. However, the same work can be looked at and described from different perspectives, and I suggest here reserving the word 'transformation' for God's perspective rather than ours. Through the Spirit we 'participate' in Christ and therefore in God's mission, but it is and remains God's mission.

107 For this recurring problem in the missional church discourse, see Guder, 'A Multicultural and Translational Approach', p. 73.

108 DeBorst, 'Integral Transformation', p. 91.

109 Ibid. Here she quotes Costas, *Christ Outside the Gate*, p. 180.

110 For a more extensive treatment, see my analysis in *Church Planting in the Secular West*, pp. 98–101. For the rather doubtful empirical assumptions behind this model, see Hunter, *To Change the World*, pp. 3–92

111 On this 'dialectic of faith and nature', see Martin, *On Secularization*, esp. pp. 3–12.

112 Sundermeier, 'Erinnern und Weitergeben', pp. 25–6.

113 Taylor, *A Secular Age*.

114 See, for example, Erdozain, *The Soul of Doubt*.

115 Smith, *How (Not) to Be Secular*, p. 50 fn. 3.

116 Smith, *How (Not) to Be Secular*, pp. 138–9, fn. 10. Cf. also Boersma, *Heavenly Participation*.

117 Flett, *Apostolicity*, p. 187.

118 Flett, *Apostolicity*, pp. 189–91.

119 Flett, *Apostolicity*, pp. 191–202.

120 Flett, *Apostolicity*, pp. 202–10.

121 Hoekendijk, 'Call', p. 170 (italics in the original).

122 Flett, *Apostolicity*, pp. 213–34.

123 Flett, *Apostolicity*, p. 232.

124 Flett, *Apostolicity*, pp. 233–4. Barth's axiom is found in *CD* IV/1, p. 185.

125 Hoekendijk, *Church Inside Out*.

126 See Engelsviken, '*Missio Dei*', pp. 481–97.

127 So too Healy, *Church, World and the Christian Life*, p. 144.

128 Literature and brief discussion in Bevans, Schroeder, *Constants in Context*, pp. 290–1.

129 I have written more extensively about this in 'Kerken vormen'.

130 *Church Planting in the Secular West*, pp. 213–17.

131 For a discussion of the Emerging Church Movement, especially regarding their different views of 'postmodernity', see Doornenbal, *Crossroads*, pp. 39–48.

132 This similarity is also noted by Tim Keller in his description of the 'Relevance Model' (*Center Church*, pp. 201–5).

133 E.g., Frost, Hirsch, *Shaping*; Hirsch, *Forgotten Ways*; McLaren, *New Kind of Christianity* (and most of his other books); Ward, *Liquid Church*. For a critical discussion of the individualism involved in this approach, see Fitch, 'The other missional conversation', pp. 470–2. Also note that some of these authors could just as well be discussed in the section on mission as transformation. Especially the more 'progressives' among them could be described as transformationists who have embraced 'movement' (together with all people of good will) instead of 'church'.

134 Cf. Marti, Ganiel, *The Deconstructed Church*, esp. pp. 134–61.

135 Here I think mainly of the folk church traditions that are (were?) common in Germany, Scandinavia and in some Southern European countries (the Church *of* the people).

136 This section follows my article 'Mission from Anywhere to Europe'.

137 Coleman, *Globalisation*, pp. 22–3.

138 Da Silva Júnior, 'The Liquid Church', p. 79.

139 Cf. Thomas, 'Selling God'.

140 Much of this doctrine can be traced back to American leaders like Kenneth Hagin, Kenneth Copeland and Oral Roberts (cf. Coleman, *Globalisation*, pp. 27–31).

141 Coleman, *Globalisation*, pp. 28, 131–3.

142 For a number of these social and cultural differences, see e.g. Hunt, 'Winning Ways'; Da Silva Júnior, 'The Liquid Church', pp. 73–5.

143 Cf. Coleman, *Globalisation*, pp. 31–40.

144 See Währisch-Oblau, *Missionary Self-Perception*, pp. 272–301.

145 Währisch-Oblau, *Missionary Self-Perception*, p. 300.

146 Coleman, *Globalisation*, p. 192.

147 Coleman, *Globalisation*, pp. 191–2, 222–5.

148 Tangen, *Ecclesial Identification*, p. 62, mentions as a 'key idea' of preaching in Hillsong London 'that the church is called to be a representative "vehicle" for God's presence in the world'. This has consequences for the moral life of believers.

149 Cf. James, *Church Planting in Post-Christian Soil*, pp. 109–11.

150 For a description and analysis of 'spiritual mapping', see Holvast, *Spiritual Mapping*.

151 Cf. Wagner, *Revival*. See also, e.g., Dennison, *City Reaching*.

152 Wagner, *Apostles of the City*.

153 On these networking types of authority, cf. Christerson, Flory, *Rise*.

154 For literature and brief discussion, see my 'Mission from Anywhere to Amsterdam', and *Church Planting in the Secular West*, pp. 177–8.

155 Coleman, *Globalisation*, pp. 109–10, 120, 122.

156 See, for example, Ruth McLean, 'Eat, Pray, Live: The Lagos Megachurches Building Their Very own Cities', *The Guardian*, 11 September 2017, accessed 6 January 2018, www.theguardian.com/cities/2017/sep/11/eat-pray-live-lagos-nigeria-megachurches-redemption-camp.

157 Maddox, 'In the Goofy parking lot', p. 148. Cf. Coleman, *Globalisation*, pp. 155–6, on the 'quantified spirituality' of neo-Pentecostalism.

158 Paas, *Church Planting in the Secular West*, pp. 175–6. Cf. Vos, *Hoop*.

159 Lyrics from the British band *Delirious*.

160 The first is from the second-century *Epistle to Diognetus*, the rest is from the Gospels.

161 A standard objection is that the Church is, after all, part of the world. From a sociological perspective this is, of course, true in a rather trivial way. I intend this distinction in a theological way. There is a part of the world that is called to serve God and follow Jesus. This part we call 'church', even if we cannot point out exactly where the 'church' ends and the 'world' begins. In fact this objection can be brought against all sorts of identities: families are part of a nation but are distinct entities at the same time; peoples are part of humanity, without coinciding with it, and so on.

162 Shenk, 'Training'. See further Paas, 'Prepared', esp. pp. 127–30.

163 More on this in Paas, 'Crisis'.

164 Cf. Nan Levinson, 'How the Everyday Use of Militaristic Jargon Makes Us More Combative', *Transformation*, 24 February 2017. Online: www.opendemocracy.net/transformation/nan-levinson/how-everyday-use-of-militaristic-jargon-makes-us-more-combative (accessed 14 February 2018).

165 Cf. 'Consultation on Mission Language and Metaphors', Fuller Theological Seminary, 1–3 June 2000 (online).

166 Schmemann, *For the Life of the World*, p. 30.

167 Thinking of mission as a form of art (creativity, beauty, abundance, inspiration) may also invite us to rethink mission from the perspective of pneumatology.

168 Corwin, 'Sociology and Missiology', p. 27.

169 Cf. Francis, *Evangelii Gaudium* (2013), §24.
170 Taylor, 'A Catholic Modernity', pp. 183–4.
171 See Paas, Roest, *Een komedie in vier bedrijven*.
172 Williams, 'Theological Integrity', p. 11.
173 Williams, 'Theological Integrity', p. 12.
174 Hunter, *To Change the World*, pp. 285–6.

4

Uprooted and Dispersed

It is extremely difficult for people in a secular culture to imagine a time when Christianity was as common as the air we breathe. People raised in Bible Belt villages may be able to form at least something of a mental picture of what Christendom looked like, but increasingly a society where religion has a central place is becoming unintelligible to us, even if we are believers ourselves. One way to get a sense of how religion functioned in those days is to look at the current place of art in many Western societies. It is not just that art for many has replaced religion as society's conscience; governments are paying respect to it in ways that remind one of the heyday of Christendom. Art is sacred, it epitomizes our cultural values. Parents who would howl about 'indoctrination' if their children learned how to pray and how to participate in religious ceremonies at school, demand that schools spend time and money on art classes, musicals or museum visits. Politicians who confess their Christian or Islamic beliefs are publicly scorned (at least, where I live), but nobody objects if they recommend a theatre show, or express their opinion that art is important for the nation's well-being. You could say, in short, that art is 'embedded' in our societies, just like church and faith in previous times. It has great symbolic power, governments feel responsible for its flourishing, it is carried out by strong institutions, and it speaks a language that everybody can relate to. Conversely, we might say – for lack of a better word – that religion is 'disembedded' from our societies. To speak with Abraham Kuyper again (see Chapter 2): there is no longer a 'sense of inevitability' about Christianity. It doesn't have the wind in its sails any more; it is no longer self-evident.

How this has come about is a long story and too complex to set out here. Scholars have mentioned many causes: increasing wealth and individualization, the pluralization of society, growing mobility and urbanization, the rise of non-religious worldviews. In this chapter, however, I am not concerned so much with describing or explaining this disembedding process, but with its *meaning* for Christians. How do the loss of Christianity's symbolic power, the erosion of its institutions and the increasing isolation of the language of faith affect us? What does it mean that faith in our times is increasingly a feature of inspired (but vulner-able) individuals and small groups who are all too aware that faith is a choice – and certainly not the most evident choice? This, I believe, is one of the most important issues in recovering Christian mission in a post-Christian society: how to make theological sense of the disembed-ding of Christianity. Innovative leadership in our times is not so much about predicting the future, articulating a 'vision', and making a plan to remedy the predicament we find ourselves in. Theological leadership, according to Michael Moynagh, is rather 'to help the organization to make sense of what it is experiencing'.[1] This happens through designing a new language, by crafting a narrative that connects our current situa-tion with the stories of the Bible and the history of God's people. Out of this new narrative, new possibilities may arise, as we have received more clarity about where we are, and what God is at in the secularization of Western culture. This is crucial, because to give up on the question of what God has to do with a post-Christian society means to allow our imagination to be secularized, and then we would really have entered a post-Christian stage of history. Conversely, so long as we can articulate a theological narrative of how God may be involved in the collapse of Christendom, a deep source of hope and creativity will remain regardless of how marginalized we are.

4.1   Exile

We can see meaning only if we can place things in a story. A narrative gives a head and a tail to the stream of events; it provides a plot and a purpose. People who can see a storyline in what happens to them are able to survive the most terrible experiences. By contrast, people who – even amid immense wealth, safety and luxury – cannot see meaning any more, lose their stomach for life and become depressed.

Which stories can help us to see meaning in this history of the disem-bedding of Christianity? Christians of all times and places have perused the Bible in such circumstances. From Adam and Eve's expulsion from Eden to John's exile on Patmos, the Bible is a book of uprooting and displacement. Christians have oriented themselves especially towards the stories and songs that were written in response to Israel's captivity in Babylon. In 597 and 586 BC the Babylonians conquered Jerusalem and they carried a large part of the people away into exile.[2] The temple was destroyed, Judah's royal dynasty was finished, and the land was no longer the property of God's people. To Israel this was not just a cultural and political trauma; it was also an attack on the foundations of their faith. With the destruction of the temple and the termination of the sacrifices

God disappeared from their midst; with the collapse of David's dynasty God's promise that there would always be a son of David on the throne was rendered undone; and with the occupation of the land God's promise to the patriarchs fell apart. In the words of Walter Brueggemann, this was for ancient Israel 'the end of privilege, the end of certitude, the end of domination, the end of viable political institutions, and the end of a sustaining social fabric'. He concludes: 'Not to overstate, *it was the end of the life with God*, which Israel had taken for granted.'[3] The cornerstones of faith had been shattered, God himself had not been able to protect his people against the gods of Babylon, and from now on many Israelites had to live among an alien people with entirely different beliefs.

Humanly speaking it was to be expected that Israel would have disappeared like so many groups and tribes have disappeared in the course of history: side-tracked, demoralized, swallowed by the sea of nations, wiped out and forgotten. But the very opposite happened. In exile Israel arrived at a new faith in God, building on its ancient traditions, but full of new discoveries. The people demonstrated the power of a good story; and its capability of keeping defeated exiles together and to give them a new perspective.[4] Therefore it is entirely understandable that Christians in times of confusion and dislocation have oriented themselves towards the exile traditions in the Bible. This may be such a time as well. Let me repeat here what I wrote in the Introduction of this book: in some way we have more in common with the Bible writers than with our own ancestors. Most of the authors of the Bible lived contested lives, under constant criticism and doubt; but our own ancestors lived in an unbroken Christian culture, where nobody really doubted the superiority of Christianity.[5] Especially when we become intimidated by the rapid disembedding of Christianity from our societies, the stories of exile begin to speak anew. I believe these stories are essential to our search for a credible missionary vision for small churches in a secular environment.

It is important, however, to keep two things in view. In the first place: history does not repeat itself. In many respects our situation cannot be compared with Israel in exile. Every historical context is unique, including ours. Nevertheless, 'exile' can be a lens through which we see our own situation in a new light, precisely because some important similarities do exist. Walter Brueggemann rightly says that a metaphor (like 'exile') does not aim at precision. It is not meant to draw an exact comparison between our time and culture and the completely different time and culture of ancient Israel. Such a metaphor does not so much *describe* our situation, but it stands 'next' to it as it were, casting a new light on things in our world, and revealing dimensions that we at first did not pay attention to. A strong metaphor brings order and meaning to a chaos of impressions, so that we are capable of seeing and experiencing new things.[6]

In the second place: especially because of this illuminating nature of a good metaphor it is important to really unpack it, by exploring its different aspects. It strikes me that Christians who compare our time with Israel's exile often confine themselves to one element of this experience. Some say that God's judgement is coming over us, that we should renounce missionary activism, and that we should repent instead. Others endorse this perspective of judgement and conversion, but in doing so they concentrate on its positive side. Just as Israel in the Bible received new opportunities whenever it repented, so should the Church renew itself so as to be relevant to a changed culture. And yet others focus mainly on the aspect of God's hiddenness and mysteriousness in exile, an aspect that miraculously concurs with the sentiment of many people in our culture. And finally there are those Christians who assert that an uprooted existence is what makes a Christian experience really Christian. Through exile God liberates his people from their entanglement with power and violence. In this way they can learn that it is possible to have their own culture and identity without possessing territory or dominating others.[7]

Such a sharp, somewhat one-sided focus endows these contributions with a prophetic élan. At the same time, they often remain rather general and undetermined. It is important to understand that especially prophetic contributions are always intended for a concrete time and place.[8] Rather than a rain shower a prophecy is a concentrated spurt of water. So the question for us is: which word is appropriate for our time? The answer may differ, depending on our own background. Clearly, folk church thinkers will see this differently from Anabaptists (see Chapter 3, sections 1–2). Older people experience this differently from the young. Therefore it is crucial that we do not try to foreclose the discussion by taking one aspect of the exilic literature as the interpretative key, regardless of how important this aspect seems to be. Below I will pay attention to various dimensions of exile that we encounter in the biblical texts. I will conclude with a number of missionary reflections on living in exile.[9]

4.2 Trauma

It does not take a great deal of imagination to see that the events at the beginning of the sixth century BC caused huge trauma among the people of Israel. Destruction, insecurity, siege, famine, conquest, arson, murder, rape, desacralization, flight, abduction, poverty, humiliation, despair – all these are ingredients of this period.[10] Therefore it is important to listen to the voices of anger and desperation that emerged from God's people.

Such voices belong just as well to the experience of 'disembedding', especially when this experience happens abruptly and violently.[11]

Take the book of Lamentations, which is packed with expressions of 'horror and grief' (Ralph Klein). It speaks vividly about life in a city under siege: the constant fear, the gnawing hunger, mothers who eat their children in desperate starvation (2.20). It speaks of massive murder and rape breaking out after the Babylonians came over the walls. In utter despair the poet complains about the 'foe' who looked on mockingly at Jerusalem's downfall (1.7). And inevitably he accuses God, who has behaved himself as an unfaithful shepherd (3.1–3, a parody of Ps. 23). God has become an enemy; he has slaughtered the people 'without mercy' (2.21). He has made himself inaccessible to the appeals of his people: 'no prayer can pass through' (3.44). This deep bitterness also leads to a confused search for those who are guilty of this terrible ordeal. Who is responsible for this? It is our own fault (3.42); no, it is the fault of our ancestors that we are now paying for (5.7); or it is the fault of the prophets who have not warned us (2.14). If there is any hope at all in this extremely gloomy poem, then it lies here: this ordeal can't become any worse (4.22). Somewhere light will appear in this ink-black darkness; once God has had enough of his own ruthlessness. Therefore, the poet calls to conversion, although it seems that he barely believes that this will lead to anything (3.22–26). His calls are peppered with cries of desperation, but nonetheless: God's mercies are new every morning (3.22–23). In his deepest despair he clings to this: God reigns for ever (5.19). And he prays for vengeance, he begs God to punish mercilessly all the crooks who have burned down his city, killed the men, raped the women and carried the children into captivity (1.21–22; 3.63–66).

Also in a number of psalms we find statements that are to be explained as the traumatized reactions of an overpowered people. Think of the furious prayer for revenge in Psalm 137, where someone (hush: let them not hear you!) sings by the rivers of Babylon: 'Happy shall they be who take your little ones / and dash them against the rock!' Also Psalm 44 is a passionate testimony of a people in desperate confusion about what has happened. God has 'rejected and abased' his people; he has 'made' them 'like sheep for slaughter' (44.9–12). Israel has become the taunt of their neighbours; they are a laughing-stock (44.14–17). Why? On the basis of what we find elsewhere in the Old Testament, you would expect that the singer might wallow in guilt. But that is far from the truth. The tone is rather rebellious and reproachful. 'All this has come upon us / yet we have not forgotten you . . . Our heart has not turned back' (44.17–22). All this destruction, slaughter and shame – it is a mystery. One can only appeal to God. 'Rouse yourself! Why do you sleep, O Lord? . . . Why do you forget our affliction and oppression?'

(44.23–25). More of such exclamations we can find in other psalms, like Psalm 74 and 79.

In this context, finally, the book of Ezekiel can be mentioned as well. Many interpreters have racked their brains about the exorbitant visions, the bizarre actions and the book's violent (masculine) language. Some exegetes even suggest that the prophet suffered from a psychiatric disorder.[12] More convincing, however, is Daniel Smith-Cristopher's proposal which seeks a connection with the traumatic events around the conquest of Jerusalem and the first abduction in 597 BC.[13] The peculiar symbolic act in Ezekiel 8.7–8, for example, where the prophet cuts a hole in the wall, can be explained as an 'acting out' of the horrors of the siege that Ezekiel has lived through or that he has heard about (see 4.1–3). In another text it is described how Ezekiel sits in his house, with tied hands (3.22–27), or that he is forced to eat unclean bread (4.9–13). It is not difficult to associate this with the experiences of life in a sieged city (see for example Lam. 3.7; 1.11, etc.). We don't have to reduce Ezekiel's prophecies to displays of post-traumatic stress disorder, but at the same time to pretend that the prophet was not a human being and a victim of violence would indeed be much to ask. In this book God's Spirit speaks through a tormented man, and this stamps his images and words.

Trauma does not look nice. Being a victim of cruel violence only very rarely makes you a kinder, more social and more balanced human being. Therefore, it is important to 'listen out' for such utterances, and not to try and take the sting out of them as soon as we can. These texts give a glimpse of uncomfortable feelings of vengeance, anger and despair. These feelings are articulated in passionate language, and sometimes in absurd, almost insane imagery. At this point the biblical exilic texts may be far away from our own experience. We feel the temptation to look away, or to explain away what we have read.[14] We almost find it irreverent; surely this is not the real meaning of these words? But this is also a part of the Bible; it shows to what extent this is a book 'from below', a book that comes up from the trampled, bloody margins of the world. And we should not forget that such experiences of insecurity and violence unfortunately are quite normal for far too many Christians in the non-Western world. Western Christians can gratefully admire persecuted Christians who pray for their persecutors and love their enemies, and rightly so. But hopefully, the reading of these texts also gives us more understanding for the grating utterances that one seldom encounters in newsletters, the cries of despair and feelings of revenge, the furious accusations that are hurled at God. This is also part of the prayers of God's people, when everything is ripped away from them.

So, what is the meaning of these texts for Western Christians, apart from breeding sympathy for victims? For starters, they may teach us not to wax too apocalyptic about the 'captivity' suffered by Christians in the secularizing nations of Europe and North America. Recently, for example, conservative American Christians have employed the exile metaphor in a call for a withdrawal from an increasingly secular culture that allows gays to marry and grants women the right of abortion.[15] However, the loss of cultural hegemony and the erosion of legislative power on the part of Christians should not be compared with imprisonment, torture or lynch mobs against evangelists – the sad fate of many Christians in other parts of the world. There is a real difference between a nation in which Christians lose their power of limiting non-Christians to make choices based on an agnostic worldview, and a nation where Christians are restricted in their own freedom of religion.[16] The pursuit of equal rights for all citizens in a post-Christian nation will of course create tensions and conflicts (think, for example, of a Christian baker who refuses to make a cake for a gay wedding), but such conflicts are inevitable in pluralistic societies and a conflict-free life has never been promised to Christians in the first place. There will always be fault lines between the realms of the private and the public (including fierce discussions about the very definitions of these concepts!), but all this is a far cry from persecution and oppression. The rapid changes in some Western countries have caused among some Christians what I would call 'resentment' for want of a better word. It may feel rather uncomfortable that the ruling powers are less impressed by Christian norms or traditional morality than they used to be. This easily creates feelings of victimhood among Christians. They feel ignored, abandoned or even ridiculed, and this is enhanced by the memory of the self-evident and uncontested nature of their former power. Such feelings are not without risk for a healthy Christian spirituality. Victimhood tends to become a hotbed for the demonization of 'enemies'; it breeds suspicion against the 'world'. Resentment against 'liberal elites' and forms of conspiracy thinking will flourish, feeding into all sorts of culture wars where respect for the truth and love of enemies are usually the first victims. The truth is that in most secularized nations the so-called 'liberal elites' are far less obsessed by conservative Christians than vice versa. Of course, there is some real hostility against orthodox religion among the 'progressive' forces in our cultures, but usually it is not so much their purpose to oppress Christianity as such, but rather to create more equality for non-Christians. Orthodox Christians might do well to concentrate less on the wrongs they are allegedly suffering in the public realm, as this usually leads to dehumanization of the opposition. And the damage that is thus done to Christian love may be a more serious threat to Christians than anything that secular elites can throw at them.

At the same time we learn from these Bible texts that such feelings are real, and that to some extent they are 'allowed' to be there. They are not to be stuffed out of some abstract idealism. And even though Christianity in the West has not been run under foot by murderous soldiers, there are certainly instances of injustice and discrimination suffered on a micro-level. In my country, for example, there is the case of so-called 'Muslim background believers', who suffer much abuse from their former friends and relatives, to the degree of outright death threats. Other Christians may be threatened or abused in other ways. But in which context do we find these feelings in the Old Testament? First and foremost in *prayer*, as Lamentations and Psalms demonstrate. Experiences of discrimination and feelings of resentment (or even hate) are a legitimate ingredient of the liturgy and of personal prayer. This is the place where they can be acknowledged, examined for their realism, and as it were 'carried away' to God. Later, the apostle Peter will call this 'entrusting it to the one who judges justly' (1 Peter 2.23). This seems to me the appropriate place for such feelings; they should not determine the public presence of Christians in society. Nowhere in the Bible do we read that Christians should enter public life in an angry and assertive way, focused on 'claiming their rights'. If there is anything to learn from the hoarse voices of the victims in the Bible, then it is this.

4.3   Explanations and Interpretations

Aside from lamentations and raw emotions, exile also provokes reflection, especially when it has become possible to create some distance from the immediate events. In the Old Testament we find several attempts to explain what has happened to the people, and to draw conclusions for the future.

Some of these interpretations are not surprising. In the book of Jeremiah, for example, we hear voices that undoubtedly will have been heard more often in those days. Thus we hear about the prophet Hananiah who, after the first abduction (597 BC), announces that God will soon break the yoke of the king of Babylon, and will end Israel's misery. Hananiah explains the exile as a business accident; such things can always happen, but God will provide a quick remedy. With the benefit of hindsight we can say that this is denial. But looking back to the post-war history of many European nations, and the optimism around secularism in the 1960s, makes it easy to understand this attitude. It may be the first reflex in such a crisis: saying that things are really not that bad after all, and that the situation in any event will not last long. In Jeremiah 28 a clash occurs between Jeremiah and Hananiah. Here we see the fragility of interpretation in the heat of the events. Who in such a moment is able to prove his views beyond refutation? It is clear, however, whom we *want* to believe in a situation like this: someone who assures us that everything will soon be over is usually preferred over someone who proclaims that the worst is still to come. But Jeremiah persists in his unpopular message, and he supports it with a historical argument that does not really sound that persuasive at all: former prophets have always announced hardship, he says. When a prophet proclaims peace, the jury is still far out. It is as if Jeremiah says: always assume the worst. Messengers of rose scent and moonshine are to be mistrusted by definition (see also Jer. 8.11).

In this book we also encounter people who have thrown in the towel completely. After the conquest of Jerusalem some groups of Israelites flee to the safety of Egypt. They take the prophet Jeremiah with them. On their arrival they start (again) worshipping other gods and the 'queen of heaven'. Jeremiah criticizes them, but they refuse to change their ways. On the contrary, they say: when we still burned sacrifices to the queen of heaven everything went well. But as soon as we began to listen to you and other prophets, and renounced the other gods, things took a turn for the worse right away (44.15–19). Undoubtedly there will have been many who in the same vein attributed the hardships of exile to God's impotence to defend his people against the powerful gods of the other nations. Also during the exile in Babylon some people turned their backs to the faith community. By far not everybody returned when the exile was over. Interpretation can go different ways, especially with such confusing and traumatic events, and we may safely assume that for a number of people the exile meant the death of Israel's God.

However, in the Bible as we have it the voice of the so-called 'deuteronomistic tradition' is the dominant one. This tradition we find in various versions, especially in the narrative books from Joshua to 2 Kings (with the exception of Ruth).[17] These books tell the history of the people of Israel from their occupation of the promised land until the destruction of Jerusalem, and they do so from the theological perspective of the book of Deuteronomy (hence 'deuteronomistic'). This tradition is also represented in a number of prophetic books, especially the book of Jeremiah. What does this deuteronomistic perspective entail? In short:

- Israel's history as a nation begins with Moses who on behalf of God makes a covenant with Israel. This covenant, that is described in the book of Deuteronomy, contains a series of stipulations to which Israel commits itself. As a reward for Israel's faithfulness God will bless the people, and he will honour his promises to the patriarchs: Israel will become a great people and it will live in the land forever. However, the covenant treaty also contains a series of threats and curses that we find

in Deuteronomy 28. An important part of this is the threat of exile. If
the people do not live up to the terms of the covenant, then God will
render the exodus from Egypt undone. He will allow the people to be
taken away into slavery again.

- The heart of the covenant is found in the temple cult. From the deuteronomistic perspective the regulations of the temple cult are all about
the pure worship of God. That is to say, this worship is only to occur
in the temple of Jerusalem ('the place that the LORD will choose' – Deut.
12.14), and it is to happen strictly according to the rules that have been
set in the covenant. Only in this way can the people truly belong to
God, and be his property.

- The deuteronomistic tradition pays extensive attention to the kings of
Israel. The narratives about these kings form in fact the burden of evidence for the judgement that God has spoken over Israel. Every king
of the Northern kingdom, the kingdom of the ten tribes, is godless
by definition. After all, all these kings have followed the example of
Jeroboam the first king of this empire, who established sanctuaries in
Dan and Bethel. This part of the people has been desecrated, as it were,
from the beginning. Therefore it is no surprise that it was taken away
into exile by the Assyrians already in 721 BC. The situation is somewhat more complex for the Southern kingdom, that of the two tribes
Judah and Benjamin. All their kings are compared with David, and
this comparison turns out to be more favourable for some kings than
for others. Moreover, Jerusalem with the temple lies in this territory.
But eventually, also here everything goes from bad to worse, until the
'measure of iniquities' is full and God puts an end to it.

- This deuteronomistic perspective, in which the cause of the exile is
sought in the persistent rebellion and unfaithfulness of the people, is
complemented by some prophets (like Amos, Hosea and Isaiah) with
other perspectives. The people did not just forget the covenant laws
on pure worship of God, but also those that referred to relations
with one another. There was an outcry of social injustice, oppression
and exploitation. Again, this could not lead to anything but God's
judgement.

- This perspective of the Deuteronomist is not without hope. In
Deuteronomy 30.1–10 a new beginning is announced, after God's
judgement and the repentance of the people. This promise is reflected
in various prophecies of salvation, such as in the book of Jeremiah
(30.31; cf. 32.1–15).[18]

This deuteronomistic explanation of the catastrophe has exerted a great
deal of influence on later exegesis. That is justified, because this tradition is strongly represented in the Bible, and it has appealed to the

imagination of generations of Christians. This approach recognizes that God is the Lord of history and that he takes sin and evil seriously. In my country several theologians have emphasized this perspective by asserting that the current erosion of Christianity in the West is not so much a 'problem' for which we need to find solutions, but rather a 'crisis' – a judgement of God.[19] The appropriate response to a divine judgement is not looking for ways to get through this as quickly as possible, but conversion and repentance. These theologians summon the Church to repent about its past sins, and to refuse quick, comfortable answers. Our first and most urgent task for now is to look for God's message in the secularization of Western culture and the Western Church. Why is God judging us? Which sins do we have to confess: Constantinianism, crusades, colonialism, or all of the above? How can our faith be deepened through all this?

These are serious questions. Rather than revelling in abstract theories of theodicy that try to explain how faith in God is justified in the face of suffering, these theologians point to the concrete, historical character of Christian faith. The Bible situates reflections on the experience of evil and loss squarely in our daily experience, and it expresses these reflections through prayer, lament and praise instead of philosophical argument. There is, in other words, no way to think about these experiences theologically outside the relationship with God. God and world, God and history need to be thought together at all times, even if this means that God is accused by his children of abandoning them – as happens so often in the psalms.[20] In my opinion it is not an option to avoid the question of what God has to say in the crisis of Western Christendom. Answering this question, if only tentatively, is not the same as claiming to know anything about the general relationship between a good and almighty God and a creation full of suffering. It is rather a spiritual exercise of accepting our helplessness and historical guilt, and entrusting ourselves to God who does not abandon his people even if he leads it into exile. This exercise may help us not to succumb to a superficial and essentially anxious response to the crisis. After all, where there is life, there is hope, right? As long as we can *do* something and develop a strategy, we may be able to fight another day. But in fact such a hasty, complacent approach is afraid to accept that even in our deepest need we are secured in God, and that the hand that strikes us is the hand that comforts us. This activism is therefore an act of unbelief; it betrays a lack of trust that we are really in God's hands – even if we have messed everything up.

At the same time I hold some reservations about this perspective, especially if it is presented as the only lens to reality. We cannot situate ourselves just like that in the position of Jeremiah in the besieged city of Jerusalem, as if our main task would now be to present everything as darkly as possible and extinguish all optimism. As Christians we are informed by the entire canon, and how we read it will depend in important ways on our own situation and history. The deuteronomistic perspective is not the only view of the exile that we encounter in the Bible.

For example, I have already pointed to a number of psalms where the people's innocence is emphatically stressed. There we find no confession of guilt whatsoever, nor summons to convert. By contrast, *God* is summoned to 'repent'; he is to wake up and finally *do* something. Such psalms show that we should be careful to make a system out of judgement. It is not so that every crisis can be traced back to sin. In the catastrophe of the exile the Israelites also encountered God as an enigma, as the God who remains hidden and keeps himself deaf. Judgement preaching and soul-searching are necessary, we cannot avoid them. There is no doubt the Western Church has much to confess. But such confessions also contain a risk, in that they tend to rationalize the crisis. In some perverted way they help us get a grip on things: if a disaster happens, this must be because of our sins. Of course, this must be said sometimes, but it should not become a fixed refrain. Ancient Israel's poets also show another perspective: that of the God whom we address in every tone and key – furiously and passionately – without us ever understanding him. Sometimes we are just truly surprised by the crisis; it is possible that we are sincerely unaware of any evil on our part that is related to this catastrophe. This does not mean that we are in the right (the judgement is God's), but it would be hypocritical in such a situation to look with all our might for sins that can explain this disaster.

We find claims of innocence in other places as well. In the books of Jeremiah and Ezekiel we find them in the form of a proverb: our ancestors have eaten sour grapes, and the children's teeth are set on edge (Jer. 31.29; Ezek. 18.2). Apparently, this reflected a general sentiment: yes, there is guilt, but it lies primarily with our ancestors. And now we are stuck with the beast.[21] Note: nowhere are these claims condemned. On the contrary, they are more or less affirmed by the Lord, when he promises in these very texts that the children will never again be punished for the sins of their parents.

Our contemporary 'deuteronomistic' perspective on secularization is in my opinion heavily charged with folk church theology. This determines both its strength and its weakness. Its strength lies herein, that it criticizes various kinds of shallow and bureaucratically driven reflexes of the ecclesiastical apparatus, whenever this tries to organize itself out of the crisis. Instead this perspective raises the deeper questions about the hand of God in history, the spiritual problem behind the decay, the character of faith when it is no longer supported by powerful institutions and symbols.

At the same time this association with folk church thinking determines its weakness. In this approach there lies so much stress on the fading of a certain ecclesiastical structure and a specific kind of faith that goes together with it, that other Christian traditions may be insufficiently in view (see Chapter 3, section 1). In this way, the fate of the people of Israel is identified too much with the experiences of nineteenth- and twentieth-century 'Christian nations'. If one rejects theocratic thinking and a sacralized national history, if one underlines more forcefully the distinction between church and world, and has a better eye for those currents of Christianity that were marginalized just by the folk church, one cannot accept this massive talk about 'judgement' and 'repentance'. Such a person may be less affected by the trauma that the collapse of the folk church means for many, and perhaps this person has a better recognition of the liberating and beneficial sides of life in exile. This may apply especially for Christians who have known for generations what it means to belong to marginal churches or who have recently immigrated to one of the Western nations. Such Christians share in the crisis of Western Christianity, but their perspective is less marked by the shock of the unexpected, the dismay that is caused by what was never seen before.

4.4   A Witnessing Faith

A faith that forms the identity of a whole nation may have strong roots, but at the same time it is limited in its scope. It is difficult for the God of Germany or America to become the God of the Inuit or Native Australians. Thus, the cultural exile of Christian faith in the West can be an invitation to learn to understand God anew. 'Our' God must become the God of everybody. In this context the Czech priest Tomás Halík writes:

> [T]the only way that God can exist for us, in our language and our world, is if we let Him exist as 'our' God. However, He exists for Himself, and we have access to Him, to the way He is in Himself, only insofar as we are prepared to forgo attempts at making Him 'our' God, our property, God in our image, the custodian of our past, who is important to us as a confirmation of our common identity – insofar as we are prepared to let Him be 'other' and exist for others.[22]

Exile, says Halík (following the French theologian Joseph Moingt) is all about leaving behind 'the God of the fathers' (insofar as he is not more than that) and to find the God and Father of Jesus Christ. Here we discover that God is not 'our' God, not the God of our Christian nation, the God of our past, the God of my favourite church or the God of my nostalgic childhood. In exile we find out that he is also the God of Babylon, the God of everywhere. In exile we can learn that God is not ours, but that we are his – wherever we are. In this way exile can become an adventure, an invitation to a life with God outside the gates, and to rediscover your own tradition in Babylon.

In ancient Israel it sometimes seemed as if God's radius did not extend beyond the boundaries of the promised land. It was in Jerusalem that God wanted to let his name dwell; to this special people he had committed himself. When David had to run away to a foreign country to escape King Saul, he accused Saul of forcing him to 'serve other gods' (1 Sam. 26.19–20). Later, the Syrian general Naaman asked the prophet Elisha for two mule loads of Israelite earth, 'for your servant will no longer offer burnt-offering or sacrifice to any god except the LORD' (2 Kings 5.17). In the book of Ruth we find the same association of people, land and worship (Ruth 1.14–16). It was commonly believed in the ancient Near East that there was a close link between a god and his city. Sometimes this link was assumed for a whole country, but usually it did not go further. When the Arameans in 1 Kings 20 claimed that the God of Israel was a 'god of the hills' rather than a god who could be effective in the plains, a prophet said to the Israelite king that God would prove the Arameans wrong. But we do not find a universal perspective here, not a God of the entire earth who rules the nations.

This is not to say that this perspective was absent prior to the exile. There are enough texts to contradict that.[23] Yet it seems that this awareness became real for Israel only when it was torn away from its own country and was spread over the nations. Precisely in and after the exile we find the most profound and far-reaching confessions that there is one God, that the other gods are 'nothing', that God is the creator of heaven and earth, that heaven and earth are his temple, that God holds the nations in his hand and moves kings as if they were chess pieces. Here we also find missionary visions of 'many nations' who one day will join themselves to the Lord, so that they will be God's people together with Israel (Zech. 2.11–12).[24]

Perhaps we encounter this universal perspective in its most elaborate form in the anonymous prophet who is held by most biblical scholars responsible for chapters 40–55 in the book of Isaiah, and who is known as 'Deutero-Isaiah' (the 'second' Isaiah).[25] His book begins with a promise of comfort to a beaten nation that feels abandoned by God (40.1, 27–28). It is remarkable how the prophet uses exactly those words of peace and comfort that Jeremiah warned against some decades earlier when he walked through the sieged city of Jerusalem. There Jeremiah struggled with the false comfort of 'peace, peace, when there is no peace' (Jer. 8.11). But for the Second Isaiah the word of God is: 'Do not fear, for I am with you . . .' (Isa. 41.10). Whoever invokes biblical texts of exile in order to interpret our own time must therefore think very carefully about the 'times' he or she speaks to. Is it important now to accuse complacent and defensive church leaders that they are magically turning God's judgement into a manageable problem? Or is our age rather about comforting defeated people, who have had their children drop out of church, and see the Church crumbling away around them? I believe that often different answers are required at the same time. These varied biblical traditions show that it takes prophetic wisdom (a sense of the text and a sense of the situation) to speak a word that 'cuts' rightly.

Most interpreters agree that two questions are central in Deutero-Isaiah: *will* God save us, and *can* he do it? In its exile Israel wondered to what extent God still thought about his promises, and whether God was capable at all to rescue his people from captivity.[26] Against these doubts and concerns the prophet sets a series of salvation oracles, all to show that God indeed thinks about his promises, and that he is fully prepared to help. It is not the Lord who has rejected Israel, but it is the other way around: Israel has repeatedly rejected the Lord. But now God is prepared to forgive and make a new start (42.18–25; 43.22–28; 50.1–3).

But then this raises the question whether God *can* help Israel at all. Surely, Babylon's power has appeared superior, and the gods of Babylon have defeated the God of Israel? Not at all, says the prophet. In a series of courtroom scenes God holds the gods of the nations accountable, and he denounces them (41.1–5, 21–29; 43.8–13; 45.18–25). Isaiah even moves on to satire: which evidence of their so-called power can the gods of Babylon actually provide (44.6–8)? And yes, for some time the armies of Babylon were allowed to run Israel under foot and keep the people captive. But that time is over now. Do not forget, says the prophet, that the Lord is the creator who holds the ends of the earth in his hands. To him the nations are like dust on the scales. He never grows weary; his power is unlimited (40.12–31). Therefore, because God can and will save, the time of salvation will come. Like Moses once brought the people from Egypt to the promised land, a new Moses will take the people home from Babylon (43.18–19). And this will happen through the orders of a pagan king, Cyrus, who is called God's 'anointed' by the prophet (45.1, 13, etc.). In this context we also find the so-called 'servant songs', a mysterious suffering figure who dedicates himself to the salvation of the world, and whose offspring will be numerous (42.1–4; 49.1–6; 50.4–9; 52.13–53.12).[27]

What would be the best way to characterize this kind of speech? Let's remind ourselves that the one who speaks is a member of a powerless people, expelled from home and relatives, an Israelite who lives among superior enemies. Walter Brueggemann points out that there are parallels here with the way Christians have to do theology now in the West.[28] No longer is their voice supported by powerful institutions and an unfragmented Christian culture. This modifies Christian speech. Someone who has power and knows no threat can speak as if everything is certain; such a person can make claims that are self-evidently universally valid. And this is how Western theology has spoken for a long time, says Brueggemann. From high pulpits it could tell how the world is, what the truth is, and how nations should behave. But for a church that is expelled from the centre it is no longer possible to 'speak from the clouds'. Christian theology can no longer assume the voice of somebody who is absolutely certain of her position and her claims. Instead, she will have to assume a *testimonial* voice.

With 'testimony' Brueggemann means a theological way of speech that is not based on how things simply are, but that refers to an identity, vision and calling that come to us, as it were, 'from the outside' or 'from the future'. There is nothing self-evident about Christian faith, just like there was nothing self-evident about Deutero-Isaiah's grand proclamations in exile. Christian faith is at odds with the reality that has manifested itself in the West in modern times. This renders it vulnerable to ridicule and doubt, but at the same time it opens up a possibility of new forms of speech: less monotonous and pompous, less 'responsible', more humoristic and more critical of the powers-that-be. This is the language of Jesus' parables, the language of the kingdom of God that settles between skyscrapers as a mustard seed, growing in the crack between two tiles. It is the language of trust against all odds, confidence that comes from being 'caught' and so creates a new reality. This is the language of the Second Isaiah and so many other voices from exile.[29]

In all this testimonial speech the ultimate question is about the true God, the one who speaks the decisive word about the world. Which gods are governing in the end? Which powers are decisive for the future of the world? Here lies the essence of the Bible's missionary consciousness: this is not about affirming again the current affairs in politics and society and claiming that we are at the successful side of history – that God is really 'ours'. By contrast, it is about the proclamation of good news that puts into question everything in our world, including our religious certainties. It seems that this consciousness could break through only when Israel was torn loose from its foundations and was to live a precarious existence, where nothing was self-evident any more. In this context the people of God learned to speak testimony, that is, not to point towards themselves, their own history and cultural superiority, but rather to expect everything from the coming Lord who has lived among us humbly and hidden, as a suffering servant. In this context the people also learned that this testimonial speech was not just directed to their own folk, but that it entailed an invitation to the world (see below, section 6). And thus they even learned that this Lord can come to us in the most unexpected ways, through pagan 'servants'. God is always greater than we think. He is also the God of the others, the seekers, the outsiders, the critics. The Church does not possess God. Precisely in exile the Church receives the freedom and relaxation to face this, without feeling threatened.[30]

4.5   How to Keep Identity

With the progression of time, the trauma of exile disappeared from Israel's memory. To live outside its own land, dispersed among the nations, became daily routine. Although a minority returned to Israel when King Cyrus gave his permission to do so, the large majority remained outside the promised land. In the New Testament we see how the Apostles in their missionary travels first focused especially on these dispersed Jewish communities that were found over the whole Roman Empire. Indeed, the apostle Paul himself came from such a community. Here we can speak of the development of a 'diaspora' identity (diaspora = dispersion), something about which I intend to say a bit more in the next chapter.

The important point to make here is that 'exile' has more than one face, and that this can be seen today as well.[31] There are many Christians in the West – particularly those from the folk churches – who still experience the traumatic aspect of exile abundantly. At the same time there are Christians – especially those from minority churches – who since time immemorial are used to a marginal existence without much power or influence. The same is true for virtually all Christians in younger generations who have grown up in a secular culture. To them, speaking of 'trauma' and 'judgement' makes far less sense than to older people.[32] Again this shows that it is impossible to draw one single message for today from the exilic texts of the Bible.

In the Old Testament we find a number of books that do not so much keep the memory of what was lost, but are rather oriented towards living and surviving in a foreign country.[33] Here we could think of parts of the book of Daniel, and of course the book of Esther. But we find traces of this kind of thinking in virtually all post-exilic Bible books (and also in apocryphal literature, such as the book of Tobit). These books are all about keeping one's own identity, often in an indifferent and hostile environment that one is unable to change. This existence is fragile and threatened, but it offers opportunities as well. Daniel became a high official in the Babylonian and Persian empires, just as long before him Joseph became the viceroy of Egypt. Esther became queen.

Life in such a context, which is indifferent at best and dangerous at worst, requires much creativity and also some degree of contrariness. In such a situation one must not be too keen on being respected and accepted by everyone, and on becoming a popular guest at literary events and academic symposia. At the same time one does not seek confrontation and is willing to contribute to society, but inspired by one's own sources and not so much to rise on the social ladder. Said texts are packed with calls for purity, separation, nonconformity and critique of idolatry. In modern eyes there is a somewhat exaggerated interest in rituals (see, for example, the books of the Chronicles) and the preservation of pure bloodlines (prohibition of 'mixed' marriages in Ezra, Nehemiah and Malachi). What we see here is a clear example of a minority group that has closed its ranks in order to maintain its identity and its faith.[34]

In this context, there grew a renewed emphasis on what one might call the 'material' or (perhaps better) 'sacramental' aspects of religion. Such dimensions will become important immediately when a community faces the challenge to keep its religious and cultural identity, while it is no longer a nation and lives in dispersion among its neighbouring peoples. In Israel's case circumcision, purity laws and the Sabbath in particular became markers of a Jewish identity. These visible structures, however, did not just function as a social cement; they also formed the answer to the question where God could be found, now that the temple had been destroyed. Deutero-Isaiah had already answered that God is everywhere, that he is the Lord of creation. He is not bound to or limited by any location or particular history. This was what the Jews expressed in their structures and rituals of local worship all over the Persian Empire. Indeed, God could be found anywhere; he could be worshipped in any place.

One of the most poignant examples of this new awareness of God's omnipresence may be the young Daniel who arrives in Babylon in 597 BC, together with his friends. Although it is to be expected that the boys will never see the temple again (ten years later it was destroyed anyway), their first concern is that they will be allowed to keep the food laws. They want to maintain their state of purity outside the land of promise, so as to approach the Lord in prayer and worship. This reflects the emerging insight in exile that the cosmos is God's temple.[35] David may have believed that he was forced to serve other gods outside the promised land; Daniel knew better. In exile the ritual customs of Israel are 'disconnected' as it were from the sacred space of Jerusalem and the temple. All over the world Israel creates sacred times, sacred places and sacred people. Thus it remains possible to approach God and to know that he is always close – perhaps even more than previously.

An important element in the struggle for identity was the relationship with political power. It is a well-known fact that ancient Eastern rulers

could crack down with extreme cruelty on anyone who resisted or dis-
sented.[36] Exiles could easily become the targets of such viciousness. The
books of Daniel and Esther show how capricious the rulers were, and
how quickly one could become the victim of their mood swings. We read
about people being burned at the stake, hacked in pieces, thrown into
a lion's den, being impaled or nailed to a beam. In such conditions one
develops a complex relationship with the ruling powers. Exiles are not
inclined to trust governments. Those who have power and cultural status find it easy to forget that the world looks very differently from the
underside. Even in the well-organized welfare states of North-Western
Europe (which represent the closest thing to heaven on earth for many
of the world's poor) much will change if you are responsible for a child
with disabilities or if you become dependent on the bureaucratic system
in some other way. One then is soon to discover that these nations are not
all that benevolent and as well organized as their reputation goes. Not
always does one receive fair and just treatment in such cases.

Refugees have the same experience. As soon as you become dependent
on institutions and offices, and you have to queue regularly in order to
wait for what an official decides about you, your view of power tends to
change. Even your language will change, as refugee studies show. Those
who always depend on the whims of rulers learn to keep a low profile;
they learn to say what others want to hear, they hide their opinions. Such
people are easily mistaken for being secretive and dishonest, but the simple truth is: 'To be a refugee means to learn to lie.'[37] Honesty is the best
policy, but only for people who can trust that they have rights, and that
they will be respected when push comes to shove.

Mockery and humour are also among the weapons of the minorities. Again the books of Daniel and Esther provide good examples of
such disguised ridicule. In both books we encounter kings who are
all-powerful on the one hand and behave like foolish children on the
other. Nebuchadnessar's moods in the book of Daniel swing back and
forth all the time. Now he wants his whole empire to worship the God of
Daniel, and then one chapter further he erects a giant statue for himself.
At some other point he crawls on the floor like a madman and eats grass
like an ox. Belsassar offers Daniel half of his kingdom, while at the very
moment of his speech the Medes and Persians are penetrating his last
fortress. And Darius, the Mede, is bound hand and foot by this funny
custom of the Medes and Persians to issue laws that cannot be revoked.
In the book of Esther, we see Artaxerxes, ruler of life and death, a man
with the mind of a toddler and the cravings of a pimp. He too is bound by
laws that no one can revoke, but at the same time we see how extremely
impressionable he is. Nowhere in the entire book does Artaxerxes say
'no'! Time and again the last one with access to him has him wrapped

around their little finger – regardless of whether this person is Haman or Esther.[38] What these narratives want to communicate is clear: the empires of the world seem all-powerful and intimidating, but on a closer look they make you laugh. Such an empire is like a giant on feet of clay. Some day a little stone will come rolling, not moved by human hands, and it will knock the giant statue out (Dan. 2).

Thus these texts grant us insight into the cruel and anxious soul of superior empires, astounding government structures and efficient bureaucracies. The permanent awareness of the shadows behind the splendour that surrounded them allowed the exiles (some of them, anyway) not to succumb, not to become a part of the world of Babylon. But at the same time this is not all there is to be said. A diaspora identity is more complex than a so-called 'counterculture'. Everywhere the exiles find cracks in the stronghold: people who want to help, a friendly face. Daniel and his friends, carried away from Jerusalem, meet a courtier who assists them at great personal risk to keep the food laws. This eunuch, Aspenaz, is not a Jew and he will not become one either, but he makes room for people who want to keep serving God when everything, even their name, is taken away. Later Daniel will work under King Darius. Regardless of how weak the king is depicted, at the same time he comes across as somebody who is sincerely fond of his old minister. Esther and her uncle Mordekai owe much to some palace guards who tell King Artaxerxes that Mordekai has saved his life, even though these servants undoubtedly know that this will antagonize the powerful Haman against them. And let us not forget Cyrus, the king of the Persians, who is referred to by God as 'my anointed servant Cyrus' (Isa. 45.1, etc.). All these people remind us of what Jesus will call later the 'person of peace', who receives the Apostles and lets them eat at his table (Luke 10.6). Everywhere in the world, regardless of how hostile it sometimes may look, the people of God encounter fellow human beings who are prepared to think with them, neighbours who create room for them. Virtually never do we read that these people come to the faith, but nonetheless they contribute to the protection of the faith community and the progress of the gospel. This remains God's world. And this means that life for exiles is complex, hopeful and constantly shaped by negotiation.

Despite proclamations that Babylon will meet the same fate as Israel, and notwithstanding vicious polemics against the gods of Babylon, the exilic critique of the empire does not become absolute. It is aimed at the violence, the powers and structures, and the ideologies that energize the empire, but never is Babylon written off entirely. This may be most evident in the famous letter that was written by the prophet Jeremiah to the group of captives who had arrived in Babylon already in 597 BC (Jer. 29). He urges them to prepare for a long stay in Babylon. The exiles are to build houses and plant gardens, they should marry and give birth to the next generation. They must assume a positive and constructive attitude: 'Seek the welfare of the city where I have sent you into exile, and pray to the Lord on its behalf, for in its welfare you will find your welfare' (verses 4–7).

It is easy to overburden this text with missionary expectations. Those who think from a transformational perspective (see Chapter 3, section 3.4) may just believe that here a programme is rolled out for 'cultural change'. But of course that is not the case; this is a letter to a threatened, weak minority who is entirely dependent on Babylon for its own survival. There is no place in the Old Testament where a vision appears for a great revival of Babylon or the transformation of Persia. On the other hand, there is no need to interpret this cynically, as if the prophet would suggest that the exiles should merely cut their losses. In that case 'seeking the peace of Babylon' would amount to nothing but self-interest: because the exiles depend on Babylon, the smart thing to do is to pray that nothing bad will happen to their jailers. The best way to read these instructions is to place them in the light of the growing realization that everything that had happened to Israel was part of God's plan. Israel is still his people, but gradually it receives a new place among the nations, and a new calling. The captives must resume their lives in the confidence that through everything that has happened God will execute his plan with Israel and Babylon. Through Jeremiah God asks his people to keep their distance from optimistic dreams that this will soon be over, but at the same time he warns against a hostile, non-constructive attitude towards Babylon. When it is impossible to escape from the world or to change it, one road is still open: a peaceful, faithful presence amid the surrounding culture.[39] The Lord asks Israel to live in Babylon as his people, a people with a future. In their daily practices they reflect that they remain God's people even in Babylon. And this means that they will not only seek their own interest, but that of many, without running hidden agendas of conquest or transformation. Fascinating parallels are present here with what we will be exploring in the next chapter on the basis of the first letter of Peter about the life of the Christian community in the world.

4.6 Mission During the Exile?

We have seen how in exile Israel became increasingly aware that God is the God of the whole earth and of all nations. At the same time Israel became obsessed with keeping its own identity more than ever. This raises the question: was there any 'missionary' consciousness among the Jews during their exile?

Scholars tend to disagree about the answer.[40] This is to do with the confusion about what exactly the word 'mission' entails. Is a community a missional community only if it actively sends out missionaries to recruit converts? Or is a community also missional if it is open to newcomers, offers them guidance and instruction, and does its best to integrate them into the community? The first missionary perspective is often called 'centrifugal' (a combination of the Latin words for 'centre' and 'fleeing'), and the second 'centripetal' (after the Latin words for 'centre' and 'seeking').[41] Undoubtedly, the first Christians found both forms of mission important. They sent out apostles and evangelists, but at the same time they strove to welcome newcomers into their congregations, and to initiate them into the faith (for example, 1 Cor. 14).[42] But what about the Jews in diaspora? Was this Christian missionary zeal a new thing, or had the first Christians adopted it from their own Jewish traditions?

That the Jewish communities in diaspora attracted converts is quite certain. These converts were called 'proselytes' (after the Greek word for 'joining'). Next to them there was presumably a much greater number of so-called 'god-fearers': people who sympathized with the Jewish religion, but without being circumcised and becoming full members of the community. They did keep the Sabbath, for instance, and some food laws, but at the same time they participated in rituals in Roman temples. One might call such people 'guest members'. In the book of Acts we find a number of references to these sympathizers, like the Roman officer Cornelius (Acts 10.2, 22).[43] The question is: were these converts and sympathizers the harvest of active mission by the Jews? Texts that seem to say this appear often unclear or ambivalent on a closer look. In a thorough analysis of all (mostly extra-biblical) so-called 'proof-texts' James Ware demonstrates that these indicate that many Jews took a positive view of conversion and did their best to further initiate converts into Judaism. Yet there are no indications that Jewish communities actively sent out missionaries to recruit non-Jews.[44] The only text suggesting this is Matthew 23.15 where Jesus accuses the scribes and Pharisees of crossing sea and land to make a single proselyte. But against the background of extra-biblical evidence this text is better explained as a reference to the practice by which Pharisees further instructed interested 'god-fearers' in order to complete their conversion to Judaism. This certainly shows an interest in the initiation of newcomers but it does not prove that Jews actively committed themselves to evangelizing the 'unreached'.[45]

Converts and sympathizers thus seem to have joined the Jewish community more or less spontaneously. There was no policy of active recruitment. At this point the early Christians did something new indeed. Yet there was some kind of missionary consciousness among Israel in exile.

If 'missional' means that a community accepts a role for itself in what God is doing in the world, and that it considers the entering of converts as an important symbol or sign of God's mission in the world and also of the community's own role in this divine work, then I would say that this community is 'missional'. In my opinion, the question whether a community is 'missional' is answered more by the *significance* that the community sees in converts than by what it does in order to recruit them. If the faith community pulls out all the stops to recruit new members, while this recruiting is motivated primarily by concern about the future of the ecclesiastical organization – a struggle for human resources and income – would that be 'missional'? I hesitate to answer 'yes' to this question.[46]

Be that as it may, converts had an important theological significance for the Jews in diaspora. Its background we find in various Bible texts dealing with a future conversion of the nations to the God of Israel. This expectation is expressed in the image of a massive pilgrimage to the temple on Mount Zion. To limit ourselves to a single example: Isaiah 2.2–5 announces that 'in days to come' all the nations will stream to the mountain of the Lord. There they will be instructed how to walk in the paths of God. Their swords they will beat into ploughshares, and they will walk in the light of Jacob's God.[47] It is this strong expectation of a future conversion of the nations that on the one hand gives theological and spiritual significance to converts who now join the community. On the other hand, this expectation also points towards the role of the Jewish community in the world until that day comes. In other words, this expectation of a pilgrimage of all nations towards the temple of the Lord forms the background of a strong missionary vision.[48]

As to converts, non-Jews who join the community or sympathize with it from some distance are signs, as it were, of the future conversion of all nations. At some time the temple will be a house of prayer for all nations (Isa. 56.7), and everybody who develops an interest in the temple here and now is a confirmation of this promise of God.[49] Since the future conversion of the nations also implies the restoration of Israel, the entry of newcomers confirms that this recovery is indeed at hand. And this explains why many Jews during the exile did have a lively interest in converts. At the same time this explains why they did not actively search for converts. The Jews in exile were not so much concerned about recruiting new members for their community as about welcoming the first signs of God's future in the world. God's work is not to be rushed. Humans cannot contribute to it; they can merely notice it and rejoice in it. Only once in a while this expectation of future events overflows into the present, when the nations are directly addressed to prepare themselves for Israel's restoration. Thus Isaiah 45.22–23 summons the gentiles: 'Turn to me and be saved, all the ends of the earth! For I am God, and there is no other . . .

"To me every knee shall bow, every tongue shall swear." However, such texts remain an exception. The future expectation remained internal most of the time; it was not shared with the outside world.

If God is working towards the restoration of Israel, together with the conversion of the nations on a massive scale, and if current converts are a sign of what is going to happen, what then does this mean for the role of the Jewish community in exile?[50] It seems that the diaspora community has specified its role primarily in terms of a prophetical and priestly vocation. For this, one could draw on Bible texts like Exodus 19.4–6 (Israel as a 'priesthood' among the nations) and the already mentioned four songs about the 'servant of the LORD' in the Second Isaiah. In later Jewish literature this latter figure was identified with the people of Israel, who thus received a kind of mediating role between God and the world. As God's servant, Israel was a 'light to the nations' (Isa. 42.6).

Such references to exilic Israel as 'priests', 'prophets' and 'light' we encounter in various texts from the second temple period. To mention a few examples: the so-called Sybilline Oracle (a Jewish text from the Egyptian diaspora, written in the second century BC) speaks about Israel as a 'holy nation of pious men'. In God's future this people will be 'exalted by the Immortal One as prophets and [they will bring] great joy to all mortals'.[51] The Wisdom of Solomon, a book from c. 100 BC, presents Israel as a 'holy nation' (see Ex. 19.6) and alludes to a mediating role of the people as 'light' and as 'priests'. This light metaphor we also find in the approximately contemporaneous book Tobit, where the future conversion of the nations is connected with a radiant light that shines until the ends of the earth. 'Many nations will come . . . to your holy name' (13.13).[52] This image reminds us of the book of Daniel (12.3) where it is said that 'those who are wise shall shine like the brightness of the sky . . . like the stars for ever and ever'.

Many of these texts most likely point first and foremost towards the future restoration of Israel. Yet we also see how this future casts its shadow here and now. At this point the Jewish philosopher Philo of Alexandria (20 BC–AD 50) is particularly interesting. For Philo too God is not limited to the temple in Jerusalem; the entire cosmos is God's temple.[53] Within this cosmos Israel holds the role of a priest for humanity's sake. Philo emphasizes that the Jewish nation stands in the same relation to the world as a priest to a city. This role the community has received by its obedience to the law of Moses and its worship of the one true God.[54] Elsewhere Philo says that he believes that Israel 'has received the office of priest and prophet on behalf of (Greek: *huper*) every nation of humanity'.[55] Here he obviously alludes to texts like Exodus 19.6 and Isaiah 61.6 ('you shall be called priests of the LORD'). What does this priesthood consist of? According to Philo it means first and foremost that the Jewish nation offers its prayers and praise to God on behalf of the whole world. Israel is 'a nation which out of all the others was ordained to be a priest, in order ever to make prayers on behalf of all humankind, that they might be preserved from evils and partake of good things'.[56]

In sum: many Jews in diaspora expected the future recovery of Israel, a restoration that would coincide with a massive pilgrimage of the nations to the temple in Jerusalem. In this future vision Israel would become the priests of humanity. Converts who joined Israel in the present were considered as signs of this future. They were as many confirmations of the reality of God's promise and of the approach of his salvation. Therefore, converts were received with joy and they were diligently initiated into the traditions of the community, however without Jews engaging in active outreach in order to recruit converts. At the same time, we see now and then that this future vision 'floods' the present, as it were. Not only are other nations summoned sometimes to prepare themselves by repentance for the coming of God's reign, but we also see that Israel receives the role of priests on behalf of humanity now already. Out of this nation the light shines already, the light of worship of the one God and the ethics of the Mosaic law.[57] Therefore, if gentiles are coming closer this can only be referred to as 'coming towards the light' (see also 1 Peter 2.9). Those who join Israel will become part of this kingdom of priests. In Isaiah 56.6–7 we read that 'the foreigners who join themselves to the LORD' will be his 'servants'. They will live on God's 'holy mountain' and bring 'offerings and sacrifices' on the altar in God's 'house of prayer'.[58]

Thus we may characterize the missionary vision of these Jewish diaspora communities as a combination of a liturgical, future-oriented and centripetal vision. Liturgical, because its emphasis was on worshipping God on behalf of all nations. Future-oriented, because they looked at the present (including the conversion of non-Jews) from the viewpoint of God's kingdom and the restoration of Israel. And centripetal, because they concentrated more on welcoming newcomers than on actively finding 'unreached' people. All three elements were rooted in a strong conviction about God's present and future work in the world.

It is clear that a vision like this can easily turn into passivity and inwardness. If, after all, God will do everything eventually, why then should we bother about mission? But this is not a necessary outcome. By contrast, this vision provides a strong basis for a positive, inviting and witnessing presence of the faith community in the world. I believe that important building blocks of a missionary identity for small Christian communities in a secular culture can be found here. I will develop this further in the next chapter by paying attention to the first letter of Peter. We will see that this apostle in particular draws extensively on the biblical traditions of Israel as a priest and light for the nations that we have discussed here.

4.7 Missiological Reflections

We are taking leave of a period when the Church, society and national culture were fused together. Increasingly Christians are waking up to the fact that as individuals and communities they are part of a society that assumes an entirely different worldview. All kinds of inherited intuitions, strategies, expectations, vocabularies and beliefs seem to 'drop dead' in the new context that has emerged. Christians notice that political, cultural and symbolic power are no longer on their side. The exile traditions from the Old Testament shed new light on this 'disembedding' of Christianity from our societies. In my opinion this occurs in at least four different ways, which I will present here as briefly as possible: (a) exile is a time of confusion; (b) exile is characterized by a loss of power; (c) exile requires looking after one's own identity; and (d) exile asks for a renewed spirituality.

Confusion

For starters, an experience of major cultural change entails deep confusion. Today we see this abundantly in theological (and other) literature. The discussion in this chapter has shown that this confusion will not magically disappear when we start listening to the Bible. On the contrary, if the Bible makes anything clear to us, it is this: more than anything else, theological contradiction is an ingredient of the exilic experience. One prophet says this, another claims that, but what is the decisive word? This person bows under God's judgement, another declares loudly his innocence – and both voices have become canonical. We have seen this contradiction in the tension between true and false prophecy in the book of Jeremiah. In hindsight it may be easy to tell, but how does one identify words of truth in the midst of a shattering crisis? Are we to assume, with Jeremiah, that in case of doubt we should always side with the bleakest scenario?

We also witnessed this confusion in the diametrically opposed words of the prophets just prior to the exile and those living in exile. Deutero-Isaiah speaks liberating and comforting words, the very words that half a century earlier were characterized as false. Apparently, it matters a great deal to whom and when words are spoken. In a different context orthodoxy can be heresy, and vice versa. It is impossible to determine what is pure theology, without making clear to which situation it responds, and to whom it is addressed. Rather than 'pure', such a theology would be sterile.

Finally, the confusion appeared in the difference between texts that are dated immediately after the catastrophe (like Lamentations) and texts that were written generations after the event – when diaspora life had become more or less a routine (like Esther). Gradually, the language of judgement preaching and complaints is replaced by the language of identity and cautious criticism of empires. Moreover, strong expectations emerge with respect to the conversion of the nations and the missionary identity of the people of God.

What does all this mean for our crisis? The confusions and contradictions that we experience have arisen, at least partly, because Christians of different stripes tend to present their own analyses as if they were independent of time and place. I see this, for instance, in the grand analyses of modern culture by neo-Anabaptists like John Howard Yoder and Stanley Hauerwas. In all their critique of hegemonic 'grand narratives' such analyses all too soon assume the features of a grand narrative themselves. 'First' we were modern, but 'now' we are 'postmodern'. 'Once' Christendom ruled by force and oppression, but 'now' we are all free to believe what we want.

Similar narratives are found with theologians who concentrate on the divine judgement in the crisis, often drawing on a folk church perspective, and usually with little regard for the perspectives of Christians who have lived in diaspora for centuries, such as the Anabaptists. Those who disagree are soon told that they are not sounding out our culture in sufficient depth. Thus, folk church theologians tend to reproduce ancient elitist perspectives over against so-called 'sects'. In fact, the trauma of the collapsing folk church is here projected on to all Christians. And yet others, possibly those who are more liberally inclined, put all their eggs in the basket of God's hiddenness and mysteriousness, while having their misgivings about other Christians who do not seem to experience much of this hiddenness at all. Pessimism and profundity are sometimes confused.

In times of contradiction it is very tempting to create order by inventing a grand narrative that excludes all other analyses. Thus we can maintain the illusion that we are theologically in control. By rebound we continue the sins of our ancestors, either by sectarian rants against all forms of 'nominal' Christianity, or by looking down arrogantly on the 'naivety' of marginal Christians. Of course, those who spray buckshot will inevitably score some points, and so there will always be something in such grand stories that rings true. But what we can learn from biblical exilic texts is this: a prophecy is a word that is spoken 'on time', it is addressed to a concrete audience, and in a specific context. Jeremiah didn't just scatter his words of judgement at random, hoping that at least some words would hit oil, while taking environmental damage for granted. He first and foremost addressed a complacent and defensive ruling class that had forgotten the Lord and allowed incredible social injustice. Deutero-Isaiah did not speak in vague generic terms, in spite of the huge scope of his words; he addressed the dispersed and desolate exiles who desperately waited for a sign of hope. We too could learn to speak 'smaller', more concretely and with more precision.[59] Whoever thinks, for example, that the current crisis is a divine judgement may have identified an important biblical truth. Yet, if one says this, he or she should also make clear which injustice and which idolatry this judgement is aimed at, and which concrete persons or groups are addressed. Only in this way can such talk be prophetic.

Apart from striving for more precision, it is also important to seek unity and reconciliation. One of the blessings of secularization in my context is that churches, however gradually, move towards one another. This happens more on local than on national levels. In local contexts churches recognize the shared challenges and questions they are facing. Insofar as they still have the human resources and finances to work independently – and this is increasingly less so – such questions urge them to dialogue and cooperation. This also provides them with the opportunity to compare theological perspectives from different contexts. Grand, generalizing narratives are easier to maintain when Christians isolate themselves in like-minded milieus, and refuse to have genuine conversations with Christians from other traditions, and with non-Christians from their neighbourhoods. We should face the theological fact that the current crisis is too complex to be understood from one single Christian perspective.[60] Therefore, if nothing else, a time of exile highlights the urgency of our quest for Christian unity. Our theologies must become more open in order to make room for perspectives that we have been uncomfortable with for a long time. This will be easier as we accept that the models that were discussed in Chapter 3 have truly run their course.

Power

Loss of power is typical of the exilic experience. Exiles are not able to make their societies respect them or to make room for them. They depend on the good will of the communities that surround them. Sometimes this good will is in good supply, and sometimes it is virtually absent, but the point is: exiles have little direct influence on this. They are weak and vulnerable. I think that here we approach the core of what the Bible means by being an 'alien' or a 'pilgrim'. These words express on the one hand that Christians have a different identity (they are pilgrims 'passing through'), and on the other hand they reflect that Christians do not usually have the instruments allowing them to arrange their societies such that life becomes easier for them. When we lived in Amsterdam, there were many such strangers around us. Some of them were very wealthy; when our Irish neighbours moved, they needed a mini-van just to transport all the shoes of the woman of the house. Others were poor and without privilege; I remember a student of mine who was a Muslim-background Christian from Ghana, who had lived on the streets as a drug addict. He was rescued by a Victory Outreach church, and had worked himself up the social ladder until he finished a Masters degree in theology. I suppose that the ancient Israelites in Babylon also had their homeless dropouts next to their Daniels and Esthers. But the point is: strangers have little power; they do not have a passport, and regardless of how rich they are, they don't have voting rights. So, the best they can hope for is a benevolent and cooperative host society, while the worst they fear is a society that is out to exterminate or assimilate them. What they usually get is a society that is more or less indifferent towards them, with individual outliers on both sides. The exile stories of the Bible give examples of all these scenarios.

If we think back for a while to the missionary models in the previous chapter, we see that the experience of 'exile' underlines the issues that were discussed there. Exile emphasizes the difference between church and world. Therefore, a folk church is unthinkable, while models of church growth, revival and cultural change also do not take seriously enough the reality of exile – and God's vocation through this reality. Exile is at odds with both the Anabaptist ideal and the ideal of the inside-out church. The first is too predicated on a negative relationship with the Church's 'host', while the other uncritically assumes a harmonious relationship. By contrast, the exilic experience emphasizes the complex and messy nature of the Church's relationship with the world. This relation is a matter of constant searching and negotiating. All-encompassing models that 'fix' the relationship once and for all do not really fit into this experience. And let me reiterate, finally, that underlining the constantly changing nature of the relationship between church and world does not contradict a vital missionary presence of the Church in the world. The desire to win souls, to serve the poor, to build just structures and to restore nature does not at all depend on paradigms in which the Church either 'owns' the world or 'counters' it all the time.

The loss of power also changes the way Christians deal with politics. We have seen how the exile traditions tend to look at history from below, as it were – from the viewpoint of refugees and strangers. Those who take this position will automatically become more critical of the way power operates in the world. The point is not that one should naively think that power is something we can do without, or that politics as such is evil, but exiles usually have a better view of the oppressive and exclusive aspects of political power. You tend to have less faith in the system once you have found out that it does not automatically work in your favour. Those who find themselves in the centre of power often speak about 'taking responsibility', 'thinking constructively', 'making a contribution', 'having confidence', and the like. They invite us to think through societal problems from the viewpoint of rulers. You should put yourself, they say, in the position of a minister. Only then can you look objectively and with nuance at refugee issues or nuclear energy, or what not. As if legislative power, having your own driver and a good salary would change a person into an angel who soars above our earthly spheres and is able to judge without prejudice or interest. Why should Christians approach societal problems from the viewpoint of rulers? Why wouldn't we approach such questions from the viewpoint of an illegal immigrant, a homeless person or an unemployed Muslim teenager?

Those who are in the centre of power tend to call such approaches 'not very constructive', 'prejudiced', 'rather one-sided', or 'unrealistic'. Insofar as Christians share such verdicts, they betray to which extent they still think that we will get a right perspective on the world only from the centre of power. The stories of exile teach us differently. Here we encounter a deep confidence that it is God who rules the world (Deutero-Isaiah), but at the same time these narratives make it clear that the world is controlled by empires with very opportunistic ideas of truth and justice. Here we do find respect for authorities, but the nature of this respect is somewhat distant and critical. The exiles always keep a realistic perspective on the stinking backside of magnificent palaces.

Again, this does not fit into a grand, comprehensive narrative that determines the relation between church and world once and for good. Politics can be relatively good and bad, and in every era Christians need to get the lay of the land. In Daniel 2, King Nebuchadnessar declares that the whole world is to worship the God of Daniel. Only one chapter further the king sets up a giant statue, and he summons the world to worship himself on pain of death. With these empires the wind blows constantly from different directions, and an exile knows this like no other. All of a sudden a new pharaoh may arise who has never heard of Joseph. Meanwhile this does not imply a dogged commitment to a 'counter culture'. The Judeans in exile are told by Jeremiah to seek the 'peace' of Babylon. They buy houses and fields and thus become involved in economic life. They marry and raise the next generation. Their first concern is to keep their own identity, but exactly this means that they commit themselves to the common good whenever this is possible. What this common good entails and how to contribute to it, however, is not primarily determined by Babylon's attitude towards Israel. Awareness of the common good emerges much more from the persistent quest how to serve the God of Israel in a foreign country.

Identity

I am tempted to say that the loss of power in combination with concern about identity are the two most pressing issues coming at the people of God in exile. The loss of power immediately draws attention to the question of how identity is maintained now that Christians are no longer able to shape the culture in their favour.

I have already pointed out that Israel in exile or diaspora developed a strong interest in circumcision, mixed marriages, the Sabbath and food laws. Put differently, more than ever before *purity* became a burning issue. Such 'ghettoization' often comes across as unsympathetic and 'sectarian' to majorities, but we might grow some understanding of it when we pay attention to the history of threatened peoples, such as the First Nations in America and Australia, or the Jews in Europe. 'Identity', says Daniel Smith-Christopher, 'is a matter of discipline.'[61] As a minority you can only keep your own identity if you are willing to invest in it. You must be prepared to make the effort to keep your children rooted in your traditions, and you must spend energy maintaining habits and rituals like churchgoing and family meals. After all, if you do not shape your children with the Christian faith, others will shape them with the stories of the cultural majority. Christians in previous generations may have had a less articulate view of this, since they and their children could benefit to some extent from a Christianized culture. But today most Western Christians know that nothing comes easy, including faith formation. Either you go for it, or you let it run its course. In the latter case this usually means that your children will pick up their worldview somewhere else.

The biblical texts, like the books of Ezrah and Nehemiah, also show that this concern about identity can easily become draconian or narrow-minded. Many Western Christians too have memories of an ecclesiastical culture where everything seemed to revolve around keeping people tobacco-free, decently dressed, at home on Sundays, and virgin until marriage. Nevertheless, it is important that we do not throw the baby out with the bath water. Christian language, customs, prayers and sacraments will only remain if people make an effort to immerse themselves in this lifestyle and pass it on to their children. This usually does not happen when you stay on your own. As the saying has it, it takes a village to raise a child. Wherever this is possible it is necessary to build such communities, that seek the peace of the city at the same time. You cannot create a culture on your own.

I don't know whether it is possible to give a general definition of such communities. But I do know churches that combine an unembarrassed commitment to a Christian identity with an open-minded presence in the world. Much of this is, I believe, to do with a loss of shyness about Christian language. This too can be a fortunate consequence of secularization. As long as we think, inspired perhaps by a thinned-out version of folk church theology, that everybody should be able to understand the language of Christian faith, we will automatically look for an ever-more generic, inclusive and secular jargon. But we could think the other way. In a world where we no longer have to be understood by everybody or have to keep everybody within the same fold, Christians can present themselves as a friendly 'tribe' with its own language. This language should not be unnecessarily complicated or esoteric, but like every language the Christian language has aspects that you can only grasp if you engage with the Christian community. Christianity has something unique to offer, and this is expressed in its language. Admittedly, not everybody will understand it, and many will merely shrug their shoulders, but that is intrinsic to exile. Regardless of what many say or think, there will always be people who are fascinated, precisely because they learn something here that cannot be heard anywhere else. This will happen especially when such communities join their Christian language with a hospitable culture and service to society.

Spirituality

What is typical of Christian spirituality in exile? In Chapter 3, I have mentioned some features: we need a spirituality of signs and foretastes (rather than instruments), a spirituality that is resilient when facing obstruction, and a spirituality that does not depend on the degree to which we are successful at realizing missional targets. Here I mention four additional matters that emerge from the exilic texts: lament; confession of guilt; the importance of sacraments and symbols; and the language of testimony.

The traumatic aspects of exile draw attention to the importance of *lament*. This pertains first and foremost to sharing in the grief and sorrow of so many Christians who are persecuted because of their faith. Naturally, this includes the fate of other people who are discriminated against because of their conscience. Wherever Christians are persecuted, other freedoms are also in trouble. The exilic texts sharpen our view of the traumatic, distorting effects for people who are affected by this. These texts also give us room to appreciate language that at first hearing sounds ugly and repulsive – like so many of the texts in Ezekiel and in some psalms. We need a liturgy in which there is plenty of room to invoke God, or even accuse him, because of the miserable fate of so many of his children. In such a liturgy there must be room also for the 'carrying away' of bitterness and anger, even feelings of revenge. Characteristic of a biblical liturgy is that such emotions are spoken, taken seriously, yet not translated into action. By contrast, they are laid down before God who judges justly. Herein lies the implicit admission that we, in spite of all our justified rage and grief, do not judge justly. In my opinion many church services would become a lot more exciting if there was something to be heard there of the fury and impotence that you can hear on the street or via the media almost every day.

Experiences of exile draw renewed attention to the role of *confession* and *repentance*. We cannot ignore that this plays a very dominant role in the biblical traditions of exile. Christians in a post-Christian culture, bearing the memory of centuries of Christendom, encounter the painful memories of this history on a daily basis. We like to point at hospitals, constitutions, cathedrals, works of art, development aid and universities as the fruits of Christendom, but it is much more difficult to face that burnings at the stake, crusades, pogroms, abusive priests and violent colonization were also part of this culture. Today, this cannot be ignored any longer. Christians in exile should generously admit that every attempt to establish a 'Christian' culture (either nationally or locally) almost inevitably produces injustice and constraint of conscience.

Of course this is a delicate matter. Confession can easily become defensive; it can be used primarily to confess the guilt of *others* (our ancestors, the conservatives, those liberals). I believe that there will be room for the recognition of guilt by Christians only when they dare to trust that Godself has led them into this cultural exile. People who have lost this confidence find it hard to deal with accusations. Those who have lost their sense-making sources will respond defensively and dismissively when they are are reminded of the problems inherent in Christianized cultures. This is precisely why we need to see a plot in the current situation, why we need to make sense of it based on the biblical sources. If we begin to see that Israel remained God's people in exile, and that it had a future despite everything, then Christians can have faith that this remains true even now. And this creates room to acknowledge generously: 'We have been wrong many times, and often we are wrong still.' This can find concrete expression in various ways. Obviously, there are the traditional options of liturgical prayer and confession, but there is a risk that they become cliché. It is more exciting, for example, when churches dare to make room for the voices of critical outsiders and intentionally create painful moments. Think of church-leavers, victims of abuse, LGBT+ people, refugees. Let their stories be heard, directly or indirectly, and let the congregation respond with a communal confession. It is not necessary to do this each Sunday; the liturgy is not an exercise in masochism, and such a routine could easily become another way to demonstrate how very tolerant and self-critical we are. Yet, such moments can be impressive now and then, and lead to repentance.

To the spirituality of exile also belongs a renewed attention to *sacramentality*. With this I mean that God is not only manifest in words, but also in images, matter, symbols and bodily actions. As indicated earlier, Israel in exile emphasized more than ever the tangible aspects of its faith, such as circumcision and the Sabbath. In a culture where God and the Bible are no longer the self-evident centre of society it is sometimes hard to notice God's presence.[62] This is even more so when the experience of God has become explicitly bound up with language and words, because especially in exile the ancient words begin to sound empty. The greatest threat of our time, says Walter Brueggemann, is not an exaggerated dependency on sacramentalism (as in the sixteenth century). Christian faith in a secular culture is threatened much more by 'technological emptiness' and by 'liturgies of consumerism and commoditization'.[63] Christians cannot resist such liturgies by words alone; they will have to think of formational practices and 'counter-liturgies'. Think of the Sabbath, 'a quiet but uncompromising refusal to be defined by the production system of Babylon, so that life is regularly and with discipline enacted as a trusted gift and not as a frantic achievement'. Think of circumcision or baptism, through which people are set apart from the empire in a bold action that says: regardless of how smart, impaired or promising you are, God's name is proclaimed together with your name, and that is more important than an IQ score or a large bank account.[64]

With this sacramentality also belongs the realization that human beings are embodied and social creatures, and that faith is appropriated via the body and processes of socialization. We are not brains in vats, nor ears on legs. A one-dimensional emphasis on correct doctrine and pure theology risks neglecting this. At least equally important are music, poetry, signs and symbols that 'touch' us in our emotions and affections. Essential too is the way in which people individually or together express their hope of the kingdom in their lifestyles.[65] Again this points to the importance of forming communities and investing in education.

Finally, I have already mentioned the new language of *testimony* (or witnessing) that arises in exile. Exiles can no longer speak as if everything around them self-evidently affirms what they are saying. The temple is burnt down, Jerusalem destroyed, sacrifices terminated, the people are scattered. There is a great temptation here to fall silent or to try and find messages that are still supported by the ruling powers. The consequence is the loss of a voice of your own; in cumbersome ways Christians are going to tell what everyone already knows and believes. Such speech is the result when Christians have unlearned how to witness, and have become used to speaking from the centre of power. Loss of nerve immediately strikes when most people (and especially important people!) do not find your words self-evident at all, or even ridicule you. In exile, Christians have to learn anew how to speak from the margins, to speak as it were 'into' the dominant thoughts and systems of this world. This is less difficult than it seems, because in exile you are likely to find out that everybody is in the same boat. Again and again, everything that seems objective, rock solid and irrefutable turns out to be the result of agreements, interests and power differences. Nobody speaks from nowhere; everybody speaks from a specific position or history – even if this is denied. Those who realize this cannot but see that witnessing is inevitable in exile; everything that rings true goes through persons and their experiences. All that is said will have to become credible in the lives of communities and individuals. Nothing is true 'just because'; and if it is, it is trivial.

Testimony is a fragile form of speech. You can't back up a testimony by offering rational proofs or by designing procedures that should lead everyone to the right conclusions. This does not mean that witnessing is irrational or concocted out of thin air, but is intimately bound up with the existential experience of the one who is giving testimony, and with the life of the community. A witness expresses confidence in the reports of earlier witnesses, all the way back to the eye-witnesses of Jesus' life on earth, the Apostles. Those who witness have experienced (or, at least, suspected) the truth of what they are saying, without being able to prove it solidly, irrefutably and objectively. Testimonial speech, therefore, is a form of speech that is the outpouring of surprise, of being overwhelmed by a new perspective. It is to be 'addressed' and hence to 'address' others, to invite them to trust this news and to live a life that is based on it.

Christian witness does not mean that you give testimony of your own faith, but of God. Witnessing is not giving an account of your own faith, but it is a response to what God has done in Jesus Christ, in concrete historical events, and to what he has promised to do in the future.[66] Therefore, witnessing happens in deeds just as well as in words. Every act, every choice of life that is a wager on the promise that Jesus will return, is a testimony of the good news. Many examples could be given. Think of living simply, voluntary celibacy, fasting and praying, giving to those who cannot give something in return, loving your enemies. All such practices are impossible to explain as strategies for success in this world. If God has not done something decisive in Jesus, if Jesus is not the living Lord, these practices are meaningless and unintelligible – regardless of how easy this can be forgotten in a post-Christian culture where vestiges of Christian moral intuitions still radiate some habitual plausibility. However, these practices are entirely rational if we believe that Jesus will return to establish his kingdom fully and permanently, a kingdom where everybody will willingly share with everybody else, where no human beings are slaves of sex or of their possessions, where former enemies are embraced. To be clear, I am not contending that Christians are the only ones (or even the most exemplary ones) who live such lives of neighbour love, forgiveness, chastity, generosity and sacrifice. All debates on natural law aside, it is not for nothing that our societies are called post-*Christian*. It would really be a miracle if centuries of Christian preaching and socialization would have left no traces at all in our cultures. My point is, simply, that in the end such lives only make sense if they are underwritten by the Christian narrative. Put differently, and perhaps overstating it a little (but only a little), there are many good folk in our societies who do not believe in Jesus' kingdom or his resurrection, but they surely live as if Jesus is alive and ruling the world. They live as if such lives have a future after all.

That said, it is inevitable that a Christian life will create conflicts with the surrounding world. This was so throughout Christendom, and it will be so in our times. However, it is important to underline that Christian faith is not primarily an act of the will to position oneself at odds with culture (drawing spiritual motivation from the Bible and the Church), but that it is a witness to another reality, a reality that is more 'real' than anything else. Christian identity is only at 'odds' insofar as the ruling culture does not understand or accept that the decisive reality is the kingdom of God. Christian witness, therefore, is far from irrational; it merely emphasizes that reality is different from what most people think. 'The believer therefore expects that the Christian values will "one day" be incontestably and abidingly established as what is most real' (Geoffrey Wainwright).[67]

By God's Spirit, people are made witnesses, animated with faith, hope and love for Jesus and his kingdom. I find it difficult to see how it is possible for someone to be a Christian witness in a post-Christian culture if this essential experience and expectation is foreign to him or her.[68] Of course, testimonies can be rendered plausible by references to the importance of Christianity for Western culture, the usefulness and necessity of 'religion', or by pointing out that faith is a helpful way to tidy up your life (at least for some). But these are all additional arguments that leave the dominant worldview untouched. At the most they say how religion in general and Christianity in particular can help us to live more successfully and effectively in Babylon. Not everything about this is to be rejected, and sometimes it may help people to cross a threshold towards faith. Yet, witnessing is different from inviting people to become (more) religious or to clean themselves up morally. It means that people receive the news that Babylon does not have the last word on reality. Witnessing is an invitation to look at reality from an entirely different perspective from now on, and to live out of this perspective. Obviously, this is also a great adventure for the witness, because who knows the consequences if we are going to take the gospel seriously? Witnessing means to invite others to share this adventure, and to learn from each other.[69]

This is why giving testimony surely is deeply personal, but never individualistic. Christian witness is not to be separated from the life of the Christian community. Of course, there will be all sorts of moments when the individual Christian testifies, but the new reality about which he or she testifies is made (somewhat) visible primarily in the life of the Church. Here the liturgy plays an important role, precisely because of its ordering of space and time from a different sense of reality. Common worship is a central act of witness, because like no other practice it shows who has priority. But the missionary and moral life too are forms of testimony. In different ways they witness about a reality that has been inaugurated in Christ and that gives meaning to whatever the community does. Only this reality of what God has done and is about to do through Jesus differentiates the Church from a mere dissenting society.[70] Because the life of a Christian and that of the Church receives significance from the future of God's kingdom, witnessing is ecumenical and multicultural by principle. Everywhere Christians achieve unity and reconciliation, and in all places where different cultures worship together, a glimpse of the inbreaking kingdom of God becomes visible (see also Chapter 6, section 5).

4.8   Summary and Conclusion

The biblical traditions of exile help us understand the current 'disembedding' of Christianity from our societies. In these texts we hear about the processing of trauma and declarations of guilt and innocence. We become familiar with new ways of theologizing and we receive the penetrating insight of God as the only God, the Lord of nations and creator of the universe. We also read about the concern to keep one's identity, and we see a new relationship being shaped with the surrounding world that is dominated by sometimes sympathetic but often indifferent or even hostile powers. In these texts looms the image of communities who are in constant negotiation with the world, without however losing their sense of particularity. These communities suffer losses and their faith is regularly challenged. Yet, they welcome seekers and converts once in a while (or perhaps often), and in this they see a sign that God is building his future. More than ever before they must learn in these fragile circumstances to trust the God of Israel who turns out to be the God of Babylon as well. They learn to live out of the future that this God is preparing. These traditions have much to tell the Christian Church in a secular culture. They provide insight into the importance of sacraments and symbols and the necessity dealing with identity in a disciplined way; they present Christian life as the life of a friendly tribe with a fragile witness, and they enrich in all sorts of ways the liturgy and the spirituality of the Christian Church.

Notes

1 Moynagh, *Church in Life*, p. 32.

2 Historical background in Oded, 'Judah and the Exile'; Van der Veen, 'Sixth Century Issues'.

3 Brueggemann, *Deep Memory*, p. 60. Italics in the original.

4 On the cruciality of identity-giving stories, see Sanders, 'The Exile and Canon Formation'.

5 I owe this insight to the Dutch theologian Wim Dekker, in his *Marginaal en missionair*, pp. 49–51.

6 Brueggemann, *Cadences of Home*, p. 1.

7 This perspective has been emphasized mainly by neo-Anabaptists, like John Howard Yoder. See, for example, his 'The Jewishness of the Free Church Vision'. But we also find it in Jewish authors who explain how the Jewish people has been able to survive for centuries without having its own territory. Finally, we often encounter such a 'diaspora theology' among Christian immigrants in the West.

8 For missionary reflections on the prophecies prior to and during the exile, see Smith, *Mission after Christendom*, pp. 32–46.

9 For some similar notions, see Beach, *The Church in Exile*.

10 Klein, *Israel in Exile*, p. 2: 'Exile meant death, deportation, destruction, and devastation.' See further Smith-Christopher, 'Reassessing'.

11 For interpretations of the exile that draw on insights from trauma studies, see Kelle, *Interpreting Exile*, pp. 253–342.

12 For such a 'psychiatric' reading, see for example Halperin, *Seeking Ezekiel*.

13 Smith-Christopher, *A Biblical Theology of Exile*, pp. 84–104. For a commentary on Ezekiel that makes extensive use of contemporary insights from trauma studies, PTSS, etc., see Bowen, *Ezekiel*.

14 Cf. Garber, 'Vocabulary', pp. 320–1.

15 E.g., Gibson, 'America's Conservative Christians'.

16 I agree with Christians who stress that their religion cannot be confined to the realm of so-called 'private' opinions, but here I am simply arguing that 'exile' and 'captivity' amount to more and worse than just being limited in your options to regulate the public square. The alternative of exile is not theocracy; it is, rather, the messy, contested public space of the pluralistic state.

17 For an introduction, see Campbell, O'Brien, *Unfolding*. For variations on this tradition in the book of Jeremiah, see McConville, *Judgment and Promise*.

18 See also McConville, '1 Kings viii'. More extensive reflections in Seitz, *Theology in Conflict*.

19 Cf. for example Van de Beek, *Lichaam en Geest van Christus*, pp. 179–80

20 See especially Lindström, *Suffering and Sin*. See also Laato, *Theodicy*.

21 We find this motive in a somewhat different way also in post-exilic prayers. There much space is made for confessions of shame about the guilt of the ancestors (e.g., Ezra 9.7; Neh. 9.16–17; Dan. 9.8, etc.). Such litanies have a double function: on the one hand they stress that it is impossible to live without sin (as history proves), on the other hand they also create some moral distance from the ancestors. The prayer is full of shame, but for the guilt of the *fathers*. Thus, such a prayer is indirectly a confession of the petitioner's own innocence (cf. Smith-Christopher, *Biblical Theology of Exile*, pp. 117–22).

22 Halík, *Patience with God*, p. 49 (here he quotes the French theologian Joseph Moingt).

23 For example, the calling of Abraham (Gen. 12.1–13).

24 On the missional significance of this text, see O'Kennedy, 'Perspectives', esp. pp. 227–9.

25 Without discussing literary and dating questions of the book of Isaiah, I simply want to point out that even if one assumes one author for the entire book, chapters 40–55 refer to the exile (in this case in a 'predictive' way).

26 See, e.g., Klein, *Israel in Exile*, pp. 97–124; Brueggemann, 'Preaching to Exiles', pp. 16–17; Brueggemann, *Cadences of Home*, pp. 1–23.

27 In recent research it is assumed that these songs form one composition with other 'servant' texts in the book of Isaiah. See a.o. Mettinger, *Farewell*. More on these songs in Chapter 4, section 6 and Chapter 5, section 3.

28 Brueggemann, *Cadences of Home*, pp. 38–56.

29 For an extensive overview of biblical and extra-biblical meanings of 'witnessing', see Baan, *The Necessity of Witness*, esp. pp. 49–80 ('Mapping the Meaning of Testimony and Witness').

30 Cf. Halík, *Patience with God*, pp. 60–5.

31 For the difference between 'exile' and 'diaspora', see for example Israel, *Outlandish*, p. ix; Wettstein, *Diasporas and Exiles*; Schiffauer, 'From exile to diaspora', pp. 69–70.

32 See also Ezra 3.11–13, where the young people cheer at the laying of the new temple's foundations, while many of the older generations (who have seen the first temple) weep.

33 Archaeologically, little is known about the life of the exiled Jews. Clay tablets containing a.o. trade contracts show, however, that they often maintained their own Jewish names, which suggests an attachment to their own identity. The Murashu texts from Nippur (from the period 445–403 BC) show that the descendants of the Jewish exiles under the Persian regime faced hardship, partly because of economic exploitation. The recently published archives from the collection of David Sopher (covering the period of 572–477 BC) suggests a more equal and prosperous existence. Both collections show that many Jews chose not to return to the land of Israel when this became possible (since 530 BC). See Pearce, Wunsch, *Documents of Judean Exiles*, pp. 3–29.

34 Smith-Christopher, 'Reassessing', p. 35. See also his *A Biblical Theology of Exile*, pp. 137–62.

35 Many interpreters assume that the creation narrative in Genesis 1 must also be read in this context. For example, there are strong parallels between ancient Eastern stories of temple construction and the seven days of creation. Remarkable also is that the creation narrative concludes with the establishment of the Sabbath. Altogether, this is primarily a doxological chapter, which represents the cosmos as the temple of the Almighty, and points all creatures towards their destiny to worship God and glorify him. See, e.g., Morrow, 'Creation as Temple-Building'; Walton, *The Lost World of Genesis One*; Walton, *Genesis 1 as Ancient Cosmology*.

36 See Kuhrt, *The Ancient Near East*, p. 517.

37 Voutira, Harrell-Bond, 'In Search', p. 216.

38 Levenson, *Esther*, pp. 12–23.

39 Cf. Hunter, *To Change the World*, pp. 276–7.

40 For a survey of (contradicting) studies of missionary consciousness in second temple Judaism, see Ware, *The Mission of the Church*, pp. 23–9.

41 For a brief introduction to both terms, see Wright, *The Mission of God*, pp. 523–5.

42 I have extensively reflected on this welcoming perspective in mission in my *De werkers van het laatste uur*.

43 Ware, *The Mission of the Church*, pp. 34–43, concludes that the term 'god fearers' in Acts does not just refer to sympathizers but also to 'real' proselytes (pp. 37, 42–3).

44 Sometimes the book of Jonah is mentioned as an example of mission across the boundaries of Israel. But Jonah is sent to censure the inhabitants of Nineveh. He is not a messenger of good news, his message does not contain a call to conversion, and he is not at all concerned about Nineveh's salvation (that God has a different view is the surprise of the book). Jonah's proclamation of destruction joins the tradition of other Old Testament prophets who accuse other nations for the injustice they have committed (see, e.g., Amos 1 – 2).

45 Ware, *The Mission of the Church*, pp. 47–54.

46 This is exactly why it is so crucial to respect the foundational structure of Christian mission, that is, the focus on what God has done and is to do through Jesus (see Chapter 1). If a church cannot explain any longer why it is important for people to follow Jesus (or however it desires to articulate this), then it can only point to itself. Sooner rather than later its own survival or success will become the implicit subject of its missionary proclamation.

47 There are many other examples of such texts. See Isa. 14.1–2; 19.18–25, etc.; Micah 4.1–5; Zeph. 2.11, etc.; Ps. 22.27; 66.4, etc.

48 Here and in the remainder of this section I follow primarily Ware's discussion in *The Mission of the Church*, chapter 2.

49 For this missionary significance of the temple, see also the prayer of Solomon at the dedication of the first temple (1 Kings 8.41–43).

50 For the remainder of this section, see especially Ware, *The Mission of the Church*, chapter 3.

51 Ware, *The Mission of the Church*, pp. 113–15.

52 Ware, *The Mission of the Church*, pp. 124–7.

53 *De specialibus legibus* 1.66.

54 Cf. Leonhardt-Balzer, 'Priests and Priesthood', pp. 150–1.

55 *De Abrahamo*, 98. For discussion, see Ware, *The Mission of the Church*, pp. 137–9.

56 *De Vita Mosis*, 1.149. See also *De specialibus legibus* 2.162, 167 (discussion in Ware, *The Mission of the Church*, pp. 138–9; Leonhardt-Balzer, 'Priests and Priesthood', pp. 150–1).

57 Cf. Ware, *The Mission of the Church*, p. 145.

58 For discussion and literature, see Ware, *The Mission of the Church*, p. 65 and fn. 27.

59 Something that is often overlooked (but certainly deserves consideration) is that most theologians who write about such issues are systematic theologians. I have the impression that such theologians are often insufficiently trained in contextual analysis. They lean more easily towards deductive, contemplative and generalizing constructions. I write this in the awareness that this too may come across as a generalizing statement!

60 I develop this argument further in 'Experimenting', pp. 188–90.

61 Smith-Christopher, *A Biblical Theology of Exile*, p. 198.

62 Part of this lies with long-term developments within Christendom and Christian theology. For a summarizing description, see, e.g., Boersma, *Heavenly Participation*.

63 Brueggemann, *Cadences of Home*, p. 9.

64 Brueggemann, *Cadences of Home*, p. 8.

65 See Smith, *Desiring the Kingdom*; Smith, *Imagining the Kingdom*.

66 In this paragraph and the next I make use of the seven marks of witness from Guder, *Continuing Conversion*, pp. 63–70.

67 Wainwright, *Doxology*, p. 2.

68 For this, see also Francis, *Evangelii Gaudium* (2013), sections 264–7.

69 Again, this shows that witnessing consists of words and deeds. A practice of evangelism that amounts to shouting good words to other people is entirely impotent, because the witness does not invest himself in the message. This may be the most important obstacle for Christians to be witnesses in a time of exile. After all, we are only all too aware that there are serious implications for ourselves if we take our own claims seriously: that God has acted decisively for the world through Jesus of Nazareth. And we have lost a lot of footing, now that we cannot any longer automatically expect that people will adapt to what the Church teaches in all sorts of ethical and social areas. At this point it might be very relaxing already if Christians would not toot their own horns too loudly, and joined their witness with the invitation to learn from each other what it means to be a Christian. To invite someone to become a Christian implies that we invite this person to make a learning community together with us, and that we promise to take the other person with utter seriousness with regard to the insights that he or she wants to share with us in following Jesus.

70 Here it is important to recall my earlier comments with regard to neo-Anabaptism in Chapter 3, section 2. Martyrdom, the extreme consequence of witness, is not the Church's calling, and it is not what the Church should strive for. Martyrdom can happen to the Church when the reality out of which she lives is fought by the rulers of the world. Sometimes the Church must say 'no', and bear the consequences. However, it is not necessarily the case that the reality of the kingdom of God is always entirely at odds with the values of a post-Christian society, or that this society will always reject this reality in every respect. Here too Christian life is a matter of understanding the times and of constant negotiation. One time you will become a minister just like that; another time you will have to face the fiery furnace.

5

Scattered and Sent

Once God lived just around the corner. Now it seems that he has left for parts unknown. In the cultural exile of Christianity in the West we are easily sneaked up on by a sense of abandonment. We fear that this is no longer God's world; he has turned a deaf ear. God has withdrawn from this world. Gradually but certainly he disappears from our thoughts and our considerations. We may still surmise him in the depths of our soul or in extraordinary signs and miracles, but his absence in daily life seems a fact. Thus the secularization of our imagination follows the secularization of society.

This modern inability to see God working in the ordinary and the mundane provokes contrary reactions. It is hardly a surprise when people give up, or muddle through even if they have actually lost their faith a long time ago. But these are not the only responses. On the contrary, feverish activity is often the consequence of this internal secularization. Since the great crisis of the 1960s Western churches seem to have doubled their efforts in an attempt to turn the tide. An endless stream of models and techniques has been poured out over us: small groups, rock masses, liturgical innovation, cell churches, church growth theory, neighbourhood mission, church planting, charismatic renewal, narrative sermons, fivefold ministry, the purpose-driven church, the Alpha course, mission-shaped communities, and so on. Of course, there is something to learn from all these approaches. The problem is that again and again they are seized to mend the unravelling carpet of a Christian culture. With every new initiative the question is: will this fix the Church? Will this bring back the people who have left? In fact, such questions show where the real pain is: *we refuse to believe that it is God who has caused this situation*. All these techniques and tools, however well wrapped in Bible texts and accompanied by prayers, are concealing a deeper spiritual problem. We look at the world as if God is no longer at work there. We think that he has dropped us off in Babylon and has then abandoned us. Now it is up to us, we believe, to find the way back to Jerusalem.

Theologians who talk about God's judgement in all of this are digging somewhat deeper. They assume that God is really present in our exile.

They refuse to have their imagination secularized. At the same time I wonder how much of their spirit has remained in Jerusalem. For me there is too much nostalgia in such analyses. I believe that there are good reasons to view the crisis of the Church and our culture as a judgement. The alternative is that we see the crisis as something that has happened to God, more or less to his surprise and against his will. To me that does not seem a real alternative for Christians. But the crucial question is: *how* is the collapse of the folk churches and the Christian nation a divine judgement? Are we to hope that God, after our repentance and conversion, will restore this great union of church and culture? Or should we believe quite the opposite, and are we experiencing now that God has judged precisely this folk church theology and national Christianity?[1] And might we believe that God is giving us a new mission through this judgement? The first perspective could be called 'deuteronomistic' and the second 'diasporic'. This diasporic perspective is all about accepting the crisis as a path that God is taking with us, while receiving our vocation by following this path. It is about learning to 'process' God's judgement into a renewed missionary calling. The current cultural exile of Christianity thus points us to a path towards a missionary consciousness that is purified from power-addiction and sectarianism. We must learn again to be weak, foolish and hopeful in the world.

In this chapter I intend to develop primarily this diasporic motive, because in my view it does more justice to the entire Bible (including the New Testament) and to the situation in which we increasingly find ourselves in the West. First, I will make a few general comments on the motive. After that I will explore it further based on the first letter of Peter. In doing so I want to show that a diaspora identity has two sides: concern about one's identity, and at the same time a positive turn towards the world. In my opinion this is an important insight for Christian communities in a secular culture.

5.1 Diaspora and Mission

Literally, the word 'diaspora' means something like 'what was sown' – a term full of missionary potential.[2] In the Bible a missionary identity always assumes mobility. Jesus orders his Apostles to 'go', as a condition for making disciples (Matt. 28.19). In this commission we hear the echo of God's assignment to Abraham to go out of his country and to be a blessing for all nations (Gen. 12.1). This mobility also finds expression in the tasks God gives to Noah and his family when they leave the ark. At the time when they find their old world destroyed and are about to make a new start, they are told: 'Be fruitful and multiply, and fill the earth' (Gen. 9.1, 7). Much later the Israelites who have been carried away to Babylon receive more or less the same instruction by Jeremiah's writing: 'Seek the welfare of the city where I have sent you into exile, and pray to the LORD on its behalf, for in its welfare you will find your welfare' (Jer. 29.6–7). Time and again we encounter people who are uprooted, living in a situation where they are 'resident aliens' on earth, and time and again they are given a task that puts them in a positive, missional commitment to the world.[3]

In the New Testament the noun *diaspora* is found three times, just like the verb *diaspeiroo*. Two texts mention the 'life in dispersion' of the Jews among the nations (John 7.35; James 1.1).[4] We find three further texts in the book of Acts where Hellenistic Jewish Christians are 'scattered' by the outbreaking of persecution, and subsequently proclaim the gospel wherever they end up (Acts 8.1, 4; 11.19).

In these texts, too, a clear connection is made between mobility and a missionary identity. At the same time the term 'diaspora' seems to relate here only to Jewish Christians. This is different in the salutation of the first letter of Peter, where the apostle addresses the 'exiles of the dispersion . . . who have been chosen and destined' (1 Peter 1.1). In this epistle Peter emphatically includes non-Jewish Christians. Thus the word 'diaspora' assumes a new meaning: it is not just about people who have been driven from their native land in a geographical sense, but about Christians who as a consequence of their Christianity have become 'alienated' from their societies.[5] In this way 'diaspora' becomes a term for the life of Christian communities as such, regardless of where they are found geographically. By definition they are 'strangers'.

The relevance of all this for the actively Christian minority in the secularized areas of the West is immense. Insofar as the experience of uprooting and displacement is still fresh in our memories, and provokes sadness, concern and feelings of guilt, we can draw hope from the fact that in the Bible a constant link is made between being driven out of an established position on the one hand and a missionary calling on the other.[6] There is a mission on the other side of the crisis. This is not only true for the Old Testament ('be a blessing', 'seek the welfare of the city'), but also for the New, as the texts that were mentioned from Acts show. Through the traumatic experience of persecution the first Christians are 'sown' all over Asia Minor. God's sovereignty over history is the presupposition of exile and dispersion in all of the Scriptures. He uses the displacement of his people to make his name known in the whole world. Today we may see this most directly in the various forms of diaspora of African and Asian Christians who have undeniably brought a new vitality to many Western (city) churches, and who as 'outsider missionaries' make the West aware of its own distortions.[7] But also the emergence of a great number of missionary initiatives in Western churches, including a growing willingness to work together, could be viewed as a fruit of the spirit of 'diaspora'.

In the remainder of this chapter I will explore this diaspora identity of the Christian minority in the secularized parts of the West. In doing so I will look first at the theological contours of this identity. I begin with the first letter of Peter, an epistle that is gaining more and more attention nowadays.[8] This 'exegetical stepchild' (John Elliott) of New Testament literature might become just as important for the contemporary Church as the letter to the Romans was for the churches of the Reformation.[9]

5.2   Strangers in 1 Peter

In what follows I first want to dwell a bit more on the diasporic identity Peter speaks about. Then I will focus on the ecclesiological core text in 1 Peter 2, where the apostle calls the Church 'a royal priesthood' (1 Peter 2.9).[10]

Aside from the opening lines, Peter speaks twice in this letter about the 'strange' identity of Christians, namely in 1.17 ('live in reverent fear during the time of your exile') and 2.11 ('I urge you as aliens and exiles').[11] What does this 'exile' entail? Two obvious connotations immediately come to the fore: exiles are *different* and they are relatively *powerless*. With respect to 'being different': in the Old Testament literature we find two terms for 'stranger', one with a hostile meaning and one with a more neutral or even friendly meaning.[12] This latter meaning resonates in the expression 'alien and exile' – or 'resident alien', as it is sometimes translated. Here the memory is envoked of the patriarchs who lived as strangers in Canaan, but also the memory of non-Israelites who later moved out of Egypt together with Israel and who continued to live among the people of God. According to various legal provisions they had to be treated well, and, after circumcision, they could participate in religious ceremonies and festivals. Yet, they continue to be referred to as strangers; somehow they remain 'different'. In the Old Testament this is very clear: regardless of how much the stranger adapts, and irrespective of how friendly and relaxed mutual relationships are, a stranger remains distinct from a born Israelite. You cannot repeat the past; your heritage cannot be rendered undone.[13]

What we see here is that the use of the term 'alien' or 'stranger' does not necessarily have a negative connotation; nor does it indicate a difficult relation between the stranger and his host society. On the contrary, 'the foreigners who join themselves to the LORD' are promised a position that is entirely equal or even better than that of born Israelites (Isa. 56.6). We could also think of the book of Ruth, where a foreigner joins Israel by her marriage and thus is included in the family tree of David and Jesus. Yet, the stranger's identity remains vulnerable. This was the case even within Israel. For example, Israelites were allowed to demand interest from a 'resident alien', while this was not permitted with fellow Israelites. Native Israelites who had become enslaved had to be released after seven years; this was not required with foreign slaves. So there was a certain degree of inequality before the law.

In Chapter 4 we saw that Bible books like Daniel and Esther keep Israel's memories of the fragility of their own sojourn as foreigners among the nations. With this we arrive at a second aspect of exile: even if being 'alien' does not necessarily imply that you are ostracized, it does mean that the boundaries of your social space are usually prescribed by others. Like Joseph, Daniel or Esther, strangers may attain a high position, become wealthy and have influence. They are not necessarily despised or persecuted. On the contrary, they may meet many friendly people and be largely accepted by the surrounding culture. Joseph received a solemn state funeral; Esther became queen; Daniel was educated in all the science of the Babylonians, and he was a regular guest at the royal palace. Yet these stories show that all this can be taken away just like that, with every whim of a ruler and every fluctuation in the public opinion. Those who know themselves to be 'strangers' also know that they will always have to look over their shoulders. They will not have blind faith in the institutions and laws of the country. The spirit of the age is capricious.

Thus, when Peter speaks about Christians as 'aliens and exiles' he primarily means that they are 'different' and 'without power'. They are 'different' in that their Christian identity is not a private matter; social consequences are attached. Peter shows this clearly, with a lot of examples, and also in the important term 'conduct' (*anastrophè* – 'walk') that he uses seven times in the first two chapters.[14] Miroslav Volf identifies this as 'an *ecclesial way of being* that is distinct from the way of being of the society at large'.[15] However, Christians are 'powerless' in that they have to flesh out their identity in a society that does not necessarily support their faith, or even obstructs it. Christians, according to Peter, do not have the power to arrange society such that their own life as Christians can be lived a bit more comfortably and consistently – if needs be at the expense of others.[16] This feature of alienhood resonates with our post-Christendom age; the actively Christian minority in the secular West is less and less supported by a generally accepted cultural inevitability of Christianity, or by legislators. No longer is the framework of our societies based on supposedly Christian principles, and no longer are these societies geared towards making life for Christians just a little easier than for other people. Sometimes it is the opposite.

It would be a mistake, however, to overemphasize the negative side of being a stranger, as if it would only reflect the historical experience of Western Christians who are disembedded from power and privilege.

This would make the term too coincidental, too dependent on historical contingency (and rather vulnerable to dreams of restoration). In accepting a status as aliens, Christians are able to rediscover their true identity in the world. The ancient term 'pilgrim', though not used by Peter, might be better able to denote this positive meaning of being a stranger.[17] This word is a clear warning sign against all missionary dreams of 'culture change' and 'church growth' (as discussed in Chapter 3). As C. S. Lewis so poignantly said: 'If you read history you will find that the Christians who did most for the present world were precisely those who thought most of the next.'[18] Yet, the term's connotations of 'looking forward' and 'passing through' (for example, Heb. 13.14) convey a positive direction of Christian pilgrimhood. Without exploring this much further, I'd like to point again to my comments on Christendom in Chapter 2. The early Christians did not intend to build a Christian culture; as pilgrims they worshipped, witnessed, suffered and served the poor. And in doing so they discovered, much to their surprise, that the rulers of the world bended their knees – reluctantly and half-heartedly perhaps, but nonetheless. Even then, they knew themselves citizens of the future city, that glorious city of God, of which Augustine has written so eloquently in his *City of God*.[19] The pilgrims of this city are prepared to cooperate with the citizens of the secular city wherever this is possible; they know the value of earthly justice and peace, and they appreciate friendship, love, discipline, security, beauty, and all other things that make life on earth tolerable or even fun sometimes. They are not out to condemn the world, even though they know that this society is not to last; they know about the different 'loves' that guide the moral lives of people, and although they seek the highest love – love for God and neighbour – they do not despise the lesser loves (such as love for honour or freedom) that create some form of virtue – or, at the very least, restrict evil. This may or may not lead to structural changes in the surrounding societies, but attaining power and influence is not on the missionary agenda of pilgrims.

Just as in the preceding chapters, I want to stress that this pilgrimhood of the Church does not necessarily imply a 'counterculture'. In that case the metaphor of alienhood would mean that Christians are constantly in an antagonistic relation with their context. In spite of the tense relation with wider society that Peter assumes, the letter never suggests that his readers should simply *oppose* the world.[20] Again Peter stays close to the exile traditions of the Old Testament. The biblical language of exile and pilgrimhood does not assume that the people of God are surrounded always and everywhere by people who are out to harm them. Even if the world is not ruled according to Christian principles, this does not mean that these principles are always and everywhere *anti*-Christian.[21]

Citizens of the kingdom of God know that their Lord is also the Lord of creation. It is quite inconceivable that a Christian identity is opposed to a non-Christian identity in every respect, and from a biblical perspective it is unimaginable that no wisdom or truth is found in the world. But the powers that rule this world do not draw on the Christian faith in shaping their societies, and some of their principles definitely clash with the values of the kingdom. It is this 'messy' situation, full of contextual decisions, that is conveyed by the first letter of Peter.

At one important point, however, the Christian 'aliens' in the first letter of Peter are different from the 'exiles and aliens' in the Old Testament. The stranger in the Old Testament was ethnically different from native Israelites; he or she was born outside the land of Israel. Reversely, it was also true that the Jews in diaspora were ethnically and historically different from their host societies. In some important ways they were foreigners. But the Christians who are Peter's audience aren't strangers because they are supposed to have entered the world *from the outside*. They are no immigrants or tourists who isolate themselves from their context in a ghetto or in a touring car, and from this isolated position choose which elements from the surrounding culture they like or don't like. Peter's readers are part of their culture all the way down, yet simultaneously they have become alienated from the world through their encounter with Christ.[22] Before their conversion, the Christians to whom Peter writes could not be distinguished from their neighbours (4.3), but now they have become different. Essential for this difference is the fact that they have been 'ransomed' from the 'futile ways' of their ancestors, 'with the precious blood of Christ' (1.18–19). They have been given 'a new birth into a living hope' (1.3). This unique connection with the life (2.21–23), death (1.2, 19; 2.24–25), resurrection (1.3; 3.18–22) and the second coming (1.7-8; 5.1) of Jesus Christ makes Christians what they are, and it makes them 'different' from their context in some ways.[23] From now on their focus is Jesus Christ; their 'home' is the kingdom of God that has erupted into the world through Jesus. This, rather than heritage or ethnicity, determines the nature of their alienhood. 'They dwell in their own countries', says the early Christian epistle to Diognetus, 'but simply as sojourners.'[24]

In my view some tension is found here with the experience of the actively Christian minority in the secularized parts of the West. The apostle Peter wrote to the first generation of Christians, converts from Judaism or from other religions. These Christians did not yet have a Christian culture, Christian art, Christian funeral rituals or marriage ceremonies, Christian architecture, literature, politics or history. They stood at the dawn of twenty centuries of Christianity, with nothing but their Jewish or gentile background, the Old Testament in a (not very

accurate) Greek translation, one or two apostolic letters, and some stories about Jesus. With these resources they had to shape their Christian
lives. But most Christians in our late-modern culture are very different. The large majority of them have been raised in Christian families,
which in turn were embedded in centuries of Christian tradition. As a
consequence of generations of socialization we are even able to speak
of 'typical' Protestants or 'obvious' Catholics. Christians differentiate
themselves from others (and in subtle ways from each other) by their
habits of speech, musical taste, political association, the designated hand
to wear a wedding ring, all the way up to (in my tradition, at least)
their preference for one kind of biscuit in church over another. All this
offers a field day to anthropologists, but it also shows how contemporary Christians have been shaped by very specific (sometimes rather odd)
histories of 'pillarization' and 'ghettoization'. In some places, especially
in the so-called Bible Belts, Christians try to make these cultures persist.
Others, however, especially those who are living in the 'diaspora' of very
secularized areas, find themselves in a situation where Christian beliefs
or lifestyles have no plausibility whatsoever. In a context were there
are no residues of cultural Christianity, everything must be argued right
from the heart of the Christian faith. If that does not succeed, there is
no way to persuade people – both inside and outside the Church – of the
importance of traditions or ethical guidelines.

To me it seems likely, therefore, that the alien nature of Christian
life as sketched in the first letter of Peter – being 'different' and 'powerless' – will be more recognized as contemporary Christians enter exile.
These are the Christians who, in the words of Michael Frost, 'find themselves falling into the cracks between contemporary secular Western
culture and a quaint, old-fashioned church culture of respectability and
conservatism'.[25] These 'exiles' are thrown back on the core questions of
a Christian identity, the disconcerting founding stories of the Church.[26]
They do so not to build a new strategy for domination by withdrawing
to the margins for a while, but to rediscover their identity as pilgrims.
Strategies for the establishment of a Christian culture, for enfolding the
world into the Church, or for reconstructing a folk church, do not make
any sense here; they do not even come up in such a situation. Other
questions present themselves: how to create distance from a culture of
excessive consumption and greed, without being bogged down in isola-
tionism and misanthropy? How to keep the faith amid a largely indifferent society? How to renew the Christian community and tradition
when you have become wary of Christian ghettoization? How to love
people and be the 'soul' of the world (thus the *Epistle to Diognetus*),
without losing yourself? How to give testimony of the 'hope' that is
among us, 'with gentleness and reverence' (1 Peter 3.15)? Peter can help

us with this. An essential element in what he writes in this regard is his emphasis on the Church as a 'royal priesthood'. In my view an important key to Christian community and Christian spirituality in diaspora is found here.

5.3   The Church as a 'Royal Priesthood'

A number of biblical scholars and theologians have drawn attention to the strong priestly dimension in biblical anthropology, that is, our mediating role between God and the rest of his creation. In the first chapters of Genesis creation is presented as a temple that is built for the glory of God, where humans are appointed as priests to lead creation into worship and extend God's blessing to creation.[27] According to Graham Tomlin the two creation stories that are sided together in Genesis 1–2 'make the point that humanity relates closely both to God and Creation. The first Creation account emphasizes the connection between humanity and divinity; the second emphasizes the connection between humanity and the earth.'[28] By this mutual participation in God and creation human beings echo the priesthood of Christ, who shares the nature of God and humanity.

> The key point . . . is that the human race on the one hand is an emphatic part of Creation, not exalted above it, made of the dust of the ground. Yet at the same time it is summoned out of that very Creation to bear the divine image and represent God within the world. If Christ is the priest of Creation, mediating between God and the world as the divine-human Son of God, then his priestly work of mediating the love of God to the world and perfecting it is carried out first and foremost through the human race itself.[29]

More than many others, the Orthodox theologian Alexander Schmemann (1921–83) has explored the priesthood metaphor to describe the calling of humans in the world. According to Schmemann, humankind is first and foremost *homo adorans*, a 'worshipping being'. Therefore, '[t]he first, the basic definition of man is that he is *the priest*'. To be called to lead God's creation in worship and thus to unify it 'in an act of blessing God' is what it means to be 'created as the priest of this cosmic sacrament'.[30] This calling to cosmic priesthood by virtue of the order of creation is restored in Christ, the second Adam. Thus the Church, as Christ's body, takes its place as a renewed priesthood, worshipping God on behalf of all creation. In Schmemann's words:

There must be someone in this world – which rejected God . . . – there must be someone to stand in its center, and to discern, to see it again as full of divine riches, as the cup full of life and joy, as beauty and wisdom, and to thank God for it. This 'someone' is Christ, the new Adam who restores that 'eucharistic life' which I, the old Adam, have rejected and lost; who makes me again what I am, and restores the world to me. And if the Church is in Christ, its initial act is always this act of thanksgiving, of returning the world to God.[31]

Schmemann points out that to refuse this calling – to refuse to bless and give thanks, to seek a perverted lifestyle of consumption and domination – is the core of our rebellion against God. To be alienated from God is thus to be alienated from ourselves and from the rest of creation; our current ecological crisis may give some testimony to that. Conversely, in accepting creation as God's incessant and abundant giving in every nano-second of time and every nano-meter of space, and accepting our role as priests of a cosmic liturgy, may be the beginning of restoration, a foretaste of the kingdom of God. To be found in Christ, to be 'wrapped' in his garment, as it were, is precisely this: to find ourselves as priests of creation.[32]

Against this rich biblical background it is fascinating that Peter does not just call the Church a community of pilgrims or 'strangers'; it is also a community of 'priests'.[33] In my view these two poles – pilgrimhood and priesthood – are indispensable for the missionary identity of small Christian communities in a secular culture.[34] While the metaphor of pilgrimhood highlights the rediscovery of the essential alien and marginalized nature of the Christian community in the world, the priesthood image helps us understand its missional calling. In this section I explore the biblical-theological background of Peter's terminology. In the next section I will give some missionary reflections about the priesthood of Christians.

Twice in chapter 2 of his letter the apostle calls his readers 'priests':[35] in verse 5 ('holy priests') and in verse 9 ('royal priesthood' or 'kingdom of priests').[36] With this term Peter points back to two crucial moments in the history of Old Testament Israel: the desert period and the exile in Babylon. Both moments are characterized by mobility and mission.

The first moment – the reference to Israel's desert journey – is found in Exodus 19.4–6, in the Greek translation of the Old Testament (Septuagint).[37] In their wanderings the people have arrived at the mountain of the covenant and the commandments. Here, at Sinai, Israel begins effectively its existence as a people. A loose alliance of tribes is forged together into a nation, now that the Lord makes a covenant and gives his laws. God then passes on these words to Moses:

You have seen what I did to the Egyptians, and how I bore you on eagles' wings and brought you to myself. Now therefore, if you obey my voice and keep my covenant, you shall be my treasured possession out of all the peoples. Indeed, the whole earth is mine, but you shall be for me a priestly kingdom and a holy nation.

While this is an intimate moment between God and his people, it occurs against the background of a universal perspective. One might say that what was established in the order of creation for all humankind is here re-established in the order of salvation for the people of God among the nations. A unique people receives a calling on behalf of all nations, with a view to restoring humanity's identity as mediators between God and his creation. Nothing more or less than 'all the peoples' and 'the whole earth' are in the picture here. Old Testament scholar and missiologist Chris Wright points to the connection with the promise to Abraham in Genesis 12: 'all the families of the earth' will be blessed in Abraham. Just like the Exodus from Egypt was motivated by God's promises to Abraham (Ex. 2.24; 6.6–8), the covenant ceremony on Mount Sinai stands under the sign of the great missionary vision from Genesis 12.1–3. Israel receives a special calling: it is separated as a priestly nation, for the salvation of God's world and of all human communities.[38] As God's precious 'property' (*segulla*), Israel will have a priestly role amid the nations. Israel's intimate relationship with God means that this people is involved in God's mission with his creation.[39]

Thus, a wealth of biblical associations – reflecting both the restoration of all creation and the particular calling of Israel among the nations – echoes in Peter's designation of the Christian community as 'priests'. There is an immediate parallel between both texts: Israel's pilgrimage through the desert corresponds with the diasporic existence of the Church as strangers in the world. Later too, when the people of Israel had settled, the priests in particular did not possess land; the Lord was their inheritance (Deut. 10.9). Rather than being bound to the land of their ancestors, the priests were bound to God. Both Israel and the Church are called to live 'holy' lives, separated for the service of God and at the same time turned towards the world, that is, God's world.

Although Peter's designation of the Church as a 'royal priesthood' can be sufficiently explained as a more or less direct reference to Exodus 19, many interpreters assume that he draws on a broader tradition that is also found in the second half of the book Isaiah.[40]

Here we encounter the second crucial moment to which the term 'priesthood' refers: the exile of Israel in Babylon. Again this is a moment in which Israel is uprooted. Precisely this is why the people is ready to receive a new assignment from God. In this context of exile, the anonymous prophet Deutero-Isaiah speaks about the suffering 'servant of the LORD' in a number of poems (Isa. 42—53). In these songs a figure is presented who is both king and priest.[41] Just like Israel in the covenant ceremony in Exodus 19 this 'servant' is a figure assigned with a mission. God has a special bond with his 'servant'. God places him in the midst of the nations in order to 'bring forth justice to the nations' (42.1) and to be a 'light' to them (42.6; 49.6). The parallel with Exodus is striking; this is about a person who is king and priest, and who is employed by God for his mission among the nations.

At the same time it is not altogether clear who this 'servant' is. If we take Exodus 19 as our interpretive key, it makes sense to identify this 'servant of the LORD' as the people of Israel. This is, for sure, how the Servant Songs have been explained in the Jewish tradition. In this case Deutero-Isaiah would present the people of Israel as a tormented man who in his captivity in Babylon receives again the ancient calling of Abraham. On the other hand, this identification of the 'servant' with Israel does not seem to work in every place. Commentators have therefore been wrestling with this mysterious figure. However, this is not really our concern here, because the question is what Peter in *his* context may have meant with his reference to these songs. And there is no doubt that in the earliest Church the 'servant' was almost unanimously identified with Jesus Christ. So, if Peter's phrase 'royal priesthood' is bound up somehow with the Servant Songs in Deutero-Isaiah it is obvious that this identification of the servant with Jesus was important to him.

In the original context, the 'servant of the LORD' seems to indicate an individual messianic figure, as appears from the remainder of the book. After the last song that mentions the 'servant' in the singular, the text switches to the plural. All of a sudden it is about 'the *servants* of the LORD' (Isa. 54.17). In the further development of the theme the emphasis is on these 'servants', that is, the 'seed' of the suffering servant (Isa. 53.10). This is his offspring, which participates in his vocation.[42] When this theme is drawn out in the latter parts of the book of Isaiah, it is emphatically said that this offspring will not only contain Israelites, but also eunuchs and foreigners (Isa. 56.1–8; compare 66.18–21).[43] Thus, the logic of these songs s eems to be like this: what the people of Israel could not perform in its calling to be a priest to the nations is fulfilled by the King-Priest. With this he opens up at the same time the way for his future offspring to become again a holy nation and a kingdom of priests for God's world (Isa. 61.6).[44] Their priesthood is twofold: they have a missional, mediating role to the nations, and they have unmediated access to the Lord in his temple.[45] In the earliest Church this was, of course, applied to Jesus and his Church.

It is in Christ, therefore, and only in him that the people of God are restored to their calling as a royal priesthood. Whoever tries to make a direct connection between Exodus 19 and 1 Peter might easily turn this into a moralistic programme, or even some sort of competition between Israel and the Church. 'Where Israel failed, the church should succeed: to live close to God and be a light to the world.' But why would the Church succeed when Israel failed? Such an approach misses the central event of the Bible: the fulfilment of God's demands and promises in Jesus Christ. It is the King-Priest from the book of Isaiah who forms the link, as it were, between the people of Israel that ran aground in Babylon, and the new people of Jews and non-Jews that is his 'offspring'. Therefore, Peter's missionary ecclesiology can be characterized as follows: Christ has done what neither Israel nor we could perform. That is: to live close to God and be a light to the world. As his 'offspring' – and only thus – the Church receives its nature and its calling.

This means that the Church does not so much 'replace' the Israel from Exodus 19 as a kingdom of priests. There is no direct link between the desert journey of Israel and the New Testament church. The Church is a royal priesthood because it is joined with the royal Priest who was born from the dispersed people of Israel. In 1 Peter 2 this bond with Christ is clearly visible. Verses 3–5 present the image of a temple, of which Jesus Christ is the 'corner stone' while Christians are 'living stones'. This temple is so organic and alive that it is priest and temple at the same time, called as it were to offer 'spiritual sacrifices' (verse 5). Thus, the organic bond between Christ and his Church produces the mixed metaphors of temple/priesthood, and 'living stones'/'offering sacrifices'. The priesthood of the Church is rooted in its organic unity with Christ; as such the Church participates in Christ's identity as high priest and temple. Christ and his Church share the same DNA, as it were.

In verse 9 this reference to Christ is more implicit. Here Peter emphasizes the special origin and calling of the Church, while he makes a sharp distinction between 'once' and 'now', between 'darkness' and 'light' (verses 9–10). In the wider context of this letter it is clear that with this Peter aims at the salvation of the Church by Christ (1.18–21). Again this new status leads to a vocation, which is now described not as 'offering spiritual sacrifices' but as 'proclaiming the mighty acts' of God (a reference to Isa. 43.21). Thus, in both texts, the Church only arrives at its identity as a royal priesthood via the connection with the royal Priest Jesus. Only through this connection could what was not a people become God's people (2.10).

Having explored the historical background of the priest metaphor, it is time to ask the next question: what does it mean to say that the Church is (like) a 'priest'? What does this mean for the role of a minority church in an overwhelmingly non-Christian culture?[46]

First and foremost it is important to look at the role of the priests in ancient Israel. They were chosen from among the people to approach God on behalf of the people. Priests stood in between God and people, as an elected minority. Priests came to God as representatives of the people out of which they were chosen; they sacrificed and worshipped on behalf of the people. Reversely, they came to the people on behalf of God; they did so through instruction (teaching the Torah) and by blessing.

This two-sided, mediating role of the priests – worshipping and sacrificing in one direction, teaching and blessing in another – is found everywhere in the Old Testament. But we can easily lose sight of how special it is that in Exodus 19 this role of the priesthood was given to all Israel. When priests are chosen out of the people of Israel to approach God, it is clear what their priesthood entails: they are to be priests for their fellow Israelites on behalf of whom they offer sacrifices and perform the temple service. But if *all Israel* is a 'priest', then what is the meaning and direction of this priesthood? Whom are they priests *for*? The answer seems obvious: their priesthood is meant for all humanity. This people is chosen out of the world of humans to be priests before God, with a view to the salvation of the world. Peter then takes the next step: if the Church through Christ receives this vocation of Israel (see 2.10), then we can see her as the priest of humanity, who offers praise to God on behalf of the world out of which she is chosen. Reversely, it is also true that she stands before the world as a priest, as God's servant. The Church is sanctified by God to represent him among the peoples of the earth. In sum, as a holy kingdom of priests, the Church represents God before humanity and humanity before God.

If we develop these two 'representations' a bit more, we can see how deeply missional this image of priesthood is. Let us look first at the first form of representation: what does it mean to appear before God as priests on behalf of humanity? In my view this means that the heart of Christian community is found in doxology, in praise.[47] This we see in an exemplary way during Sunday worship (the liturgy), where the 'priestly people' gathers to 'proclaim the mighty acts of God' (1 Peter 2.9). You could say that this is the most visible, structured and public expression of the priesthood of the Church.[48] But, as I have emphasized more than once in this book, we can also see this doxological nature of the Church in the daily life of the congregation and in the personal spirituality of its members (Rom. 12.1; Heb. 13.15).[49] Liturgy is much more than a cultic category; it is what defines the Church as church: to become a corporate entity that ministers on behalf of the whole community. In its communal action for God and for the world, the Church *is* a liturgy.[50]

The Church praises God on behalf of a world that does not know God. It 'is an expression and embodiment of the world's response to the gospel of Jesus Christ', or, more briefly: the Church 'is called to be the world's Christian expression' (Nicholas Healy).[51] Out of this part of humanity, praise to God will ascend in every place and every moment – in every congregation, because of the gift of life, because of his salvation and grace. And it will invite others to join in this praise: to offer themselves as a sacrifice to God and glorify him.[52] Before anything else mission is doxological; it is aimed at paying gratitude to God and glorifying him. This is how priests fulfil their task.

Apart from this passage in 1 Peter, a clear association is made between this liturgical existence and mission in various New Testament texts. An example is Acts 14.8–18, where Paul and Barnabas arrive in Lystra. When Paul heals a paralytic man, a spontaneous liturgy bursts out: the town people declare Paul and Barnabas to be gods, and they want to offer them sacrifices. Next, the Apostles tear their clothes, and they summon the people to convert to the living God. They encourage this by pointing to the 'rains from heaven and fruitful seasons' which God has given, 'filling you with food and your hearts with joy'. The implication is obvious: rather than worshipping idols you are to give glory and gratitude to the true God for the overwhelming abundance he pours out on you. The Apostles see this as their task: to summon people to glorify God together with them. Fascinating is the positive relationship with the world that is displayed here, quite contrary to the traditional revivalistic evangelism that many modern Christians are familiar with. Apparently the Apostles do not find it necessary to point out to these gentiles what they are *lacking* (and then present Jesus as the solution); rather they describe the abundance of *blessing* in their lives, and they invite them to give a proper liturgical response to such abundance.[53]

Even more telling is Romans 15.16, where Paul describes his own missionary work as temple service.[54] He calls himself a 'minister' of the temple (*leitourgos*) 'in the priestly service of the gospel of God, so that the offering of the Gentiles may be acceptable, sanctified by the Holy Spirit'. Here Paul recognizes his own apostolic role in the fulfilment of the Old Testament promises about the gathering of the nations at Mount Zion where they will praise God.[55] Mission work is priestly work; it is about the gathering of the 'first fruits' and then offering these as a sacrifice to God.

A beautiful example of this liturgically tinted speech is, finally, found in Philippians 2.14–18.[56] Here Paul addresses the Christian church first as a typical diaspora community; they 'shine like stars in the world in the midst of a crooked and perverse generation' (verse 15). This idiom reminds us of the images that I have discussed in the previous chapter, about the missionary vision of the Jewish people in exile. The whole atmosphere of the text reflects this tradition of the future restoration of Israel, when 'every knee shall bend' (verse 10; compare Isa. 45.23), and when light will shine from Israel to the ends of the earth.[57] In this context Paul speaks about his own possible death as a 'libation' that is shed 'over the sacrifice and the offering of your faith' (verse 17). With these terms Paul pictures the congregation of Philippi as people who bring sacrifices and perform a 'liturgy'. In other words, he pictures them as a community of priests.[58]

To wrap this up: if the Church as a priest represents humanity before God, this means that her existence is essentially doxological. The Church gives thanks and praise to God, as the redeemed part of creation, and she invites others to join her in doing this. This does not mean that the Christian community denies the existence of evil in the world; on the contrary, it praises God for the very reason that his mercies have entered this world where so much evil occurs. The Church's joy about 'rains from heaven and fruitful seasons' is *joy* precisely because she knows how fragile and undeserved such gifts are. Nobody is grateful for what is ordinary or experienced as a right; gratitude is born in the discovery that everything good that happens to us is a surprising gift. Knowing God means primarily to recognize God's gracious gifts.[59]

That, then, is the first meaning of priesthood, in which the Church represents the world before God. Next we look at the second meaning: as a priest, the Church also represents God to the world. What does this mean? Above all, this: the Church is a 'showcase', a sign of God's purposes with his creation. As a kingdom of priests, Israel was to be a model of dedication to God; it was to be transparent towards God for all peoples.[60]

At the same time it is crucial to see how this gets a concrete shape with Peter.[61] The Church in this epistle is not a radiant, white city on a high mountain, gaped at with admiration by the people below. The Church is not an exclusive community of untouchable saints who travel through the wilderness of this world. Their priesthood gets concrete form first and foremost in response to questions, accusations, slander, curiosity; and it is rooted in the example of Christ. The Christian community is committed to its environment by blessing, service and prayer. Peter does not allow any misunderstanding about the thoroughly missional intention of this priestly identity of the Church. Immediately after he has called the Church a 'priesthood' he expresses his desire that non-believers 'may see your honorable deeds and glorify God when he comes to judge' (1 Peter 2.12). He urges women who are married to non-Christian husbands to 'win' their spouses through their conduct, without words (3.1). As true priests, Christians will 'repay abuse with a blessing' (3.9). Because the priesthood of the Church flows directly from its bond with Christ, the suffering King-Priest, Peter can present the missionary lifestyle of the Church as following the example of Jesus. A priest does no harm, and does not repay abuse with abuse. By contrast, a priest brings love and tolerance into the world (2.21–25). Just as Jesus gave himself for the salvation of God's world, the Church is called to give itself as a token of God's love. 'In your hearts sanctify Christ as Lord,' says Peter. 'Always be ready to make your defence to anyone who demands from you an account of the hope that is in you; yet do it with gentleness and reverence' (3.15–16).

In sum: as a representative of God among humanity the Christian community has a serving, friendly, patient, witnessing, blessing lifestyle, just like Jesus Christ who leads it as a priest. Its existence is characterized by hope for God's salvation, but also by the hope that people around her will glorify God.

To me these two directions of the priesthood – representing the world before God and God before the world – form the core of what it means to be a missionary community of 'aliens'. Here lies in my opinion a wealth of meaning – to be explored further in the next chapters – by which we can get beyond the problems that cling to outdated models of mission (see Chapter 3). The metaphor of the priesthood allows us to accept our minority existence as a hopeful calling, without necessarily heading towards a collusion with the world. In the next chapter I want to draw attention to another important aspect of the Church as a priesthood – its deeply relational nature.

5.4 Summary and Conclusion

In our search for a missional identity of Christian communities in a largely post-Christian culture we have arrived at two core metaphors, those of 'pilgrim' and 'priest'. Both metaphors have been derived from the first letter of Peter. This letter lines up well with the Old Testament discourse of 'exile' and (especially) 'diaspora'. The description of the Christian community as 'strangers' or 'pilgrims' who live in 'dispersion' resonates with the experience of the Western Church as largely 'disembedded' from its surrounding culture, while at the same time re-emphasizing its orientation towards God's future kingdom breaking in to the world. The term 'stranger' also underlines the importance of caring about your own identity, something which requires purposeful maintenance – especially in a secular context. This emphasis on identity maintenance is reinforced by another important metaphor: the Church as a holy 'kingdom of priests'. By embracing this identity the Church accepts a positive relationship with the world through which it travels as a pilgrim. The Church receives its identity as a priest from Christ, the suffering Priest-King who is the link between Old Testament Israel (Ex. 19) and the New Testament community. The priest metaphor defines the missionary nature of the Church as a dual movement: the Church represents the world before God and she represents God before the world. She comes into the presence of God as a worshipping, praising, liturgical community and she engages with the world in a witnessing, inviting, friendly way. In short, while passing through the world as pilgrims, Christians bless God on behalf of the world, and they bless the world on behalf of God.

Notes

1 To be clear: in writing this I do not join uncritically an Anabaptist view of the folk church (see Chapter 3, section 2). Such a vision easily assumes sectarian traits in that it – when speaking about God's judgement – applies this judgement solely on the 'other'. Those who do so can reconstruct their own position as a beam of light through the dark history of Europe, and the current crisis can be presented as a divine affirmation that 'we were right after all'. But, as has been argued in Chapter 3, the Anabaptist perspective is just as well part of the great vision of unity of Christendom. The sins of the past are not only represented by the folk church's arrogance, but also by the lust for purity on the part of dissenting churches. The so-called 'free' and 'seceded' churches share in the malaise of the unravelling Christian culture.

2 In the Old Testament we do not find a neat terminological distinction between 'exile' and 'diaspora', even though distinct traditions are clearly suggested. The Septuagint (Greek translation of the OT) uses *diaspora* to indicate the 'dispersion' and exile of the Jews among the gentiles (Deut. 28.25; 30.4; Neh. 1.9, etc.). In the intertestamentary literature *diaspora* is used both for dispersion as a consequence of forced deportation, and for dispersion as a consequence of voluntary migration. For all this, see Santos, '*Diaspora* in the New Testament', pp. 6–8.

3 On the relationship between diaspora and mission, see Cruchley-Jones, 'Entering Exile'.

4 Opinions differ on the meaning of the 'twelve tribes in the dispersion' in James 1.1, but the majority view tends to see this as a reference to Jewish Christians who lived dispersed in the Roman Empire. It is also possible to think of a more specific reference to Jewish Christians who had escaped Jerusalem after the first persecutions (Acts 8.1–4; 11.19). See Floor, Jakobus, pp. 46–7.

5 Santos, '*Diaspora* in the New Testament', pp. 5–6, who presents the majority view.

6 See, e.g., Groody, 'The Church on the Move', who mentions a 'theology of migration'.

7 Literature on this subject is abundant. See, e.g., Wan, *Diaspora Missiology*.

8 It is rather peculiar that the first letter of Peter has been ignored for so long in missiology and cultural theology. In his famous book *Christ and Culture* (1951), for example, H. Richard Niebuhr discusses five different relations between the Christian community and its surrounding culture, invariably based on biblical or early Christian 'paradigms'. Miroslav Volf points out how the first letter of Peter is remarkably lacking in the book, despite the fact that the letter is entirely devoted to exploring the life of Christians in the world (Volf, 'Soft Difference', p. 16). The Dutch theologian Klaas Schilder, who preceded Niebuhr with the similarly titled

study *Christus en Cultuur* (1947), does not discuss Peter either. It is possible that both authors (and others as well) were still too captured by an attempt to 'think together' the whole world and society, and to relate it to 'Christ' (emphatically not: Jesus). The modest piecemeal approach that Peter presents to us, seems to fit more into the experience of a minority community, to whom such a comprehensive vision of society is less appropriate or relevant (for an extensive description and discussion of different Christian church–world paradigms, see Keller, *Center Church*, pp. 194–217). Understandably this modesty and lack of comprehensiveness did not appeal to theologians of previous generations, who were living in a Christian culture. Yet, it is striking that 1 Peter is also virtually absent where you would not expect it, namely in the most influential missiological textbook of the twentieth century, *Transforming Mission* by David J. Bosch (1991; reprinted for the twenty-fifth time in 2011). For this, see Jennings, 'Christian Mission'. One would expect that someone who dedicates more than a hundred fascinating pages to New Testament 'models' of mission (*Transforming Mission*, pp. 15–178) would have spent a few lines on the epistle that thematizes this more than most other texts in the New Testament. Incidentally, Bosch is aware of the fact that 1 Peter 2.9 is the background of much contemporary writing about the missional church (*Transforming Mission*, pp. 372, 374, 493).

9 While older research routinely characterized the first letter of Peter as a late, pseudepigraphical text that was dependent on the epistles of Paul to a high degree, the original and relatively independent nature of the letter is recently much more emphasized, while the date has been pushed backwards (Elliott, 'Rehabilitation'). Consequent on this rehabilitation, the number of studies on 1 Peter has hugely increased. For a survey since 1985, see Dubis, 'Research'. For a series of Bible studies based on 1 Peter, and focused on post-Christendom America, see Thompson, *The Church in Exile*. Much literature on the missionary significance of 1 Peter can be found in Stenschke, 'Reading First Peter'.

10 Peter uses many different terms to designate the Church. For an overview, see Gangel, 'Pictures'.

11 Peter employs two concepts for 'alienhood', which both refer to the Old Testament 'resident alien' or the non-Israelite who was allowed to live in the land of Israel (1.1: *parepidèmos*; 1.17: *paroikia*; 2.11: *paroikoi kai parepidèmoi*). This contains a clear salvation historical reference to the acceptance of the gentiles into the people of God, as appears from the Hosea citation in 2.10. Another Old Testament parallel is the wandering existence of the patriarchs in Canaan (cf. Deut. 26.5: 'a wandering Aramean'). Think also of Lev. 19.34 (and similar texts), which ground the commandment to love the stranger on Israel's own sojourn 'as a stranger in the land of Egypt'. Here the emphasis lies on the identity of the people of God in a gentile culture. For the use of such concepts in the New Testament, see Feldmeier, *Die Christen als Fremde*; Wassenaar, *Vreemdelingschap*, pp. 18–53.

12 Stefan Paas, 'Vreemd, vreemdeling'.

13 At the same time it must be stressed that precisely the fact that the stranger, upon circumcision, was allowed to join native Jews in every cultic and ritual dimension, shows how the ethnic distinction between the native Israelite and the stranger is strongly relativized in the Old Testament. Eventually, the boundary between those who belong to God's people and those who don't is determined by acceptance of God's law rather than ethnic descent. See, for example, the book of Ruth.

14 Cf. 1.15, 17, 18; 2.12; 3.1, 2, 16.

15 Volf, 'Soft Difference', p. 20 (italics in the original).

16 Cf. Fagbemi, 'Living for Christ'.

17 Cf. Stroope, *Transcending Mission*, pp. 373–6.

18 Lewis, *Mere Christianity*, p. 135.

19 For an extensive discussion of Augustine's views of politics, see my *Vrede stichten*.

20 So too Van Houwelingen, *1 Petrus*, pp. 36–8. Volf, 'Soft Difference', pp. 20–1, points here to three important aspects: (1) Nowhere in 1 Peter is the Church urged to distance itself from the surrounding *culture*; Christians should just distance themselves from their own *past*, and from human (not 'worldly') 'desires' (1.18; 2.11; 4.2). So, the identity formation is positive rather than negative; it is namely oriented towards the example of a holy God (1.15–16) and the suffering Christ (2.21–24). (2) The image of the devil as a lion that 'prowls around' (5.8) indicates that evil to Peter is not primarily a realm or a culture outside the Church, but that it is 'mobile', capable of ambushing us in the most unexpected places (including the Church). (3) Nowhere is Peter busy cursing or threatening the world outside the Church. He rather points to the special place of Christians before God (2.9–10). 'Christian hope, not the damnation of non-Christians, figures centrally in the letter (see 1:3; 3:15).'

21 Cf. Volf, 'Soft Difference', p. 26: 'The stress on Christian difference notwithstanding, the "world" does not seem a monolithic place in 1 Peter. We encounter evil people who persecute Christians and who will continue to do the same, blaspheming what is most holy to Christians (4:4, 12). We come across ignorant and foolish people who will be silenced by Christian good behaviour (2:15). We meet people who know what is wrong and what is right and are ready to relate to Christians accordingly (2:14). Finally, we encounter people who see, appreciate, and are finally won over to the Christian faith (2:12; 3:1) . . . This testifies to a sensitivity in 1 Peter for the complexity of the social environment.' NB: we find the same complexity in Luke 10.1–12, where Jesus sends out his disciples in pairs. He sends them 'like lambs into the midst of wolves' (v. 3), but apparently this does not exclude that they will meet 'persons of peace' (v. 6).

22 Volf, 'Soft Difference', pp. 18–19.

23 Cf. the Encyclical *Deus Caritas est* (God is love) by Benedict XVI (25 December 2005): 'Being Christian is not the result of an ethical choice or a lofty idea, but the encounter with an event, a person, which gives life a new horizon and a decisive direction' (Introduction, section 1).

24 Anyway, this second-century letter is a wonderful illustration of what it means for Christians to be 'alien', in the ecclesiological way in which this concept is used in 1 Peter.

25 Frost, *Exiles*, p. 3.

26 Cf. also Brueggemann, *Cadences of Home*.

27 For an extensive discussion of these chapters in their Ancient Near Eastern context, see Walton, *The Lost World of Genesis One*, esp. pp. 71–106; Walton, *The Lost World of Adam and Eve*, esp. pp. 104–27.

28 Tomlin, *The Widening Circle*, p. 75.

29 *The Widening Circle*, p. 76. See also Anizor, Voss, *Representing Christ*.

30 Schmemann, *For the Life of the World*, p. 15. Italics in the original.

31 *For the Life of the World*, pp. 60–1. Cf. pp. 92–3.

32 Williams, 'Changing', pp. 178–9.

33 Cf. Rev. 1.6; 5.10; 20.6.

34 Here I continue my discussion from Chapter 4, section 6, on the development of a missionary vision among second temple Judaism. With his emphatic

reference to the role of the faith community as 'priests' in the world, Peter is close to this Jewish diaspora tradition.

35 Peter uses the Greek word *hierateuma*. The singular that is used indicates the identity of an entire group, and is usually translated as 'priesthood'. Note, however, that this word can mean two things in English: a reference to the *office* of priesthood (function) and also a reference to a social or professional *group* acting together as priests (collective; cf. 'brotherhood'). The second, collectivist, meaning is assumed here: the Christian community is a community of priests.

36 Most interpreters prefer this translation (Van Houwelingen, *1 Petrus*, p. 82). Van Houwelingen also suggests that the 'sprinkling' with Christ's blood in 1.2 is a reference to the ordination of priests in Ex. 29.19–21; Lev. 8.30 (*1 Petrus*, p. 49).

37 The Septuagint adds the same phrase in Ex. 23.22 ('kingdom of priests and holy nation'). The expression 'holy community of priests' in 1 Peter 2.5 is a contraction of 'kingdom of priests' and 'holy nation' in Ex. 19.6. See further Isa. 61.6.

38 Wright, *The Mission of God*, pp. 224–5.

39 Wright, *The Mission of God*, pp. 256–7. Cf. Köstenberger, 'Mission in the General Epistles', p. 202; Bartholomew, 'Introduction', pp. 2–3; Goheen, *A Light to the Nations*, pp. 36–40.

40 This is developed extensively and, in my opinion, convincingly by Voss, *The Priesthood of All Believers*, chapter 2. In the remainder of this section I draw on his study, which employs a large amount of early Christian and modern scholarly literature.

41 Thus many interpreters, cited by Voss, *Priesthood*, pp. 83–4, fn. 34–6. A similar royal-priestly figure ('according to the order of Melchizedek') is encountered in Ps. 110, the most-cited Old Testament text in the New. This again suggests a dominant tradition in which kingship and priesthood were projected on a messianic figure.

42 Voss, *Priesthood*, pp. 88–95, discusses five texts that attribute priestly titles to the offspring of the messianic servant. Their priesthood gives them a 'new level of priestly access to Yahweh and his divine instructions' (p. 91). For this transition of 'servant' to 'servants', see also Dekker, 'Servant'.

43 In this context it is striking that the eunuch/stranger in Acts 8 is reading the book of Isaiah, and has just arrived at the fourth Servant Song (Isa. 53) when he meets the evangelist Philip. We may assume that Luke has included this story exactly because of this, as an indication that the messianic time of salvation has appeared.

44 Cf. Voss, *Priesthood*, p. 98.

45 Voss, *Priesthood*, pp. 100–4.

46 To be clear: this book is not a biblical-theological study but a missiological one. I do not pretend to produce a balanced or complete exegesis of these Bible texts, nor that my view is the end of all debate. My concern is merely that what I have to say about God, the world, the Church and priesthood is theologically responsible and contextually relevant.

47 This is underlined by the centrality of cultic images of the Church and Christian life in the New Testament. On the ecclesiological structure 'priest' – 'temple' – 'sacrifice', see Voss, *Priesthood*, passim. Cf. further Beale, *Temple*.

48 Without exploring this further: the word 'liturgy' is derived from Greek *leitourgia* ('ministry on behalf of the people'). When in ancient Greece, for example, a warship needed to be equipped, and a wealthy citizen donated the money that was required, this action was called a 'liturgy'. In the Greek translation of the Old

Testament (the Septuagint) this word is subsequently used to describe the priestly ministry in the temple (see Wolterstorff, 'The Reformed Liturgy').

49 See especially §3.7.3 and §7.5.

50 Schmemann, *For the Life of the World*, p. 25.

51 Healy, 'Ecclesiology, Ethnography, and God', pp. 198–9.

52 It a debated issue whether this 'proclaiming the mighy acts of God' has a missionary significance, that is, whether humans may be the address of this proclamation too. Several authors point out that this 'proclaiming' (*exaggelein*) is a cultic term and emphatically directed towards God. Therefore, '[v]on einer missionarischen Verkündigung an die Mitwelt kann an dieser Stelle (noch) keine Rede sein', concludes Gäckle (*Allgemeines Priestertum*, p. 449), even though he admits that in this praise to God a missionary echo can be heard, and that this does not do anything to diminish the missionary claim of other texts in 1 Peter (Gäckle, *Allgemeines Priestertum*, p. 450). This exclusive identification as cultic praise is contested, however, by other authors such as Seland, 'Resident Aliens', pp. 583–5, who points out that *exaggellein* in the Septuagint does not always have a clear cultic meaning (cf. Ps. 9.15; 72.78; Sir. 39.10; 44.15), whereas Isa. 43.21 (the text cited by Peter) has *diègeomai*, where Peter writes *exaggellein*. This can mean that Peter wanted to emphasize the cultic meaning of this sentence, but also that for him both terms were synonyms. Probably it is sensible not to play out these two directions of 'proclaiming' against each other: the congregation praises God by a holy life that at the same time provokes missionary questions in its neighbourhood (cf. Fagbemi, 'Transformation', pp. 216–17).

53 For this passage, cf. Flemming, *Contextualization in the New Testament*, pp. 66–72.

54 For a recent discussion, see Gäckle, *Allgemeines Priestertum*, pp. 347–61.

55 Wright, *The Mission of God*, pp. 525–6.

56 My discussion of this text is based on Ware, *The Mission of the Church*, pp. 251–82.

57 For this text, see §4.6. Apparently, Paul opines that the coming of Jesus Christ ushers in God's future and thus the restoration of Israel.

58 Ware, *The Mission of the Church*, p. 272.

59 Gratitude is the essence of a classical Reformed spirituality, thus Wolterstorff, *Until Justice & Peace Embrace*, pp. 14–15.

60 Goheen, *A Light to the Nations*, p. 38.

61 Cf. Seland, 'Resident Aliens', pp. 565–89 (for a survey of missiological studies of 1 Peter, see p. 567, fn. 5). See also Cailing, '"That You May Proclaim"'.

6

All Together and Each One in Person

A colleague of mine once shared a story, and I still don't know whether it was meant as a joke. She described a church service where Communion was celebrated. In this congregation it was customary to invite the visitors and guests to stand up first, and introduce themselves. The invitation was something like this: 'Please, tell us who you are, why you want to share Communion with us, and whether you live in peace with your own church.' An elderly man stood up, mentioned his name, and then solemnly said: 'I am not a member of any congregation, because I belong to the invisible and universal Church of Christ.' A reverent silence descended on the congregation, because what can you say after such a pious statement? But the pastor responded wittily: 'Perhaps you should then celebrate Communion in that church, brother.'

Modern Christians – and Protestants in particular – more often than not tend to separate their Christian identity from participating in a concrete, earthly community of faith. 'Church', at best, is an addition to Christian identity, or a tool to improve and protect it, but it is not a genuine part of what it means to be a Christian. In the present chapter, therefore, I want to pay attention to another important aspect of the priesthood of the Church: its nature as a community. I believe this aspect is immensely important for contemporary religious consumers. Here I will first develop this communal nature of the priesthood a bit further. Next, I will try and show how this is relevant for spirituality, our understanding of salvation, and for evangelism.

6.1 'Priesthood' and 'Priests'

The term 'priest(hood)' in 1 Peter 2 has been interpreted by many Christians as a reference to the 'priesthood of all believers'. If all believers are priests, then the distinction between clergy and laity is relativized. To Martin Luther, and others in his trail, this insight appeared to function primarily within the Christian community. As priests who are joined with Christ, Christians have unlimited access to the Father. They intercede, they bring sacrifices of gratitude and holy lives, they are all allowed to participate in Holy Communion, and in emergency situations every Christian has permission to preach and administer the sacraments.[1] In this way there was, at least in theory, a tremendous emancipation of the 'ordinary' church member, whereas the life of a Christian was redefined based on his or her connection with Christ. The role of the 'special' priestly office – priests, pastors, bishops and such officials – thus became less important. Believers could approach God directly, without mediation of an ordained office-holder.

In a world that was fundamentally understood as 'Christian' this common priesthood could not be developed further than 'upward' (the relationship with God) and 'inward' (relationships with one another). Only with the work of the twentieth-century theologian Karl Barth we see a widening of the priesthood of the believer in 'outward' direction (the relationship with the world). According to Barth, this priesthood is intimately bound up with the testimony of the Church in the world: each member of the Church has, by virtue of his or her baptism, the liberty to proclaim the gospel here and now, depending on his or her gifts and vocation.[2] This missional revisiting of the doctrine of the general priesthood by Barth has exerted a huge influence on missiologists like Hendrik Kraemer,[3] Lesslie Newbigin,[4] David Bosch[5] and Darrell Guder.[6] In their missionary ecclesiologies the witness of the congregation is crucial, and this receives concrete shape by equipping 'ordinary' members of the Church for serving and evangelizing their neighbours.[7]

This emphasis on the individual calling of the faithful to be witnesses is an essential and necessary enrichment of the doctrine of the priesthood of all believers. Yet, it is important to reason carefully, as mistakes are easily made. There is a kind of hyper-Protestantism that uses the priesthood of all believers to question the phenomenon of 'church' as such. In late-modern missionary literature this has almost become routine. Currently, much attention is focused on 'post-church Christians'. For one reason or another such people have become frustrated about the actual life of concrete congregations, and they continue their 'faith journey' beyond the church.[8] Often they organize themselves in forms of community, but these are usually loose and provisional. Their identity as Christian does not appear to be determined by these groups; on the contrary, precisely their identity as Christians has led them to seek their salvation outside the church. According to George Barna, such 'revolutionaries' experience that they can only grow in their relationship with Christ when they look outside the church for new forms of spirituality, community and mission.[9] The dominant metaphor in such descriptions is usually that of a 'journey': the individual has been touched directly by God, is individually empowered by the vision of the kingdom, and decides to hit the road based on this experience – hopefully together with some fellow travellers but if needs be without them. In this journey the church is nothing more than an intermediate station – and often a source of irritation above all.

I don't want to claim that it is impossible to be a Christian without going to church.[10] Also I don't want to deny that many people may have very good reasons why they never want to darken the doors of a church again. Sadly, churches can be unsafe places for people who deviate from unwritten norms of religious exaltation, fundamentalism, heterosexuality, etc. As far as I am concerned it is a good thing if such people find each other and can support each other in their faith. Furthermore, I am glad that there are opportunities to hear a good sermon via the Internet or the television, or to sing in a choir. And let me reiterate that theologians and church leaders would do the smart thing if they listen to Christians who have ended up outside the church. There is much to be learned from them.[11] But I do not agree with the tough anti-institutional language of Barna. I am not at all convinced that these groups of Christian church-leavers are the vanguard of Christianity, a priesthood generation par excellence. There is certainly a place for Christians who perform their pilgrimage and mission at or even outside the unruly margins of the institutional church, but I do not believe that this is where the future of Christianity in the West must be sought. For that, I see too many practical odds and ends.

Under certain conditions such an extra-ecclesial group may surely develop into a community that is rooted within the Christian tradition, offers a safe and inspiring home for the soul, engages missionally with its neighbourhood, and maintains fruitful relations with other Christian communities. But if that happens, then in my view this group is no longer *outside* the Church. Unfortunately, what I also often get to see is that such groups run aground somewhere halfway through this development. For example, I remember a visit once to a post-evangelical group of rather wounded Christians in London, together with some mission-minded friends from the Netherlands. When we left, we were quite astounded about the conversations we'd had: somehow they all seemed to revolve around issues like beer drinking (apparently, a big thing for former Baptists and lapsed Pentecostals), using the f-word a lot (undoubtedly very liberating), and the constant venting of frustrations about the churches they had left behind. When asked if there was anything *positive* they believed and strove for, the answers were rather vague and included a lot of references to 'mystery' and 'inclusion'.[12] This and similar experiences have left me with the lasting impression that a Christian community needs a positive missional vision above all, and that too many so-called 'fresh' or 'experimental' Christian communities are predominantly therapeutic groups, where damaged people manage to maintain some fragments of their former faith, but without much appeal and witness to those who don't share their background and sensitivities. Thus, relationships with other

Christian communities are also in peril, especially when these communities smack too much of 'denominations' and 'traditions'. Such groups may be a useful safety net for people who cannot take the church any more, but they are not a fully fledged expression of the 'kingdom of priests' Peter writes about. Christian identity in such post-ecclesial faith journeys easily assumes a gnostic character: the individual bonds with an invisible, spiritual church or with an idealistic kingdom of God, without engaging with a concrete, human community of Christ in a local congregation that is connected with other congregations.[13]

At this point we could learn from the way Jewish communities in diaspora cared about their identity (see Chapter 4, section 5). From a purely sociological point of view it is highly doubtful that serious Christian faith can flourish in a secular culture without being embedded in a firm community, spiritual practices and a liturgical tradition. Every study in this field proves otherwise.[14] But theologically there are also major questions: this thrust towards post-ecclesial faith journeys seems rather dependent on the model of the 'church inside out', where the distinction between church and world is insufficiently acknowledged (see Chapter 3, section 5). Its advocates seem to say that people can be just as good (or even better) Christians if they separate from a visible faith community. Perhaps this was possible once, when the whole culture was soaked in Christianity. But in the current post-Christian society this is very difficult for most people – except perhaps for some prophetic figures with a specific calling.[15] In this sense this whole approach is still firmly wedded to a Christendom mindset.

In 1 Peter 2.4–9 we clearly receive some push-back at this point. It must be asserted that the term 'priesthood' in this passage does not primarily denote *individual* believers, but it is a *collective* term. Peter is not talking about 'priests' in the plural, as the sum of many individuals, but he employs a word in the *singular*: 'priesthood'. Insofar as believers participate in the Church they are members of the 'priestly community' (*hierateuma*), and consequent on this they are also priests individually.[16] But the order is crucial. God does not appoint individuals as priests in order to bring them subsequently together in a congregation. Precisely the opposite is true: by virtue of their baptism Christians are joined with Christ, embedded in the Church, and only thus they receive priestly status.

This does not mean that the Protestant emphasis on the priesthood of every believer is unbiblical, but we must stress that the believer receives this priesthood by virtue of his or her membership of Christ's body. In said hyper-Protestant views more often than not the Church is seen as the sum of (saved, sanctified) individuals who join together based on their own preferences. The Church receives its existence, as it were, from these individuals and thus always has a somewhat secondary, derived nature. In short:

God has first and foremost a relationship with isolated individuals, and through them he builds the Church. The Church is God's Church to the extent that the individuals out of which the Church is composed belong to God. Opposed to this view, however, is an ecclesiology that is based on recent (twentieth-century) explorations of early Christian literature and a renewed reading of the New Testament through the lens of the Church Fathers. Here it is said that the Church precedes the individual, and that the individual receives his or her Christian identity through participation in the Church. In short: God has first and foremost a relationship with the Church, and through the Church he builds relationships with individuals. To be a Christian means to belong to the Church, and so to belong to God.

This bears important missionary consequences. After all, if God builds the Church through saved individuals, the Church will always lack something as long as there are still people outside the Church. In some sense, the Church will only be fully realized if every single individual on earth has been saved and enfolded into a church body. An emphasis on church growth is the logical consequence of this view. At the same time, the peculiar fact presents itself that it is hard to explain *why* these saved individuals would become members of a church in the first place. Surely, salvation has already happened between God and the individual; membership of a church does not make an essential difference. Typical of this missiology is thus a functionalist approach of ecclesiology: the Church is not really necessary, but sometimes it comes in handy. Young believers can find support, resources can be used more efficiently, church planting is an effective instrument of evangelization, Christians can find some protection against the world, they can organize missions together, and so forth. Salvation is not ecclesial in nature, but for salvation to have its optimal effect on people, the Church – or at least some form of community – can be useful.

However, if God relates with individuals through the Church rather than the other way around, then the Church is also fully realized when it counts only a small minority of the world population as its active membership. It is fully church even if only a fraction of the village attends on Sunday. Even if there are very few *priests* (perhaps only two or three), there is a complete priest*hood*. Then the emphasis lies less on numerical church growth or on attempts to define non-Christians within the Church by sophisticated semantics; instead it lies much more on the quality of the Church's mediation between God and its context. The New Testament metaphors of 'salt', 'yeast' and 'light', but also the image of 'priesthood', make this clear. By definition these metaphors picture a minority, but it is a minority that serves the surrounding world in various ways.

Moreover, this approach explains why the Church is important; being a Christian implies above all participation in the Church. You receive your identity as a Christian through baptism, connecting you with the community of the Church. Salvation is ecclesiological; it means being incorporated into the people of God, the body of Christ. To belong to Christ is to belong to his Church; there is no other way. As the early Christian bishop Cyprian said: 'Outside the church there is no salvation' (*extra ecclesiam nulla salus*).[17] This should not be misunderstood as an arrogant claim for exclusivity by the all-powerful umbrella Church of Christendom; nor should it be framed as a billboard of a late-modern 'consumer-oriented vendor of salvation' (Bryan Stone).

> But [this slogan] is quite right as a post-Constantinian expression of the ecclesiological shape of salvation and Christian practice. Salvation is impossible apart from the church, not because the church has received salvation as a possession and is now in a position to dispense it or withhold it from others. *It is instead because salvation is, in the first place, a distinct form of social existence.* To be saved is to be made part of a new people and a new politics, the body of Christ.[18]

What does this 'ecclesiological shape of salvation' mean for being a missional church in a post-Christian context? To this question we now turn.

6.2 Experiencing God in Community

Some readers may have felt some irritation while reading the previous section. Individualization has stamped our minds and lives so profoundly that we have serious problems in imagining what it means to receive a Christian identity above all through the church community. To some extent this theology runs counter to the Protestant imagination, while it may trigger some (post-)Catholic frustrations at the same time. Therefore, I want to draw out this perspective a bit more in this section and the next.

At the beginning of Chapter 5 I suggested that the lack of experience of God is one of the characteristics of life in exile. The entire symbolic and institutional framework that rendered God close and present has crumbled away. Faith in God is no longer a matter of common decency or normality (obligation). Instead we are thrown back on our own motivation and desire (see Chapter 2, section 1). If faith no longer comes from the outside, it must be fanned from the inside. Late-modern spirituality is profoundly individualized: everybody is to find his or her own private connection with God. For some this connection is made of philosophical arguments and empirical evidence (including signs and miracles); for many others this consists of positive inner experiences (feel-good spirituality).

Within Christian tradition this type of spirituality has found an ally in pietism. In this stream of faith it has always been stressed that true faith is a matter of the individual and his or her God. Real spirituality is a matter of the heart; it is an intimate sense that the gospel is true *for me*. This assurance of spiritual truth can only be attained individually; we cannot receive it from others. Surely, God does not have grandchildren, right? This shows that we cannot just attribute this individualization of spirituality to the cultural exile of Christianity in the modern age. Within Christianity itself there is a thrust towards individuality, as for example Larry Siedentop has argued.[19] Early modern pietism, however, pushed this to the extreme, while this individualizing tendency of Christianity accelerated by the rapid erosion of the Christendom framework in the twentieth century.

However, regardless of whether the chicken came first or the egg, serious problems ensue from such an extremely individualized spirituality. To begin with, it isolates us from the community of believers by pushing us into an atmosphere of spiritual competition. If it is true that God first relates to the community, and through the community with individuals, then there is something strange in this striving to find an individual connection with God for each and every one. An important part of the Christian faith experience has always been that God demonstrates himself to the community of the Church, whereby he gives more light to some than to others. Perhaps, we can call such especially graced people 'saints'. Other believers have by no means always direct experiences of God, but they rely on the testimony of others – Bible writers, Apostles, the saints in every generation, the mothers in Israel. This is why faith is, by definition, communal; it is structured as a covenant. Faith is certainly personal, but it is not individual. The idea that everyone should have his or her own, unique, high-quality experience of God is a product of a modern consumer society rather than an authentic Christian thought. The result of this consumers' spirituality is that testimonies of special experiences of God are often encountered with a mixture of envy and scepticism. One person thinks: 'I wish I had that.' The other thinks: 'There's another religious nut.' More or less the same response is seen when the Joneses buy a nice new car, while the rest of the neighbours still drive a second-hand model.

In such an individualized, and thus competitive, spiritual climate people prefer to remain silent about their experiences with God (if scepticism is the spirit of the group) or – and this also happens – they pretend to have experiences with God (fake it if you can't make it). There are a lot of churches where people feverishly bid against each other with spectacular sensations of the Spirit, and where miracles and signs are the buzz of every Sunday. I see this mostly as an effect of an individualized spirituality; we cannot live with the thought that God reveals his special presence only now and then, and only to some people. An unhealthy spiritual climate follows suit. In some churches people no longer dare to believe that God sometimes privileges people with his special grace; in other churches people shout down their doubt, or they drop out because of the hypocrisy they see on stage in every worship event.

We should realize that we are first and foremost *persons*, not individuals. To be a person is to be in relation, to be given to each other. Personal knowledge of God is not the same as individual knowledge of God. It is quite normal that for many believers, *individually speaking*, special and powerful experiences of God are scarce or virtually non-existent. Especially graced individuals are rare. In the Bible too we see that God sometimes doesn't call any prophets for generations at a stretch. However, if the congregation is not primarily a loose collection of individual 'priests', but a priestly *community*, then spiritually there is an 'us' that precedes 'me'. God is in a relation with 'us' and through this with 'me' – not the other way around. In loving mutual relations, in the path of following Jesus together (see John 7.17) and in the gatherings of the congregation, our faith in God grows. And as to 'special' experiences of God, even though they are revealed to the few, they are meant for the upbuilding of the whole community. In this sense they are nobody's property; they are gifts to be shared. Nobody receives such an experience only for herself; God demonstrates himself to all via the few. My personal experience with God is also (and sometimes only) the experience that God has given to me *via the testimony of others*. Therefore, we must foster a culture where stories about experiences can be shared, without raising the impression that everyone should have such experiences. Our first response to such testimonies must not be envy or scepticism (unless in the event of an unhealthy spiritual climate), but wonder: what is it that God wants to tell us through this testimony? Sharing testimonies of such experiences should lead to joyful gratitude: the proclamation of the 'mighty acts' of God in past and present (1 Peter 2.9). Christian spirituality thus assumes that we live in community with the Church, both the living Church on earth and the Church of previous generations. We can only experience what God does, if we meet him where he is: in the community of his people, in authentic relations where faith is shared. That is why sincere, warm, loving bonds are so crucial to a rich spiritual life.

With this we have arrived at another problem of an individualized spirituality. Precisely this modern quest for an individual experience of faith cuts us off from one of the most important ways to experience God: other human beings. If we are indeed on our own, it is obvious that we must seek God in our own soul or in argumentation or in all sorts of special occurrences. We will have to mistrust everything that we have not devised with our own minds or experienced in our own lives. Such

a quest actually amounts to the same thing every time: we position ourselves as individuals over against reality, and we try to find God there.
We 'objectify' God, as it were, rendering him into an object of examination and study. But is this how we can find God? Without exploring this
in detail, I would point out that in the Bible God is presented as a person.
You cannot meet a person as the conclusion of an argument, or as a link
in a chain of evidence. Of course, we can examine someone or describe
him or her through argumentation, but in doing so we will never meet
him or her as a *person*. In examining a person we make her a thing; 'we
murder to dissect' (Wordsworth). It is characteristic of a person that we
can only experience him or her in an encounter 'from face to face'. This
is what the Bible means by living 'before the face of God'. It is impossible
to objectify or 'reify' someone's personality; you cannot study it from a
distance. Precisely then the other's being-a-person will elude you. That
what is necessary in scientific analysis, namely disengagement and objec-
tification, precludes a personal encounter.

This is the same with God. We live 'before God's face', in his personal
presence. In this world he is present, not as an object of study but as the
one who wants to be encountered in and through his creation. We see this
most clearly in the Incarnation: God became human in Jesus Christ. It is
the Incarnation that renders every personal relationship into a sacrament
of encountering God.

For a healthy Christian spirituality this is extremely important.
Christian faith directs us towards the God who became human, who
'faces' us, and who calls himself 'I am'. Christian spirituality does not
mean that we get a grip on God through reasoning and experience, but
that we meet him – incarnationally and sacramentally – in the reality of
this world.[20] And this encounter happens, above all, in a real human contact. In the words of author Marilynne Robinson:

> One of the things I like about John Calvin is that he always talks about
> people as being presented to us, or even given to us. What he means is that
> any encounter with another human being is like God posing a question . . .
> [T]o me it's much more meaningful than Zen or something like that. It
> opens the world. It's not a place of refuge, it's a place where the exhilara-
> tions of reality are presented to you, almost at the level of demand.[21]

An encounter like this with a fellow human can unsettle us. It can be a
moral appeal to us, and impress on us a sense of guilt. Who can look into
the eyes of a starving child for more than a heartbeat? Rather than blaming
God (how can he allow this to happen?), as modern Western people tend
to do, we sense that God looks at us through these breaking eyes, asking us:
how on earth could *you* let this happen? How can you live with the death

of even a single child, while you have all the resources to rescue it from starvation and malaria? In such encounters God speaks to us, he judges us and appeals to us. But a true human encounter can also be a sacrament of God's love. Or, perhaps better put, God's love that became flesh in Jesus underwrites every gentle human touch and gives it a meaning beyond itself. Something of this notion is expressed by the poet Christian Wiman who, through a serious and very painful disease, saw the way to Jesus.

> I am a Christian . . . because I understand that moment of Christ's passion to have meaning in my own life, and what it means is that the absolutely solitary and singular nature of extreme human pain is an illusion. I'm not suggesting that ministering angels are going to come down and comfort you as you die. I'm suggesting that Christ's suffering shatters the iron walls around individual human suffering, that Christ's compassion makes extreme human compassion – to the point of death, even – possible. Human love can reach right into death, then, but not if it is merely human love.[22]

Insofar as our society prevents genuine human encounters, it is a society where the experience of God is fading. The secularization of our imagination is much to do with the modern quest for autonomy. This quest leads us to disengagement, to functional relationships, to objectifying persons rather than engaging them and becoming dependent on them. All too often we are placed in competitive relations with our fellow human beings. Work stress and pressure for efficiency will do the rest. In such a formalized world God gets out of sight, because true relationships become scarce. The more we are on our own, the more we will be metaphysically lonely. Precisely by the other person we are placed before God and touched by him. 'God', writes Roger Scruton, 'is understood not through metaphysical speculations concerning the ground of being, but through communion with our fellow humans.' It is in this community that God is no longer an 'it', but a 'thou' and an 'I' who meets us as a person.[23]

Of course, this is by far not everything that can be said about Christian spirituality, but in my view this shows how important it is to understand Christian spirituality from the perspective of community. Here, an important key might be found for recovering the experience of God in an age of exile.

6.3   Salvation and the Church

Outside the Church there is no salvation, Cyprian said. And he was not the only one. But what, then, is this salvation? Above I have said something about spirituality, but that is not enough. Salvation is not the same as *experiencing* God; to receive salvation means that we enter a forgiving and healing *relationship* with God. An incarnated, sacramental spirituality can penetrate us with a sense of responsibility and guilt. It can touch us profoundly with an awareness of superhuman love and patience. Yet the kind of salvation the Christian tradition speaks about touches deeper levels: it is about forgiveness, reconciliation, intimacy and adoption as God's child, together with your brothers and sisters. Therefore, I think it is good to add something on the relation between community and salvation, as it is understood in the Christian faith.

At this point it is fascinating to see how in the twentieth century almost all major Christian traditions have come closer together in their discovery of what is often called *koinonia* ecclesiology.[24] *Koinonia* is the Greek word for 'community', and this is exactly what God's salvation is about. Surely, community begins with and flows from God: Father, Son and Spirit are mutually related through eternal love. The three persons of the Trinity never exist or act in isolation; they always exist and act in mutual dependency. Relationality is essential for a Christian understanding of who God is. Thus we can also begin to understand who we are as humans. As God's image-bearers, humans are *relational* beings. People are destined to partake in the life of the divine Trinity (John 17.22). This happens most visibly and tangibly in the worship of the creature to her creator – she is *homo adorans* (Alexander Schmemann). Here, in worship, a human being responds to the eternal gift of God's love, and thus he or she returns into the loving community of Godself. Praising God, as creation's priesthood, is to express the very essence of our being. Again we see why doxology (worship) is central in a theology that takes the Church seriously as community with Christ. Here too we may think of Peter who writes about the Church that she is a 'priesthood', called to 'offer spiritual sacrifices' (1 Peter 2.5) and to 'proclaim the mighty acts of God' (verse 9).

We can therefore say that salvation is essentially this: the restoration of community. It is social by nature. People reach their destiny and thus God, when they are united with God in worship and reconciled to each other. Here we see the structure of the Great Commandment being reflected: love God above all and your neighbour as yourself. This structure is relational; it is aimed at the establishing and reinforcing of a community bound together by love and oriented towards God in loving praise. The same principle is visible in the Lord's Prayer, when we ask God to 'forgive us our trespasses, as we forgive those who trespass against us'. Again, this is all about the restoration of relationship; it is about being brought into communion. The principal feature of sin is, after all, a lack of love; it is the human tendency to autonomy, the desire to define yourself independent of relationships, and thus to make the 'other' secondary to yourself. This is a major obstacle in becoming a true person.[25] Hell, as Sartre has said so poignantly, is where the 'other' becomes my enemy by his sheer presence, and remains so in all eternity. Throughout the history of salvation God is working at the restoration of humanity; he is building a kingdom of love and justice. The coming of Jesus Christ to this world was the core event in this work: 'In Christ God was reconciling the world to himself' (2 Cor. 5.19). Salvation takes place when people are incorporated in Christ, that is, in his body. Christ is the true human, who embodies what a restored community is about.

If we accept this, we can also see that God's mission to his world is *ecclesiological* in shape. The Orthodox theologian John Zizioulas expresses this eloquently:

> [E]cclesial being is bound to the very being of God. From the fact that a human being is a member of the Church, he becomes an 'image of God', he exists as God Himself exists, he takes on God's 'way of being'. This way of being is not a moral attainment, something that man accomplishes. It is a way of *relationship* with the world, with other people and with God, an event of *communion*, and that is why it cannot be realized as the achievement of the individual, but only as an ecclesial fact.[26]

If salvation is indeed the restoration of community and if it is to be more than pie in the sky, then there must be a place where this really happens. There must be a community where salvation is real, even if provisionally and partially. This community is the Church. Here it becomes clear how a theology of community and relationality will inevitably lead to an 'upgrading' of the Church. The Church is not an 'extra' or a useful addition to the real thing. She belongs essentially to what God does with humans. To be saved in the New Testament means that one belongs to the community of salvation, the body of Christ. As I have said above, faith is personal but it is never individual. The Church is the form chosen by God through which his final plan for humanity and the world is realized. This means that we are to take the Church very seriously. At the same time the Church is not the last word. She is the visible form that God's mission now assumes, but she is not the full restoration of creation. The Church is the 'foretaste' or 'sign' (rather than 'instrument') of the eventual restoration, but she does not coincide with it (see also Chapter 3, section 7).

A community ecclesiology, as it is described here, finds its natural centre in the tangible celebration of community: the Eucharist.[27] This is where Peter's 'holy kingdom of priests' gathers as a community to glorify and give thanks to God. The Eucharist is more than the celebration of

Communion;[28] it is the service of Word, prayer and sacrament that constitutes the community of the Church and renders it visible at the same time (1 Cor. 10.6–17). We should not think of the Eucharist as the celebration of a previously existing community, more or less like a neighbourhood having an annual barbecue to congratulate itself on its good fellowship. Nor should we think of the Eucharist as an anchor place for individual religious needs, much like a spiritual fast-food outlet where strangers meet and pass by each other like ships in the night. In the eucharistic event of Word, prayer and sacrament, Christ continually creates the community of the Church; this is where the personal character of our existence is made visible, and where we are given to each other time and again. And this is what it means to become the body of Christ: to be joined together as a body by being joined to his body (cf. 1 Cor. 10.16–17).[29] Also, precisely because the Eucharist is not the affirmation of an existing 'natural' community (like a family or a neighbourhood), it is always open and inviting. The network of relationships that begins here will continue into the world, extending salvation through human contact to the ends of the earth and until the end of time. In other words, the Eucharist is the core of the missional identity of the Church; it is the constant sacrament of its openness to Christ who builds community out of strangers by sharing himself with them. By celebrating the eucharistic event the Church confesses that its community is never finished, that it will never become a 'natural' community based on blood, soil or lifestyle options.

Thus, through prayer, proclamation, attentive listening and worship, the congregation – depicted in the New Testament as priesthood, temple and sacrifice – arrives at its destiny in God.[30] To be clear, nothing of what has been said so far assumes a specific liturgical *style*, even less an old-fashioned or traditional style. It is not the exact style of the liturgy that is crucial (although its quality and beauty are important), but the fact that there is a structured encounter with Christ through Word, sacrament and prayer. If someone wants to know what Christianity is about, the best way to find out is to participate in Christian worship (cf. 1 Cor. 14.14–17, 23–25).[31] From a missionary perspective this is extremely relevant in a post-Christian culture, as Sunday worship is one of the very few places where Christian language is spoken and passed on without limitation. With this, the church service is a reservoir of 'God-talk' for all of society.[32] It is one of the few remaining places where words for God, prayer, sin, grace, glory, non-monetary value and eternal life are freely used.

Of course, this does not mean that being church amounts to a series of Sunday worship meetings. The Eucharist says what the Church is in its essence, but it does not delimit the extent of its reach or its actions. The community of the Church also exists outside communal worship; she is a workplace of the Spirit during weekdays as well. As priests Christians are called to serve their fellow priests and to build them up with their gifts. They are called to extend the life of the community into the lives of others who do not yet belong to the community of salvation. The life of worship and celebration is radiated outside the Sunday worship, into the other days of the week and outside the community. All activities of the Church are considered as expressions of the same reality that is celebrated during the Eucharist – the community with Christ and one another.[33]

6.4 Mission and Community

Viewed through this lens of koinonia theology, the mission of the triune God may be defined as the restoration of his fallen creation in his image. Or, more briefly, God's mission is about the *restoration and renewal of relationships*. This bears on human relationships first. God is out to build a humanity that is characterized by mutual giving and receiving, by forgiveness and reconciliation, by bringing out the best in one another through joyful service – a humanity that is characterized by God's reign. In other words, it is God's plan to restore the priesthood of humanity, renewing our calling to lead creation in the worship of its creator. For this priesthood to be effective, priests must be in peace with their communities and with non-human creation.

Here we might recall the holistic character of mission, as set out in Chapter 1, exploring the so-called 'five marks of global mission'. Regardless of whether there should be exactly five marks rather than four, six or nine, the crucial point is that the different dimensions of mission – evangelism, discipleship, seeking justice, serving the poor, caring for the planet – are joined at the roots. For example, it is impossible to have true compassion for the poor without paying attention to the ecological damage that is often the cause of their poverty in the first place – as pope Francis has argued convincingly in his Encyclical *Laudato Si'* (2015). And how could churches evangelize credibly in the secular, post-Christian city without being involved in justice and environmental issues? Conversely, how could the Church be a witness to Christ without making explicit in whose name she cares about pollution or the plight of the poor? The point is, all these dimensions fall into perspective once we have accepted humanity's role as the priesthood of creation. To bless creation on God's behalf is much more than extending a 'gospel invitation' to unbelievers (although it certainly includes that as well), and to bless God on behalf of creation is much more than offering him the souls of the 'saved'.

In terms of local communities this may mean that some accept evangelism and discipleship as their first calling, while exploring justice, service and ecological care as consequences of discipleship and understanding the gospel of Christ. Other churches may come across God's mission through the needs of the poor, through suffering under unjust regimes, or via their shared love of non-human creation, but wherever they begin they are to discover that all these dimensions assume each other somehow, and give depth to each other. Perhaps the worst thing that could happen to churches is that these different dimensions of God's mission become bones of contention, dividing the Church between 'liberals' who love justice, and 'evangelicals' who prefer evangelism. Rather they should be seen as different stepping-stones towards the abundance and totality of God's mission, both for churches and individual Christians, depending on their gifts, experiences and spirituality. Let one church enter God's mission through accepting its ecological responsibility, and then find out how this relates to discipleship, serving the poor, finding justice and proclaiming Christ as the high priest of creation. Let another church organize Alpha courses, and find out how God's grace opens our hearts for the poor and to responsible lifestyles. Rather than locking ourselves up in our own perspective on God's mission, and use this as a moral high ground from where to judge others, we might accept the particular dimension that has touched our hearts as a first step towards wider explorations into God's mission and our priesthood. And this will inevitably lead us towards a common search, together with Christians of different stripes, learning from each other what it means to be priests of creation.

Let us now take one step back and ask how one becomes a member of such a community. In other words, if the restoration of relationships is key to God's mission, how does this work out on the level of a local church? Perhaps the best way to imagine the missional vision that is bound up with koinonia ecclesiology is to view the eucharistic event as a lamp that shines its light in various directions, or as a well that overflows into a great number of streams. The Sunday worship brings the congregation into God's presence as priests, to praise him, to receive his grace and to offer him sacrifices; but it also sends out the congregation as priests into the world to give tangible, concrete shape to community with Christ and one another. To be clear, this runs counter to a view of mission that lays all emphasis on individual salvation, isolated from the restoration of community. As we have seen above, there is no individual salvation without reconciliation and renewed relationships. God saves people by bringing them into community with Christ and thus with others. The mission of the Church is aimed at bringing people into a relationship with a eucharistic community, or to plant such a community where it is not yet present. Mission is about 'initiation' into salvation. Moreover, the Church in its mission to the world will make every effort for the restoration of communities and against everything that blocks this reconciliation.

This view of the Church as a priestly community may lead to a more relaxed approach to the question as to what extent people should be actively involved in the Church in order to enjoy God's salvation.[34] Communities tend to be messy around the edges; relationships are usually widely ramified and difficult to map with much precision. Around the biblical temple there were also forecourts and outbuildings, there were temple servants and suppliers, and beggars lay at the gates. In the Gospel of John, chapter 15, Jesus says about his disciples that they are connected with him like branches to the vine. And he says that the Father will cut off every branch that bears no fruit. But a vine can be immensely ramified, creeping along walls and over wooden carriers in various ways, some-times stretching out so far that it is impossible to see where it ends. Yet the juice stream reaches the extreme end, even if this is much thinner than the branches close to the trunk. Who can say that he or she knows exactly how many fruits the Father wants to see and how long he is prepared to wait before they appear? Who can tell for sure how far the Spirit is willing to go into the world outside the boundaries of the Church? At this point we are to pay our respects to an ancient folk church idea: even if there is a theological distinction between the Church and the world, we should not be too concerned about the exact location of the dividing line. Precisely the view that salvation happens in and through the community, should make us wary of limiting this salvation to the community of active churchgoers. Essentially, this approach is too dependent on individualism, as it limits the community to those who have chosen to belong via an explicit and well-informed confession. A more collective approach is open towards the countless ways in which the eucharistic community ramifies itself in its environment – via spouses who are 'holy' through their partners (1 Cor. 7.14–15), through friends and colleagues who request prayer, through 'outsiders' and 'unbelievers' who attend worship services now and then (1 Cor. 14), and through those who are tarrying on the threshold.

By saying that salvation operates in all these relationships, I do not advocate 'universal salvation' as if everybody purely on the basis of his or her humanity shares in God's salvation.[35] In my view this is a mech-anistic, dogmatic position that renders evangelism superfluous. Such an armchair theology removes all creative tension. Remember, this book is not a dogmatic study of soteriology; it is first and foremost a study into missional spirituality. Rather than trying to present a more or less authoritative view of who belongs in God's kingdom and who doesn't, I want to encourage missional practitioners not to give up on reaching out to people even if they are often quite unwilling to become members of a church. When people are not 'converted' and refuse to develop an interest in churchgoing, it is worthwhile in itself to make friends with them, to share each other's lives, to have genuine conversations, to serve and bless them as priests. In and through all this the 'juice stream' of God's salvation is flowing, and only God knows how far and to what effect. I would like to discourage abstract reflections on the precise criteria as to counting someone as 'saved'. Such discussions are often remarkably removed from a truly missional practice. By contrast, I advocate a practice that does justice to the fact that God relates primarily to communities, and that the outside edges of communities are always frayed. Developing such a practice is what it means to *walk* in the truth, rather than have discussions about it. And if anybody has borne with me so far it should also be clear that all this is far from saying that evangelism is not required any more. This would be claiming the exact opposite of what I wrote about God's mission. If God predominantly works through community, salvation will just happen via genuine contacts, through real relationships. If anything, this will encourage us to embrace the cruciality of going and reaching out to people, to serve them and witness to them in daily life, hoping and trusting that this will somehow be used by the Spirit to reconnect people with the eucharistic heart of creation – if only indirectly and remotely. Evangelism, therefore, is all about making friends, creating relationships and making these relationships a channel of deep and rich human contact, a location for witness. The congregation is created by the Word, through which the Spirit works. And in every meaningful relationship where words and deeds of salvation are happening, the Spirit flows even to the most extreme branches.

Therefore it is necessary that the community actively seeks to expand its relational network, that it invests in building true contacts through which the gospel can be shared. Without mission the community will not extend its reach, and there is no mission without evangelism. Only a more collective view does not consider evangelism a failure when people won't become active members. They are carried and lifted up by the community of priests with whom they are personally connected through bonds of love and friendship. If salvation occurs through relations, if the Spirit flows into the farthest branches, we are not to patrol constantly the outward boundaries, but we should guard the core eucharistic event and build paths towards this core. I repeat: all this is impossible to realize without an actual priesthood. Without active, pastoral and evangelizing interference of the congregation with its context there is no use speculating about people and their relation with God's salvation.

Seeing the Church as a foretaste and sign of the full restoration of creation (rather than a project that we must bring to completion) contains hope for the future of the world. Just like the Church is not the perfect community with Christ and one another, the world is certainly not yet restored. But God is active in both, and he works towards his purpose in mysterious ways. Christ is not just the Lord of the Church, but also of creation (Eph. 1.10). And if the Eucharist is the heart and engine of ecclesial life, then there must be an effect of this in all sorts of visible and invisible ways far beyond the boundaries of the community. Undoubtedly it is better if people regularly participate in worship, but it is difficult to explain why people would be outside salvation if they show up only once every year. The question of salvation is approached more 'objectively' in this view; it is realized primarily in the community with Christ and each other. Salvation does not depend on our 'subjective' stance or on our effort to attend as many meetings as possible. At the same time, the emphasis on community with each other implies that people are naturally missed when they are not there, and that it is important for their community with Christ to be in community with fellow Christians. Everybody is needed, because salvation is realized in the reconciliation and growth of mutual love.

As said, this view agrees well with Peter's metaphor of 'priesthood'. The organic unity of the Church with Christ and the central character of the liturgy are core moments, both for Peter and in this 'community ecclesiology'. What attracts me above all in this approach is the missionary potential of the Church as a priestly community, especially in a culture where only a minority can be bothered with (organized) Christianity. This potential is what the next chapter is about.

6.5   Summary and Conclusion

The term 'priest(hood)' points to the nature of salvation: to be a Christian means, first and foremost, to belong to Christ's Church. Salvation means that we are restored into community with God and each other, and this does not happen outside the body of Christ. What Christianity is becomes most visible in the celebration of a liturgical community, which subsequently has its fallout in the world in all sorts of ways. Especially in the development of a serious practice of evangelism, it becomes concrete that salvation happens in and through community.

Notes

1 For an overview of Luther's theology of the general priesthood, see Voss, *Priesthood*, pp. 186–208.

2 Discussion in Voss, *Priesthood*, pp. 223–45.

3 See Kraemer, *Het vergeten ambt*. Translated as *A Theology of the Laity*.

4 For this, see esp. the extensive study of Newbigin's ecclesiology by Goheen, *As the Father Has Sent Me*.

5 See, e.g., Livingston, *A Missiology of the Road*, pp. 253–359.

6 E.g., Guder, 'The Church as Missional Community', p. 122, who states that the 'first resources' of a missional ecclesiology 'can be traced in Luther's vision of the priesthood of all believers'.

7 As I have explained in section 3.5, the neo-Calvinist model of 'cultural trans-formation' and the neo-Barthian approach show family resemblance.

8 Cf. Jamieson, *A Churchless Faith*.

9 Barna, *Revolution*.

10 Fascinating principled debates on this topic have been conducted in missiology, esp. with regard to the so-called 'Jesus Hindus' and 'Jesus Muslims'. As for India, I refer to the debate between M. M. Thomas and Lesslie Newbigin on 'conversion' and 'community' (see Hunsberger, 'Conversion and Community'). As regards Muslims, see the so-called 'C1 – C6 spectrum' (John Travis), as explained and discussed in a.o. *Evangelical Missions Quarterly* 34.4 (October 1998). Both discussions are about the question as to what extent a Hindu or a Muslim is able to follow Jesus if he or she does not join a Christian community, keeps attending the mosque or the temple, and so on.

11 As, for example, Tomáš Halík shows time and again in his books.

12 Christopher B. James points out similar features of so-called 'New Community' churches in his study of church planting in Seattle. Such churches, often of an emerging nature and entertaining more or less 'liberal' theologies, are defined to a large extent by their rejection of evangelicalism (and are often populated by people with an evangelical background). The burden of their frustrations clearly hampers them in the performance of actual mission, both in terms of evangelism and social justice – despite a lot of rhetoric about justice, inclusion and peace (*Church Planting*, pp. 112–25).

13 Cf. Newman, 'Priesthood'. On catholicity (i.e., connection with other churches) as an important point of attention for 'emerging' faith communities, see Gay, *Remixing*, pp. 69–70, 99–102, 111–13.

14 Research in Western societies show a firm correlation between regular church attendance and orthodox Christian beliefs. Moreover, it appears that such beliefs usually erode if someone leaves the church, while there is solid evidence that little success is to be expected from a faith education without churchgoing. See, e.g., Gill, *Churchgoing and Christian Ethics*, esp. pp. 59–93; Walker, *Testing Fresh Expressions*, esp. pp. 111–24. As to India, see Hoefer, *Churchless Christianity*, and Jeyaraj, *Followers of Christ*, who both describe how followers of Jesus in India may remain outside the organized church, yet form communities that gather regularly around a Christ-centred liturgy. For this, see also Duerksen, *Ecclesial Identities*.

15 To me it seems probable that some prophetic individuals are called by God to give expression to their Christian identity outside the institutionalized church. Especially in our post-Christian culture such figures, who are in between the Church and the world, as it were, are required. But even they will somehow be connected with a form of Christian community (friendships, retreats, literature, etc.).

16 Van Houwelingen, *1 Petrus*, pp. 83–5. It is important, though, to add this individual dimension. Some interpreters seem to derive from the collective nature of the priesthood in Ex. 19.6 and 1 Peter 2.4, 9 that an individual application is out of the question even secondarily (cf. e.g., Elliott, *Elect and the Holy*, pp. xiii–xiv, 63–70; Elliott, *1 Peter*, pp. 406–55; Gäckle, *Allgemeines Priestertum*, p. 445, but also pp. 469–70). Excluding the individual dimension altogether would contradict a series of claims in early Church literature (see, extensively, Voss, *Priesthood*, pp. 40–60). Therefore it would amount to overstating the case to dismiss an

individualizing interpretation as the consequence of modern developments. Surely, the collective precedes the individual here, but it does not replace the individual (see also Voss, *Priesthood*, pp. 290–3, where Voss warns against individualistic and collectivistic perversions of the priesthood of all believers).

17 *Ep.* 72, §21.

18 Stone, *Evangelism after Christendom*, p. 188 (my italics).

19 Siedentop, *Inventing the Individual*.

20 More on this sacramental worldview in Boersma, *Heavenly Participation*.

21 Sarah Pulliam Baily, 'Interview: Marilynne Robinson on the Language of Faith in Writing', *Religion News Service*, 8 October 2014 (online).

22 Wiman, *My Bright Abyss*, p. 15.

23 Scruton, *The Face of God*, p. 21.

24 For the remainder of this section, see esp. Ploeger, *Celebrating Church*, pp. 459–541.

25 I have written on the relationship between 'freedom' and 'equality' in the context of a Christian understanding of the person (building on the theological work of Colin Gunton, Alistair McFadyen and others) in *Vrede stichten*, chapter 4.

26 Zizioulas, *Being as Communion*, p. 15.

27 'Eucharist' is derived from Greek *eucharistein*, which means 'giving thanks'. It is the classical term for Holy Communion or the Mass. When applied to ecclesiology, the term 'eucharistic' is generally used in a wider sense so that it denotes a way of ecclesial being in which gratitude and praise are the core of a common Christian existence. We might translate it here as 'worship service' or 'celebration'.

28 Cf. Schmemann, *For the Life of the World*, pp. 32–3: '[T]he liturgy of the Word is as sacramental as the sacrament is "evangelical". The sacrament is a manifestation of the Word . . . The proclamation of the Word is a sacramental act par excellence because it is a transforming act. It transforms the human words of the Gospel into the Word of God and the manifestation of the Kingdom.'

29 For some discussion of this relationship between the 'eucharistic body' of Christ shared in the bread and wine of communion, and the 'ecclesial body' of the Church that originates from this, see Boersma, *Heavenly Participation*, pp. 112–14.

30 With regard to the sermon, Ploeger emphasizes that this is not the centre of the liturgy but certainly an indispensable component. In some sense the whole liturgy can be seen as proclamation of the Word, both in words and images. Preaching in this context is not merely an exercise of the mind or the transmission of information, but 'one instance of the way in which God through Christ and the Spirit, draws people to himself' (Ploeger, *Celebrating Church*, p. 492).

31 With this I do not mean that every instance of Christian worship is just as appropriate. Unfortunately, there are cold, distant, boring and inward-focused performances of liturgy. Here I advocate a Christian celebration where the prayers and praise of God's creation are brought before God by the priestly community in a reflective and careful way, and out of a heartfelt involvement and compassion with the congregation's surrounding community. In the worship ceremony there must be clear 'links' with the world in the worship service. This should appear from the prayers, the songs, the conversations, the proclamation, the people who are there. It is obvious that such contextuality requires liturgical flexibility and creativity. See further Chapter 7, sections 3–5.

32 I have expanded on this further in 'Religious Consciousness'.

33 In the tradition of the Orthodox Church the term that is often used here is 'the liturgy after the liturgy', in reference to the Church Father John Chrysostom.

He distinguished two altars: the altar in the church and the altar in the marketplace. The Church performs its liturgy in both contexts. Cf. Bria, *The Liturgy after the Liturgy*.

34 Cf. Ploeger, *Celebrating Church*, p. 429.

35 In its most basic form 'universal salvation' means that all people are saved regardless of whether they believe in Jesus Christ, or have even heard of him. For some advocates of this view this means that there is indeed salvation outside Christ, for others it means that there is only salvation through Christ, but that people can be saved in Christ without knowing it.

7

The Priestly Church

A good friend of my family grew up as a Catholic boy in a predomin-antly Protestant context, back in the heyday of Dutch pillarization – when Catholics and Protestants had organized themselves in antagonistic ghettos of self-righteousness. After university he started a law firm in the west of the Netherlands. Now, as a retired attorney well into his eighties, he lives in the deeply secularized rural area south of Amsterdam. The large majority of his friends and former colleagues aren't believers, but he and his wife attend Mass every Sunday and they sing in the church choir. When I asked him how he had managed to keep the faith, while so many of his generation had dropped out, he answered: 'I guess, what you need is to see the fun of being a bit contrary.'

Being contrary and seeing the fun of it: that may be pretty much what this book is about. I have described a church that understands itself increasingly as a stranger in a post-Christian culture, and yet is not all too depressed about it. By contrast, it is perfectly possible to embrace a minority identity and in so doing find a new mission, through and beyond judgement, as it were. In the previous chapter I have characterized this Church as a priestly Church, inspired by the first letter of Peter. In my view we find in this metaphor an important beginning of identity forma-tion for small Christian communities in a secular culture.

In this concluding chapter I want to draw together a number of lines that have been sketched earlier so as to present my view as coherently as possible. First, I want to show that the idea of a priestly church fits well within a post-Christian culture. At the same time it is biblically respon-sible and ecumenically sensitive. I believe these are both good reasons to take this approach seriously. Then I will explore the practice of a priestly church a bit further. I do this based on three core concepts: community, mission and worship. Of course, my treatment is far from complete or even balanced; I merely want to touch on a few issues that render the priestly church somewhat more tangible. In doing this I hope to show that this 'model'[1] is not only theologically interesting, but that it has something to offer to pastors or mission workers who face the harsh realities of their context.

7.1 Minority

The image of the Church as a priestly community does full justice to the experience of the New Testament writers and many contemporary Christians in the West that the Church is a minority, and that this is the rule rather than the exception (see Chapter 2). Priests are a minority community *by definition*, who find their calling in seeking the peace of the city. There is nothing odd or imperfect about a minority church; on the contrary, it is its 'natural' position.

Therefore, this 'model' fits extremely well into our increasingly post-Christian situation. It takes distance from the grand vision of unity that animates virtually every model that was discussed in Chapter 3. The world is not Christian, and it will not become Christian. At the same time the priestly church accepts (as indicated in the previous chapter) the folk church emphasis on different degrees of involvement and the relative unimportance of sharp organizational distinctions between 'church' and 'world' (which is, after all, God's world). It is clear what salvation is and where it comes from, but it is not so clear where it ends.

Conversely, it is also true that the Church is called out of the world to be distinguished from the world as a 'kingdom of priests' in commitment to God. The priestly church does not express this by positioning itself 'against' the world, but rather by devoting itself to the world of God, working to restore relationships and inviting people to join the worshipping community. Because of its emphasis on the communal character of the Church and salvation (Chapter 6, sections 2–3), the priestly church is quick to say that people are on a path towards Christ, and simultaneously it will always stress that this path must be *gone*, and that it is in some sense never completed. Growth, sanctification, discipleship – they are important words in the priestly church, while it is at the same time very open towards everyone who has a 'link with God'.

On this view the Church is called out of the world and made distinct from the world, without ending up in a position where she necessarily opposes the world. Because she is called to glorify God as the priesthood of humanity, the Church will always look for new sacrificial gifts to offer to God: converts, the gratitude of people inside and outside the Church. She will have a critical view of the liturgies in our culture that alienate people from God and each other, and she will make her own liturgical heart flexible so as to involve people who are seeking God. In this view the Church does not focus its energy first and foremost on answering the question who belongs (if only just) and who doesn't. Instead it will take a centripetal stance: who is and who isn't a Christian is determined above all by the direction people are going, by their orientation towards the eucharistic heart of the Church. The priestly church will concentrate on this core more than on its outward boundaries.[2]

7.2 Biblically Structured and Ecumenically Sensitive

In this 'model' of a priestly church a great number of biblical topics are joined, which together provide a rich and deep identity. In Chapter 4 I already pointed to the traditions of exile and diaspora that are echoing through the entire New Testament, and particularly through this 'model' of the Church as pilgrim and priest. The point is that the priestly church is not just based on a few texts from 1 Peter 2. This ecclesiology is firmly anchored in the Scriptures. This is not just true as far as exile and diaspora are concerned, but also with regard to the liturgical and eucharistic nature of the priestly church. It is no use denying that the Bible speaks in many places about the faith community as a cultic community. The Church is the body of Christ, the Priest-King, she offers herself as a living sacrifice, she is a temple and a community of priests. This is not merely an isolated image or a single metaphor, but a rich, variegated and consistent biblical vocabulary.

Besides, this 'model' accords well with ecumenical insights that see the Church as a community (*koinonia*). I have elaborated on this in the last chapter. This is important for various reasons. On the one hand, the Church must retrieve its original 'script' in a secular, post-Christian age, and this requires a reorientation towards the Bible. On the other hand, the emphasis on the Western mission field and its concurring church models should not lead to ecclesiological isolation. The quest for a missional church doctrine that provides an adequate response to a post-Christian culture should not be absorbed by its own problematic to such an extent that contact with the world Church is lost. This sometimes happens in all-too-Protestant versions of the priesthood of all believers, where the individual believer in fact becomes an ecclesial 'microcosmos' – equipped with everything that the Church needs and therefore essentially autonomous. Such an approach renders the Church superfluous, and therefore it alienates many other Christians around the world. It remains necessary, inside and outside the West, to maintain a recognizable and ecumenically sensitive theological terminology. The 'model' of the priestly church, with its rich biblical content and strong ecumenical echoes, meets this condition.[3]

7.3 Community

Now that the 'model' of the Church as a community of pilgrims and priests has been justified contextually and theologically, I will sketch a number of concrete implications in the remainder of this chapter. I set out with 'community'.

In the previous chapter 'community' came forward as a crucial theme in thinking about what it means to be a church in a post-Christian society. Community is important because as human beings we only reach our destiny in relationships. Salvation is realized through the community in which we learn to love and to be loved, to serve and to be served. Former Anglican archbishop Rowan Williams puts it this way: 'The life of the Christian community has as its rationale – if not invariably its practical reality – the task of teaching us to so order our relations that human beings may see themselves as desired, as the occasion of joy.'[4] If we take this seriously, a congregation must give priority to facilitating deep human relations. Establishing, keeping and expanding community must really be high on the agenda. Without this, salvation cannot be realized.

In my view small communities are better qualified for this than larger ones. The larger an organization is, the more formal its relations and policy, and the more specialized and bureaucratic its functions and offices. Therefore, it may be a good thing that church plants in the more secular areas of the West (especially Europe) rarely grow beyond 50–80 people. And what about older congregations? I remember an expert meeting on church and mission in the Netherlands, where I was on the panel together with a representative of a shrinking small church somewhere in the rural north of the country. His story was rather depressing: the congregation had fallen to no more than 70 members. There was no money for a full-time pastor, and the costs for building maintenance pressed heavily on the dwindling membership. Already a request for dissolution had been made at the denomination's headquarters. I must confess that I was absolutely astonished. Apparently, his entire narrative rested on the assumption that a 'real' church must be big enough to pay for a pastor, to equip a complete church council (and some committees for good measure), and to maintain a building. Theologically these assumptions have very little to do with being church.[5] I am among the last to find such things unimportant, but especially in a time of decline we might rediscover what church is truly about: a celebrating community through which God's salvation manifests itself. It is very possible that many churches must become much smaller in order to see this. The accent on community can thus help us to see opportunities in situations of decline. We may learn to see such a situation as a path through which God leads us into exile, not to abandon us there, but to give us new visions of the future. We often tend to find churches too small, while we should be more concerned whether they are not too big.[6]

In a small church, community can emerge more naturally and more self-evidently. At this point best practices abound, such as a frequent (monthly, weekly or even daily) celebration of Holy Communion, a more interactive or multi-voiced worship service,[7] drinking coffee before and after worship, having meals (whether or not integrated into the liturgy),[8] doing neighbourhood mission (possibly combined with some form of liturgy),[9] retreats and the like. Community is also indispensable for processes of church development and forming a missional vision. At this point I want to join writers such as Pat Keifert and Alan Roxburgh who explain in different ways that a missional vision can never be imported from the outside via successful models or be imposed on a church by a visionary leader. Vision for God's mission emerges among the people of God through a careful process of 'dwelling in the Word' and 'dwelling in the world', in which concrete small-scale experiences of neighbourhood service are brought into conversation with the biblical narrative. Its aim is a profound culture change, not some cosmetic adaptations.[10] Recently, Christopher James has pointed out, based on his careful fieldwork in new churches in Seattle, that this 'neighbourhood' or 'community' church may in fact be the most promising approach of missional ecclesiology today.[11]

Writers like Roxburgh and Keifert are not just well-educated theologians, they also have dozens of years of experience with leading and studying shrinking (mainline) churches in North America. Much of what they write makes sense in the more secularized areas of the West, like where I live. Their point of departure is always that it is God who has led his Church into exile; it is not some alien fate that has struck us. Therefore, we may have confidence that God will speak again in this situation just like he spoke before, if only we are prepared to wait and listen. Waiting, let's have that clear, is an active attitude. The Church will have to embark on a quest to find out what God is doing in this new age for Christianity. This quest should begin very close by, in the daily and mundane life of the neighbourhood. Its approach is based on forming some simple routines in the life of the congregation, routines that allow certain questions to be asked and, above all, to have conversations between the Scriptures and the life of the community in its neighbourhood. Such routines may be compared with cultivating a garden.[12] After all, the Church is not a machine that can be fixed with some blueprints and smart interventions. Rather it is a field, where people surely work hard, but realize at the same time that the growth process is a mystery – fully God's work (1 Cor. 3.6). We cannot make plants grow faster by pulling them out of the soil, or by imposing our will on them.[13] The 'gardening routines' in the Church consist of shared Bible reading, based on spiritual traditions such as *lectio divina*,[14] and on concrete forms of engagement with the neighbourhood. After all, one of the major obstacles for missional work is the lack of meaningful contacts between the Church and its context. This, more than anything else, hinders the realization of a truly missional priesthood.

So this approach is all about a simple, unspectacular way to connect a prayerful engagement with the Word with listening to questions and needs from the context of the Church, trusting that through all this God has something to say, and that he will lead the congregation into missional experiments. The common quest to understand God is here embedded in seeking better relations with each other and the neighbourhood. From this, new questions arise for common reflection: what is God doing in our neighbourhood? How does he want to involve us? How can we as a priesthood present the questions, the joy and the needs of this neighbourhood to God in worship, and how can we bless the lives of people on behalf of God and his story?

7.4 Mission

With these last questions we arrive at a next dimension of the practice of the priestly church. In this section I want primarily to address a number of aspects that are to do with the relationship of the Church with the world. Here too, by the way, I am not talking about a rigid category, as if we should now only talk about the 'outside' of the Church. Just as the section on 'community' also discussed the community with God and relations with the neighbourhood, so is this part not only about the Church's 'external' orientation but just as much about the orientation of the congregation towards God and one another.

Meanwhile I assume it to be clear by now that the priestly church does not choose between being a church 'of', 'for' or 'over against' the people. She is all of these simultaneously, because she represents the people to God and God to the people. In my view this defines priesthood as a motivating and challenging way of being church. The priestly church applies itself to a kind of mission that does not alienate Christians from God, but makes them more dependent and hopeful instead. This is so because this approach does not see the minority situation of the Church as a problem first, but rather as a privilege and a calling.

Much doubt and dropping out happens when young Christians begin to realize that so many people are looking at life very differently, and are very happy nonetheless. So many missionally inspired people get disappointed or burnt out, because they experience that very few people are converted without prior religious socialization. Assuming that everybody should actually be a Christian, these people begin to doubt when they see how few people in very secular contexts really become Christians. However, they should be addressed instead as priests, and be encouraged to take up this calling. To be a priest does not primarily mean that we are constantly worried about people who are not (yet) priests, and likely do not want to become one; it means above all that we apply ourselves to giving God the praise that he deserves also on their behalf. If I go to church as the only one from my street or my family, then I do this also on behalf of my street or my family. To be a Christian at that moment means to be a priest on behalf of those who live in my neighbourhood, to offer sacrifices on behalf of the family. Parents go to represent their children, children to represent their parents, neighbours to represent each other.

This more or less 'substitutionary' churchgoing may provoke questions. However, I fear that many of such questions emerge from our deeply individualized worldviews. We find it extremely difficult to conceptualize what it means to have faith 'for' someone else, or to go to church 'in the name of' another person. The whole symbolic world of 'representation' that underwrites this has become alien to us. In faith, like in most other things, the motto is: each to his or her own. Whoever disagrees will immediately raise suspicion that he or she does not value personal conversion and membership of a faith community. Before we know it, the idea of the 'anonymous Christian' pops up again (see Chapter 3, section 1). Yet it is of the utmost importance to reintroduce this corporate sensitivity into our (missionary) theology. I indicate a few biblical notions that may be helpful here.

In the first place, there is, of course, the priest metaphor itself. In the previous chapter I demonstrated that there is a clear parallel between the priests who were chosen out of Israel on behalf of this people, on the one hand, and Israel that was chosen as a nation of priests out of the world on behalf of humanity, on the other hand. This parallel is suggestive at the least, as also Chapter 4 showed (section 6). Priests approached God 'on behalf of' the people. This people contained all sorts of individuals, and not necessarily only those who agreed with what the priests did in their name.

Second, we may think of a variety of biblical examples in which the faith of one person 'carries' others in one way or another. Here I think especially of Abraham's intercession for the city of Sodom (Gen. 18.16–33). It appears that God is prepared to spare the city because of a small group of righteous people. Apparently this was so even though the inhabitants of the city couldn't care less about the righteous flock in their midst. Their sheer presence could have held back God's judgement of the city, even if Sodom did not repent.

We can also think here of the example of Job who brought sacrifices on behalf of his children when they had partied together. He did this because they might have sinned 'and cursed God in their hearts' (Job 1.5). Nowhere do we read that his children had asked him to do so, and they might not even have known about Job's offerings. His sacrifice could justifiably be called 'substitutionary'; he substitutes what his children possibly have neglected to do. From a more collective understanding of faith this makes sense, but our individualized mind is mystified.

In Acts 15.21 we find a text that is difficult to interpret, where James, the leader of the church in Jerusalem, explains the decision that had just been taken not to circumcise the gentile Christians. There he says: 'For in every city, for generations past, Moses has those who proclaim him, for he has been read aloud every Sabbath in the synagogue.' The Dutch biblical scholar Rob van Houwelingen suggests that we should think here of a representative function of the synagogue: 'Reading the Torah has never been a merely internal Jewish event . . . but it affects the well-being of all society.'[15] In Chapter 4 (section 6) we saw that this thought lines up well with streams in diaspora Judaism where the dispersed people of God are described as 'priests' and 'prophets' of humanity. Their lives and prayers contribute to the well-being of everyone.

Finally, I also think of 1 Corinthians 7 where Paul writes that an unbelieving spouse of a believer 'is made holy' through his wife or her husband. If this would not be the case, writes Paul, their children would be 'unclean'. 'But as it is, they are holy' (verse 14). Again the identity of the believer extends itself, so to speak, over the people with whom he or she is related. Through him or her they are 'holy' and 'clean'. Humans are fundamentally relational beings, to such an extent that even the people with whom a Christian is intimately connected 'benefit' from the bond the Christian has with Christ. God does not pour out his salvation in isolated tubes, but in networks and relationships, abundantly (see also Chapter 6, section 4). In order to fully understand what it means that God loves us as human beings, we should consider that we are *persons*, not individuals. And this means that God loves our relationships.

Summarizing this, we could say that in all these texts a faithful minority performs the liturgy (in its widest sense) for the benefit of a majority who does not share this faith. This performance 'on behalf of' is salvational, even without the knowledge or sympathy of those who benefit from it. I don't know how far we can stretch this. I certainly do not want to play this out against the importance of evangelism and conversion, as this is an emphatic line in the Bible as well (see Chapter 6, section 4; and below). People are to be invited and challenged to entrust themselves to Jesus Christ, and to join a worshipping community. It may be best, therefore, to read these texts precisely in this context of witness and evangelism. Otherwise, they might easily become an excuse for refraining from the proclamation of the good news. Within the context of evangelism such texts are an encouragement for believers. They should know that their faith does play a role in God's upholding of the world. In some way, their faith and prayer 'supports' many more people than they are aware of. What will happen to people who do not worship God is something we should leave to God. Christians can only say: apparently, with God it is not true that each is on his or her own.

This also means that Christians have a much larger evangelizing repertoire at their disposal than merely inviting people to come to church. A priestly attitude creates intimacy with fellow humans. Priests can drop by their neighbours or the city council, and ask them if they can pray for them in the Sunday worship celebration. Priests can praise God on behalf of their non-churched relatives for all the beauty they have received in each other. They can offer the guilt of the world, the neighbourhood and their family to God in the ministry of reconciliation. Some people may appreciate that Christians do this for them, while others don't care or are annoyed. But this provides the Christian minority with a fundamentally important task that they can always perform, regardless of whether the people around them are interested. Praise and intercession in the worship service are *always* on behalf of the world too. Christians worship God in the name of God's world that does not recognize God.[16] This lends a strong and positive identity to people who are not successful in terms of church growth or changing the world. Christians are to believe that they matter in God's world, whether their society recognizes it or not. It creates in them a constant, attentive involvement with their societies, with what matters to people. Thus their love for others grows, and their prayers become stronger and richer.

In the third chapter I called it a great risk for Christian spirituality to think that Christians are placed in the world to change it. Especially where the Church is seen as an 'instrument' for a better world the emphasis often lies on the moral quality that Christians are supposed to demonstrate. What, after all, does it mean to change the world if Christians have nothing 'better' to show for it? With some regularity I talk with young Christians who grew up in a vital congregation in one of the Bible Belt areas of the country and ended up in Amsterdam. Nearly all experience a certain helplessness. It is one thing to know that many people are not interested in the gospel (the gospel, after all, is not 'of human origin' – Gal. 1.11), but it is something else entirely to find out that there are a good number of non-Christians who are kinder, more social and more humanitarian than they will ever be. In a post-Christian society, which is permeated with Christian intuition, it is not easy to make a moral difference. Often this results in Christians who feel that they have to trick the world into believing that it is much worse than it thinks, or in Christians who lose heart. 'What do you mean by "mission"? I am not better than my neighbours!' Part of the crisis of the Church lies exactly here: in the desire to be 'relevant' at all costs. Its outcome is easily guessed: if Christians do not stand out morally, this immediately undermines their mission; but if they do stand out, people will say: 'But surely, you don't have to be a believer to do this.' And of course, examples can always be found of morally gifted people who outperform any Christian without belief in God. This can cause deep despair and eventually loss of faith. After all, what is faith good for if believers are not demonstrably 'better' than others?

A priestly approach of the Church gets us out of this spasm. The Church does not need to confront the world constantly with its immorality. On the contrary, a priestly church can recognize humbly that the post-Christian world, by its radicalized post-Christian morality, often performs 'better' than the Church. She can admit this joyfully and, on behalf of God's world, praise the God whom the world does not know. In this way missionary spirituality arrives at a basic tone of gratitude. Let us thank God every day for all the good that he achieves through believers and unbelievers. Thus we can overcome the pietist heritage that always wants to point the world towards its deficits, offering Jesus as the solution to fill the gaps. This model may not be wrong as such, but it only appeals to the desperate and not to 'strong' and happy people – like so many nowadays. This 'model' of the priestly church thus meets the requirements about doing mission in a culture that we no longer dominate morally or in any other way. What might have been a source of embarrassment and frustration (the goodness of so many non-Christians) now becomes a source of gratitude to a God of so much mercy.

For this thanksgiving on behalf of humanity, people are needed who can represent humanity in the liturgy. This underlines another aspect of evangelism, an aspect that often remains neglected. In our age of world Christianity an awareness begins to grow in the Western Church that the gospel is richer and more multi-coloured than was often thought. In this context Andrew Walls speaks of an 'Ephesian moment', that is, an opportunity to grasp for the first time in a long time what it means to know Christ 'with all the saints' (see Eph. 3.18–19).[17] In his view this is a return to the roots of Christianity, preceding the 'colossal ecumenical failure' of the sixth century.[18] In the first age of world Christianity, between the year AD 70 and the Council of Chalcedon (AD 451), Christianity consisted of a rich variety of cultural and linguistic expressions, while at the same time a sense of community existed between these variations: the conviction that there was, in essence, one Church that was 'diasporically' scattered over the world (1 Peter 1.1). Walls opines that our time more than ever presents the opportunity to restore a sense of 'an intercontinental and crosscultural community of Christians'.[19] Referring to Ephesians 3, he speaks about the 'fullness' of Christ that is revealed through the 'translation of the life of Jesus into the lifeways of all the world's cultures and subcultures through history. None of us can reach Christ's completeness on our own.'[20] Or, in the often-cited words of Kenneth Cragg, '[i]t takes a whole world to understand a whole Christ'.[21]

In my view, this 'Ephesian principle' not only has a bearing on the level of worldwide Christianity, but on every neighbourhood as well. Thus, the priesthood nature of the Church points in a concrete direction when 'direct' evangelism – the practice of invitation to the community and its worship – is concerned. It is not so much the quantitative growth of the Church (the fullness of pews) that is the key issue here, but the growth of its diversity (the fullness of Christ). From a doxological perspective evangelism is about the Church's capacity to represent humanity before God, and its potential to be a truly universal community (regardless of its size in numbers) that displays the fullness of Christ to the world. A 'kingdom of priests' should ask itself in every place and time whether it is really a church that can offer the sacrifices and thanksgivings of the local community to God, and at the same time it should wonder if her community is sufficiently rich in texture and colour to show Christ to humanity. This pertains to the whole range of human diversity: ethnicity, social class, gender and age. Are there groups, generations, classes who are underrepresented or even absent (compare Gal. 3.28)? Are there people in this city who are so lonely that they 'have no one' to carry them to the pool (John 5.7), nobody who praises, prays, sings and speaks in their name?

This approach of evangelism essentially highlights different dimensions from the models (discussed in Chapter 3) that have 'transformation' (through church growth or cultural influence) as their main purpose. Evangelism that is inspired by a transformation model can hardly avoid prioritizing outreach to influential persons, people with some cultural weight. One aims at people who are 'normal' and 'strong', because in this model evangelism is inevitably instrumentalized to achieve cultural transformation. And shouldn't you try to reach these 'normal' and 'strong' people if you want to see serious culture change?

However, when diversity and multi-colouredness become central in evangelism, as only these will show the fullness of Christ, the focus will almost naturally move towards people who are 'deviant' or 'weak'. To make myself clear: I am not here advocating some kind of 'preferential option' (for the poor or whatever group); I merely indicate that the theology of evangelism that is presented here is far less concerned about who is relevant or important in the eyes of the world (without excluding such people, though). There can be real joy here about *every* 'sinner who repents' (Luke 15.10), regardless of whether this sinner is an influential government official or an anonymous refugee. Every human being adds something to the social and cultural variety of the congregation and thus to the fullness of Christ. Therefore, a priestly church is almost self-evidently rooted in the local context, and it focuses at least as much on weak people as on the strong.

Especially for churches who are struggling with great effort to persist within a deeply secularized society, it is important to approach evangelism in this way. When the survival of the church becomes the core issue, questions of quantitative growth tend to prevail. For example, an ageing church will try to attract teenagers in all sorts of ways – and often quite forced. When this does not work out as planned, such churches may easily embrace a theology where evangelism is dismissed as sectarian, something that 'others' (read: evangelicals) do, who place recruitment before the kingdom. However, an ageing church can and should evangelize, not to safeguard its institutional survival, but because in its environment there may be precisely this one person who – regardless of his or her age, fertility and vitality – can add something to the worship of the Church and its knowledge of Christ. And thus a diverse, locally rooted group of ten persons can be more church than a homogeneous group of two thousand who drive their cars in from far and wide every Sunday. Let me make it clear here that I have nothing against large churches as such, but also that size does not really matter for this 'model'. Five elderly women in a rural retirement home can be a priestly church, containing the fullness of Christ in their context, just as well as a thriving multi-generational church in an inner-city neighbourhood.

With this evangelizing dynamic of the priesthood, the Church is characterized as a search to connect people in all possible ways (directly or indirectly) with the eucharistic heart of the Church. It is a 'model' that responds flexibly to the pluralistic multicultural society, and presents a positive ideal: to form a local, representative, worshipping community, 'together with all the saints'. Therefore, this 'model' has ample place for evangelism and conversion, even if Christians know that usually only a minority of humanity will be priests. The desire for the conversion of people is not so much rooted in anxiety about their eternal destiny as in a longing for multi-coloured and variegated worship of God and a rich witness to Christ.

With regard to evangelism, this perspective may be an important correction of much missionary thinking. The traditional practice of evangelism, rooted in the revival experiences of the eighteenth and nineteenth century, took its point of departure in unbelief as a state of rebellion against God, and it stressed the crucialness of escaping God's judgement. Evangelism in this style aims at addressing, or even confronting, all people with a call to conversion, and thus snatch souls from hell. Later this approach was popularized (and sometimes trivialized) into a call to 'make a personal decision for Jesus', so as to be saved from the consequences of sin.

The strength of this approach is that it insists on the importance of evangelism. In Chapter 1 I expressed my surprise about the fact that sharing the good news is currently approached with so much suspicion, both on the left and the right. In one wing of the Church it is considered as outdated, fundamentalist proselytism, while others of a more conservative ilk think that evangelism sacrifices the gospel on the altar of consumerism and activism. At the very least, this pietist school of evangelism tries to do justice to the missionary tradition of Jesus and the Apostles, a tradition that seems rather forgotten in large sectors of the contemporary Western Church. Only, the problem is that the good news is here all too often packaged in fire and brimstone. In my view a much more powerful motivation for evangelism is found in the desire to achieve the 'fullness of Christ', the longing that God be praised by different voices. Nevertheless, the traditional approach of evangelism remains influential, meaning that people are assured that they will be damned as they continue their unconverted lives, but that the gospel (that is, an individualized version thereof) is the entrance to eternal bliss, provided that they will respond to it with sincere repentance. I am not at all asserting that this 'judgemental stream' is entirely absent in apostolic preaching (although it is far less dominant than has often been claimed), but I don't think that this approach is the key to the lock of evangelism.

First, there are serious biblical-theological problems implied in such an evangelistic practice. Is the gospel really a message of 'you will be thrown into the eternal fire, unless you believe', or 'God loves you, but if you don't respond to his love, you will be tortured for all eternity'? Doesn't that amount to a form of spiritual blackmail? What sort of divine 'love' is this? Which image of God do Christians communicate by this practice? How can such an approach lead to sincere, loving worship? The Apostles presented a gospel, 'good news', a tiding of great *joy*. Moreover, is it not too big a claim for us to say that everyone who does not confess Jesus personally is therefore lost? What in the Bible gives us the right to draw such an exact boundary-line between the 'saved' and the 'lost'? Isn't this knowledge God's prerogative? And finally, wouldn't this approach lead people – at least those who believe in it – to an unhealthy obsession with themselves and their own salvation? To what extent is this practice really about God rather than us? Isn't God here subordinated to our human need of soul peace and an assured afterlife?

At the same time, we need to emphasize that our response to the gospel is indeed relevant. With this I don't mean that our response *decides* what God is going to do (God will decide that for himself), but in any case it is relevant for *ourselves*. Typically, biblical language about salvation is process-language. In this context Paul speaks about 'those who are being saved' and 'those who are perishing' (1 Cor. 1.18). In other words, he indicates a *process* through which salvation and damnation are realized in human beings. Perhaps this is the way to put it: 'There is a risk, indeed, that we become harder, that we make our resistance against grace grow. If you don't respond to the message of hope, you run the risk of becoming increasingly hopeless. God's sovereignty and mercy will sound more and more unlikely to your ears. Increasingly, your heart will become "curved in on itself" (*incurvatus in se*). You will resist more and more the reality of God's kingdom, until this reality appears to you as mere foolishness, not worth another thought. And this means that eventually you will be lost. In that stage you don't even *want* to be saved.'

Whatever the force of this example, I only want to make clear that it certainly matters in which direction people are moving – even when their 'lostness' as such may not be the best inspiration for evangelism. I don't know how big those steps in the right direction should be. Also, I don't know how many steps there should be. I don't even know if we can always tell whether someone goes in the right direction at all.[22] That is up to God. Above, I wrote that we may believe that people, even when they keep their distance from Sunday worship, are 'supported' by the faith and prayers of the congregation. Nevertheless, we can underline with the utmost sincerity that it does indeed matter how we respond to the gospel. And at this point any move in the right direction is a movement of salvation.

In my view this approach does justice to two fundamental strands in the biblical witness. The first is the emphasis on human responsibility. It does indeed matter how we respond to God's offer of grace. But there is another strand as well: the irresistibility of God's plan of salvation. God does not depend on us to perform his plan. If we emphasize the first line at the expense of the second, Arminianism looms large. We then end up with a weak God who cannot do anything if humans don't cooperate; we don't take God's will to salvation seriously enough. But if we stress the second line at the expense of the first, universalism comes closer; we then don't take human rebellion seriously enough. At the cross God shows himself as the judging and forgiving God at the same time. Here he shows how seriously he takes our sin and at the same time to what ends he is prepared to go in order to fulfil his plan of salvation. Therefore it is crucial to keep emphasizing that the core of the gospel is 'Christ crucified' (1 Cor. 1.23). This will not solve our theological dilemmas, but it will at the very least help us to keep both lines in view.

Aside from theological problems, the motive of 'saving souls from hell' also confronts Christians with an immense practical challenge. How are we to live with the thought that every single individual who has not yet taken a personal decision for Jesus is hell-bound? Shouldn't we then constantly evangelize, seven days a week and 24 hours a day? How could we sleep, knowing that our neighbour (or a child far away in Nepal) may die tonight? Aren't we obliged to bother our own adult children incessantly, even if this damages relationships? After all, is there any kind of temporary earthly peace, harmony or love that outweighs the prospect of eternal torture? I can see how this approach can motivate Christians into evangelistic activity, but I find it much more difficult to see how it avoids legalism and activism. And usually this will result in hypocrisy, that is, a gap between theology and life. After all, nobody can meet the demand that is implied by this 'saving the lost' rhetoric, so that there is always blood on our hands – and not because of our reluctance or rebellion, but simply as a consequence of the fact that we cannot be everywhere at the same time, and that we need our sleep now and then. Thus, this particular theology of evangelism seems to create a serious gap between a highly idealistic love that wants to save people from hell, and the daily neighbourly love that we are indebted to give to our children, friends, colleagues and ourselves. This is the sort of theology that tends to create less-than-human evangelists who talk about love all the time, but are experienced by virtually all people around them as quite unloving and inflexible. Furthermore, this theology inspires a superficial kind of evangelism, geared towards speed and efficiency, and resulting in baptizing with a sprinkler. Is someone evangelized if he or she has heard a radio message, or if he or she was given a tract by a hurried evangelist who is on his way already to the next lost soul? Let us admit that an incarnational, personal, witnessing style of evangelism is 'slow', and that it cannot meet the demand that every individual must have received a gospel invitation before he or she dies.

Much more fundamental is it to take our starting point in the *gloria Dei*, the glory of God. This doxological approach stimulates evangelism just as well, but it does not begin with the question who is or isn't going to hell. Instead it begins with the question how the congregation can glorify God, as a royal priesthood, the first fruits of the harvest. Also, this way of evangelism is less susceptible to manipulation and pressure, because it wants to glorify God also in its methods. In the concluding section I want to dig this out a bit further.

7.5 Doxology

According to Peter's first letter, the Church does not exist to change the world or to expand constantly. The Church exists 'to proclaim the mighty acts (or 'virtues') of God' (2.9). With a theological phrase you could therefore say that 'doxology' is the purpose of the Church. This word is derived from the Greek *doxa* (glory, honour), and it means something like 'to give honour' or 'to give praise'. This does not mean that Christians always walk around with big smiles, or that the Church's worship services are to be an ecstatic wall of sound. Doxology is all about the recognition of God as God; it is to acknowledge him as the creator and sustainer of all that is alive, the one who has saved us from sin and judgement. Certainly, this recognition begins with gratitude, with the joy that arises from the awareness of God's good will towards us. Praise is a grateful response towards the one who has come to us in freedom and love. The bottom line of doxology is joy and gratitude. But exactly this also gives rise to questions and laments. After all, if there were no reason to be grateful to God, there would be no reason to accuse him. If God were indifferent or impotent, there would be no point in praising him, but nor would there be anything to complain about. Precisely this fact that we recognize God as our loving creator, sustainer and redeemer means that we also question him and take issue with his governance. Even when we assail him with our sadness and rage, we address him as the God of heaven and earth, the Father of Jesus Christ.

To live doxologically, therefore, does not at all mean that we suppress everything that disturbs our happy-clappy peace of mind. By contrast, it means that we bring *all* of our lives and that of our loved ones – everything we are and own – before God, and leave it there, out of a deep sense that God is merciful and loving (but not necessarily more intelligible because of that). Even if we accuse him or cry out to him in anger and grief, we give him honour. Indeed, we then recognize him as the God who holds this creation in his hand, and leads it to its future. In the right pitch, the outcry 'How long, O Lord, will you forget us?' is more doxological than many a pious statement of resignation.

So, the Church is on earth to glorify God, in every tone and every form. This purpose of the Church is concentrated most in the liturgy, the Sunday worship gathering. I have called this the 'eucharistic heart' of the Church: you can see best what a church is by attending a celebration of this community of exiles and priests who in all sorts of ways are meaningfully connected to their neighbourhood. They sing, sigh, lament, shout, pray, cheer to God on behalf of a world that does not know or recognize him. And they invite others to join.

This purpose of the Church also determines the theology and practice of mission.[23] In this book I have tried to explore what it means to be missional in a culture that does not, or only very rarely, ask for God. Already in the seventeenth century the Dutch theologian Gisbertus Voetius (1589–1676) wrote about the 'glorification of divine grace' as the most important goal of mission, even more important than conversion or church planting. Other Reformed theologians, like Johan Herman Bavinck (1895–1964), have followed him in this. But in fact this emphasis is found in every serious reflection on mission.[24] In the end such reflection must get beyond a practical strategy or optimism about what we can do. When it comes to 'proclaiming the mighty acts of God' we might also get beyond the constant dilemmas in mission, such as that between words and deeds, or between evangelism and social justice. God's glory surpasses them all.[25]

At the conclusion of this book I only return to the most important doxological motives that I have touched on. As far as the meaning and importance of doxology go, it is easy to fill a library, so I will try to keep it as brief as possible. Here I am mostly interested in aspects that are important for small churches in a predominantly secular context. I summarize these as: looking back, looking around and looking ahead. With a bit of good will we might recognize the most important 'lines of sight' of the Eucharist (or Holy Communion): looking back to remember the death of the Lord, looking around to become aware of each other, and looking ahead to wait for the Lord.

Looking Back

Glorifying God begins with looking back, 'remembering'. Doxology keeps the memory of the congregation alive of what God has done in Jesus Christ. However, this is something not just to remember; in worship the Church 'internalizes' this event. By prayer and song, by listening and sharing, the Church allows herself to be influenced by God's gracious act of salvation. What God has done through Christ is above all a *free* act. That is, God was not forced or obliged to perform it. We haven't had any influence on it, and we cannot enforce it. The reverse side of this is that we cannot lose this gift by our failures. Loving us is entirely a matter of God's free choice. Next, what God has done is *merciful*, unmerited. By saying this, I don't mean that God has thrown this gift to us carelessly, without another thought, more or less as we throw a coin in a beggar's hat when we visit an old church in Italy. No, 'mercy' means that this is a *joyful* present, a spontaneous gift. The Greek word *charis*, from which our word 'grace' is derived, also means 'joy'. God enjoys this giving; he is love. He likes giving to people who do not deserve his gifts, and he gives generously.

Doxology is the Church's response to this free and gracious gift of God. Here mission begins, with 'an explosion of joy' (Lesslie Newbigin). I love this metaphor, since it expresses so beautifully what makes for the core of Christian life. If God's gift is given completely freely and joyfully, then our praise should have the same characteristics. It is not meant to achieve anything but simply to glorify God, to recognize him as our creator, sustainer and redeemer. Joy 'is' simply 'there'; it is not good 'for' anything. It is silly to ask someone: 'What is the point of your joy? What do you hope to achieve with it?' (The same is true, by the way, for our grief or our anger about injustice. The vocabulary of lamentation and accusation is not strategic either, but doxological.) Christians do not glorify God to achieve something that is even more important than God, such as changing the world or themselves. Doxology is the response to undeserved love, to generous grace. It is to love God *above all*. That is why Christian life itself – starting with the Eucharist – assumes the nature of generosity and abundance.

All this is important to underline, because in various theological proposals the liturgy is sometimes instrumentalized. Christians, so it goes, should be equipped in and through the liturgy to go into the world, and establish signs of God's kingdom.[26] The liturgy, according to many neo-Anabaptists, is supposed to be focused on shaping 'virtuous' people of 'character', a community of true saints.[27] According to neo-Pentecostals, to take another example, doxology should be effective in terms of combating invisible evil powers, and thus contribute to the transformation of the world. Of course I don't contest that the liturgy has a formative effect on Christian characters and communities, and that it does change the world in some way, but that is not its purpose or its justification. We must not confuse the purpose of praise with the effects it possibly has. In this respect, character formation can be compared with health or happiness: they are mostly the byproduct of something else. A good marriage certainly contributes to our health, but we should not marry to keep the doctor away. So, too, motivation for mission and the shaping of Christian virtues are by-products of true doxology, but not its purpose.

This is good news, especially for small Christian communities in their cultural exile. When doxology becomes an instrument to inspire us for action, we are yet again thrown back on what we can achieve. Or, more likely in this context, we are constantly frustrated about what we fail to achieve. And by rebound, all this talk about the formational, equipping and motivating effects of the liturgy becomes ever more implausible – so that even the worship of God is undermined. A spirituality of exile must learn to celebrate 'freely'; it must learn to glorify God's grace as an unforced and free gift. Just like someone who embraces her spouse should not wonder whether this helps against stress, but simply enjoy her lover's presence. 'The worship of God', says the German missiologist Henning Wrogemann, 'is first and foremost about recognizing the glory of God, a God who is at work even when my little ego has perished long ago.' Every instrumentalization of doxology leads us into obsession with ourselves – without me this will not succeed. 'The worship of God keeps in view that God surely wants to make us participants in his mission, but that its success will always be dependent on Godself.'[28]

By reminding us of what God has done in Jesus Christ the doxology works in a liberating and relaxing way. Our hope lies with God who raises the dead. For people who have to learn again what it means to be weak and foolish in the world, that is liberating news. For so many Christian leaders who have come to the end of their strength and inspiration, this is their only hope. The apostle Paul emphasized this when he wrote: 'I will boast all the more gladly of my weaknesses, so that the power of Christ may dwell in me' (2 Cor. 12.9). This is not masochism, as if Christians should talk themselves into the pit all the time. Paul does not mean that weakness as such is something to be happy about or to wish for. His point is this: especially when we are somehow confronted with our own impotence or that of others, then this is the place where God's power will be revealed.[29] At this point we can only set our hopes on him. 'Mortal, can these bones live?', asked the Lord to the prophet Ezekiel in the valley of dry bones. He answered: 'O LORD God, you know.' And he prophesied to skeletons (Ezek. 37.1–7).

Looking Around

Next to this non-instrumental character of the doxology, I have worked out another aspect in some detail: glorifying God instils contextual sensitivity in the Church. After all, as priests they represent God to the people, and the people to God. Doxology thus works in two directions. From the world the Church reaches out to offer all of life to God. And from God her desire is nourished that the world will be a place of praise: that there will be communities everywhere that glorify him with a multitude of voices and cultural variations.

As regards the representation of God to the people around us: the free and gracious gift of his love works through the love of Christians for others. In Chapter 3, section 7, I have said something about the scribe who asked for the one and 'greatest' commandment, and who in response received *two* commandments as homework: love God above all, and your neighbour as yourself. The entirely selfless, non-instrumental, liberating love of God requires a fitting response: love for God and the neighbour. These two loves do not compete, because both are an echo of God's love for us. A missionary approach to people, therefore, does not treat them as subjected to a higher purpose. We don't evangelize to fill our churches, and we don't organize foodbanks to change the world. If this is our purpose, we turn love into an instrument, and we set ourselves on a course towards disappointment and spiritual exhaustion. Of course, we take into account that evangelism can lead to church growth and that foodbanks can trigger processes of social change. There is nothing wrong with praying for this to happen, and to work for it. But to a doxologically motivated mission these are extras; they are neither the justification nor the purpose of missional activity.[30] If they were, we would soon become tired of doing good and we would no longer be happy about one sinner (only one?) who repents. Christians do good, not to be effective or create opportunities for success, but in order to glorify the generous, merciful God who has brought about the world out of nothing and who creates life out of death. They do not work on the basis of optimism, but on the basis of faith, hope and love.

This also implies a judgement over any missionary methods that exploit human dependency, like the ones that were mentioned in Chapter 1. To glorify God in his mission means that we use methods that recognize him for his grace and generosity, his non-calculating love. Our strategies must give witness to that. Whoever is hungry, gets food. Period. Of course we will look for opportunities to testify about the good news in doing so, but we do this only to people who don't feel compelled to listen to us, and we will do it 'with gentleness and reverence' (1 Peter 3.16). Manipulative methods demonstrate suspicion towards God; they display our fear that he cannot reach people if we don't assist him with our tricks. Such methods testify about a God for whom nothing comes for free. And this is not the God Christians believe in.

As a community of priests the Church also represents the world before God. Therefore it is always out to collect the gratitude, the complaints and the grief of the world, to offer them to God. She proclaims 'the Name' by giving thanks to God for all the good he does through people – whether they are Christians or not. Christians ask their neighbours, relatives and friends to pass on their prayers or to join them in worship to bring these before God. They become involved in the lives of their fellow humans; they share their joy, power, sadness and fragility; and they bring their songs, sighs, anger and questions before the creator of life. In their engagement with the poor and oppressed of this world they experience more than ever the human impotence that reminds us of the power of God. In their evangelizing efforts they are out to find especially those people who add something to the diversity of the Church, since only 'with all the saints' can we penetrate the love of Christ; and because nobody is better able to thank God and worship him on behalf of the world who does not know him than someone who can represent this particular part of the world. The worship of the Church is therefore principally open to all sorts of cultures, and it makes room for diversity.

It wants to provide opportunities for people to glorify God in their own languages.

Looking Ahead

To look doxologically means, finally, that we look ahead to what God is still going to do in Jesus Christ. In Chapter 4, section 6, we dwelt on the expectation of Israel in exile that, with the recovery of Israel, other nations too would worship God. In the New Testament we see how Peter and Paul see the promise of Israel's restoration being fulfilled in the coming of Jesus Christ, the King-Priest. His 'offspring' of Jews and gentiles, a kingdom of priests, forms the renewed people of God. You could say that in New Testament perspective the future of God's rule is 'stretched out', as it were, into the here and now. On the one hand the people of God celebrates the dawning of this future, on the other hand it eagerly awaits the final arrival of this future – the day when every knee will bend for Jesus and every tongue confess that he is Lord (Phil. 2.10–11). Meanwhile, the future role of the faith community as priests has become reality in the present. The Christian Church praises God, also on behalf of those who do not (yet) praise him it welcomes converts as first signs of the harvest that is to come, and it goes out to invite the nations to the great wedding feast. And all this stands under the sign of God who works at the perfect restoration of his creation.

In this context I have talked about a spirituality of signs and foretastes (Chapter 3, section 7). I do not deny that our effort can be an instrument through which God builds his kingdom – surely, in the Lord our work is not in vain – but how this happens almost always escapes our understanding. In the secularized areas of the West we see a convert only now and then, but the community of priests can rejoice about this person (like the angels in heaven), because he or she is a sign of the wedding meal of the Lord. A community of priests has all kinds of contacts with people who would not call themselves Christians, but it may believe that through these relations God works his salvation in hidden ways (see Chapter 6, section 4). Full of expectation she looks ahead to God's future, hoping and expecting to be surprised by God's grace. A community of priests builds signs of justice and service (visiting the lonely, reconciliation between enemies, help for the poor, working for justice), without expecting that this will immediately bring forth a better world. But she invests in these things, because she believes that love, peace and justice will at some time be the most ordinary aspects of the world. It is all about how you define reality, not how you calculate for success.

Let's face it: many Christian values and habits are rather pointless if we want to use them to achieve success or increase our reputation. Love for enemies is risky; caring for illegal immigrants is controversial; turning the other cheek is pretty stupid. We must be very optimistic indeed, or rather naive, if we really believe that this lifestyle will infect so many people that the world will become a paradise. But from a spirituality of signs and foretastes such behaviour is nothing more or less than the glorification of God who will usher in his kingdom. We don't do it to be successful; we do it to demonstrate the reality we believe in and hope for.

7.6 Summary and Conclusion

In my search for an attractive missional vision for small Christian communities in a secular culture I have arrived at the 'priesthood Church'. This vision is realistic, it has ample biblical support and it is ecumenically sensitive. Furthermore, it provides many leads for practical action. This is particularly about the significance of small communities, a way of church development that revolves around listening to God and establishing meaningful relationships with the neighbourhood, and a realistic and theologically responsible approach of evangelism and service. All this is bound together and receives its meaning from the worship of God.

> Now to him who by the power at work within us is able to accomplish abundantly far more than all we can ask or imagine, to him be glory in the church and in Christ Jesus to all generations, for ever and ever.

> Amen.
> (Eph. 3.20–21)

Notes

1 For various reasons I object to the word 'model', but I use it nonetheless, as shorthand for 'the Church as a community of pilgrims and priests'. In order to indicate the problematic character of the word, I will place it between quotation marks.

2 Compare the distinction made by Paul G. Hiebert between a 'bounded' and a 'centred' set ('Category'). I have explored and defended this extensively in my *De werkers van het laatste uur*, pp. 169–86.

3 Without exploring this further, I believe that this 'model' can also point towards a middle road between Free Church, Reformed and Roman Catholic views of the Church. In a certain way I try here to connect the Free Church and Reformed emphasis on the local congregation and the priesthood of all believers with

important elements of a Roman Catholic and Orthodox ecclesiology, such as the primacy of the Church over the individual believer, and the Eucharist as the heart of the Church. One might call such an attempt, with Doug Gay, the 'remixing' of the Church (*Remixing the Church*). Gay too looks for connection with Free Church and Roman Catholic ecclesiological views from his own Reformed position.

4 Williams, 'The Body's Grace', p. 312.

5 To be clear: I do not mean that a 'real' church can do just as well without offices. A community is not an amorphous mass, but it is structured and governed. Thus, salvation is realized in the community by employing these structures and means. My point is that it would be ecclesiologically irresponsible to make ecclesiality dependent on a particular implementation of the structure of offices or an overburdened organization.

6 'Modern denominations tend to think of any congregation less than 100 as failing, and to despair over chapels with membership less than 20. But the congregations in the beginning of Christianity were mostly as small, and even when the whole church in a city like Corinth could assemble in one house, they can only have been about 40 strong ... Where *we* think of congregations as too small, perhaps the real danger is that they are too *large*!' – Dunn, 'Is there evidence', p. 62.

7 See, e.g., Kreider, Kreider, *Worship and Mission*.

8 Examples in Paas et al., *Eten met Jezus*.

9 See, for example, the Sant'Egidio community that has extended its presence in many Western (European) cities (www.santegidio.org/pageID/1/langID/en/HOME.html).

10 Cf. Keifert, *We Are Here Now*; Roxburgh, Romanuk, *The Missional Leader*; Roxburgh, *Missional Map-Making*.

11 James, *Church Planting*.

12 Cf. McGrath, 'Cultivation'.

13 'In that planting process, I was making something, not by the imposition of my will, but by working with and becoming part of a process that was much greater than myself and my tools. Cultivation is a process that is, at its heart, profoundly mysterious' (Roxburgh, *Missional Map-Making*, p. 184). I have elaborated on this point in *Church Planting in the Secular West*, pp. 199–224.

14 See esp. Rooms, Keifert, *Forming a Missional Church*.

15 Van Houwelingen, *Apostelen*, p. 59.

16 A nice example is the Basilique du Sacré-Coeur (Montmartre, Paris). In this landmark place uninterrupted intercession for church and world has been made since 1 August 1885 ('une mission d'intercession constante pour l'Eglise et le monde'). See www.sacre-coeur-montmartre.com, sub 'la prière d'adoration'.

17 Walls, 'The Ephesian Moment'. See also Walls, 'Evangelical and Ecumenical'.

18 Walls, 'Rise', pp. 27, 33.

19 Walls, 'Rise', p. 30.

20 Walls, 'Ephesian Moment', p. 79. In this context the expression 'ontic expansion of God in Jesus Christ' is sometimes used, that is, 'our understanding and insight into the full nature of God in Jesus Christ is continually expanding as more and more people groups come to the feet of Jesus' (Tennent, 'Challenge', pp. 174, 176).

21 Cragg, *Call*, p. 168.

22 I don't mean that nothing can be said about it at all, but that we should be careful not to identify the path of salvation with the path of conformity. Christians, after all, are just human and, especially when churches are shrinking, we are all

too inclined to construct 'steps forward' as 'being more like us' or 'becoming better adapted'. The principal step is that people have meaningful contacts with the community of priests. In these meaningful contacts, however, even words and deeds of (apparent?) unbelief and alienation can be ways through which God works in the other person and speaks to us. Here I have learnt much from Tomáš Halík, who in his *Patience with God* presents the figure of Zacchaeus (the seeker who climbs a tree and looks at Jesus from a distance) as the 'patron saint' of those who have a more distant relationship with the institutional Church. By the way, for Halík this does not imply that the Church is relativized.

23 On this threefold structure of 'worship', 'doctrine' and 'life', see Wainwright, *Doxology*, pp. 5–6.

24 See, for example, the study of the Lutheran missiologist Wrogemann, *Den Glanz widerspiegeln*, esp. pp. 46–113.

25 On this, cf. Jongeneel, 'Voetius' zendingstheologie', p. 146, who agrees critically with Voetius's doxological motive for mission. Translated as 'The Missiology of Gisbertus Voetius'.

26 Cf. Wrogemann, *Den Glanz widerspiegeln*, p. 46, with a critique of the 'Verzwecklichung des Gotteslobes' (instrumentalization of worship) in the missionary reflections of the 1960s.

27 This last view is prominently present in neo-Anabaptist theologies, like those of John Howard Yoder and Stanley Hauerwas (cf. Chapter 3, section 2). Here the Church is seen as a countercultural community, a particular 'political' entity. Thus, liturgy soon becomes instrumentalized as a means to build up the Church. Except for this instrumentalization of the Eucharist, another disadvantage is that the missionary calling of the congregation becomes secondary. The liturgy is, at best, a means to equip the congregation for mission, but essentially the Church is inward-focused. For all of this, see Kerr, *Christ, History and Apocalyptic*, pp. 169–73.

28 Wrogemann, *Den Glanz widerspiegeln*, p. 48.

29 Cf. Wrogemann, *Den Glanz widerspiegeln*, pp. 48–51.

30 See further what I have discussed in Chapter 3, section 7.

Bibliography

Al-Azmeh, Aziz and Effie Fokas (eds), *Islam in Europe: Diversity, Identity and Influence*, Cambridge: Cambridge University Press, 2007.

Ammerman, Nancy Tatom, *Sacred Stories, Spiritual Tribes: Finding Religion in Everyday Life*, Oxford: Oxford University Press, 2014.

Anizor, Uche and Hank Voss, *Representing Christ: A Vision for the Priesthood of All Believers*, Downers Grove, IL: InterVarsity Press, 2016.

Archbishop's Commission on Evangelism, *Towards the Conversion of England: Being the Report of a Commission on Evangelism Appointed by the Archbishops of Canterbury and York Pursuant to a Resolution of the Church Assembly Passed at the Summer Session, 1943*, London: Westminster Press, 1945.

Arnold, Bill T. and Richard S. Hess (eds), *Ancient Israel's History: An Introduction to Issues and Sources*, Grand Rapids, MI: Baker Academic, 2014.

Baan, Ariaan, *The Necessity of Witness: Stanley Hauerwas's Contribution to Systematic Theology*, BOXPress, 2014.

Barna, George, *Revolution: Finding Vibrant Faith beyond the Walls of the Sanctuary*, Wheaton, IL: Tyndale, 2005.

Baron, Jürgen, 'Back from the Brink – Zurück vom Abgrund: Warum die Kirche in England hoffnungsvoll in die Zukunft schauen kann', *Theologische Beiträge* 41 (2010), 54–67.

Bartels, Matthias and Martin Reppenhagen (eds), *Gemeindepflanzung: Ein Modell für die Kirche der Zukunft?*, Neukirchener Verlag: Neukirchen-Vluyn, 2006.

Bartholomä, Philipp, *Freikirche mit Mission: Eine explorative Studie zum freikirchlichen Gemeindebau im säkularen Zeitalter*, Leipzig: Evangelische Verlagsanstalt GmbH, 2019.

Bartholomew, Craig (ed.), *A Royal Priesthood? A Dialogue with Oliver O'Donovan*, Grand Rapids, MI: Zondervan, 2002.

Bartholomew, Craig, 'Introduction', in Bartholomew, *Royal Priesthood*, pp. 1–45.

Beach, Lee, *The Church in Exile: Living in Hope after Christendom*, Downers Grove, IL: InterVarsity Press Academic, 2015.

Beale, G. K., *The Temple and the Church's Mission: A Biblical Theology of the Dwelling Place of God*, Downers Grove, IL: InterVarsity Press, 2004.

Beek, Abraham van de, *Lichaam en Geest van Christus: De theologie van de kerk en de Heilige Geest*, Zoetermeer: Meinema, 2012.

Bekkum, Koert van, 'Coexistence as Guilt: Iron I Memories in Judges 1', in Gershon Galil (ed.), *The Ancient Near East in the 12th–10th Centuries BCE*, Münster: Ugarit-Verlag, 2012, pp. 525–47.

Bender, Kimlyn, *Karl Barth's Christological Ecclesiology*, Aldershot: Ashgate, 2005.

Benedict XVI, *Encyclical Deus Caritas Est*, 25 December 2005.

Berg, Johannes van den, *Constrained by Jesus' Love: An Inquiry into the Motives of the Missionary Awakening in Great Britain in the Period between 1698 and 1815*, Kampen: J. H. Kok, 1956.

Berkman, John and Michael Cartwright (eds), *The Hauerwas Reader*, Durham, NC: Duke University Press, 2000 (2nd edn).

Bevans, Stephen B. and Rogers P. Schroeder, *Constants in Context: A Theology of Mission for Today*, Maryknoll, NY: Orbis, 2011 (7th edn).

Bevans, Stephen B. and Roger P. Schroeder, *Prophetic Dialogue: Reflections on Christian Mission Today*, Maryknoll, NY: Orbis, 2011.

Boersma, Hans, *Heavenly Participation: The Weaving of a Sacramental Tapestry*, Grand Rapids, MI: Eerdmans, 2010.

Bolt, John et al. (eds), *The J.H. Bavinck Reader*, Grand Rapids, MI: Eerdmans, 2013.

Bosch, David J., 'Evangelism: Theological Currents and Cross-Currents Today', *International Bulletin of Missionary Research* 3 (1987), 98–103.

Bosch, David J., *Transforming Mission: Paradigm Shifts in Theology of Mission* (1991), Maryknoll, NY: Orbis, 2008 (24th edn).

Bowen, Nancy R., *Ezekiel*, Nashville, TN: Abingdon, 2010.

Bria, Ion, *The Liturgy after the Liturgy: Mission and Witness from an Orthodox Perspective*, Geneva: WCC, 1996.

Brown, Peter, *The Rise of Western Christendom*, Oxford: Blackwell, 2003 (2nd edn).

Bruce, Steve, 'Secularization and Church Growth in the United Kingdom, *Journal of Religion in Europe* 6 (2013), 273–96.

Brueggemann, Walter, *Cadences of Home: Preaching among Exiles*, Louisville, KY: Westminster, 1997.

Brueggemann, Walter, 'Preaching to Exiles', in Clarke, *Exilic Preaching*, pp. 9–28.

Brueggemann, Walter, *Deep Memory, Exuberant Hope: Contested Truth in a Post-Christian World*, Minneapolis, MN: Fortress Press, 2000.

Bruijne, Ad de, 'Not without the church as institute: The relevance of Abraham Kuyper's ecclesiology for a faithful and contextually sensitive execution of Christian public and theological responsibilities in the 21st century', *Kuyper Review* 5 (2014).

Bruijne, Ad de, '"Colony of Heaven": Abraham Kuyper's Ecclesiology in the Twenty-First Century', *Journal of Markets and Morality* 17 (2014), 445–90.

Burgess, Richard, 'Bringing Back the Gospel: Reverse Mission among Nigerian Pentecostals in Britain', *Journal of Religion in Europe* 4 (2011), 429–49.

Burkimsher, Marion, 'Is Religious Attendance Bottoming Out? An Examination of Current Trends Across Europe', *Journal for the Scientific Study of Religion* 53 (2014), 432–45.

Bury, J. B., *St. Patrick: The Life and Work of Ireland's Saint*, London: Tauris, 2010.

Buskes, J. J., *Hoera voor het leven*, Amsterdam: Ten Have, 1963.

Cahill, Thomas, *How the Irish Saved Civilization: The Untold Story of Ireland's Heroic Role from the Fall of Rome to the Rise of Medieval Europe*, New York: Doubleday, 1995.

Cailing, Rolex, '"That You May Proclaim His Excellencies": The Missional Use of the Old Testament in 1 Peter', *Torch Trinity Journal* 16 (2013), 138–55.

Callagher, Robert L., 'The Integration of Mission Theology and Practice: Zinzendorf and the Early Moravians', *Mission Studies* 25 (2008), 185–210.

Calvin, John, *Institutes of the Christian Religion* (1559).

Cameron, Euan, *Enchanted Europe: Superstition, Reason, & Religion*, 1250–1750, Oxford: Oxford University Press, 2010.

Campbell, Antony F. and Mark O'Brien, *Unfolding the Deuteronomistic History: Origins, Upgrades, Present Text*, Minneapolis, MN: Fortress Press, 2000.

Cartwright, Michael G. and Peter Ochs (eds), *John Howard Yoder: The Jewish-Christian Schism Revisited*, Scottdale, PA: Herald Press, 2008.

Chilcote, Paul W. and Laceye C. Warner (eds), *The Study of Evangelism: Exploring a Missional Practice of the Church*, Grand Rapids, MI: Eerdmans, 2008.

Christerson, Brad and Richard Flory, *The Rise of Network Christianity: How Independent Leaders are Changing the Religious Landscape*, Oxford: Oxford University Press, 2017.

Clarke, Erskine (ed.), *Exilic Preaching: Testimony for Christian Exiles in an Increasingly Hostile Culture*, Harrisburg, PA: Trinity Press, 1997.

Coleman, Simon, *The Globalisation of Charismatic Christianity: Spreading the Gospel of Prosperity*, Cambridge: Cambridge University Press, 2000.

Comaroff, Jean and John Comaroff, *Of Revelation and Revolution: Christianity, Colonialism, and Consciousness in South Africa*, Vol. 1, Chicago, IL: University of Chicago Press, 1991.

Corwin, Gary R., 'Sociology and Missiology: Reflections on Mission Research', in Rommen and Corwin, *Missiology*, pp. 19–29.

Costas, Orlando, *Christ Outside the Gate: Mission beyond Christendom*, Maryknoll, NY: Orbis, 1982.

Cragg, Kenneth, *The Call of the Minaret*, Oxford: Oneworld, 2000 (3rd edn).

Cramer, David, 'Scandalizing John Howard Yoder', *The Other Journal* (July 2014). Online: https://theotherjournal.com/2014/07/07/scandalizing-john-howard-yoder/ (accessed 4 August 2019).

Cray, Graham et al. (eds), *New Monasticism as Fresh Expression of Church*, London: Canterbury Press, 2010.

Croft, Steven (ed.), *Mission-Shaped Questions: Defining Issues for Today's Church*, London: Church House Publishing, 2008.

Cruchley-Jones, Peter, 'Entering Exile: Can There Be a Missiology for "Not My People"?', in Foust, *Scandalous Prophet*, pp. 23–36.

Davie, Grace, 'Religion in Europe in the 21st Century: The Factors to Take into Account', *European Journal of Sociology* 47 (2006), 271–96.

Davie, Grace, 'Vicarious Religion: A Methodological Challenge', in Nancy T. Ammerman (ed.), *Everyday Religion: Observing Modern Religious Lives*, Oxford: Oxford University Press, 2007, pp. 21–35.

Davie, Grace, *The Sociology of Religion*, London: SAGE, 2007.

Dekker, Jaap, 'The Servant and the Servants in the Book of Isaiah', *Sárospataki Füzetek* 16 (2012), 33–45.

Dekker, Wim, *Marginaal en missionair: Kleine theologie voor een krimpende kerk*, Zoetermeer: Boekencentrum, 2011.

Dennison, Jack, *City Reaching: On the Road to Community Transformation*, Pasadena, CA: William Carey Library, 1999.

Deursen, A. Th. van, *Bavianen en Slijkgeuzen: Kerk en kerkvolk ten tijde van Maurits en Oldenbarnevelt*, Franeker: Van Wijnen, 1998 (3rd edn).

Deursen, A. Th. van, *Een dorp in de polder: Graft in de zeventiende eeuw*, Amsterdam: Bert Bakker, 1994.

Dombois, Hans, *Das Recht der Gnade: Ökumenisches Kirchenrecht III*, Bielefeld: Luther Verlag, 1983.

Doornenbal, Robert, *Crossroads: An Exploration of the Emerging-Missional Conversation with a Special Focus on 'Missional Leadership' and Its Challenges for Theological Education*, Delft: Eburon, 2012.

Dreher, Rod, *The Benedict Option: A Strategy for Christians in a Post-Christian Nation*, New York: Penguin Random House, 2017.

Drost, Daniël, *Diaspora as Mission: John Howard Yoder, Jeremiah 29, and the Shape and Mission of the Church*, PhD dissertation VU University Amsterdam, 2019.

Dubis, Mark, 'Research on 1 Peter: A Survey of Scholarly Literature Since 1985', *Currents in Biblical Research* 4 (2006), 199–239.

Duerksen, Darren Todd, *Ecclesial Identities in a Multi-Faith Context: Jesus Truth Gatherings (Yeshu Satsangs) among Hindus and Sikhs in Northwest India*, Eugene, OR: Pickwick Publications, 2015.

Dulles, Avery, *The Reshaping of Catholicism: Current Challenges in the Theology of the Church*, San Fransisco, CA: Harper, 1988.

Dunn, James D. G., 'Is there evidence for fresh expressions of church in the New Testament?', in Croft, *Mission-Shaped Questions*, pp. 54–65.

Elliott, John H., *Elect and the Holy: An Exegetical Examination of 1 Peter 2:4–10 and the Phrase basileion hierateuma*, Leiden: Brill, 1966.

Elliott, John H., 'The Rehabilitation of an Exegetical Step-Child: 1 Peter in Recent Research', *Journal of Biblical Literature* 95 (1976), 243–54.

Elliott, John H., *1 Peter*, New York: Doubleday, 2000.

Engelsviken, Thormod, 'Missio Dei: The Understanding and Misunderstanding of a Theological Concept in European Churches and Missiology', *International Review of Mission* 92.367 (2003), 481–97.

Engen, Charles van, *The Growth of the True Church: An Analysis of the Ecclesiology of Church Growth Theory*, Amsterdam: Rodopi, 1981.

Erdozain, Dominic, *The Soul of Doubt: The Religious Roots of Unbelief from Luther to Marx*, Oxford: Oxford University Press, 2016.

Fagbemi, Stephen Ayodeji A., 'Living for Christ in a Hostile World: The Christian Identity and Its Present Challenges in 1 Peter', *Transformation* 26 (2009), 1–14.

Fagbemi, Stephen Ayodeji A., 'Transformation, Proclamation and Mission in the New Testament: Examining the Case of 1 Peter', *Transformation* 27 (2010), 209–23.

Feldmeier, Reinhard, *Die Christen als Fremde: Die Metapher der Fremde in der Antiken Welt, im Urchristentum und im 1. Petrusbrief*, Tübingen: J. C. B. Mohr, 1992.

Feldtkeller andreas, 'Missionswissenschaft und Interkulturelle Theologie', *Theologische Literaturzeitung* 138 (2013), 3–12.

Fiddes, Paul S., 'Versions of Ecclesiology: Stanley Hauerwas and Nicholas Healy', *Ecclesiology* 12 (2016), 331–53.

Fitch, David E., 'The Other Missional Conversation: Making Way for the Neo-Anabaptist Contribution to the Missional Movement in North America', *Missiology* 44 (2016), 466–78.

Fitzgerald, Frances, *The Evangelicals: The Struggle to Shape America*, New York: Simon and Schuster, 2017.

Flemming, Dean, *Contextualization in the New Testament: Patterns for Theology and Mission*, Downers Grove, IL: InterVarsity Press, 2005.

Fletcher, Richard, *The Barbarian Conversion: From Paganism to Christianity*, New York: Henry Holt, 1997.

Flett, John G., *The Witness of God: The Trinity, Missio Dei, Karl Barth, and the Nature of Christian Community*, Grand Rapids, MI: Eerdmans, 2010.

Flett, John G., *Apostolicity: The Ecumenical Question in World Christian Perspective*, Downers Grove, IL: InterVarsity Press, 2016.

Floor, L., *Jakobus: Brief van een broeder*, Kampen: Kok, 1992.

Foust, Thomas S. et al. (eds), *A Scandalous Prophet: The Way of Mission after Newbigin*, Grand Rapids, MI: Eerdmans, 2002.

Francis, *Apostolic Exhortation Evangelii Gaudium* ('The Joy of the Gospel'), 2013.

Frost, Michael, *Exiles: Living Missionally in a Post-Christian Culture*, Grand Rapids, MI: Baker Books, 2006.

Frost, Michael and Alan Hirsch, *The Shaping of Things to Come: Innovation and Mission for the 21st-Century Church*, Peabody, MA: Hendrickson, 2003.

Gäckle, Volker, *Allgemeines Priestertum: Zur Metaphorisierung des Priestertitels im Frühjudentum und Neuen Testament*, Tübingen: Mohr Siebeck, 2014.

Gangel, Kenneth O., 'Pictures of the Church in 1 Peter', *Grace Theological Journal* 10 (1989), 36–46.

Garber, David G., 'A Vocabulary of Trauma in the Exilic Writings', in Kelle, *Interpreting Exile*, 309–22.

Gay, Doug, *Remixing the Church: Towards an Emerging Ecclesiology*, London: SCM Press, 2011.

Gelder, Craig van, 'A Great New Fact of Our Day: America as a Mission Field', in Hunsberger and Van Gelder, *The Church between Gospel and Culture*, pp. 57–68.

Gibaut, John and Knud Jørgensen (eds), *Called to Unity: For the Sake of Mission*, Oxford: Regnum, 2014.

Gibson, David, 'America's Conservative Christians Ponder a "Babylonian Exile" to Save Their Faith', *The Huffington Post*, 26 August 2014 (online).

Gill, Robin, *Churchgoing and Christian Ethics*, Cambridge: Cambridge University Press, 2004.

Goheen, Michael, *'As the Father Has Sent Me, I Am Sending You': J.E. Lesslie Newbigin's Missionary Ecclesiology*, Zoetermeer: Boekencentrum, 2000.

Goheen, Michael, *A Light to the Nations: The Missional Church and the Biblical Story*, Grand Rapids, MI: Baker Academic, 2011.

Goossen, Rachel Waltner, '"Defanging the Beast": Mennonite Responses to John Howard Yoder's Sexual Abuse', *The Mennonite Quarterly Review* 89 (January 2015), 7–80.

Graaf, Jan van der, *Volkskerk in de marge: Een actuele bezinning*, Heerenveen: Groen, 2012.

Greeley, Andrew, *The Catholic Imagination*, Berkeley, CA: University of California Press, 2000.

Green, Stanley W. and James R. Krabill (eds), *Fully Engaged: Missional Church in an Anabaptist Voice*, Harrisonburg, VA: Herald Press, 2015.

Greenman, Jeffrey P. and Gene L. Green (eds), *Global Theologies in Evangelical Perspective: Exploring the Contextual Nature of Theology and Mission*, Downers Grove, IL: InterVarsity Press Academic, 2012.

Gregory, Brad S., *The Unintended Reformation: How a Religious Revolution Secularized Society*, Cambridge, MA: Harvard University Press, 2012.

Groody, Daniel G., 'The Church on the Move: Mission in an Age of Migration', *Mission Studies* 30 (2013), 27–42.

Guder Darrell L. (ed.), *Missional Church: A Vision for the Sending of the Church in North America*, Grand Rapids, MI: Eerdmans, 1998.

Guder, Darrell L., *The Continuing Conversion of the Church*, Grand Rapids, MI: Eerdmans, 2000.

Guder, Darrell L., 'The Church as Missional Community', in Husbands and Treiter, *Community*, pp. 114–30.

Guder, Darrell L., 'A Multicultural and Translational Approach', in Ott, *The Mission of the Church*, pp. 21–40.

Gutiérrez, Gustavo, *We Drink from Our Own Wells: The Spiritual Journey of a People*, Maryknoll, NY: Orbis, 1984.

Halík, Tomáš, *Patience with God: The Story of Zacchaeus Continuing in Us*, New York: Doubleday, 2009.

Halperin, David J., *Seeking Ezekiel: Text and Psychology*, University Park, PA: Pennsylvania State University Press, 1993.

Hamilton, Bernard, *Religion in the Medieval West*, London: Hodder Arnold, 2003.

Hart, Addison Hodges, *Strangers and Pilgrims Once More: Being Disciples of Jesus in a Post-Christendom World*, Grand Rapids, MI: Eerdmans, 2014.

Hart, David Bentley, *Atheist Delusions: The Christian Revolution and Its Fashionable Enemies*, New Haven, CT: Yale University Press, 2009.

Hauerwas, Stanley, *A Community of Character: Toward a Constructive Christian Social Ethic*, Notre Dame, IN: Notre Dame Press, 1981.

Hauerwas, Stanley, 'On Keeping Theological Ethics Theological' (1983), in Berkman and Cartwright, *Hauerwas Reader*, pp. 51–74.

Hauerwas, Stanley, 'A Christian Critique of Christian America' (1986), in Berkman and Cartwright, *Hauerwas Reader*, pp. 459–80.

Hauerwas, Stanley, 'Why the "Sectarian Temptation" is a Misrepresentation: A Response to James Gustafson' (1988), in Berkman and Cartwright, *Hauerwas Reader*, pp. 90–110.

Hauerwas Stanley, *After Christendom: How the Church is to Behave if Freedom, Justice and a Christian Nation Are Bad Ideas*, Nashville, 1999 (2nd edn).

Hauerwas, 'In Defence of "Our Respectable Culture": Trying to Make Sense of John Howard Yoder's Sexual Abuse', *ABC Religion and Ethics* (October 2018). Online.

Hauerwas, Stanley and William H. Willimon, *Resident Aliens: Life in the Christian Colony*, Nashville, TN: Abingdon Press, 1996.

Hayes, John H. and J. Maxwell Miller (eds), *Israelite and Judaean History*, Philadelphia, PA: Trinity Press, 1990 (3rd edn).

Healy, Nicholas, *Church, World and the Christian Life: Practical-Prophetic Ecclesiology*, Cambridge: Cambridge University Press, 2000.

Healy, Nicholas, 'Ecclesiology, Ethnography, and God: An Interplay of Reality Descriptions', in Ward, *Perspectives*, pp. 182–99.

Healy, Nicholas, *Hauerwas: A (Very) Critical Introduction*, Grand Rapids, MI: Eerdmans, 2014.

Hellemans, Stef and Peter Jonkers (eds), *A Catholic Minority Church in a World of Seekers*, Washington, DC: The Council for Research in Values and Philosophy, 2015.

Heitink, Gerben, *Een kerk met karakter: Tijd voor heroriëntatie*, Kampen: Kok, 2008.

Herbst, Michael, *Missionarischer Gemeindeaufbau in der Volkskirche*, Neukirchen-Vluyn: Neukirchener Verlag, 2010 (4th edn).

Hiebert, Paul G., 'The Category "Christian" in the Mission Task', *International Review of Mission* 72 (1983), 421–7.

Hirsch, Alan, *The Forgotten Ways: Reactivating the Missional Church*, Grand Rapids, MI: Brazos, 2006.

Hoefner, Herbert E., *Churchless Christianity*, Pasadena, CA: William Carey Library, 2002.

Hoekendijk, J. C., *Kerk en volk in de Duitse Zendingswetenschap*, Utrecht, 1945.

Hoekendijk, J. C., 'The Call to Evangelism', *International Review of Mission* 39.154 (1950), 162–75.

Hoekendijk, J. C., *The Church Inside Out*, Philadelphia, PA: Westminster Press, 1966.

Hoekendijk, J. C., *Kirche und Volk in der deutschen Missionswissenschaft*, Munich: Kaiser, 1967.

Hof, Eleonora Dorothea, *Reimagining Mission in the Postcolonial Condition: A Theology of Vulnerability and Vocation at the Margins*, Zoetermeer: Boekencentrum, 2016.

Hogebrink, Laurens, *Europe's Heart and Soul: Jacques Delors' Appeal to the Churches*, Globethics.net: Geneva, 2015 (online).

Hollinghurst, Steve, *Mission Shaped Evangelism: The Gospel in Contemporary Culture*, London: Canterbury Press, 2010.

Holvast, René, *Spiritual Mapping in the United States and Argentina, 1989–2005*, Leiden: Brill, 2008.

Houwelingen, P. H. R. van, *1 Petrus: Rondzendbrief uit Babylon*, Kampen: Kok, 1991

Houwelingen, P. H. R. van, *Apostelen: Dragers van een smaakmakend evangelie*, Kampen: Kok, 2010.

Huber, Wolfgang, 'Volkskirche I.', *TRE* 35 (2003).

Hunsberger, George R., *Bearing the Witness of the Spirit: Lesslie Newbigin's Theology of Cultural Plurality*, Grand Rapids, MI: Eerdmans, 1998.

Hunsberger, George R., 'Conversion and Community: Revisiting the Lesslie Newbigin – M.M. Thomas Debate', *International Bulletin of Missionary Research* 22 (1998), 112–17.

Hunsberger, George R. and Craig van Gelder (eds), *The Church between Gospel and Culture: The Emerging Mission in North America*, Grand Rapids, MI: Eerdmans, 1996.

Hunt, Stephen, '"Winning Ways": Gobalisation and the Impact of the Health and Wealth Gospel', *Journal of Contemporary Religion* 15 (2000), 336–42.

Hunter, James Davison, *To Change the World: The Irony, Tragedy, & Possibility of Christianity in the Late Modern World*, Oxford: Oxford University Press, 2010.

Husbands, Mark and Daniel J. Treier (eds), *The Community of the Word: Towards an Evangelical Ecclesiology*, Downers Grove, IL: InterVarsity Press, 2005.

Irvin, Dale and Scott Sunquist, *History of the World Christian Movement I: Earliest Christianity to 1453*, Maryknoll, NY: Orbis, 2001.

Irvin, Dale and Scott Sunquist, *History of the World Christian Movement II: Modern Christianity from 1454–1800*, Maryknoll, NY: Orbis, 2012.

Israel, Jonathan I., *The Dutch Republic: Its Rise, Greatness and Fall, 1477–1806*, Oxford: Clarendon Press, 1998 (4th edn).

Israel, Nico, *Outlandish: Writing between Exile and Diaspora*, Stanford, CA: Stanford University Press, 2000.

BIBLIOGRAPHY

James, Christopher B., *Church Planting in Post-Christian Soil: Theology and Practice*, Oxford: Oxford University Press, 2018.

Jamieson, Alan, *A Churchless Faith: Faith Journeys beyond the Churches*, London: SPCK, 2002.

Janssen, Allan J., *Kingdom, Office, and Church: A Study of A.A. van Ruler's Doctrine of Ecclesiastical Office*, Grand Rapids, MI: Eerdmans, 2006.

Jenkins, Philip, *God's Continent: Christianity, Islam, and Europe's Religious Crisis*, Oxford University Press: Oxford, 2007.

Jennings, J. Nelson, 'Christian Mission and "Glocal" Violence in 2006 A.D. / 1427 H.', *Missiology* 35 (2007), 397–415.

Jeyaraj, Dasan, *Followers of Christ Outside the Church in Chennai, India*, Zoetermeer: Boekencentrum, 2009.

Joas, Hans, *Glaube als Option: Zukunftsmöglichkeiten des Christentums*, Freiburg: Herder, 2012.

Jongeneel, Jan A. B., 'Voetius' zendingstheologie, de eerste comprehensieve zendingstheologie', in Van Oort, *De onbekende Voetius*, pp. 117–147.

Jongeneel, Jan A. B., 'The Missiology of Gisbertus Voetius: The First Comprehensive Protestant Theology of Mission', *Calvin Theological Journal* 26 (1991), 47–79.

Jongeneel, Jan A. B., '"Mission and Evangelism" (1982) and "Together Towards Life" (2013)', *Exchange* 43 (2014), 273–90.

Keifert, Patrick, *We Are Here Now: A Missional Journey of Spiritual Discovery*, St. Paul, MN: Church Innovations Institute, 2006.

Kelle, Brad E. et al. (eds), *Interpreting Exile: Displacement and Deportation in Biblical and Modern Contexts*, Atlanta, GA: SBL, 2011.

Keller, Timothy J., *Center Church: Doing Balanced, Gospel-Centered Ministry in Your City*, Grand Rapids, MI: Zondervan, 2012.

Kendall, Calvin et al. (eds), *Conversion to Christianity from Late Antiquity to the Modern Age: Considering the Process in Europe, Asia, and the Americas*, Minneapolis, MN: University of Minnesota, 2009.

Kerr, Nathan R., *Christ, History and Apocalyptic: The Politics of Christian Mission*, London: SCM Press, 2008.

Keum, Jooseop (ed.), *Together towards Life: Mission and Evangelism in Changing Landscapes*, Geneva: WCC, 2013.

Kirk, J. Andrew, *What is Mission? Theological Explorations*, Minneapolis, MN: Fortress Press, 2000.

Klein, Ralph W., *Israel in Exile: A Theological Interpretation*, Philadelphia, PA: Fortress Press, 1979.

Knibbe, Kim, 'Nigerian Missionaries in Europe: History Repeating Itself or a Meeting of Modernities?', *Journal of Religion in Europe* 4 (2011), 471–87.

Köstenberger, A. J., 'Mission in the General Epistles', in Larkin and Williams, *Mission in the New Testament*, pp. 189–206.

Krabill, James R. et al. (eds), *Evangelical, Ecumenical, and Anabaptist Missiologies in Conversation*, Maryknoll, NY: Orbis, 2006.

Kraemer, Hendrik, *Het vergeten ambt in de kerk: Plaats en roeping van het gewone gemeentelid*, 's-Gravenhage: Boekencentrum, 1960.

Kraemer, Hendrik, *A Theology of the Laity*, Vancouver: Regent, 2005.

Krause, Johannes, *A Soul for Europe? Contributions of European Churches to the Forum of the Convention on the Future of Europe*, MA Thesis, Helsinki University, 2007 (online).

Kreider, Alan (ed.), *The Origins of Christendom in the West*, Edinburgh: T&T Clark, 2001.

Kreider, Alan and Eleanor Kreider, *Worship and Mission after Christendom*, Scottdale, PA: Herald Press, 2011.

Kuhrt, Amély, *The Ancient Near East: c. 3000–330 BC*, vol. 2, London: Routledge, 1995.

Kuyper, Abraham, *Geworteld en gegrond: De Kerk als organisme en instituut*, Amsterdam: H. de Hoogh & Co., 1870.

Kuyper, Abraham, 'Sphere Sovereignty: Inaugural Address at the Dedication of the Vrije Universiteit Amsterdam' (1880), in James D. Bratt (ed.), *Abraham Kuyper: A Centennial Reader*, Grand Rapids, MI: Eerdmans, 1998.

Kuyper, Abraham, 'Calvinism and the Future', in Abraham Kuyper, *Lectures on Calvinism*, Lafayette, LA: Sovereign Grace Publishers, 2001.

Kuyper, Abraham (trans. Nelson D. Kloosterman), *Rooted and Grounded: The Church as Organism and Institution*, Grand Rapids, MI: Christian Library's Press, 2013.

Kwiyani, Harvey C., *Sent Forth: African Missionary Work in the West*, Maryknoll, NY: Orbis, 2014.

Laatto, Antti et al. (eds), *Theodicy in the World of the Bible*, Leiden: Brill, 2003.

Larkin, W. J. and J. F. Williams (eds), *Mission in the New Testament: An Evangelical Approach*, Maryknoll, NY: Orbis, 1998.

Leonhardt-Balzer, Jutta, 'Priests and Priesthood in Philo: Could He Have Done Without Them?', in Schwartz and Weiss, *Was 70 CE a Watershed*, pp. 127–54.

Levenson, Jon D., *Esther: A Commentary*, Louisville, KY: Westminster John Knox Press, 1997.

Lewis, C. S., 'Myth Became Fact', in Walter Hooper (ed.), *C. S. Lewis: God in the Dock. Essays on Theology*, London: HarperCollins, 1990 (7th edn).

Lewis, C. S., *Mere Christianity: Revised and Amplified Edition* (1952), New York: HarperCollins, 2001.

Lewis, C. S., *Surprised by Joy: An Accidental Journey from Atheism to Christianity* (1955), London: William Collins, 2016.

Lichterman, Paul, *Elusive Togetherness: Church Groups Trying to Bridge America's Divisions*, Princeton, NJ: Princeton University Press, 2005.

Lieburg, Fred van, 'Nederlands protestantisme op weg naar 2040', *Kontekstueel* 28 (2014).

Lindbeck, George, *The Nature of Doctrine: Religion and Theology in a Postliberal Age*, Philadelphia, PA: Westminster Press, 1984.

Lindström, Fredrik, *Suffering and Sin: Interpretations of Illness in the Individual Complaint Psalms*, Lund: Almqvist and Wicksell, 1994.

Livingston, J. Kevin, *A Missiology of the Road: Early Perspectives in David Bosch's Theology of Mission and Evangelism*, Cambridge: James Clarke & Co, 2013.

Lockhart, Ross A., *Beyond Snakes and Shamrocks: St. Patrick's Missional Leadership Lessons for Today*, Eugene, OR: Cascade, 2018.

Lodberg, Peter, 'Studying the ecclesiology of a national church: The Danish context', *International Journal for the Study of the Christian Church* 16 (2016), 126–35.

Luther, Martin, *Von weltlicher Obrigkeit* (1523), WA 11.251.

MacGavran, Donald A., *Understanding Church Growth: Fully Revised*, Grand Rapids, MI: Eerdmans, 1980.

MacGavran, Donald A., *Understanding Church Growth: Third Edition, Revised and Edited by C. Peter Wagner*, Grand Rapids, MI: Eerdmans, 1990.

MacIntyre, Alasdair, *After Virtue: A Study in Moral Theory*, London: Bloomsbury, 2007 (3rd edn).

MacIntyre, Alasdair, *Whose Justice? Which Rationality?*, Notre Dame, IN: University of Notre Dame Press, 2014 (6th edn).

Maddox, Marion, '"In the Goofy Parking Lot": Growth Churches as a Novel Religious Form for Late Capitalism', *Social Compass* 59 (2012), 146–58.

Marti, Gerardo and Gladys Ganiel, *The Deconstructed Church: Understanding Emerging Christianity*, Oxford: Oxford University Press, 2014.

Martin, David, *Pentecostalism: The World Their Parish*, Oxford: Wiley-Blackwell, 2001.

Martin, David, *On Secularization: Towards a Revised General Theory*, Aldershot: Ashgate, 2005.

Mason, Mark, 'Living in the distance between a "community of character" and a "community of the question"', in Nelstrop and Percy, *Evaluating Fresh Expressions*, pp. 85–104.

McClendon Jr., James, *Ethics: Systematic Theology I*, Nashville, TN: Abingdon, 1986.

McConville, J. Gordon, '1 Kings viii and the Deuteronomic Hope', *Vetus Testamentum* 42 (1992), 67–79.

McConville, J. Gordon, *Judgment and Promise: An Interpretation of the Book of Jeremiah*, Winona Lake, IN: Eisenbrauns, 1993.

McGrath, Alister E., 'The Cultivation of Theological Vision: Theological Attentiveness and the Practice of Ministry', in Ward, *Perspectives*, pp. 107–23.

McKim, Donald K. (ed.), *Major Themes in the Reformed Tradition*, Eugene, OR: Wipf & Stock, 1998.

McKnight, Scott, *Kingdom Conspiracy: Returning to the Radical Mission of the Local Church*, Grand Rapids, MI: Baker, 2014.

McLaren, Brian, *A New Kind of Christianity: Ten Questions that are Transforming the Faith*, New York: HarperCollins, 2010.

McLeod, Hugh and Werner Ustorf (eds), *The Decline of Christendom in Western Europe*, Cambridge: Cambridge University Press, 2003.

McLeod, Hugh, 'Introduction', in McLeod and Ustorf, *Decline*, pp. 1–26.

Mettinger, T. N. D., *A Farewell to the Servant Songs: A Critical Examination of an Exegetical Axiom*, Lund: Gleerup, 1983.

Michael, Goodich, *Vita Perfecta: The Ideal of Sainthood in the Thirteenth Century*, Stuttgart: Anton Hiersemann, 1982.

Morrow, Jeff, 'Creation as Temple-Building and Work as Liturgy in Genesis 1–3', *The Journal of the Orthodox Center for the Advancement of Biblical Studies* 2 (2009), 1–13.

Moynagh, Michael, *Church in Life: Innovation, Mission, and Ecclesiology*, London: SCM Press, 2017.

Murray, Stuart, *Church after Christendom*, Milton Keynes: Paternoster Press, 2004.

Murray, Stuart, *Post-Christendom*, Milton Keynes: Paternoster Press, 2004.

Nation, Mark Thiessen and Samuel Wells (eds), *Faithfulness and Fortitude: In Conversation with the Theological Ethics of Stanley Hauerwas*, Edinburgh: T&T Clark, 2000.

Nation, Mark Thiessen, 'Stanley Hauerwas: Where Would We Be Without Him?', in Nation and Wells, *Faithfulness and Fortitude*, pp. 19–36.

Nelstrop, Louise and Martyn Percy (eds), *Evaluating Fresh Expressions: Explorations in Emerging Church*, Norwich: Canterbury Press, 2008.

Newbigin, Lesslie, *The Open Secret: An Introduction to the Theology of Missions*, Grand Rapids, MI: Eerdmans, 1978 (revised edn 1995).

Newbigin, Lesslie, 'Can the West be Converted?', *International Bulletin of Missionary Research* (January 1987), 2–7.

Newbigin, Lesslie, *The Gospel in a Pluralist Society*, Grand Rapids, MI: Eerdmans, 1989.

Newman, Elizabeth, 'The Priesthood of All Believers and the Necessity of the Church', in Thompson and Cross, *Recycling*, pp. 50–66.

Nielsen, Marie Vejrup, 'The Danes: The Church in the eyes of its members', in Svenningsen, *Evangelical Lutheran Church*.

Nissen, Peter, 'De kerstening van christenen', in Charles Caspers et al. (eds), *Wegen van kerstening in Europa: 1300–1900*, Budel: Damon, 2005, pp. 7–15.

Noordegraaf, A., *Vijf broden en twee vissen: Missionair gemeentezijn in een (post) moderne samenleving*, Zoetermeer: Boekencentrum, 1998.

Noort, Gerrit and Stefan Paas, Kyriaki Avtzi (eds), *Sharing Good News: Handbook on Evangelism in Europe*, Geneva: World Council of Churches, 2017.

Oded, Bustenay, 'Judah and the Exile', in Hayes and Miller, *Israelite and Judaean History*, pp. 469–76.

O'Donovan, Oliver, *The Desire of the Nations: Rediscovering the Roots of Political Theology*, Cambridge: Cambridge University Press, 1996.

O'Kennedy, Daniel F., 'Perspectives on the Book of Zechariah', *Missionalia* 41 (2013), 223–38.

Oort, J. van et al., *De onbekende Voetius: Voordrachten wetenschappelijk symposium Utrecht 3 maart 1989*, Kampen: Kok, 1989.

Ott, Craig (ed.), *The Mission of the Church: Five Views in Conversation*, Grand Rapids, MI: Baker Academic, 2016.

Paas, Stefan, *Jezus als Heer in een plat land: Op zoek naar een Nederlands evangelie*, Zoetermeer: Boekencentrum, 2001.

Paas, Stefan, *De werkers van het laatste uur: De inwijding van nieuwkomers in het christelijk geloof en de christelijke gemeente*, Zoetermeer: Boekencentrum, 2003.

Paas, Stefan, 'Vreemd, vreemdeling', in A. Noordegraaf et al. (eds), *Woordenboek voor bijbellezers*, Zoetermeer: Boekencentrum, 2005.

Paas, Stefan, 'Kerken vormen: De gemeenschappelijke structuur van het Evangelie anno nu', *Soteria* 23 (2006), 6–26.

Paas, Stefan, *Vrede stichten: Politieke meditaties*, Zoetermeer: Boekencentrum, 2007.

Paas, Stefan, 'Prepared for a Missionary Ministry in 21st Century Europe', *European Journal of Theology* 20 (2011), 119–30.

Paas, Stefan, 'The Making of a Mission Field: Paradigms of Evangelistic Mission in Europe', *Exchange* 41 (2012), 44–67.

Paas, Stefan, 'Religious Consciousness in a Post-Christian Culture: J.H. Bavinck's *Religious Consciousness and Christian Faith* (1949), Sixty Years Later', *Journal of Reformed Theology* 6 (2012), 35–55.

Paas, Stefan, 'The Crisis of Mission in Europe: Is There a Way Out?', *Scandinavian Evangelical e-Journal* 3 (2012), 16–51.

Paas, Stefan, 'Mission among Individual Consumers', in Ryan K. Bolger (ed.), *The Gospel after Christendom: New Voices, New Cultures, New Expressions*, Grand Rapids, MI: Baker, 2012, pp. 150–63.

Paas, Stefan, 'Experimenting with Mission and Unity in Secular Europe: Networking for Mission, Client-Based Mission, and Ecumenical Mission', in Gibaut and Jørgensen, *Called to Unity*, pp. 186–99.

Paas, Stefan, 'Mission from Anywhere to Europe: Americans, Africans and Australians Coming to Amsterdam', *Mission Studies* 32 (2015), 4–31.

Paas, Stefan, *Vreemdelingen en priesters: Christelijke missie in een postchristelijke omgeving*, Boekencentrum: Zoetermeer, 2015.

Paas, Stefan, 'The Discipline of Missiology in 2016: Concerning the Place and Meaning of Missiology in the Theological Curriculum', *Calvin Theological Journal* 51 (2016), 37–55.

Paas, Stefan, *Church Planting in the Secular West: Learning from the European Experience*, Grand Rapids, MI: Eerdmans, 2016.

Paas, Stefan, 'Evangelism and Methods', in Noort, *Sharing Good News*, pp. 275–89.

Paas, Stefan, 'Intercultural Theology and Missiology', *Interreligious Studies and Intercultural Theology* 1 (2017), 133–9.

Paas, Stefan, 'The Countercultural Church: An Analysis of the Neo-Anabaptist Contribution to Missional Ecclesiology in the Post-Christendom West', *Ecclesiology* 15 (2019), 271–89.

Paas, Stefan and Gert-Jan Roestz *Een komedie in vier bedrijven: Jona*, Zoetermeer: Boekencentrum, 2015.

Paas, Stefan, Gert-Jan Roest and Siebrand Wierda, *Eten met Jezus: Bijbelstudies over maaltijden in Lucas*, Zoetermeer: Boekencentrum, 2012.

Paas, Stefan and Marry Schoemaker-Kooy, 'Crisis and Resilience among European Church Planters', *Mission Studies* 35 (2018), 366–88.

Paas, Stefan and Siebrand Wierda, *Ontworteld: Bijbelstudies over Daniël*, Zoetermeer: Boekencentrum, 2011.

Padilla, C. René, *Mission between the Times: Essays on the Kingdom*, Grand Rapids, MI: Eerdmans, 1985.

Padilla, C. René, 'Integral Mission and Its Historical Development', in Tim Chester (ed.), *Justice, Mercy, and Humility*, Carlisle: Paternoster Press, 2003.

Padilla, C. René and Harold Segura (eds), *Ser, Hacer y Decir: Bases Bíblicas de la Misión Integral*, Buenos Aires: Ediciones Kairos, 2006.

Padilla DeBorst, Ruth, 'An Integral Transformational Approach', in Ott, *The Mission of the Church*, pp. 41–69.

Pearce, Laurie E. and Cornelia Wunsch, *Documents of Judean Exiles and West Semites in Babylonia in the Collection of David Sofer*, Bethesda: CDL Press, 2014.

Peel, John D. Y., *Religious Encounter and the Making of the Yoruba*, Bloomington, IN: Indiana University Press, 2000.

Ploeger, Matthijs, *Celebrating Church: Ecumenical Contributions to a Liturgical Ecclesiology*, Groningen: Instituut voor Liturgiewetenschap, 2008.

Roest, Henk de, *Een huis voor de ziel: Gedachten over de kerk voor binnen en buiten*, Zoetermeer: Meinema, 2010.

Rogers Jr., Eugene F. (ed.), *Theology and Sexuality: Classic and Contemporary Readings*, Oxford: Blackwell, 2002.

Rommen, Edward and Gary Corwin (eds), *Missiology and the Social Sciences: Contributions, Cautions and Conclusions*, Pasadena, CA: William Carey Library, 1996.

Rooden, Peter van, *Religieuze regimes: Over godsdienst en maatschappij in Nederland, 1570–1990*, Amsterdam: Bert Bakker, 1996.

Rooms, Nigel and Pat Keifert, *Forming a Missional Church: Creating Deep Cultural Change in Congregations*, Cambridge: Grove Books, 2014.

Roschke, Volker (ed.), *Gemeinde pflanzen: Modell einer Kirche der Zukunft*, Neukirchener Verlag: Neukirchen-Vluyn, 2001.

Roxburgh, Alan J., *Missional Map-Making: Skills for Leading in Times of Transition*, San Francisco, CA: Jossey-Bass, 2010.

Roxburgh, Alan and Fred Romanuk, *The Missional Leader: Equipping Your Church to Reach a Changing World*, San Francisco, CA: Jossey-Bass, 2010.

Ruler, A. A. van, 'A Theology of Mission', in John Bolt (ed.), *Calvinist Trinitarianism and Theocratic Politics: Essays Toward a Public Theology*, Lewiston, ME: Edwin Mellen, 1989, pp. 199–226.

Samuel, Vinay and Chris Sugden (eds), *Mission as Transformation: A Theology of the Whole Gospel*, Eugene, OR: Regnum Books, 1999.

Sanders, James, 'The Exile and Canon Formation', in Scott, *Exile*, pp. 37–61.

Sanneh, Lamin, *Translating the Message: The Missionary Impact on Culture*, Maryknoll, NY: Orbis, 1989.

Sanneh, Lamin, *Whose Religion is Christianity? The Gospel beyond the West*, Grand Rapids, MI: Eerdmans, 2003.

Santos, Narry F., '*Diaspora* in the New Testament and Its Impact on Christian Mission', *Torch Trinity Journal* 13 (2010), 3–18.

Savage, Sara and Eolene Boyd-MacMillan, *The Human Face of Church: A Social Psychology and Pastoral Theology Resource for Pioneer and Traditional Ministry*, Norwich: Canterbury Press, 2007.

Scherer, James A., *Gospel, Church, Kingdom: Comparative Studies in World Mission Theology*, Eugene, OR: Wipf & Stock, 1987.

Schiffauer, Werner, 'From exile to diaspora: The development of transnational Islam in Europe', in Al-Azmeh and Fokas, *Islam in Europe*, pp. 68–95.

Schilder, Klaas, *Christus en Cultuur*, Franeker: Wever, 1947.

Schmemann, Alexander, *For the Life of the World: Sacraments and Orthodoxy*, Crestwood, IL: St. Vladimir's Seminary Press, 1998.

Schnabel, Eckhard J., *Urchristliche Mission*, Wuppertal: Brockhaus Verlag, 2002.

Schnabel, Eckhard J., *Early Christian Mission*, Downers Grove, IL: InterVarsity Press, 2004.

Schwartz, Daniel R. and Zeev Weiss (eds), *Was 70 CE a Watershed in Jewish History? On Jews and Judaism before and after the Destruction of the Second Temple*, Leiden: Brill, 2011.

Scott, James M. (ed.), *Exile: Old Testament, Jewish & Christian Conceptions*, Leiden: Brill, 1997.

Scruton, Roger, *The Face of God: The Gifford Lectures 2010*, London: Continuum, 2012.

Seitz, Christopher R., *Theology in Conflict: Reactions to the Exile in the Book of Jeremiah*, Berlin: DeGruyter, 1989.

Seland, Torrey, 'Resident Aliens in Mission: Missional Practices in the Emerging Church of 1 Peter', *Bulletin for Biblical Research* 19 (2009), 565–89.

Shenk, Wilbert R., 'The Training of Missiologists for Western Culture', in Woodberry, *Missiological Education*, pp. 120–9.

Siedentop, Larry, *Inventing the Individual: The Origins of Western Liberalism*, Cambridge, MA: Harvard University Press, 2014.

Silva Júnior, Nelson da, 'The Liquid Church: A Reading of the Modern Church through Neo-Pentecostalism', *Ciberteologia* 7 (2011), 63–80.

Skreslet, Stanley H., *Comprehending Mission: The Questions, Methods, Themes, Problems and Prospects of Missiology*, Maryknoll, NY: Orbis, 2012.

Smith, David, *Mission after Christendom*, London: Darton, Longman & Todd, 2003.

Smith, James K. A., *Desiring the Kingdom: Worship, Worldview, and Cultural Formation*, Grand Rapids, MI: Baker Academic, 2009.

Smith, James K. A., *Imagining the Kingdom: How Worship Works*, Grand Rapids, MI: Baker Academic, 2013.

Smith, James K. A., *How (Not) to be Secular: Reading Charles Taylor*, Grand Rapids, MI: Eerdmans, 2014.

Smith, Julia M. H., *Europe after Rome: A New Cultural History 500–1000*, Oxford: Oxford University Press, 2005.

Smith-Christopher, Daniel L., 'Reassessing the Historical and Sociological Impact of the Babylonian Exile (597/587–539 BCE)', in Scott, *Exile*, pp. 7–36.

Smith-Christopher, Daniel L., *A Biblical Theology of Exile*, Minneapolis, MN: Fortress Press, 2002.

Spaans, Joke, *Haarlem na de Reformatie: Stedelijke cultuur en kerkelijk leven 1577–1620*, Den Haag, 1989.

Stanley, Brian (ed.), *Christian Missions and the Enlightenment*, Grand Rapids, MI: Eerdmans, 2001.

Stark, Rodney, *The Rise of Christianity*, San Francisco: HarperCollins, 1997.

Stenschke, Christoph, 'Reading First Peter in the Context of Early Christian Mission', *Tyndale Bulletin* 60 (2009), 107–26.

Stoffels, Hijme, 'Opkomst en ondergang van de buitenkerkelijke: Enige historische ontwikkelingen', in Gerben Heitink, Hijme Stoffels (eds), *Niet zo'n kerkganger: Zicht op buitenkerkelijk geloven*, Baarn: Ten Have, 2003.

Stone, Bryan, *Evangelism after Christendom: The Theology and Practice of Christian Witness*, Grand Rapids, MI: Brazos Press, 2007.

Stroope, Michael W., *Transcending Mission: The Eclipse of a Modern Tradition*, Downers Grove, IL: InterVarsity Press, 2017.

Sundermeier, Theo, 'Erinnern und Weitergeben: Die Kraft missionarischer Erzeugung', in *Der Faden die nicht reißt*, Augustana, 2007. Online: https://augustana.de/fileadmin/user_upload/dokumente/ertraege/ertraege_neu/sonderheft%202007%20Prof.%20Wagner%2080%20ganz.pdf (accessed 4 August 2019).

Sunquist, Scott, *Understanding Christian Mission: Participating in Suffering and Glory*, Grand Rapids, MI: Baker Academic, 2013.

Svenningsen (ed.), Rebekka Højmark, *A Brief Guide to the Evangelical Lutheran Church in Denmark*, Frederiksberg: Aros Forlag, 2013.

Tangen, Karl Inge, *Ecclesial Identification beyond Late Modern Individualism? A Case Study of Life Strategies in Growing Late Modern Churches*, Leiden: Brill, 2012.

Taylor, Charles, *A Secular Age*, Cambridge, MA: Harvard University Press, 2007.

Taylor, Charles, *Dilemmas and Connections: Selected Essays*, Cambridge, MA: Harvard University Press, 2011.

Taylor, Charles, 'A Catholic Modernity?', in Taylor, *Dilemmas*, pp. 167–87.

Tennent, Timothy, 'The Challenge of Churchless Christianity: An Evangelical Assessment', *International Bulletin of Missionary Research* 29 (2005), 171–7.

Thomas, Pradip, 'Selling God/saving souls: Religious commodities, spiritual markets and the media', *Global Media and Communication* 5 (2009), 57–76.

Thompson, James W., *The Church in Exile: God's Counterculture in a Non-Christian World*, Abilene, TX: Leafwood, 2010.

Thompson, Philip E. and Anthony R. Cross (eds), *Recycling the Past or Researching History? Studies in Baptist Historiography and Myths*, Waynesboro, GA: Paternoster Press, 2005.

Tomlin, Graham, *The Power of the Cross: Theology and the Death of Christ in Paul, Luther and Pascal*, Carlisle: Paternoster Press, 1999.

Tomlin, Graham, *The Widening Circle: Priesthood as God's Way of Blessing the World*, London: SPCK, 2014.

Üffing, Martin, 'Catholic Mission in Europe 1910–2010', in Stephen Bevans (ed.), *A Century of Catholic Mission*, Oxford: Regnum, 2013, pp. 34–43.

Valentine, Daniel E. and John C. Knudsen (eds), *Mistrusting Refugees*, Berkeley, CA: University of California Press, 1995.

Vanier, Jean, *An Ark for the Poor: The Story of L'Arche*, Ottawa: Novalis, 1995.

Veen, Peter van der, 'Sixth Century Issues: The Fall of Jerusalem, the Exile, and the Return', in Arnold and Hess, *Ancient Israel's History*, pp. 383–405.

Veer, Peter van der (ed.), *Conversion to Modernities: The Globalization of Christianity*, New York: Routledge, 1996.

Volf, Miroslav, 'Soft Difference: Theological Reflections on the Relation Between Church and Culture in 1 Peter', *Ex Auditu* 10 (1994), 15–30.

Vos, Alrik, *Hoop: Een onderzoek naar de missionaire effectiviteit van kerkplantingen binnen de NGK, CGK en GKV in Nederland*, MA Thesis, VU Amsterdam, 2012.

Voss, Hank J., *The Priesthood of All Believers and the Missio Dei: A Canonical, Catholic and Contextual Perspective*, PhD Thesis, Wheaton College, Wheaton, 2013.

Voutira, Eftihia and Barbara Harrell-Bond, 'In Search of the Locus of Trust: The Social World of the Refugee Camp', in Valentine and Knudsen, *Mistrusting Refugees*, pp. 207–24.

Wagner, C. Peter, *Revival! It Can Transform Your City*, Wagner Publications, 1999.

Wagner, C. Peter, *Apostles of the City: How to Mobilize Territorial Apostles for City Transformation*, Wagner Publications, 2000.

Währisch-Oblau, Claudia, *The Missionary Self-Perception of Pentecostal/Charismatic Church Leaders from the Global South in Europe: Bringing Back the Gospel*, Leiden: Brill, 2009.

Wainwright, Geoffrey, *Doxology: The Praise of God in Worship, Doctrine, and Life*, New York: Oxford University Press, 1980.

Walker, John, *Testing Fresh Expressions: Identity and Transformation*, Aldershot: Ashgate, 2014.

Walls, Andrew, *The Missionary Movement in Christian History: Studies in the Transmission of Faith*, Maryknoll, NY: Orbis, 1996.

Walls, Andrew F., 'Culture and Conversion in Christian History', in Walls, *The Missionary Movement*, pp. 43–54.

Walls, Andrew F., 'The Eighteenth-Century Protestant Missionary Awakening in Its European Context', in Stanley, *Christian Missions*, pp. 22–44.

Walls, Andrew, *The Cross-Cultural Process in Christian History*, Maryknoll, NY: Orbis, 2002.

Walls, Andrew F., 'The Ephesian Moment: At a Crossroads in Christian History', in Walls, *The Cross-Cultural Process*, pp. 72–81.

Walls, Andrew F., 'Evangelical and Ecumenical: The Rise and Fall of the Early Church Model', in: Krabill, *Evangelical, Ecumenical*, pp. 33–7.

Walls, Andrew F., 'Afterword: Christian mission in a five-hundred years context', in Walls, Ross, *Mission in the 21st Century*, pp. 193–204.

Walls, Andrew F., 'The Rise of Global Theologies', in Greenman and Green, *Global Theologies*, pp. 19–34.

Walls, Andrew and Cathy Ross (eds), *Mission in the 21st Century: Exploring the Five Marks of Global Mission*, Maryknoll, NY: Orbis, 2008.

Walton, John H., *The Lost World of Genesis One: Ancient Cosmology and the Origins Debate*, Downers Grove, IL: InterVarsity Press Academic, 2009.

Walton, John H., *Genesis 1 as Ancient Cosmology*, Winona Lake, IN: Eisenbrauns, 2011.

Walton, John H., *The Lost World of Adam and Eve: Genesis 2–3 and the Human Origins Debate*, Downers Grove, IL: InterVarsity Press Academic, 2015.

Wan, Enoch, *Diaspora Missiology: Theory, Methodology, and Practice*, Portland, OR: Institute of Diaspora Studies of USA, 2011.

Ward, Pete, *Liquid Church*, Grand Rapids, MI: Baker, 2001.

Ward, Pete (ed.), *Perspectives on Ecclesiology and Ethnography*, Grand Rapids, MI: Eerdmans, 2012.

Ware, James P., *The Mission of the Church in Paul's Letter to the Philippians in the Context of Ancient Judaism*, Leiden: Brill, 2005.

Warneck, Gustav, *Evangelische Missionslehre: Ein missionstheoretischer Versuch. Dritte Abteilung: Der Betrieb der Sendung*, Gotha: Friedrich Andreas Berthes, 1896 (2nd edn, 1902).

Wassenaar, J. D. Th., *Vreemdelingschap: Historische en hedendaagse stemmen uit kerk en theologie*, Zoetermeer: Boekencentrum, 2014.

Wessels, Anton, *Europe: Was It Every Really Christian?*, London: SCM Press, 2012.

Westphal, Merold, *Suspicion and Faith: The Religious Uses of Modern Atheism*, New York: Fordham University Press, 1998.

Wettstein, Howard (ed.), *Diasporas and Exiles: Varieties of Jewish Identity*, Berkeley, CA: University of California Press, 2002.

Williams, Rowan, *On Christian Theology*, Oxford: Blackwell, 2000.

Williams, Rowan, 'Theological Integrity', in Williams, *On Christian Theology*, pp. 3–15.

Williams, Rowan, 'The Judgement of the World', in Williams, *On Christian Theology*, pp. 29–43.

Williams, Rowan, 'Trinity and Revelation', in Williams, *On Christian Theology*, pp. 131–47.

Williams, Rowan, 'The Body's Grace', in Rogers, *Theology and Sexuality*, pp. 309–21.

Williams, Rowan, *Tokens of Trust: An Introduction to Christian Belief*, London: Canterbury Press, 2007.

Williams, Rowan, *Faith in the Public Square*, London: Bloomsbury, 2012.

Williams, Rowan, 'Changing the Myths We Live By', in Williams, *Faith*, pp. 175–84.

Wilson, Jonathan R., *Living Faithfully in a Fragmented World: Lessons for the Church from MacIntyre's After Virtue*, Harrisburg, PA: Trinity Press, 1997.

Wiman, Christian, *My Bright Abyss: Meditation of a Modern Believer*, New York: Farrar, Straus and Giroux, 2013.

Winter, Ralph D., 'The Two Structures of God's Redemptive Mission', in Winter and Hawthorne, *Perspectives*, pp. 220–30.

Winter, Ralph D. and Steven C. Hawthorne (eds), *Perspectives on the World Christian Movement: A Reader*, Pasadena, CA: William Carey Library, 2009 (4th edn).

Wolterstorff, Nicholas, *Until Justice & Peace Embrace*, Grand Rapids, MI: Eerdmans, 1983.

Wolterstorff, Nicholas, 'The Reformed Liturgy', in McKim, *Major Themes*, pp. 273–304.

Woodberry, J. Dudley et al. (eds), *Missiological Education for the Twenty-First Century: The Book, the Circle, and the Sandals*, Maryknoll, NY: Orbis, 1997.

World Council of Churches, *The Church: Towards a Common Vision*, Faith and Order Paper 214, Geneva: WCC, 2013.

Worthen, Jeremy, 'What's New about Renewal in *Evangelii Gaudium?*', *Ecclesiology* 12 (2016), 73–90.

Wright, Christopher J., *The Mission of God: Unlocking the Bible's Grand Narrative*, Downers Grove, IL: InterVarsity Press, 2006.

Wright, N. T., *Surprised by Hope: Rethinking Heaven, the Resurrection, and the Mission of the Church*, New York: HarperCollins, 2008.

Wright, N. T., *After You Believe: Why Christian Character Matters*, New York: HarperCollins, 2010.

Wrogemann, Henning, *Den Glanz widerspiegeln: Vom Sinn der christlichen Mission, ihren Kraftquellen und Ausdrucksgestalten: Interkulturelle Impulse für deutsche Kontexte*, Berlin: LIT Verlag, 2012.

Wrogemann, Henning, *Interkulturelle Theologie und Hermeneutik: Grundfragen, aktuelle Beispiele, theoretische Perspektive*, Gütersloh: Gütersloher Verlagshaus, 2012.

Yoder, John Howard, *The Politics of Jesus: Vicit Agnus Noster*, Grand Rapids, MI: Eerdmans, 1972.

Yoder, John Howard, *The Royal Priesthood: Essays Ecclesiological and Ecumenical*, Grand Rapids, MI: Eerdmans, 1994.

Yoder, John Howard, 'To Serve Our God and to Rule the World', in Yoder, *Royal Priesthood*, pp. 127–42.

Yoder, John Howard, 'Let the Church be the Church', in Yoder, *Royal Priesthood*, pp. 168–80.

Yoder, John Howard, 'Christ the Hope of the World', in Yoder, *Royal Priesthood*, pp. 192–220.

Yoder, John Howard, *For the Nations: Essays Public and Evangelical*, Grand Rapids, MI: Eerdmans, 1997.

Yoder, John Howard, 'The New Humanity as Pulpit and Paradigm', in Yoder, *For the Nations*, pp. 37–50.

Yoder, John Howard, 'The Believers Church and the Arms Race', in Yoder, *For the Nations*, pp. 148–61.

Yoder, John Howard, 'The Jewishness of the Free Church Vision', in Cartwright and Ochs, *John Howard Yoder*, pp. 105–19.

Zizioulas, John D., *Being as Communion: Studies in Personhood and the Church*, Crestwood, IL: St. Vladimir's Seminary Press, 1997.

Index of Scripture References

Index of Names